Hungry Nation

This ambitious and engaging new account of independent India's struggle to overcome famine and malnutrition in the twentieth century traces Indian nation-building through the voices of politicians, planners, and citizens. Siegel explains the historical origins of contemporary India's hunger and malnutrition epidemic, showing how food and sustenance moved to the center of nationalist thought in the final years of colonial rule. Independent India's politicians made promises of sustenance and then qualified them by asking citizens to share the burden of feeding a new and hungry state. Foregrounding debates over land, markets, and new technologies, *Hungry Nation* interrogates how citizens and politicians contested the meanings of nation-building and citizenship through food, and how these contestations receded in the wake of the Green Revolution. Drawing upon meticulous archival research, this is the story of how Indians challenged meanings of welfare and citizenship across class, caste, region, and gender in a new nation-state.

Benjamin Robert Siegel is Assistant Professor of History at Boston University. In 2014, he won the Sardar Patel Award for "the best doctoral dissertation on any aspect of modern India."

Hungry Nation
Food, Famine, and the Making of Modern India

Benjamin Robert Siegel
Boston University

Shaftesbury Road, Cambridge CB2 8EA, United Kingdom

One Liberty Plaza, 20th Floor, New York, NY 10006, USA

477 Williamstown Road, Port Melbourne, VIC 3207, Australia

314–321, 3rd Floor, Plot 3, Splendor Forum, Jasola District Centre, New Delhi – 110025, India

103 Penang Road, #05–06/07, Visioncrest Commercial, Singapore 238467

Cambridge University Press is part of Cambridge University Press & Assessment, a department of the University of Cambridge.

We share the University's mission to contribute to society through the pursuit of education, learning and research at the highest international levels of excellence.

www.cambridge.org
Information on this title: www.cambridge.org/9781108425964

DOI: 10.1017/9781108605397

© Benjamin Robert Siegel 2018

This publication is in copyright. Subject to statutory exception and to the provisions of relevant collective licensing agreements, no reproduction of any part may take place without the written permission of Cambridge University Press & Assessment.

First published 2018

A catalogue record for this publication is available from the British Library

Library of Congress Cataloging-in-Publication data
Names: Siegel, Benjamin Robert, author.
Title: Hungry nation : food, famine, and the making of modern India / Benjamin Robert Siegel, Boston University.
Description: Cambridge, United Kingdom; New York, NY:
Cambridge University Press, 2018. |
Includes bibliographical references and index.
Identifiers: LCCN 2018000024 | ISBN 9781108425964 (hardback)
Subjects: LCSH: Agriculture and state – India – History. |
Famines – India – History. | Food security –
India – History. | India – History – 1947–
Classification: LCC HD2073.S595 2018 | DDC 338.10954–dc23
LC record available at https://lccn.loc.gov/2018000024

ISBN   978-1-108-42596-4   Hardback
ISBN   978-1-108-44196-4   Paperback

Cambridge University Press & Assessment has no responsibility for the persistence or accuracy of URLs for external or third-party internet websites referred to in this publication and does not guarantee that any content on such websites is, or will remain, accurate or appropriate.

Contents

List of Figures	*page*	vii
Acknowledgments		ix
	Introduction	1
1	The Bengal Famine and the Nationalist Case for Food	21
2	Independent India of Plenty	50
3	Self-Help Which Ennobles a Nation	86
4	The Common Hunger of the Country: Merchants and Markets in Plenty and Want	119
5	All the Disabilities Which Peasant and Land Can Suffer	152
6	The Ideological Origins of the Green Revolution	183
	Conclusion: Landscapes of Hunger in Contemporary India	220
	Select Bibliography	234
	Index	267

Figures

1 Ram Nath Puri's "Photo of India" was printed in an Urdu-language magazine in 1905. Next to a fulminating poem and scenes of various colonial deprivations, it depicts the country as an emaciated prisoner, wasting away from hunger as British officials tuck into a sumptuous feast; it was this drawing that led to Puri's long exile in California. *page 2*

2 The artist Chittaprosad Bhattacharya published his account of a voyage to famine-ravaged Midnapur district in November 1943 as *Hungry Bengal*, illustrating it with his harrowing sketches. Here, he depicts "the five corpses that I counted one morning in the short stretch of road." (Credit: DAG Modern / Chittaprosad / Hungry Bengal) 38

3 The February 1946 issue of the Hindi newsweekly *Sansar* asks whether famine will return to India, displaying photographs of victims of the Bengal famine. At bottom, Jawaharlal Nehru is quoted decrying a world where "one man dies of hunger, and another drowns in food." (Credit: author's collection) 55

4 The Grow More Food campaign of 1949 reanimated the strategies and publicity efforts of its wartime antecedent. This film, *Grow More Food*, was directed by A. Bhaskar Rao and produced by Ezra Mir for the Department of Information and Broadcasting. Urging Indians to take up "kitchen gardening," it depicts the expenses of purchasing food from the trader against a backdrop of scarcity. The husband's skepticism about the kitchen garden his wife plants is overcome by the beautiful eggplant it yields. (Credit: Films Division, Ministry of Information and Broadcasting, Government of India) 72

vii

viii   List of Figures

5 Indian politician Uma Nehru and Lilavati Munshi, wife of Food Minister K.M. Munshi, oversee cooking and nutrition classes at the Annapoorna restaurant in Delhi, September 1951. (Credit: Photo Division, Ministry of Information and Broadcasting, Government of India)   111

6 Government publicity campaign reminding Indian citizens that "Every third chappati you eat is made from imported wheat," c. 1965–1966. (Credit: Ministry of Information and Broadcasting, Government of India)   116

7 Customers purchase wheat at a "fair price shop" in Delhi, 1959. (Credit: Photo Division, Ministry of Information and Broadcasting, Government of India)   134

8 Mockup by American officials of the emblem to be used on grains distributed in India under Public Law 480. In the margins, an official has put forth different options and has given suggested breakdowns of the languages in which this emblem should be printed. The Hindi version reads "Strength from America to the Free World." (Credit: United States National Archives, College Park, Maryland)   137

9 The cover of the *Zamindar-Kisan Natak [Landlord-Peasant Drama]*, a short Hindi-language play on land reform written by two students in Varanasi in 1950. (Credit: University of Chicago Library)   153

10 Prime Minister Jawaharlal Nehru examines corn grown on an Illinois farm, October 1949. (Credit: Department of State, Courtesy of Harry S. Truman Library)   184

11 A Rockefeller Foundation photographer captured this image (c. 1965–1966) of a farmer whose maize was now towering above him, thanks to the returns of the new agricultural strategy. (Credit: Rockefeller Archive Center)   211

12 The "new farmers' movement" of the 1980s saw ascendant peasants assert their newfound political preeminence through massive demonstrations. Here, Uttar Pradesh's M.S. Tikait addresses one such rally.   229

Acknowledgments

It is a pleasure to thank the friends whose support has been so vital to the completion of this project, and to the good cheer of its author. I am grateful to my earliest mentors for the gift of big questions and the words to work through them: David Watson in Detroit, Dodie McDow and Tatiana Seijas in New Haven, and Alex Perry and Aryn Baker in the PTI Building in New Delhi. Barney Bate, gone too soon, shared his wit, his wisdom, and his effervescent love for the subcontinent; rare is the day when I do not hear his guiding voice.

I am grateful to my doctoral supervisor at Harvard University, Sugata Bose, for his sterling mentorship and support, and to Sunil Amrith, Caroline Elkins, Emma Rothschild, and Ajantha Subramanian, for their friendship, guidance, and counsel. Over the years, my research has been underwritten by Harvard University's History Department, Asia Center, and South Asia Institute, as well as Hong Kong University's Centre for Medicine and the Humanities, the American Institute of Indian Studies, the Indian Agricultural Research Institute, and the Harvard Academy for International and Area Studies; I am particularly grateful to Jorge Dominguez, Kathleen Hoover, Purnima Mehta, and Larry Winnie for their support. I thank the many archivists and librarians whose work underwrote my own, and wish to single out Ikbal Ahmed, Shazia Faridi, Sanjeev Gautam, Kevin Greenbank, Lee Hiltzik, Jyothi Luthra, Jim Nye, Dharmender Singh Rawat, and Barbara Roe for their gracious assistance. Shreya Goswami and Pranjali Srivastava of Jawaharlal Nehru University offered stellar research assistance at various points in this project.

I have benefited enormously from presenting parts of this work at the University of California, Berkeley, Cambridge University, Harvard University, Harvard Business School, Harvard Law School, Hong Kong University, the Institute for European Global Studies at the University of Basel, Lahore University of Management Sciences, Massachusetts Institute of Technology, New York University, the University of North Carolina, Chapel Hill, Penn State University, Princeton University,

x   Acknowledgments

and Yale University, as well as at meetings of the American Society of Environmental History, the Annual Conference on South Asia at the University of Wisconsin, Madison, and the Association of Asian Studies. Lucy Rhymer of Cambridge University Press has been a superlative editor; I am grateful to the two anonymous reviewers whose careful and generous comments dramatically improved this text. I would also like to offer thanks to Priya Paul for permission to use the image that graces this book's cover, and to Kishore Singh of DAG Modern for permission to use Chittaprosad Bhattacharya's drawing in this book's first chapter.

This book is richer for the astute feedback I have received from the late C.A. Bayly, Rachel Berger, Vivek Chibber, David Engerman, Munis Faruqui, William Gould, Ramachandra Guha, Akhil Gupta, Prakash Kumar, David Ludden, Purnima Mankekar, Paul McGarr, Rochisha Narayan, Francesca Orsini, Rob Paarlberg, Susan Pennybacker, Gyan Prakash, Mridu Rai, Mahesh Rangarajan, Krishnendu Ray, James C. Scott, Amartya Sen, K. Sivaramakrishnan, and A.R. Venkatachalapathy. My colleagues at Boston University have been superlative interlocutors as I have completed this work and begun new undertakings; I am grateful to Betty Anderson, Brooke Blower, Arianne Chernock, Ashley Farmer, Lou Ferleger, Phil Haberkern, Jim McCann, Eugenio Menegon, Alexis Peri, Sarah Phillips, Jon Roberts, Jeff Rubin, Ed Russell, Bruce Schulman, and Jonathan Zatlin for their friendship and support.

A coterie of fellow travelers commented on drafts, offered new ideas and insights, and countered sagging morale with adventure, food, and cheer. Thank you to Sana Aiyar, Alessandro Angelini, Sam Asher, James Baer, Dwai Banerjee, Mou Banerjee, Naor Ben-Yehoyada, Yael Berda, David Boyk, Clare Cameron, Rebecca Chang, Chandrahas Choudhury, Stephanie Davidson, Rohit De, Richard Delacy, Namita Dharia, Hardeep Dhillon, Diana Doty, Daniel Elam, Eve Fine, Pete Fishman, Bjorn Fredrickson, Jen Fucile, Anny Gaul, Greg Goodman, Maitri Gopalakrishna, Radhika Govindrajan, David Guss, Philippa Hetherington, Lilly Irani, Jason Jackson, Radhika Jain, Jeff Kahn, Nachy Kanfer, Hayden Kantor, Roanne Kantor, Alicia Ringel, Anush Kapadia, Mary Kuhn, Nicole Labruto, Elizabeth Leake, Miriam Liebman, Andy Liu, Noora Lori, Johan Mathew, Nikhil Menon, Yael Merkin, Ross Mulcare, Jyothi Natarajan, Ariel Nierenberg, Tim Nunan, Naamah Paley, Dharini Parthasarathy, Mircea Raianu, Shruti Ravindran, Tehila Sasson, Bart Scott, Ornit Shani, Melissa Shin, Sarah Shortall, David Roth Singerman, Josh Specht, Julia Stephens, Chiara Superti, Tara Suri, Anand Vaidya, T.T. Venkatesh, Lydia Walker, Joanna Ware, Hannah Watson, Kate Wheeler, and Jeremy Zallen. I owe you all one.

Acknowledgments

I dedicate this book to my family – in Detroit, Chicago, Madison, and Boston – with boundless love and gratitude. My aunts Pam and Eve, my cousins Amy, Pam, Nathan, and Noah, and family members further afield have lent sanity, succor, and support in equal measure. Jack and Joyce Cohen and Sid and Naomi Siegel gifted me their curiosity for the world, and the insight and humor to weather its uncertainties. My brother and sister-in-law, Joshua Siegel and Katie Palusci, are fonts of cheer and encouragement; they inspire me daily with the clarity of their purpose and the warmth of their partnership. My parents, David and Sharon Siegel, have borne a wayfaring son with unstinting grace; there is little that I do not owe to their love and encouragement. Finally, Caterina Scaramelli has brought to this project that which she brings to every one of our shared undertakings: crystalline insight, riotous laughter, and the transubstantiation of daily life into something no less than magical. To shared adventures yet to come – *andiamo*!

Introduction

In February 1947, a Punjabi farmer stood in a packed room in California, a newly issued ticket in his hand.[1] Ram Nath Puri was 7000 miles and four decades removed from his birthplace in Lahore. But growing up in colonial Punjab, Puri had been a nationalist firebrand. Outraged by tales of famines that had ravaged India in the decades before his birth, and antagonized by the plunder of the nation's produce by rapacious colonial officers, Puri had been moved to publish a seditious cartoon, "Photo of India," in an Urdu-language magazine.

His scathing drawing, with a fulminating poem attached, depicted the country as an emaciated prisoner, wasting away from hunger as British officials tucked into a sumptuous feast. The caricature, published in 1905, was met with censure from a nervous provincial government. And after a brief detour through Japan to meet with other exiled radicals, Puri had escaped to northern California to join a growing number of Punjabi expatriates there.

Far from home, Puri had begun work as a hospital watchman, then as a fruit-picker and manager of a boarding house for fellow exiles. His radical instincts never abated: for many years, Puri underwrote the publication of an Urdu newsletter, the *Circular-i-Azadi*, which was smuggled to Europe and back to India, where it riled the colonial censors again.[2] Yet as the decades passed, Puri wrote less and planted more, enrolling in agricultural courses and establishing a successful farm. Its abundant harvest reminded him of the meager ones he had left behind: news of the Bengal famine, which had claimed 3.5 million lives, vexed Puri. And when word arrived of India's imminent independence, the exiled farmer knew what he had to do.

---

[1] Ram Nath Puri, *How to Conquer Poverty and Famine in India by American Methods* (Baroda: Padmaja Publications, 1947).

[2] Maia Ramnath, *Haj to Utopia: How the Ghadar Movement Charted Global Radicalism and Attempted to Overthrow the British Empire* (Berkeley: University of California Press, 2011), 25–26.

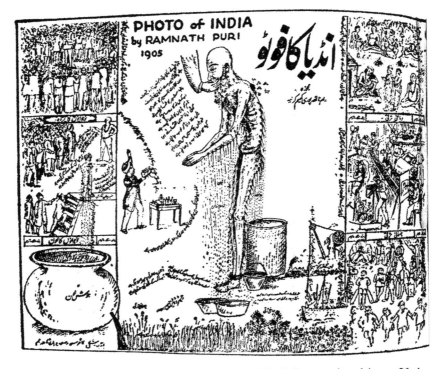

Figure 1 Ram Nath Puri's "Photo of India" was printed in an Urdu-language magazine in 1905. Next to a fulminating poem and scenes of various colonial deprivations, it depicts the country as an emaciated prisoner, wasting away from hunger as British officials tuck into a sumptuous feast; it was this drawing that led to Puri's long exile in California.

Six months before independence, Ram Nath Puri made a plea to the other members of the California Hindu Farmers' Association. After four decades in exile, Puri announced that he would be returning home to free India. There was work to be done on countless barren fields, and California's Indian farmers, he contended, had the knowledge to make them bloom. If they would join him, he announced, India might free itself permanently from the disgrace of food imports, and the horrors of recurrent famine. He brandished his ticket, and asked who among them would return home to feed a hungry nation.

If Puri had managed to arrive by August 15, he would have seen the Union Jacks as they were lowered across the length and breadth of

Introduction

British India, and the independent nation's saffron, green, and white tricolor flags hoisted triumphantly in their place. He would have heard India's new Prime Minister, Jawaharlal Nehru, declaim India's "tryst with destiny" on tinny transistor speakers. In cities and towns across the nation, he would have seen food stalls doling out sweets in celebration, and bands blaring fusillades of patriotic tunes. And perhaps, considering the mission which had called him back, he might have seen a solemn and germane flag-raising in Delhi.

Early in the morning, Congress statesman Rajendra Prasad had arrived at the leafy campus of the Indian Council of Agricultural Research, his motorcade rolling past a blur of horses' legs and bulls' horns painted in the national colors.[3] A year earlier, Prasad had been appointed Minister of Food and Agriculture in the interim national government; soon, he would become the nation's first president. For now, he stood beside the rows of millet and maize inching skywards, which hinted at the promise of the autumn crop. And as the new flag was raised, Prasad declared that India's most pressing task would be "to conquer that dread evil – hunger."[4] *Indian Farming* reported on Prasad's speech with approval, decrying the "nationwide surge of hunger which is sapping the energy and vitality of our people," and lauding the future president for realizing that sustenance would be the chief measure of free India's success. Yet there was deepening doubt, in homes and offices and on fields, that this goal would be met. India's food stocks were dwindling, its foreign reserves were sapped, and its most productive lands were suddenly across the border, in Pakistan. A few days before independence, India's government would ask members of the press to help quash an outbreak of food riots, declaring "that India's political freedom must not be allowed to prove illusory by a complete collapse on her food front."[5]

Yet no press directives were needed for new citizens across India to sense the challenges ahead. While Rajendra Prasad spoke, a more modest flag-raising was taking place near Madras, 1300 miles away. The *tiranga*, an Indian journalist reported, had been raised proudly in the center of a small village. But the moment's "idealistic delight was mellowed considerably when the villagers pointed to the flag and asked: 'There is the flag, but where is the food?'"[6] Independence, these villagers knew, would

[3] "Oh Lovely Dawn," *Time* 50, no. 8 (August 25, 1947): 30–31.
[4] "Flag Hoisting Ceremony at the Indian Council of Agricultural Research," *Indian Farming* 8, no. 8 (August 1947): 380–381.
[5] Department of Information and Broadcasting, Government of India, "Guidance for Food Publicity," August 8, 1947, IOR/L/I/1/1104.x.
[6] George Kuttickal Chacko, *India: Toward an Understanding (A de Novo Inquiry into the Mind of India in Search of an Answer to the Question: "Will India Go Communist?")* (New York: Bookman Associates, 1959).

4   Introduction

mean little if free Indians remained as hungry as they had been through two centuries of foreign rule.

In the weeks and months that followed, millions of hungry refugees would stream across new borders in Punjab and Bengal. Shrewd hoarders would bump up the prices of wheat and rice, aware that India's food stores had dwindled dramatically over years of uncertainty. Indian bureaucrats would travel to countless world capitals to petition for food assistance, worried about a fragile rationing system strained to the breaking point. Communists and radicals would issue secret memoranda calling for the forcible seizure of food at gunpoint, while prosperous farmers would pen angry petitions to New Delhi to protest the commandeering of their crops. Agronomists would struggle to make sense of a nation bereft of much of its arable land, and bureaucrats would debate the tradeoffs between encouraging agricultural growth and promoting rural equity. The leaders who had midwifed India's independence would fret as their promises of abundance foundered on the hard realities of a failing food system. And India's citizens would ask themselves what it meant to be participants in a democratic experiment that had offered a solemn promise of sustenance in place of want, but struggled to realize it.

This is a book about independent India's efforts to feed itself. It considers politicians' and planners' schemes and plans oriented towards that end, and the hopes and fears of new citizens struggling with want. It asserts that the goal of sustenance was central to the structure and language of postcolonial nation-building itself. In the decades after independence, India's national leadership would work to actualize the vows of sustenance made during the struggle for self-rule. They would debate the role that land reform and technological change had in the search for more food, and what obligations citizens would need to undertake to be worthy of that promise. Bureaucrats and planners would argue over the role that food rationing and regulation had in a free economy, and dispute what exactly it would mean for India to become "self-sufficient" in food.

Yet these were not debates for planners and politicians alone. As this book traces India's struggle to feed its citizens, it asks how and to what extent those citizens, across divisions of class, caste, gender, and region, could become participants in those debates. Within the confines of archival restraints, it interrogates how Indian citizens used India's "food question" to explore more abstract questions about the meaning of rights, citizenship, and welfare. And it suggests that participating in those debates helped Indian citizens imagine that state, and nationhood itself, in ways that other subjects did not so readily invite.

Introduction   5

To contend that food was a primary locus for Indian citizens to understand nation-building is not to deemphasize other major debates that enjoyed primacy in public life. Indians, in the mid twentieth century as today, wrestled with questions of caste and religion. They worried about broader standards of living, fought for access to infrastructure, courts, and consumer goods, pondered India's role in the world, and negotiated the tensions between country and city, group, and nation. Yet they often touched upon these questions through the problem of food, whose severity hit them viscerally as they stood in ration lines, worked in fields, or bought grains in the marketplace.

Even in a predominantly agrarian nation, it was not a given that India's food question would assume such a major role in postcolonial public life. Rather, this overriding concern with food sprung from colonial experiences of hunger and malnutrition, and the lamentably late administrative responses to them. For nearly two centuries, India's British administrators had presided over innumerous famines, each dismissed in turn as a Malthusian inevitability. Hunger had begun to emerge as a site of political contestation in the decades before independence, but it was in the wake of the Bengal famine of 1943 that Indian nationalists tied the promise of independence to the guarantee of food for all, drawing upon novel critiques of India's political economy. Assuming power, these nationalists found themselves struggling with the staggering difficulty of that promise. Faced with stagnant agriculture, global food shortages, a dearth of foreign reserves for food imports, and a population growing with alarming speed, free India's politicians and bureaucrats began to examine and qualify their earlier assurances, even as they, and citizens, explored radically divergent models for ensuring sustenance.

For two decades after independence, India's politicians, planners, and citizens debated these models with urgency, collectively advancing the premise of a political solution to India's food crisis. A complex rationing system, borne of wartime experience, sought to determine how Indians procured and sold their food, and in a larger sense, engage with their fledgling economy. Through a network of interlinked schemes, the state sought to harness agricultural expertise and authority over the food problem. Seeking to conserve rice and wheat, and the scarce foreign reserves needed to purchase them from abroad, India's leadership appealed to Indians to change their diets, replacing these cereals with tubers, bananas, alternate grains, and *ersatz* foodstuffs. And as they sought to redistribute land on more equitable lines, India's planners debated whether the nation should follow Chinese and Soviet models or Gandhian ones, or whether equity might be sacrificed in the name of abundance. Debating and experimenting, and imagining the functioning and the limits of their

6   Introduction

economy, Indian planners and citizens came to see the nation with new cohesiveness.[7]

By the mid 1960s, a transformation was taking place. India's efforts to grow more food and preserve the value of social equity had faltered. After decades of imports, a precarious food situation was of increasing interest to planners overseas. "There is no nation on earth far enough from India," the American Secretary of Agriculture contended in 1966, "to be immune from hunger there."[8] As the work of agricultural scientists on maize, wheat, and rice began to yield results, and India faced a new moment of crisis, the nation's planners resuscitated the marginalized notion that the concentrated application of resources could yield far larger harvests than schemes which sought to preserve equity at all costs. These Green Revolution paradigms were not new, and drew upon available models and Indian expertise. Yet Indian planners' belated embrace of these paradigms served to decouple questions of sustenance and good governance, rendering productivity an overriding goal. The unequal gains that followed did not cause the Green Revolution to "go red," as commentators had initially predicted. Yet they did engender the ascendance of a new class of wealthy farmers whose lobbying would reshape Indian politics, and ended an era when the food problem was inextricably tied to larger questions of governance and citizenship.

This separation helps explain some of the most vexing paradoxes of contemporary India. The independent nation has repeatedly defied gloomy predictions of outright famine. Yet India has remained in the thrall of pervasive malnutrition since independence, its citizens less food secure than those of any sub-Saharan African state.[9] In spite of quantitative surplus and grain exported overseas, India's nutritional indicators are among the worst in the world. Alongside a national grain store that would reach to the moon and back, and the "dual burden" posed by its mounting obesity epidemic, India is still home to a quarter of the world's acutely malnourished population – around 230 million people.[10] This book locates the origins of India's contemporary food crisis in

[7] See Manu Goswami, *Producing India: From Colonial Economy to National Space* (Chicago: University of Chicago Press, 2004).
[8] Orville L. Freeman's statement before US House Committee on Agriculture, United States Congress, Secretary of Agriculture, March 31, 1966, in *Emergency Food for India* (Washington, DC: United States Government Printing Office, 1966).
[9] Peter Svedberg, *Poverty and Undernutrition: Theory, Measurement, and Policy* (Oxford: Oxford University Press, 2000), 13.
[10] Revati Laul, "The Politics of Hunger," *Tehelka*, July 3, 2013; Arvind Virmani and Charan Singh, "Malnutrition, Not Hunger, Ails India," *Livemint*, September 22, 2013.

Introduction 7

the contestations of the recent past, and in the foreclosure of the many solutions which officials and citizens explored in an era of postcolonial nation-building.

The centrality of food to Indian political life is a product of very modern political transformations, and this book takes as its starting point the Bengal famine of 1943. Yet the transformations wrought by this late colonial famine owe much to earlier colonial failures in the realm of food management. Famines were part of the Indian ecological and social landscape prior to British rule, though scarcity was accelerated by its onset: the "Great Bengal Famine" of 1770 saw somewhere between a fifth and a third of the region's people felled by hunger, their food entitlements disrupted by massive political transformation.[11] Yet famine and hunger did not take on broader political salience until these deprivations were adopted by economic nationalists at the dawn of the twentieth century.

The provision of adequate sustenance had long been seen as the purview of sovereigns and privileged intermediaries across the subcontinent. Premodern ethical texts routinely exhorted potentates to see to the food needs of the governed. The Jain philosopher Somadeva Suri related the imperative poetically in the *Nitivakyamrtam*, an influential medieval treatise on good governance. "Of what use is the barren cow, which gives no milk?" he asked. "Of what use is the king's grace, if he does not fulfill the hopes of suppliants?"[12] The sixteenth-century *Amuktamalyada*, a Telugu epic poem proffering ethical wisdom, advised rulers to invest in agriculture for the prosperity of the realm and the *dharma* borne of good wardship.[13] India's Mughal emperors were exhorted to dig wells, procure and distribute grains, and open *langars* during times of famine.[14]

Folk literature across the subcontinent alternately praised and pilloried the *baniya* and the *mahajan*, the creditor and intermittent usurer who held the Indian peasantry in bonds of debt and obligation, yet also saw to their sustenance with acts of munificence during moments of scarcity. Legends circulated in thirteenth-century Gujarat about a *baniya*, Jagdusha, who imported grain from distant countries upon hearing

---

[11] Sugata Bose, *Peasant Labour and Colonial Capital: Rural Bengal since 1770* (Cambridge: Cambridge University Press, 1993), 17–24.

[12] Myron Weiner, *The Politics of Scarcity: Public Pressure and Political Response in India* (Chicago: University of Chicago Press, 1962), vii.

[13] Prasannan Parthasarathi, *The Transition to a Colonial Economy: Weavers, Merchants, and Kings in South India, 1720–1800* (Cambridge: Cambridge University Press, 2001), 48.

[14] Prithwis Chandra Ray, *Indian Famines: Their Causes and Remedies* (Calcutta: Cherry Press, 1901), 7–10.

8   Introduction

a prediction of famine; in Western India, the *baniya*'s bazaar taxes were said to pay for famine-time stockpiles.[15]

Late nineteenth and early twentieth-century anthropologists and administrators perceived in Indian villages complex systems of reciprocal obligation centered around food distribution. The colonial Dufferin Enquiry of 1888, an examination into the condition of Indian farmers, detailed codes for the public distribution of grains within villages after threshing.[16] By the 1930s, anthropologists in India had identified the *jajmani* system as the characteristic feature of economic life in the Indian village, with landlords – *jajmans* – paying barbers, potters, washermen, carpenters, and blacksmiths in grain.[17] It is perhaps too much to gird a distinct "moral economy of the peasant" – a purported willingness on the part of peasants to accept rapacious crop taxation in exchange for succor in times of dearth – upon an entire subcontinent.[18] Yet it is clear that across premodern India, sovereigns saw themselves as beholden to diverse codes of conduct that governed food distribution, from the textual Hindu ideal of *annadhan*, or food-giving, to the Bengali practice of *kangali bhojan*, the ritual feeding of the poor.[19]

Traditional patron–client relationships were decoupled by the onset of colonial rule, severing the bonds of obligation governing these practices. Grain riots predated British domination in India, but grew more frequent in the wake of late nineteenth-century famines.[20] The upheavals

---

[15] David Hardiman, *Feeding the Baniya: Peasants and Usurers in Western India* (New Delhi: Oxford University Press, 1996), 154–162.

[16] P.B. Mayer, "Inventing Village Tradition: The Late 19th Century Origins of the North Indian 'Jajmani System,'" *Modern Asian Studies* 27, no. 2 (May 1, 1993): 372; R.C. Temple, "Agricultural Folk-Lore Notes," *The Folk-Lore Record* 5 (January 1, 1882): 35–37.

[17] The existence of the *jajmani* system was first posited by William Henricks Wiser, *The Hindu Jajmani System* (Lucknow: Lucknow Publishing House, 1936). See Mayer, "Inventing Village Tradition."

[18] James C. Scott, *The Moral Economy of the Peasant: Rebellion and Subsistence in Southeast Asia* (New Haven: Yale University Press, 1976).

[19] R.S. Khare, "Hospitality, Charity, and Rationing: Three Channels of Food Distribution in India," in *Food, Society, and Culture: Aspects in South Asian Food Systems*, ed. R.S. Khare and M.S.A. Rao (Durham: Carolina Academic Press, 1986), 277–296.

[20] On market disruptions and protest, see Ravi Ahuja, "State Formation and 'Famine Policy' in Early Colonial South India," *Indian Economic Social History Review* 39, no. 4 (2002): 351–380; David Hall-Matthews, "Colonial Ideologies of the Market and Famine Policy in Ahmednagar District, Bombay Presidency, c. 1870–1884," *Indian Economic and Social History Review* 36, no. 3 (1999): 303–333; Hardiman, *Feeding the Baniya*, 254–271; Sanjay Sharma, "The 1837–38 Famine in U.P.: Some Dimensions of Popular Action," *Indian Economic and Social History Review* 30, no. 3 (September 1, 1993): 337–372; and Sanjay Sharma, *Famine, Philanthropy, and the Colonial State: North India in the Early Nineteenth Century* (Oxford: Oxford University Press, 2001). On nineteenth-century famines more generally, see Mohiuddin Alamgir, *Famine in South Asia: Political Economy of Mass Starvation* (Cambridge: Oelgeschlager, Gunn & Hain, 1980); Mike

Introduction

which erupted across Madras Presidency during the First World War, for example, were fueled by the expansion of colonial meddling in a traditional grain economy, with peasants resorting to insurrectionary protest to defend their continued subsistence.[21] The deeper penetration of market forces into agrarian India further altered the relationships between ideals of good governance and the material provision of foodstuffs, fueling more explicit critiques mounted in the name of hunger.[22]

By the late nineteenth century, Indians and Britons were advancing divergent accounts of India's worsening hunger. India's colonial officials went to pains to situate famines as a natural feature of the Indian ecological landscape, and as evidence of Indian's incapacity for self-rule. As early as the first Bengal famine, British administrators saw millions of deaths as evidence of a weak society too moored in fatalism to lift itself to prosperity.[23] Malthusian hubris underwrote these nineteenth-century beliefs, and imperial administrators conveniently ignored the seven decades of abundance predating their rule.[24] Yet as a new century dawned, Indian economic thinkers, alongside writers, artists, and poets, brought famines from the shadow of ecology and culture into the domain of history and political economy.[25] The Parsi educationist and parliamentarian Dadabhai Naoroji, in his 1901 *Poverty and Un-British Rule in India*, framed India as an economic space drained of its agricultural and monetary wealth by a rapacious foreign regime.[26] India, to Naoroji, had become a space where the "natural laws of economy" had

Davis, *Late Victorian Holocausts: El Niño Famines and the Making of the Third World* (London: Verso, 2001); Michelle Burge McAlpin, *Subject to Famine: Food Crises and Economic Change in Western India, 1860–1920* (Princeton: Princeton University Press, 1983); and Hari Shanker Srivastava, *The History of Indian Famines and Development of Famine Policy, 1858–1918* (Agra: Sri Ram Mehra, 1968).

[21] David Arnold, "Looting, Grain Riots and Government Policy in South India 1918," *Past & Present*, no. 84 (August 1, 1979): 114.

[22] See Arjun Appadurai, "How Moral Is South Asia's Economy? A Review Article," *The Journal of Asian Studies* 43, no. 3 (May 1, 1984): 481–497.

[23] David Arnold, "Hunger in the Garden of Plenty," in *Dreadful Visitations: Confronting Natural Catastrophe in the Age of Enlightenment*, ed. Alessa Johns (London: Routledge, 1999), 82.

[24] S. Ambirajan, *Classical Political Economy and British Policy in India* (Cambridge: Cambridge University Press, 1978).

[25] Sugata Bose, "Pondering Poverty, Fighting Famines: Towards a New History of Economic Ideas," in *Arguments for a Better World: Essays in Honor of Amartya Sen*, ed. Kaushik Basu and Ravi Kanbur, vol. 2: *Society, Institutions, and Development* (Oxford: Oxford University Press, 2009), 425–426.

[26] Dadabhai Naoroji, *Poverty and Un-British Rule in India* (London: S. Sonnenschein, 1901). See Darren C. Zook, "Famine in the Landscape: Imagining Hunger in South Asian History, 1860–1990," in *India's Environmental History: Colonialism, Modernity, and the Nation*, ed. Mahesh Rangarajan and K. Sivaramakrishnan, vol. 2 (Ranikhet: Permanent Black, 2012), 412–413.

10 Introduction

been distorted; only recognition of the "un-British" nature of this misrule would lift Indian subjects out of poverty.[27] Naoroji's contemporary, the economist and civil servant Romesh Chunder Dutt, saw in an emaciated populace the stark consequences of colonial underdevelopment. Indians, he wrote, "attest to semi-starvation by their poor physique; numbers of them suffer from a daily insufficiency of food; and the poorer classes are trained by life-long hunger to live on less food than is needed for proper nourishment."[28]

Dutt and Naoroji's analyses sought to turn imperial logic on its head, and vernacular writers were advancing a similar body of critique. The Marathi nationalist Bal Gangadhar Tilak's paper *Kesari* published a despondent poem in 1896 in the voice of the warrior-king Shivaji, lamenting the desolation of his hungry land; Tilak was promptly charged with sedition.[29] Five years earlier, Calcutta's *Hitavadi* had lambasted foreign merchants "snatching away the bread from the mouths of the people."[30] Short famine stories circulated widely across India: Hari Narayan Apte's popular Marathi famine novel *Kal Tar Motha Kathin Ala* was translated into English as *Ramji: A Tragedy of the Indian Famine* and was circulated widely in India and the United Kingdom.[31] An Urdu pamphlet issued by the Ghadar Party in San Francisco around 1915 decried the colonial government's military expenses in the face of preventable poverty and famine, calling for insurrection.[32] And images like *Bharat ki Lut* – the "Plunder of India" – circulated widely across India itself, showing a British official in a Union Jack cap pilfering food from an emaciated family. This "plunder" was superimposed over a map of India, damning quotes from British and Indian political figures, and a short poem on the ravages of hunger.[33]

The proliferation of these grim visions came as colonial idioms of governance were themselves being reworked in the name of stability. The

[27] Manu Goswami, "From Swadeshi to Swaraj: Nation, Economy, Territory in Colonial South Asia, 1870 to 1907," *Comparative Studies in Society and History* 40, no. 4 (October 1, 1998): 615.

[28] Romesh Chandra Dutt, *The Economic History of India Under Early British Rule*, vol. 1 (London: Kegan Paul, Trench, Trübner, 1902), xxiii–xxiv. See also Romesh Chandra Dutt, *Famines in India: Their Causes and Possible Prevention* (London: P.S. King & Son, 1876); and Romesh Chandra Dutt, *Open Letters to Lord Curzon on Famines and Land Assessments in India* (London: Trübner, 1900).

[29] Bose, "Pondering Poverty, Fighting Famines," 425–426.

[30] Bipin Chandra, *The Rise and Growth of Economic Nationalism in India* (New Delhi: People's Publishing House, 1996), 162–167.

[31] Hari Narayan Apte, *Ramji: A Tragedy of the Indian Famine* (London: T.F. Unwin, 1897).

[32] *Hindson Ki Gavahi: Angrezi Raj Mein Parja Ke Dukh Ki Kahani [India's Testimony: The Story of Sorrow Under British Rule]* (San Francisco: Ghadar Press, 1915).

[33] Devanarayan Varma, *Bharat ki Lut [The Plunder of India]* (Calcutta: Deva-Citralaya, 1930).

Introduction

ravages of the Great Depression saw colonial officials cast old ecological paradigms as new scientific idioms: the commissioning of a *Report on the Improvement of Indian Agriculture* and the establishment of the Imperial Agricultural Research Institute, for example, still relied upon the traditional bogey of stagnant Indian productivity.[34] A new, intertwined concern over population, nutrition, and conjugality was less a palliative for hunger and poor health than a means of fixing subjects, regulating bodies, and advancing new interventions into markets and land in the name of continued extraction.[35] The founding of the Nutrition Research Laboratories in Coonoor, the publication of India's first nutrition textbooks, and village surveys like the one undertaken in 1933 by John Megaw, director of the Indian Medical Service, helped quantify the percentage of Indians said to be malnourished.[36] Yet these projects were designed to strengthen the bodily foundations of colonial rule, and had

[34] M.S. Randhawa, *A History of Agriculture in India*, vol. 3: *1757–1947* (New Delhi: Indian Council of Agricultural Research, 1983). The classic account of India's productivity in the last half-century of colonial administration is George Blyn, *Agricultural Trends in India, 1891–1947: Output, Availability, and Productivity* (Philadelphia: University of Pennsylvania Press, 1966).

[35] The ample and important literature on biopolitics in late colonial India stems from research on nineteenth-century antecedents in David Arnold, *Colonizing the Body: State Medicine and Epidemic Disease in Nineteenth-Century India* (Berkeley: University of California Press, 1993). On the rise of population as a global ideology, with reference to Indian thought, see Alison Bashford, *Global Population: History, Geopolitics, and Life on Earth* (New York: Columbia University Press, 2014). On health, nutrition, and malnutrition, see Rachel Berger, *Ayurveda Made Modern: Political Histories of Indigenous Medicine in North India, 1900–1955* (Basingstoke: Palgrave Macmillan, 2013); Nick Cullather, "The Foreign Policy of the Calorie," *The American Historical Review* 112, no. 2 (April 1, 2007): 337–364; David E. Ludden, "The 'Discovery' of Malnutrition and Diet in Colonial India," *Indian Economic and Social History Review* 31, no. 1 (1994): 1–26; and Michael Worboys, "The Discovery of Colonial Malnutrition between the Wars," in *Imperial Medicine and Indigenous Societies*, ed. David Arnold (Manchester: Manchester University Press, 1998), 208–225. On sex, sex work, and the body, see Sanjam Ahluwalia, *Reproductive Restraints: Birth Control in India, 1877–1947* (Urbana: University of Illinois Press, 2008); Anjali R. Arondekar, *For the Record: On Sexuality and the Colonial Archive in India* (Durham: Duke University Press, 2010); Sarah Hodges, *Contraception, Colonialism and Commerce: Birth Control in South India, 1920–1940* (Farnham: Ashgate Publishing, 2016); Stephen Legg, *Prostitution and the Ends of Empire: Scale, Governmentalities, and Interwar India* (Durham: Duke University Press, 2014); and Ashwini Tambe, *Codes of Misconduct: Regulating Prostitution in Late Colonial Bombay* (Minneapolis: University of Minnesota Press, 2009). On new conjugal ideals, see Mytheli Sreenivas, *Wives, Widows, and Concubines: The Conjugal Family Ideal in Colonial India* (Bloomington: Indiana University Press, 2008); and Eleanor Newbigin, *The Hindu Family and the Emergence of Modern India Law, Citizenship and Community* (Cambridge: Cambridge University Press, 2013).

[36] John Megaw, *An Inquiry into Certain Public Health Aspects of Village Life in India* (New Delhi: Government of India Press, 1933).

12   Introduction

the unintended consequence of inspiring anti-colonial nationalism in the name of a healthy body politic.

For nationalists, the deprivations of the interwar years underscored the imperative of combating agrarian poverty and bolstering internal markets.[37] As Indian thinkers increasingly conceptualized the incipient nation itself as a "body" comprising healthy citizens, malnutrition and hunger emerged as potent sites of anti-colonial foment.[38] And as the specter of a free India came into focus, food emerged as a site for nationalist planners to articulate the cleave between colonial deprivations and the material promise of self-rule. Works like *Starving India Under the Aegis of Great Britain*, written by the Congress organizer C.N. Zutshi in 1925, asserted that only self-rule would be "the panacea of all economic ills with which India is for long sorely afflicted. A free India will be better able to cope with such problems by enacting laws to check the export of her foodstuffs which go to feed other nations abroad at the cost of bringing starvation upon her own people."[39] In his 1938 *Food Planning for Four Hundred Millions*, economist and sociologist Radhakamal Mukerjee appealed to the promise of centralized planning that would only be possible under self-rule.[40] And Nagendranath Gangulee, a former member of the Royal Commission on Indian Agriculture, castigated an alien government in his 1939 primer *Health and Nutrition in India*. Decrying the rapaciousness of colonial rule, he dedicated his work to "Pandit Jawaharlal Nehru and other leaders of the Indian National Congress, who have undertaken the responsibility of shaping a national policy [for] my Country, where 'for every three mouths, there are only two rice bowls.'"[41] The colonial government, belatedly, was moving food and agriculture towards the center of its planning. Yet its formation of a Central Food Advisory Council and the initiation of a Grow More Food campaign in 1942 came as famine was already descending upon Bengal; these belated moves did little to claim the weight of moral authority back from India's nationalists.

The nationalist vision of a healthy India free of famine was split over the question of how India's agriculture was to be "reconstructed."[42]

---

[37] David E. Ludden, *An Agrarian History of South Asia*, The New Cambridge History of India 4 (Cambridge: Cambridge University Press, 1999), 167–168.

[38] Benjamin Zachariah, "Uses of Scientific Argument: The Case of 'Development' in India, c. 1930–1950," *Economic and Political Weekly* 36, no. 39 (2001): 3689–3702.

[39] C.N. Zutshi, *Starving India under the Ægis of Great Britain* (Muzaffarnagar, 1925).

[40] Radhakamal Mukerjee, *Food Planning for Four Hundred Millions* (London: Macmillan, 1938).

[41] Arnold, *Colonizing the Body*, 246; Nagendranath Gangulee, *Health and Nutrition in India* (London: Faber and Faber, 1939).

[42] Sunil S. Amrith, "Food and Welfare in India, c. 1900–1950," *Comparative Studies in Society and History* 50 (2008): 1021–1022.

Introduction 13

Congress modernizers emphasized the need to eliminate taboo and custom, pushing aside vegetarianism, cultural preferences, and vestigial sentiment in the name of a national crisis. By contrast, Gandhian thinkers sought to affirm the connections between agricultural and moral reconstruction, urging planners to "think small." Yet the cleft between these two visions did not alter the fundamental critique of India's colonial political economy: by the time of the Bengal famine, Indian nationalists knew that the nation's hunger stemmed not from the caprices of ecology, but from fundamental misrule and exploitation.

The pages that follow pick up the story of India's search for plenty from the moment when independence was all but inevitable. This story is told in six roughly chronological chapters which stretch from the 1940s to the 1970s, and which glance forward and backwards in the interests of more theoretical excursions.

An opening chapter, "The Bengal Famine and the Nationalist Case for Food," demonstrates how the 1943 famine galvanized nationalist thought and brought food to the fore of national consciousness. Chapter 2, "Independent India of Plenty" examines the new state's efforts to import, grow, and procure food on the cheap, contrasting these efforts with the proliferation of popular visions of plenty in the wake of independence and the contested location of expertise itself. A third chapter, "Self-Help Which Ennobles a Nation," interrogates Indian planners' quixotic efforts to remake the Indian diet in the name of self-sufficiency, as they saddled citizens with the burden of their own development. "The Common Hunger of the Country," this book's fourth chapter, explores India's byzantine rationing and food control system, demonstrating how provision and restriction prompted Indian citizens to imagine the workings and limits of their own economy. A fifth chapter, "All the Disabilities Which Peasant and Land Can Suffer," examines the debate over agrarian reform in India, and the ways in which leftist planners' schemes for collective and cooperative farms were contested and defeated by wealthy peasants, conservative politicians, and free-market businessmen. A final chapter, "The Ideological Origins of the Green Revolution," demonstrates how, at a moment of crisis, India reanimated earlier, technocratic schemes for agricultural growth, upending earlier paradigms of social equity among its citizens. And a brief conclusion traces the subsequent rise of a wealthy peasantry and the emergence of India's confounding, present-day food crisis.

As this book wends through three decades of political development, it will remain attentive to three key bodies of literature: on nation-building and the state, on development expertise, and the role of food in modern political and economic histories. First, *Hungry Nation* considers the

14   Introduction

nature of postcolonial nation-building and the Indian state itself, remaining keenly aware of parallel and connected developments far away from India. Bringing contestations over food's procurement, consumption, and provision to the center of a story about state-making and nation-building highlights the affective and political differences which separate the postcolonial Indian state from its colonial predecessor. If Indian nationalism has been cast as a "derivative discourse" modeled upon European antecedents, this book joins other recent interventions in demonstrating how late colonial Indian nationalism drew upon these antecedents, while advancing fundamentally different notions of what the nation itself was to be.[43] The story of India's search for plenty highlights the ways in which these notions drew upon colonial models, as well as a complex global network of ideas and institutions.[44] By interrogating the meaning of "economic nationalism" and self-sufficiency, this book situates the quest for material well-being as central to the process of Indian nation-building.[45] And in looking to everyday experience when possible, it highlights how the state was encountered, perceived, and contested by Indian citizens themselves.[46]

[43] On Indian nationalism as a "derivative discourse," see Partha Chatterjee, *Nationalist Thought and the Colonial World: A Derivative Discourse?* (London: Zed Books, 1986); and C.A. Bayly, *Origins of Nationality in South Asia: Patriotism and Ethical Government in the Making of Modern India* (New Delhi: Oxford University Press, 1998). On postcolonial nationalism and nation-building, see Ritu Birla, *Stages of Capital: Law, Culture, and Market Governance in Late Colonial India* (Durham: Duke University Press, 2009); Srirupa Roy, *Beyond Belief: India and the Politics of Postcolonial Nationalism* (Durham: Duke University Press, 2007); and Vazira Fazila-Yacoobali Zamindar, *The Long Partition and the Making of Modern South Asia: Refugees, Boundaries, Histories* (New York: Columbia University Press, 2007).

[44] Work on the circulation of South Asian ideas through diverse international networks has proliferated in recent years; see Muhammad Ali Raza, Franziska Roy, and Benjamin Zachariah, eds., *The Internationalist Moment: South Asia, Worlds, and World Views, 1917–39* (New Delhi: Sage Publications, 2016); Sugata Bose and Kris Manjapra, eds., *Cosmopolitan Thought Zones: South Asia and the Global Circulation of Ideas* (Basingstoke: Palgrave Macmillan, 2010); T.N. Harper and Sunil S. Amrith, eds., *Sites of Asian Interaction: Ideas, Networks and Mobility* (Cambridge: Cambridge University Press, 2014); and Carolien Stolte and Harald Fischer-Tiné, "Imagining Asia in India: Nationalism and Internationalism (ca. 1905–1940)," *Comparative Studies in Society and History* 54, no. 1 (January 2012): 65–92.

[45] The classic account of "economic nationalism" in India is Chandra, *The Rise and Growth of Economic Nationalism in India*; see also Andrew Wyatt, "Building the Temples of Postmodern India: Economic Constructions of National Identity," *Contemporary South Asia* 14, no. 4 (December 2005): 465–480. On economic thought in India more generally, see Ajit Kumar Dasgupta, *A History of Indian Economic Thought* (London: Routledge, 1993). The first two chapters of this book, in particular, have been influenced by my reading of T.H. Breen, *The Marketplace of Revolution: How Consumer Politics Shaped American Independence* (Oxford: Oxford University Press, 2004).

[46] On citizenship practices and the everyday, see Sarah Ansari, "Everyday Expectations of the State during Pakistan's Early Years: Letters to the Editor, Dawn (Karachi),

Introduction 15

Secondly, this book looks critically to the broader course of development, planning, and expertise in the twentieth century. As independence neared, India's nationalist leadership drew freely upon colonial and international paradigms of development and planning.[47] Indian planners were inspired by Soviet and Chinese development schemes and American New Deal projects, and their own efforts would soon be caught up in the machinations of Cold War politics.[48] And as Indian politicians and planners looked with admiration to collective farms and massive dams overseas, the nation's agronomists, economists, and other experts became

1950–1953," *Modern Asian Studies* 45, Special Issue 1 (2011): 159–178; Rohit De, *Litigious Citizens, Constitutional Law and Everyday Life in the Indian Republic*, forthcoming; C.J. Fuller and Véronique Bénéï, *The Everyday State and Society in Modern India* (London: Hurst & Co., 2001); William Gould, *Bureaucracy, Community, and Influence in India: Society and the State, 1930s–1960s* (London: Routledge, 2009); Akhil Gupta, *Red Tape: Bureaucracy, Structural Violence, and Poverty in India* (Durham: Duke University Press, 2012); and Tarangini Sriraman, "Revisiting Welfare: Ration Card Narratives in India," *Economic and Political Weekly* 46, no. 38 (2011): 52–59.

[47] See Sugata Bose, "Instruments and Idioms of Colonial and National Development," in *International Development and the Social Sciences*, ed. Frederick Cooper and Randall Packard (Berkeley: University of California Press, 1997), 45–63; Partha Chatterjee, "The National State," in *The Nation and Its Fragments: Colonial and Postcolonial Histories* (Princeton: Princeton University Press, 1993), 200–219; David Washbrook, "The Rhetoric of Democracy and Development in Late Colonial India," in *Nationalism, Democracy, and Development: State and Politics in India*, ed. Sugata Bose and Ayesha Jalal (New Delhi: Oxford University Press, 1997), 36–49; and Benjamin Zachariah, *Developing India: An Intellectual and Social History, c. 1930–50* (New Delhi: Oxford University Press, 2005).

[48] On American and Soviet influence and competition in Indian development, see David C. Engerman, "Learning from the East: Soviet Experts and India in the Era of Competitive Coexistence," *Comparative Studies of South Asia, Africa and the Middle East* 33, no. 2 (2013): 227–238; David C. Engerman, *Planning for Plenty: The Economic Cold War in India* (Cambridge, MA: Harvard University Press, forthcoming); Daniel Immerwahr, *Thinking Small: The United States and the Lure of Community Development* (Cambridge, MA: Harvard University Press, 2015); Daniel Klingensmith, *One Valley and a Thousand: Dams, Nationalism, and Development* (New Delhi: Oxford University Press, 2007); Nicole Sackley, "The Village as Cold War Site: Experts, Development, and the History of Rural Reconstruction," *Journal of Global History* 6, no. 3 (2011): 481–504; Nicole Sackley, "Foundation in the Field: The Ford Foundation New Delhi Office and the Construction of Development Knowledge, 1951–1970," in *American Foundations and the Coproduction of World Order in the Twentieth Century*, ed. John Krige and Helke Rausch (Göttingen: Vandenhoeck & Ruprecht, 2012), 232–260; Nicole Sackley, "Village Models: Etawah, India, and the Making and Remaking of Development in the Early Cold War," *Diplomatic History* 37, no. 4 (2013): 749–778; Benjamin Siegel, "Fantastic Quantities of Food Grains: Cold War Visions and Agrarian Fantasies in Independent India," in *Negotiating Independence: New Directions in the History of Decolonization and the Cold War*, ed. Elisabeth Mariko Leake and Leslie James (London: Bloomsbury, 2014), 21–42; and Subir Sinha, "Lineages of the Developmentalist State: Transnationality and Village India, 1900–1965," *Comparative Studies in Society and History* 50, no. 1 (2008): 57–90.

16   Introduction

part of international networks of research and development.[49] Yet all the while, "planning" continued to enjoy a privileged space in the Indian political imagination as a site of knowledge and power ostensibly removed from the tumult of participative democracy.[50] In the stories that follow, highlighting within archival constraints how Indian citizens' hopes and ideas interacted with more formal categories of expertise, it is possible to see the competing and contested notions of development planning as they played out in India's first several decades of independence.[51]

Finally, this book foregrounds central debates over food procurement and consumption in the South Asian context, suturing questions of politics and economic life to important debates over the role of food in history and anthropology. Moving food to the center of a story of political and economic life demonstrates how contestations over sustenance are not questions of aesthetics or identity alone, but rather, constituent debates over how a nation is itself to function. The vibrant contemporary study of food in South Asia draws upon a rich and voluminous body of literature on the region's agrarian pasts.[52] So, too, does it reference important foundational work on Indian foodways, ecology, and religious life, beginning with seminal investigation into caste and ritual life

[49] On these networks, see Robert S. Anderson, *Nucleus and Nation: Scientists, International Networks, and Power in India* (Chicago: University of Chicago Press, 2010); Jahnavi Phalkey, *Atomic State: Big Science in Twentieth-Century India* (Ranikhet: Permanent Black, 2013).

[50] Partha Chatterjee, "Development Planning and the Indian State," in *The State, Development Planning and Liberalisation in India*, ed. T.J. Byres (New Delhi: Oxford University Press, 1998), 82–103; Sunil Khilnani, *The Idea of India* (New York: Farrar, Straus and Giroux, 1998), 78–90. The classically trenchant critique of development as an apolitical category of knowledge and action is James Ferguson, *The Anti-Politics Machine: "Development," Depoliticization, and Bureaucratic Power in Lesotho* (Minneapolis: University of Minnesota Press, 1994).

[51] The salient critique of high modernist planning schemes is James C. Scott, *Seeing Like a State: How Certain Schemes to Improve the Human Condition Have Failed* (New Haven: Yale University Press, 1998); an important critique which has been influential in this reading is Tania Murray Li, "Beyond 'the State' and Failed Schemes," *American Anthropologist* 107, no. 3 (2005): 383–394.

[52] David Ludden's thorough account is capped by an exhaustive review essay; see Ludden, *An Agrarian History of South Asia*. Other important interventions include Amiya Kumar Bagchi, "Reflections on Patterns of Regional Growth in India During the Period of British Rule," *Bengal Past and Present* 95, no. 1 (1976): 247–289; Sumit Guha, ed., *Growth, Stagnation, or Decline? Agricultural Productivity in British India* (New Delhi: Oxford University Press, 1992); David E. Ludden, ed., *Agricultural Production and South Asian History* (New Delhi: Oxford University Press, 2005); Peter Robb, ed., *Meanings of Agriculture: Essays in South Asian History and Economics* (New Delhi: Oxford University Press, 1996); and Eric Stokes, "Dynamism and Enervation in North Indian Agriculture," in *The Peasant and the Raj: Studies in Agrarian Society and Peasant Rebellion in Colonial India* (Cambridge: Cambridge University Press, 1978), 228–242.

Introduction 17

undertaken by anthropologists rooted in debates over structuralism.[53] The emerging anthropological concerns of space and care, drawing upon this early work, have birthed vital new ethnographic investigations into food and public life.[54] And historians of South Asia, more recently, have come to see the primacy of food in twentieth-century India, examining practices of consumption, political contestation, and international linkages alike.[55] This book reflects extensively upon this literature, and a wider body of scholarship on food and nation-building across the globe.

[53] R.S. Khare, *Culture and Reality: Essays on the Hindu System of Managing Foods* (Simla: Indian Institute of Advanced Study, 1976); R.S. Khare, *The Hindu Hearth and Home: Culinary Systems Old and New in North India* (Delhi: Vikas Publishing House, 1976); and McKim Marriott, "Caste Ranking and Food Transactions: A Matrix Analysis," in *Structure and Change in Indian Society*, ed. Milton B. Singer and Bernard S. Cohn (New York: Wenner-Gren Foundation for Anthropological Research, 1968), 133–172. This early work preceded a broader investigation, in the 1980s, into the symbolism, politics, and ecological orientation of Indian foodways; see Arjun Appadurai, "Gastro-Politics in Hindu South Asia," *American Ethnologist* 8, no. 3 (August 1, 1981): 494–511; Carol Appadurai Breckenridge, "Food, Politics and Pilgrimage in South India, 1350–1650 A.D.," in *Food, Society, and Culture: Aspects in South Asian Food Systems*, ed. R.S. Khare and M.S.A. Rao (Durham: Carolina Academic Press, 1986); Marvin Harris, "The Cultural Ecology of India's Sacred Cattle," *Current Anthropology* 33, no. 1 (February 1, 1992): 261–276; R.S. Khare and M.S.A. Rao, *Food, Society, and Culture: Aspects in South Asian Food Systems* (Durham: Carolina Academic Press, 1986); R.S. Khare, *The Eternal Food: Gastronomic Ideas and Experiences of Hindus and Buddhists* (Albany: SUNY Press, 1992); and Francis Zimmermann, *The Jungle and the Aroma of Meats: An Ecological Theme in Hindu Medicine* (Berkeley: University of California Press, 1987).

[54] Most recently, see Jonathan Shapiro Anjaria, *The Slow Boil: Street Food, Rights and Public Space in Mumbai* (Palo Alto: Stanford University Press, 2016); Hayden S. Kantor, "'We Earn Less than We Eat': Food, Farming, and the Caring Family in Bihar, India" (Ph.D. diss., Cornell University, 2016); and Harris Solomon, *Metabolic Living: Food, Fat, and the Absorption of Illness in India* (Durham: Duke University Press, 2016).

[55] Much of this work was instigated by Arjun Appadurai's classic provocation; Arjun Appadurai, "How to Make a National Cuisine: Cookbooks in Contemporary India," *Comparative Studies in Society and History* 30 (1988): 3–24. Recent and important studies include Rachel Berger, "Between Digestion and Desire: Genealogies of Food in Nationalist North India," *Modern Asian Studies* 47, no. 5 (2013): 1622–1643; E.M. Collingham, *Imperial Bodies: The Physical Experience of the Raj, c. 1800–1947* (Cambridge: Polity Press, 2001); Utsa Ray, "Eating 'Modernity': Changing Dietary Practices in Colonial Bengal," *Modern Asian Studies* 46, no. 3 (2012): 703–729; Utsa Ray, "The Body and Its Purity: Dietary Politics in Colonial Bengal," *Indian Economic and Social History Review* 50, no. 4 (October 1, 2013): 395–421; Krishnendu Ray and Tulasi Srinivas, *Curried Cultures: Globalization, Food, and South Asia* (Berkeley: University of California Press, 2012); Jayanta Sengupta, "Nation on a Platter: The Culture and Politics of Food and Cuisine in Colonial Bengal," *Modern Asian Studies* 44, Special Issue 1 (2010): 81–98; and Benjamin Siegel, "Learning to Eat in a Capital City: Constructing Public Eating Culture in Delhi," *Food, Culture and Society: An International Journal of Multidisciplinary Research* 13, no. 1 (2010): 71–90. Short studies of food and politics include Amrith, "Food and Welfare in India"; Taylor C. Sherman, "From 'Grow More Food' to 'Miss a Meal': Hunger, Development and the Limits of Post-Colonial Nationalism in India, 1947–1957," *South Asia: Journal of South Asian Studies* 36, no. 4 (December 2013): 571–588; and Zook, "Famine in the Landscape: Imagining Hunger

18   Introduction

The patchy nature of the Indian archive itself means that this book is limited in the representative claims that it can make about Indian citizenship and experience. But with this constraint in mind, the stories that follow highlight the constant interplay between planners and politicians and citizens themselves – as well as the emergence, and then foreclosure, of a certain model of participatory citizenship in postcolonial India.

In 1947, two Hindi books asked citizens to take on a new responsibility befitting a country in charge of its own fate. *Hamari Khurak aur Aabadi ki Samsaya* – "Our Food and Population Problem" – gave a brief account of the quantity and quality of food the new nation would need to build up as its population continued to grow.[56] Its introduction was written by Lakshmi Chand Jain, a veteran Congressman charged with feeding the residents of Delhi's overflowing Kingsway Refugee Camp. "The complex food problem that our country faces today," Jain declared, "is a secret to no one. If a country cannot give its citizens proper food, and enough of it, is not its economic organization useless?"

India's new leaders, he vowed, would be ecumenical in their thinking about the food problem. Even if the war with Japan had only recently ended, there was nothing wrong with looking towards their new agricultural methods, or towards any other nation's example. India, Jain averred, had no meaningful shortage of land or implements, only "a lack of knowledge as to how to make use of them correctly and in consort." Towards that end, India's new leaders would need to empower citizens to think critically about the food problem. "For the first time," Lakshmi Chand Jain concluded, "our country is in the hands of its own peoples' representatives. The most important thing is to make our problems known to the common people, so that an informed public can help officials decide on the best course." Self-rule meant that citizens themselves would be allowed, and perhaps obligated, to weigh in on the nation's most pressing matters.

Yet citizens, another writer contended, needed little prompting to think critically about food. Jagdishchandra Jain's *Hamari Roti ki Samasya* – "Our Food Problem" – was dedicated to the victims of the Bengal

---

in South Asian History, 1860–1990." A small body of work attuned to international connections include Kristin L. Ahlberg, *Transplanting the Great Society: Lyndon Johnson and Food for Peace* (Columbia, MO: University of Missouri Press, 2008); Dennis Merrill, *Bread and the Ballot: The United States and India's Economic Development, 1947–1963* (Chapel Hill: University of North Carolina Press, 1990); and Robert L. Paarlberg, *Food Trade and Foreign Policy: India, the Soviet Union, and the United States* (Ithaca: Cornell University Press, 1985).

[56] Shri Omprakash, *Hamari Khurak aur Aabadi ki Samasya [Our Food and Population Problem]* (New Delhi: Rajkamal Publications, 1947), 3–4.

Introduction   19

famine, in whose memory the nation's food crisis should be resolved.[57]
"Wherever you go these days," he maintained, "everyone speaks constantly of food." Congress was now in control of the country, yet the
transfer of power had done nothing by itself to fill bellies. "You must keep
your ration card safe," he continued,

> since if you were to lose it by mistake, you would have no option but to starve.
> And even if you stand in line at the ration depot for hours, you still can't get your
> full quota. There is not enough to fill your stomach: you use up the sugar by the
> fifth day, *dal* is incredibly scarce, and you wonder what you will end up eating to
> keep yourself alive.

Yet Jain sounded an optimistic tone: citizens were already viscerally aware of the magnitude of India's most pressing crisis. "Our food
problem," Jain wrote, "is not only a problem of the farmer's field, but
a problem worldwide, and one which the common man must approach
seriously." An informed citizenry would help the nation's "bread-givers"
forge better policy, ultimately actualizing the promise of food for all.

Writing on the eve of independence, writers like Lakshmi Chand Jain
and Jagdishchandra Jain imagined a citizenry engaged in vital learning and debate on India's food problem. And India's citizens, across
boundaries of class, caste, region, and politics, met these appeals with
urgency and enthusiasm. In this book, alongside tales of political and
economic transformation, there are stories of some of the Indian citizens
who thought carefully and critically about the nation's food problem.
These include an astrologer in Bombay using lucky numbers to predict
the end of India's food crisis, and a housewife in the same city lamenting that the Congress leadership had abandoned its pledge to end the
hunger of the common man and woman. In the pages that follow, a frustrated merchant writes to the Prime Minister to protest India's byzantine
restrictions on trade in foodgrains, and a wealthy landlord pens a similar
letter to lament the breakup of his hereditary lands. These pages highlight some of the many plans that citizens wrote as they dreamed of agricultural abundance, distributing them via cyclostyle, mimeograph, and
small runs on printing presses. These plans include the detailed scheme
of a retired lawyer in Kohlapur, the outlandish fantasy of a barely liter-
ate *Dalit* laborer in a Madras village, and the petition filed by villagers in
north India who, unable to sign their own names, protested mandatory
grain procurement with 6000 thumbprints.

---

[57] Jagdishchandra Jain, *Hamari Roti ki Samasya [Our Food Problem]* (Bombay: National
Information and Publications, 1947), iv.

20   Introduction

These stories help us see how the ideas, aspirations, and disappointments of citizens interacted with the larger social and political contexts in which they were forged. None of these encounters can be fully satisfying. The postcolonial Indian archive is patchy, and frustrating in its lacunae. In the absence of the more comprehensive repositories, historians of India and South Asia must rely upon fragmentary collections: moldy papers in state-run archives, books, newspapers, and pamphlets which made their way to libraries overseas, and privately held materials acquired by grit and happenstance in equal measure.[58]

Yet even if these citizens and their plans too often disappear into a historical miasma, the record that does remain suggests that citizens were rarely silent, or quiescent.[59] Within some limits, this book shows how they could and did speak back to the planners, bureaucrats, and politicians hatching schemes undertaken in their name. If this story is confined by the limits of the archive, and by the limits of language – this book draws from Hindi, Urdu, and English sources, as well as a smattering of Bengali documents – it is still vital to take these citizens and their ideas seriously, not condemning them to silence. And while critically interrogating their specific visions, it is still evident that the food debate, for a fertile moment, invited and impelled Indian citizens to make their voices heard. As politicians and bureaucrats schemed and planned, so too did citizens consider the struggles of the past and the challenges of the present. They considered the promises made in the struggle for freedom, and the possibility of a brighter future finally free from hunger.

---

[58] On the South Asian archive and problems of history-writing, see Sugata Bose, "Post-Colonial Histories of South Asia: Some Reflections," *Journal of Contemporary History* 38, no. 1 (2003): 133–146; and Saloni Mathur, "History and Anthropology in South Asia: Rethinking the Archive," *Annual Review of Anthropology* 29 (2000): 89–106. More generally, on the challenges of postcolonial historiography and the archive, see Frederick Cooper, "Conflict and Connection: Rethinking Colonial African History," *The American Historical Review* 99, no. 5 (1994): 1516–1545; and Ann Laura Stoler, *Along the Archival Grain: Epistemic Anxieties and Colonial Common Sense* (Princeton: Princeton University Press, 2009). An examination of the migration of Indian materials to the United States is Maureen L.P. Patterson, "The South Asian P.L. 480 Library Program, 1962–1968," *The Journal of Asian Studies* 28, no. 4 (August 1, 1969): 743–754.

[59] To answer the question famously posed in Gayatri Chakravorty Spivak, "Can the Subaltern Speak?," in *Marxism and the Interpretation of Culture*, ed. Cary Nelson and Lawrence Grossberg (Urbana and Chicago: University of Illinois Press, 1988), 271–313. A reflection upon the ensuing "Subaltern Studies" project is Sumit Sarkar, "The Decline of the Subaltern in Subaltern Studies," in *Writing Social History* (New Delhi: Oxford University Press, 1997), 82–108.

1 The Bengal Famine and the Nationalist Case for Food

> Hunger is a fierce Durga
> with innumerable limbs and faces
> and a boundless appetite.
> When hunger roams the earth,
> the earth shakes and staggers.
> She chews up injustice, and eats the unjust.
> And in an instant, consumes their intolerable rule.

In a decade of global depression, there were few brighter stars in India than the Hindi poet Harivansh Rai Bachchan, a young Allahabad University professor whose epic poem had catapulted him to stardom. *Madhushala*, a lyrical retelling of Omar Khayyam's *Rubaiyat*, had offered romance to north Indian audiences eager for distraction as the nationalist movement staggered forward, and the poet's readings packed lecture halls across north India.

Yet war had changed Bachchan no less than it had changed India itself: it was impossible to write of ardor when famine had ravaged the country. Three and a half million Bengalis had died needlessly of hunger, and in his 1946 *Bengal ka Kal*, "The Bengal Famine," Bachchan had traded love for insurrectionary fervor. "Be rid of complacency," he urged India's starving, likening hunger to the ferocity of Durga, Bengal's most revered goddess. "Raise the call of dissatisfaction, and sound the cry of revolution."[1]

Hunger, Bachchan insisted, offered a transformative power largely unrealized by Bengal's decimated peasantry, who had streamed into Calcutta from the hinterlands three years prior. Dying on the pavement next to regal hotels, Bengal's "hunger marchers" had come to empire's second city to stage a feeble protest against imperial rapaciousness. Few Bengalis believed the British officials who blamed the famine deaths on flood, cyclone, and drought. When rice rotted in warehouses, and left

---

[1] Harivansh Rai Bachchan, *Bangal ka Kal [The Bengal Famine]* (Allahabad: Bharati-Bhandara, 1946).

on freighters destined for British soldiers overseas, it was hard to see the famine as the consequence of anything but an odious political arrangement borne on the backs of Bengal's rural poor. A professor of English at the University of Calcutta watched in horror as peasants collapsed next to Gothic colonnades and Art Deco cinemas, vowing that no one who had watched them would ever forget their shameful deaths.[2] "Hunger marchers confronted those who had made them hungry and had made them march," Humayun Kabir would write a year later. Their cries "rent the sky and at last penetrated the complacency of the masters who toiled under the self-imposed task of doling out freedom and democracy to the colored peoples of the world."

As those colonial masters debated how to staunch the political damage wrought by famine, a cloud of rage had settled over the green lawns of Cambridge's Trinity College. Since the 1890s, expatriate students had met there to debate the future of their homeland, and Indian leaders of all persuasion courted support in the rooms abutting the Great Court. Separated by 8000 miles, news nonetheless galloped from Calcutta to Cambridge: well before the famine had appeared in the *Times* of London, it was being debated and decried by Cambridge's Indian students.

Late in 1943, it was these students who produced a slim pamphlet on Bengal authored by Jyoti Basu, a Communist firebrand then studying law in London, and who would later serve as West Bengal's Chief Minister.[3] *The Man-Made Famine* recounted stories of starving Bengalis "sharing food with the animals in the gutter," fleeing from British troops who shot at hungry crowds and retreated to feast in well-appointed hotels. Basu did not dwell upon the less flattering aspects of the Communist Party's complicity in British misrule: the Muslim League government in Bengal had been a great deal more effective in organizing famine relief than the Party, which touted radical food committees but had collaborated extensively with the British administration. But his key assertion was one that Harivansh Rai Bachchan, Humayun Kabir, and Indians the world over could agree upon: only India's legitimate leaders, the nationalist Congressmen held in detention for the duration of the war, possessed the stature and vision needed to prevent famine's recurrence. "The unanimous demand of the Indian people today," Basu wrote, "is for food and freedom."

After decades of marches, boycotts, and strikes in protest of the economic consequences of imperial rule, the Bengal famine marked, in

---

[2] Kalyani Bhattacharjee and Humayun Kabir, *War against the People: A Sharp Analysis of the Causes of Famine in Bengal* (Calcutta: People's Book Club, 1944).

[3] Jyothi Bose, *The Man-Made Famine* (Cambridge: Cambridge University Majlis, 1943).

The Bengal Famine

Jawaharlal Nehru's words, "the final judgment on British rule in India."[4] As India's citizens and politicians reflected upon the famine, they saw in it the clearest failure of colonial politics and economics, tying the promise of self-rule to the project of sustenance for every Indian. Famine had long been central to Indian understandings of imperial injustice, but after 1943, the elimination of hunger emerged as a nationalist imperative.

The ascendance of famine to political preeminence did not preclude a proliferation of visions for how the independent Indian state would function. In the years that followed, Indians imagined their nation as a cooperative socialist republic, a country powered by capitalist industry, a loose confederation of self-sustaining villages, or a modernizing polity that would yoke Indians forward from custom and superstition. But their plans converged around the imperative of providing all Indians with sustenance. Nor, of course, did the famine flatten contentious internecine fighting among Indian nationalists of different hues. But if Congress activists continued to hurl invective at Communists for their wartime collaboration, and members of both parties saw the Muslim League as complicit in misadministration and incompetent in delivering relief, these barbs served to underscore the political centrality that the provision of food and the elimination of famine had come to occupy.

Histories of the turbulent decade preceding independence have understated the Bengal famine's transformative effect on Indian politics and national aspirations. These histories relegate the famine to a gruesome wartime footnote, overlooking the ways in which a provincial atrocity was transformed into a key site for political claim-making. As a result, the 1943 famine has been used more frequently by historians, economists, and political scientists to advance divergent positions over the causes of famines in general. Amartya Sen's 1981 *Poverty and Famines: An Essay on Entitlement and Deprivation* famously used the Bengal famine to deflate the notion that famines stemmed from an overall shortage of food, focusing instead upon the role of political entitlements; subsequent work has largely affirmed this position.[5]

---

[4] Jawaharlal Nehru, *The Discovery of India* (New Delhi: Oxford University Press, 1989), 499.

[5] Amartya Sen, *Poverty and Famines: An Essay on Entitlement and Deprivation* (Oxford: Clarendon Press, 1981). The persistent reexamination of the "food availability decline" model suggests scholarly reluctance to engage with the political consequences of the famine. See Omkar Goswami, "The Bengal Famine of 1943: Re-Examining the Data," *Indian Economic and Social History Review* 27, no. 4 (December 1, 1990): 445–463; Auriol Weigold, "Famine Management: The Bengal Famine (1942–1944) Revisited," *South Asia: Journal of South Asian Studies* 22, no. 1 (1999): 63–77; M. Mufakharul Islam, "The Great Bengal Famine and the Question of FAD Yet Again," *Modern Asian Studies* 41, no. 2 (March 1, 2007): 421–440; Mark B. Tauger, "The Indian Famine Crises of World War II," *British Scholar* 1, no. 2 (2009): 166–196; and Cormac Ó Gráda, "*Sufficiency*

24 Hungry Nation

Some recent accounts have eschewed more granular work on the famine, deploying it primarily as proof of the British leadership's deliberate mendacity.[6] But a small number of sophisticated historical treatments have examined the events of the famine with great care. Paul Greenough's *Prosperity and Misery in Modern Bengal: The Famine of 1943–44*, published a year after Amartya Sen's *Poverty and Famines*, situated the events of the famine against the backdrop of a longer decline in the Bengal peasantry.[7] More recently, in examining the machinations of starvation and relief more closely and accounting for the violence which beset Bengal in starvation's wake, Janam Mukherjee's *Hungry Bengal: War, Famine and the End of Empire* demonstrates with great elegance how devastation long outlived the famine itself.[8]

In broadly failing to account for how a provincial tragedy came to be seen as a national injustice, historians have also missed how the larger case for self-rule came to be animated by particular material claims. As news of the famine traveled throughout India and the world, Indian journalists, artists, politicians, and planners could articulate, with clarity and force, the need for an independent government which would attend unfailingly to their sustenance. These claims, in time, came to be shared by an even broader swath of India's citizenry, animating dreams of how free India might best be governed.

Long before independence was assured, the zealous editors of *Independent India*, true to name, had begun to make plans for freedom. Followers of M.N. Roy, the charismatic expatriate revolutionary who had been a founder of both the Mexican Communist Party and the Communist Party of India, the Bombay-based cadre had published a storm of articles outlining a radical developmental trajectory for the incipient republic. Yet by the middle of 1943, there were no more blueprints: reports of famine filled the pages of the broadsheet, crowding out more forward-looking visions.

The June dispatch of Vasudha Chakravarty, a young female journalist reporting from Bengal, told of horrors far grimmer than those of India's

---

and Sufficiency and Sufficiency": Revisiting the Bengal Famine of 1943–44 (Dublin: UCD School of Economics, 2010).

[6] Madhusree Mukerjee, *Churchill's Secret War: The British Empire and the Ravaging of India during World War II* (New York: Basic Books, 2010).

[7] Paul R. Greenough, *Prosperity and Misery in Modern Bengal: The Famine of 1943–1944* (New York: Oxford University Press, 1982). Sugata Bose places the famine in the broader context of the collapse of Asian subsistence agriculture in Sugata Bose, "Starvation amidst Plenty: The Making of Famine in Bengal, Honan and Tonkin, 1942–45," *Modern Asian Studies* 24, no. 4 (October 1990): 699–727.

[8] Janam Mukherjee, *Hungry Bengal: War, Famine and the End of Empire* (New York: Oxford University Press, 2015).

The Bengal Famine

25

earlier famines.[9] The province's rural areas were an endless graveyard. Men and women were sneaking into neighbors' plots by cover of night to steal rice and potatoes, meeting death by pistol or fist, while widespread suicides compounded the ravages of starvation and disease. Bengal's tortured countryside contrasted mightily with the venal scenes of private life in Calcutta, where corrupt British and Indian officials made merry with profiteers and society girls in the city's leading hotels. "Who is the enemy of the people?" Chakravarty asked as she surveyed the gruesome disparity. "Is it the foreigner? Is it the native? Or is it both? The imperialist, the fascist, the profiteer, the corrupt official – or all together?"

Bengal's revolutionary fervor had made it the site of an insidious territorial stratagem four decades prior. Lord Curzon, preparing to divide the restive province in two, decried the Bengalis "who like to think themselves a nation, and who dream of a future when the English will have been turned out, and a Bengali Babu will be installed in Government House, Calcutta."[10] The ensuing partition of Bengal in 1905, aimed at staunching the province's mounting political force, had instead inspired an outpouring of *Swadeshi* protest, infusing the nationalist movement with new techniques of anti-colonial mobilization. The British were forced to rescind the partition in 1911, but the province's tradition of protest had been sutured to the legacy of divisive communal politics. This fractious political landscape meant that even the most astute observers of the famine struggled, at first, to mete out responsibility for the mounting death toll.

Yet few Indians believed the imperial spokesmen in New Delhi and London who blamed the famine on the environmental misfortunes of a stormy delta. And the further gruesome news traveled from Bengal itself, the more Indians and their allies were able to voice what the Famine Inquiry Commission of 1944 would partially affirm and what economists would demonstrate four decades later: that the famine had been both avoidable and manmade.

Bengal's major political parties – the Muslim League, the Hindu Mahasabha, the Communist Party, and the Indian National Congress – agreed on little. The debate over how much culpability the governing Muslim League bore for the famine remained a vehement one, and the proclamations of Communists were rendered unavoidably suspect by the

---

[9] Partha Sarathi Gupta, ed., "Article by Basudha Chakravarty in Independent India: Bengal Awaits Revolution," in *Towards Freedom 1943–1944, Part II* (New Delhi: Indian Council of Historical Research, 1997), 1854–1856.

[10] Sumit Sarkar, *The Swadeshi Movement in Bengal, 1903–1908* (New Delhi: People's Publishing House, 1973), 418.

26   Hungry Nation

Party's wartime collaboration. Yet increasingly, Indian observers agreed with what Jyoti Basu had asserted in Cambridge: that the "real blame [for the famine] rests on the government, and that government is British."[11]

The charismatic Chief Minister of Bengal at the beginning of the famine, Fazlul Huq, had come to power on a populist and grimly ironic slogan of *dal* and rice for all. Huq, a former secretary of the Indian National Congress who had helped found the All India Muslim League, had campaigned in 1937 on the promise of an end to inequitable land holdings, eschewing what he saw as divisive communalist rhetoric.[12] Winning the first provincial elections under the banner of his new Krishak Praja Party – "The Farming Peoples' Party" – Huq presided over an unstable coalition with the Muslim League before their resignation led to an even shakier alliance with the Hindu Mahasabha.

Yet the thundering of provincial politics in Bengal belied the fact that the preponderance of political power in India rested with the colonial Indian administration. India's "Governors-General" managed the province from New Delhi, cooled by wooden fans in the sprawling South Block of the Secretariat Building. In Calcutta, shielded by the whitewashed balustrades and Cuban palms of Government House, the Conservative parliamentarian John Herbert oversaw provincial machinations from a velvet divan, before his death from appendicitis saw him replaced by the Australian politician Richard Casey. Clad in wing collars and harlequin insignias, these men presided confidently over the complete collapse of Bengal's food position.

Burma, by the 1930s the world's largest rice-exporting territory, had long provided a buffer stock for India and Ceylon. Its wartime fall to the Japanese in the winter of 1941–1942 deprived Bengal of only around 15 percent of its imports, but the panic that ensued was more damning. Landlords and traders who had once loaned grain and cash to poor peasants shuttered their godowns, panicked by the specter of war; those peasants, no less agitated, looted paddy to plant and eat.[13] These problems were compounded by the abuse of infrastructure: Bengal's tracks shuddered under the weight of trains ferrying rice to soldiers and industrial workers, and fearful of a Japanese invasion, British officials confiscated boats and bicycles along the coast in a maladroit "denial policy," oblivious to their role in moving grain.[14]

---

[11] Bose, *The Man-Made Famine.*
[12] Greenough, *Prosperity and Misery in Modern Bengal*, 66.
[13] Sugata Bose, *Agrarian Bengal: Economy, Social Structure, and Politics, 1919–1947* (Cambridge: Cambridge University Press, 1986), 245.
[14] Rakesh Batabyal, *Communalism in Bengal: From Famine to Noakhali, 1943–47* (New Delhi: Sage Publications, 2005), 73.

The Bengal Famine

In Delhi, the central government busied itself with organizational filibuster. In March 1942, the Department of Education, Health, and Lands convened a conference to debate the best ways of encouraging greater wartime production, agreeing on the initiation of a Grow More Food campaign and the formation of a Central Food Advisory Council.[15] But before that Council met for the first time in August, an exasperated Fazlul Huq had already written to Delhi urging a recognition of the "rice famine in Bengal" – a mention that itself was assuredly too late.[16] Meanwhile, India's political landscape was descending into its wartime nadir. Six days after Huq's letter, the failure of the Cripps Mission to secure Congress' support for the war effort led to the declaration of a "Quit India" movement. Within hours of issuing their demand that the British leave India immediately, nearly 60,000 Congress leaders and activists had been arrested, many remaining in detention until the war's end.[17]

The spindly casuarina trees fringing the Bengal coast did little to impede the ferocious cyclone that made landfall near the village of Contai in October 1942. Tens of thousands of residents of Midnapore district died in a region already wracked by political disorder: many of the district's police stations had been burnt down, and thousands of jailed activists watched the storm from their prison cells. The enterprising civil servant B.R. Sen, later Director-General of the Food and Agriculture Organization, watched the storm from his verandah in Calcutta. Days later, he was surveying the remains of villages which had been washed away in preparation for relief efforts, in defiance of a District Officer who gloated that the unruly province had received what it deserved.[18] Sen courted the support of groups like the Friends' Society of Britain and the Ramkrishna Mission to clear corpses and repair embankments. But no relief team could replant the *aman* [winter] rice crop, washed away by

---

[15] John D. Tyson, "Need to Increase the Food and Fodder Supplies of India," March 10, 1942, Baroda Residency – War – W-215, 1942 (Vol. I), NAI; "Constitution of a Central Food Advisory Council Consisting of Both Officials and Non-Officials," June 30, 1942, Home – Public – 221/42, NAI; *Summary of Proceedings of the First Meeting of the Central Food Advisory Council Held at New Delhi on the 24th and 25th August 1942* (New Delhi: Government of India Press, 1942).

[16] Mukherjee, *Hungry Bengal*, 11.

[17] Lizzie Collingham has asserted that the Congress leadership's detention meant that "the Bengal famine played far less of a role in the debates about independence than one might have expected of such a devastating event." Other Indian citizens, however, brought the famine to the fore of political consciousness; Collingham's assertion that news of the famine, overshadowed by news of the Nazi holocaust, "faded into obscurity and was quickly forgotten," is most incorrect. Lizzie Collingham, *The Taste of War* (New York: Penguin, 2011), 154.

[18] B.R. Sen, *Towards a Newer World* (Dublin: Tycooly International Pub., 1982), 44–47.

28   Hungry Nation

torrential rain; nor could anyone scrape the green paddy of the devastating fungus which grew in the cyclone's wake. Midnapore, once verdant with rice, was a waterlogged graveyard. Its blight portended miserably for the troubled province.

A week before the end of the year, a group of underground Congress organizers circulated an insurrectionary leaflet across Bengal, urging activists who had stayed out of prison to rise up. "There is famine," the leaflet's author declared. "Why are our people – the worker, the peasant, the city-poor – starving or semi-naked or living in horrid conditions? Because the British Administration is so corrupt that there is no equal to it."[19] British censors did their best to confiscate flyers like these. Yet they struggled to contain popular outlets like the *Hindustan Times*, where a January cartoon showed a British "food expert" who had arrived in India promising a solution to Bengal's food problem. Instead, he was too sidetracked by a massive buffet to notice a swarm of groveling peasants.[20] If this cartoonist had thoroughly lambasted British officialdom, he would have had nothing more charitable to say about the American propaganda film produced that same season, which showed Calcutta dock workers unloading a feast of dried eggs, canned apples, corned beef hash, Tootsie Rolls, and Schlitz Beer for army canteens.[21]

Hunger was not merely Bengal's purview. Smaller shortages had pockmarked Malabar and Travancore throughout the war, and relief workers fretted that the scale of Bengal's deprivation would divert scant resources away from their hungry districts.[22] A team of Bombay Congress activists who had stayed out of prison likened India's hunger marchers to those in Milan and Florence said to be protesting in a similar manner: both were fighting against the abuse of foreign fascists.[23] In each case, the activists proclaimed,

the usurper Government does not care a whit for the hunger stricken stomachs, so long as it is able to carry on its loot of food for its own purposes. But blind as

---

[19] Partha Sarathi Gupta, ed., "Note of the Intelligence Bureau about a Leaflet Free India (January 1943)," in *Towards Freedom 1943–1944, Part II* (New Delhi: Indian Council of Historical Research, 1997), 1821.

[20] "One More Mouth to Feed [Cartoon]," *Hindustan Times*, January 14, 1943.

[21] *Supplies for India* (War Department Bureau of Public Relations, 1943).

[22] All Kerala Grama Seva Sangham, "An Appeal," July 6, 1943, Purshottamdas Thakurdas papers, folder 315, NMML; Servindia Travancore Relief Centre, Alleppy, "Our Present Needs," January 4, 1944, Purshottamdas Thakurdas papers, folder 315, NMML. Relief workers in Travancore lamented that, in spite of a mortality rate that dwarfed Bengal's, the famine of the same period had been equally ignored by the Government of India. K.G. Sivaswamy, *The Exodus from Travancore to Malabar Jungles* (Coimbatore: Servindia Kerala Relief Centre, 1945).

[23] Partha Sarathi Gupta, ed., "Bombay Congress Bulletins: Phillip's Visit to India," in *Towards Freedom 1943–1944, Part III* (New Delhi: Indian Council of Historical Research, 1997), 2805–2807.

The Bengal Famine

such usurpers are, they do not see the monster of hunger that they themselves have created, and it will not be very long now when this monster takes a jump and crashes upon them with a bang.

Those usurpers were, in fact, watching the monster of hunger with alarm. In January, Calcutta's municipal government wondered if rationing the city would help staunch the arrival of hunger marchers.[24] In Delhi, the central government issued lame promises to check prices and facilitate transportation of grains, while reminding provincial governments that food was, ultimately, their concern.[25] And in London, the War Cabinet belatedly took note of India's "serious food shortage," establishing a Department of Food after two centuries of rule.[26] Yet this shuffling did little to calm matters at home, where, the *New Statesman and Nation* noted, the British government was facing "an enemy more formidable than Congress – famine."[27]

Bengal, never quiescent, was a hotbed of political quarreling as much as a scene of ghastly starvation. Calcutta's streets were lined with corpses and the province's rice prices were sky-high.[28] Meanwhile, Fazlul Huq had been hounded from the Chief Ministry, replaced by Khawaja Nazimuddin; a new Muslim League ministry formed in April saw the new famine strategy led by the prominent, and incompetent, politician H.S. Suhrawardy.[29] As district officers appealed to Suhrawardy to direct grains to famine areas, the new Civil Supplies minister focused doggedly on the hoarding he believed to be responsible for shortages. The raids and invective of his "anti-hoarding" drive, however, simply drove stocks further away from the market. Bengal's political opposition was livid at Suhrawardy's unwillingness to declare a famine and thereby invoke the famous famine codes.[30] And the appointment of the Calcutta tycoon M.A.H. Ispahani, an ardent Muslim League supporter, as the sole dealer of rice in Bengal was proof, if ever there were, that the League would rather repay political patrons than manage a worsening catastrophe.[31]

---

[24] "Rationing of Foodstuffs in Calcutta," *Hindustan Times*, January 28, 1943.

[25] "Members' Statement to the Press Conference on Food Production," January 11, 1943, Education – Food Production – 20–6/43, NAI.

[26] "Conclusions of a Meeting of the War Cabinet," January 12, 1943, War Cabinet Secret W.M. (43) 7th Conclusions, UKNA.

[27] "Editorial," *New Statesman and Nation*, January 23, 1943.

[28] Batabyal, *Communalism in Bengal*, 80.

[29] Lance Brennan, "Government Famine Relief in Bengal, 1943," *The Journal of Asian Studies* 47, no. 3 (August 1, 1988): 541–566.

[30] "Declare Bengal a Famine Area," *Times of India*, June 28, 1943.

[31] J.N. Uppal, *Bengal Famine of 1943: A Man-Made Tragedy* (New Delhi: Atma Ram, 1984), 221–222.

30   Hungry Nation

The political atmosphere was poisonous. Bengal's Communists, the Krishak Praja Party, and the Hindu Mahasabha assailed the impuissant Muslim League, demanding the release of the detained Congress leadership and the formation of a "unity government" in the name of relief. Yet that term held vastly different meanings for Bengal's opposition parties.[32] The Hindu Mahasabha, lacking a robust provincial base, used this call to piggyback on popular support for the Congress; its premier, Shyama Prasad Mookherjee, decried the Muslim League for conspiring with the imperialists to starve Bengal.[33]

India's Communists emphasized their long connection to India's *kisan* [peasant] movements and joined the call for "unity," even as they had secretly collaborated with the British and worked to oust underground Congress organizers.[34] And they worked diligently to make capital from the famine in Bengal and in provinces far away. *People's War*, an incendiary Party weekly, vexed the censor's office: the Food and Home Departments launched a coordinated effort to suppress or shutter the paper for "publishing alarmist headlines, and reports and pictures calculated to arouse horror."[35] Party workers in Bombay distributed a grisly model speech to commemorate the first anniversary of the Quit India movement.[36] "Bengal," they wrote, "the cradle of our National movement, has become one vast graveyard. National disunity has meant millions of deaths; it has meant destitution and famine all round. It is today the only passport of the present regime to rule over our land as it likes." Party leaders in Punjab, the United Provinces, Bombay and Travancore papered their respective provinces with combustible pamphlets, each variants on the same theme: without "unity," famine would be the purview of all of India, not merely Bengal.[37]

---

[32] On communal politics in Bengal in this period, see Joya Chatterji, *Bengal Divided: Hindu Communalism and Partition, 1932–47* (Cambridge: Cambridge University Press, 1994).

[33] Kali Charan Ghosh, *Famines in Bengal: 1770–1943* (Calcutta: Indian Associated Publishing, 1944), 103; Bimal Chandra Sinha and Haricharan Ghosh, *Food Problem in Bengal* (Calcutta: H.C. Ghosh, 1943), iii.

[34] On the linkages between the CPI and the Kisan Sabha, see E.M.S. Namboodiripad, *With the Ploughshare and the Sickle: Kisan Sabha in the Campaign for More Food* (Bombay: Sharaf Athar Ali for the People's Publishing House, 1943).

[35] Sanjoy Bhattacharya, *Propaganda and Information in Eastern India, 1939–45: A Necessary Weapon of War* (Surrey: Curzon, 2001), 32.

[36] Partha Sarathi Gupta, ed., "Communist Propaganda," in *Towards Freedom 1943–1944, Part II* (New Delhi: Indian Council of Historical Research, 1997), 1670–1671.

[37] Gangadhar M. Adhikari, *Food in the Punjab* (Bombay: People's Publishing House, 1944); Romesh Chandra, *Who Starves Bengal To-Day Punjab To-Momorrow?: An Indictment of the Unionist Ministry* (Bombay: People's Publishing House, 1943); P.C. Joshi, *Who Lives If Bengal Dies?* (Bombay: People's Publishing House, 1943); E.M.S. Namboodiripad, *Food in Kerala* (Bombay: People's Publishing House, 1944); Bhalchandra Trimbak Ranadive, *Food in Bombay Province* (Bombay: People's Publishing House, 1944); and S.G. Sardesai, *Food in the United Provinces* (Bombay: People's Publishing House, 1944).

The Bengal Famine   31

The further political claim-making was from the province, the more it eschewed internecine squabbles to zero in on the role of empire itself. Even before the extent of Bengal's misfortunes were fully known, the radical activist Jayaprakash Narayan, who had cut his teeth studying social theory at Berkeley and Iowa, was connecting famine to imperial rule. "The British," he wrote in a letter to freedom fighters in early 1942, "partly by their incompetence and partly by design, have created [the food] problem, and so long as they are here there is no alternative to starvation. Therefore, the fight for freedom is the real fight for food."[38] Veteran Congressman C. Rajagopalachari had urged his party to reconcile with the British for the duration of the war; by 1944, he, too, was declaring that only an immediate transfer of power to "popular leaders" would allow for a solution to the problem of food.[39] Humayun Kabir, in a second pamphlet on the famine, echoed the call for "a National Government at the Centre and broad-based Governments in the provinces, formed with the support of every important section of political opinion in the country."[40] Loyalist Indian representatives in the legislature in Delhi balked at the central government's insistence that the Bengal famine be discussed without reference to the country's political situation.[41] The call for a "unity" government did not enjoy universal appeal. M.N. Roy, whose followers had had continued to chronicle the mounting disaster on the pages of *Independent India*, declared that no "National Government" could conjure up food without a commitment to complete revolution.[42] Muslim League leader Muhammad Ali Jinnah decried calls for the party to be stripped of provincial power, but agreed that the central government was criminally wrong in blaming the famine on population growth and natural disaster.[43] The responsibility, he held, was solely that of the British administration, "incapable of meeting any crisis."

As news of the famine traveled across India, it stoked the notion that only a free, national government could staunch the damage and prevent

[38] Jayaprakash Narayan, "Letters to Freedom Fighters," in *Jayaprakash Narayan: Struggle with Values: A Centenary Tribute*, ed. Madhu Dandavate (New Delhi: Allied Publishers, 2002), 83.

[39] C. Rajagopalachari, *The Way Out, a Plea for Constructive Thought on the Present Political Situation in India* (London: H. Milford, Oxford University Press, 1943).

[40] Humayun Kabir, *Bengal Famine* (Calcutta: Bengal Students' Federation, 1944).

[41] Partha Sarathi Gupta, ed., "Motion Regarding the Food Situation: Debate in the Central Legislative Assembly – November 1943," in *Towards Freedom 1943–1944, Part II* (New Delhi: Indian Council of Historical Research, 1997), 1908–1955.

[42] M.N. Roy, *National Government or People's Government?* (Bombay: Renaissance Publishers, 1946), 17–19.

[43] Mohammad Ali Jinnah, *Quaid-i-Azam Mohammad Ali Jinnah: Speeches, Indian Legislative Assembly, 1935–1947* (Karachi: Quaid-i-Azam Academy, 1991), 527–537.

32   Hungry Nation

a recurrence. That idea traveled back to Calcutta, too, reaching the most stalwart members of Bengali society. Home Ministry officials in Delhi gritted their teeth in frustration as they read the speech of a well-respected jurist who had inaugurated a private relief kitchen in August 1943. Hoarders and profiteers, future Law Minister C.C. Biswas had declared, had little responsibility for the famine when compared with the "stupid and scandalous bungling" of officials in Delhi.[44]

The waterlogged fields of estuarial Bengal are far removed from the Punjab plains, its wheat crop irrigated by five rivers. Both bear little resemblance to the fishing villages of the Malabar coast, or the rainshadowed Coromandel coast which flanks it. They are all worlds apart from the snowpeaked Himalayas, the scorched Thar desert, and the rocky Sindh coast. From craggy fortresses on the Deccan Plateau, four dynasties of potentates presided over the sprawling Vijayanagar domain; further north, from the fertile Gangetic Plain, a dynasty of Central Asian rulers reigned over the Mughal Empire. Beneath them, and other polities, a coterie of agrarian and mercantile regimes vied for control of capital, goods, and people.

Yet over the centuries, these disparate environmental and political regions inched closer towards one another, forging a sense of commonality hewn of political and technological transformation. Historians debate the moment at which inhabitants of far-off regions began to see themselves as part of a shared "India," and the moment at which nationalists could use the idea of a shared national space to propel the struggle for self-rule.[45] Yet by the time of the Bengal famine, India was inarguably knit together by a common political struggle, new technologies of communication, and a retinue of transformative ideas. The nation was criss-crossed by telephone wires, telegram cable, and thousands of miles of railroad track. Terrestrial radio waves bounced across the length and breadth of the subcontinent, and for a century or more, a capable postal service had ferried letters from place to place. Markets bound together the country through bonds of commerce, and textbooks chronicled a whiggish national history. And as the twentieth century dawned, new technologies of representation let residents of the subcontinent see other people whom they were coming to see as their countrymen – first in daguerreotype, and then with cheaper and smaller Kodak and Graflex cameras.

---

[44] Partha Sarathi Gupta, ed., "Official Notings on Justice C.C. Biswas' Speech (Dt. 21.8.1943–7.9.1943) (Extracts)," in *Towards Freedom 1943–1944, Part II* (New Delhi: Indian Council of Historical Research, 1997), 1872–1873.

[45] See Bayly, *Origins of Nationality in South Asia*; Chatterjee, *Nationalist Thought and the Colonial World*; Goswami, *Producing India*.

The Bengal Famine

The notion that Bengal's suffering was the concern of Indians in Punjab, or Bombay, or far-off Travancore, was animated by the material and ideological transformations wrought of colonial rule. Similarly, news of the famine and charitable responses from across India and the world furthered the idea that India was a national space with a shared purpose and future, with a tragedy in one region becoming an injury to the nation as a whole. "Whether it is Bengal or Kerala," the Bombay *Sentinel* concluded in July 1944, "Frontier or Orissa, Bihar or Bombay, the problem is the same: how to feed the people."[46]

India's colonial administration had tried desperately to keep news of the famine from spreading outside of the province, with the exigencies of war making this imperative more urgent.[47] As early as January 1943, Delhi's Chief Commissioner had asked editors to err on the side of "circumspection" in their coverage of the food situation.[48] But it was impossible to conceal the wrenching scenes for long. By summer, the sympathetic British editor of the Calcutta *Statesman*, Ian Stephens, was festooning his broadsheet with photographs that exasperated the central government: corpses, children with kwashiorkor, and emaciated bodies lining city streets.[49] As other papers followed suit, Stephens traveled to Delhi armed with a stack of visiting cards, these photographs printed on their obverse.[50] It could not stop the determined Stephens, but the Censor's Office buzzed with activity. In early 1944, its representatives arrived at the Calcutta home of Ku Chih-chung, editor of the *Yindu Ri Bao*. The community newspaper of the city's 20,000 Chinese residents had reported too explicitly upon the famine, and British officials insisted that the dispatches cease.[51] Later that year, an antagonized British correspondent in India lamented that his dispatch on the "hungry and dumb millions" of India had reached London with the word "hungry" expunged.[52]

Increasingly, Indians' determination made the work of the Censor's Office a waste of good ink. Indians armed with Zenith Clippers and

---

[46] "Shall Kerala Perish?," *Bombay Sentinel*, July 11, 1944.
[47] On press and the nationalist struggle, see Milton Israel, *Communications and Power: Propaganda and the Press in the Indian Nationalist Struggle, 1920–1947* (Cambridge: Cambridge University Press, 1994).
[48] Chief Commissioner, Delhi, "Instruction Issued to Newspaper Editors in Delhi," January 1943, Home – Political – 33/3/43 – POLL (I) 1943, NAI.
[49] Bhattacharya, *Propaganda and Information*, 32.
[50] Zareer Masani, *Indian Tales of the Raj* (Berkeley: University of California Press, 1988), 45.
[51] "Censorship Interceptions: Letter from T.T. Koo, Calcutta to M.T. Chen, Chungking," 1944, External Affairs – War – 42(38)-W, 1944(Secret), NAI.
[52] Partha Sarathi Gupta, ed., "Editorial in the Hindu Dt. 17.6.1944 – Censorship Methods Exposed," in *Towards Freedom 1943–1944, Part I* (New Delhi: Indian Council of Historical Research, 1997), 818–819.

34   Hungry Nation

other receivers could tune into the broadcasts on Axis stations excoriating the British for starving Bengal.[53] Rumors swirled on shortwave that the freedom fighter Subhas Chandra Bose was personally arranging for 100,000 tons of rice to be sent as relief.[54] In London, a Conservative parliamentarian lamented that the Axis Powers' lies were being "quickly absorbed by a people with empty stomachs."[55] Censorship seemed futile when these politicians, and even the most loyal Indian civil servants, were decrying the central government for suppressing news of Bengal's lamentable state.[56]

It was not merely that news of the famine was shooting past the censor's gaze. Indians far from Bengal were tying themselves affectively to the province through their relief efforts. Calcutta's network of nearly 500 private grain depots and relief kitchens, managed by the Bengal Relief Coordination Committee, was supported by donations from a wide swath of society.[57] The nationalist physician Bidhan Chandra Roy appealed for aid across "barriers of class, creed, and nationality," declaring that "for the first time in Bengal's recent history, men from so many different sections, with such divergent political allegiances, have responded together to the call of humanity."[58]

Given the political squabbling in Bengal, the unity of these appeals was assuredly overstated. Yet moved by word and picture, Indians responded magnanimously. Volunteers from the student wing of the Communist Party of India traveled to Bengal to open their own relief kitchens.[59] Women took to the streets of Lahore with collection tins, asking for donations of rings and bangles. The president of Ludhiana's Sikh Missionary College published a poem in the pages of the daily *Akali*, asking the people of Punjab to "reduce your intake by a fraction and send it to Bengal."[60] Karachi's merchants banded together to form a Famine

---

[53] "Indian Food Situation: Memorandum by the Secretary of State for India," September 10, 1943, War Cabinet Secret W.P. (43) 393, UKNA.

[54] Sugata Bose, *His Majesty's Opponent: Subhas Chandra Bose and India's Struggle against Empire* (Cambridge, MA: Belknap Press of Harvard University Press, 2011), 250.

[55] "Food Situation in India," *Hansard*, HL Deb, October 20, 1943, vol. 129, cols. 253–286.

[56] Partha Sarathi Gupta, ed., "Censorship on Publication of News about Famine in Bengal," in *Towards Freedom 1943–1944, Part I* (New Delhi: Indian Council of Historical Research, 1997), 766–767; J.P. Srivastava, "Speech at the Debate on Food in the Council of State," August 13, 1943, IOR/V/27/830/5, British Library.

[57] *Relief Organisations Fight Bengal Famine* (Calcutta: Relief Co-ordination Committee, 1943).

[58] Bengal Medical Relief Coordination Committee, "Bengal Faces Second Crisis," March 13, 1944, Purshottamdas Thakurdas papers, folder 315, NMML.

[59] Vimla Dang, "Some Glorious Struggles of AISF," *New Age Weekly: Central Organ of the Communist Party of India* 52, no. 6 (February 8, 2004).

[60] Partha Sarathi Gupta, ed., "An Appeal to Punjabi Brethren for Help to Famine Stricken Bengalis," in *Towards Freedom 1943–1944, Part III* (New Delhi: Indian Council of Historical Research, 1997), 2584–2586.

The Bengal Famine

Relief Committee, sending thousands of bags of rice, wheat, and cloth to Bengal. "That this disaster should have taken place," the merchants wrote, "in the present age of civilization with modern quick rail, road and sea communications, and in a country where food could be secured to avert the tragedy, is deplorable, and one which does little credit to the administration."[61] The young socialist mayor of Bombay, M.R. Masani, who had earlier authored a popular pamphlet on India's food problem, spoke at a fund-raiser for the All-Bengal Flood and Famine Relief Committee.[62] From Poona, the Servants of India Society deputed relief workers to Bengal, who provided rice, milk, cloth, and medicine in famine-stricken districts.[63] The *Hindustan Times* announced the formation of a relief fund, soliciting donations from its readers and from those of its Hindi-language counterpart, *Hindustan*.[64] Perhaps the most remarkable response came from Nairobi, where members of the East African Indian National Congress collected half a million shillings from Indians in Kenya and Tanganyika.[65] With their second donation of £40,000, the Congress' assistant treasurer added his hope "that we Indians, who have adopted this part of the world as our home, have not forgotten the mother country."[66]

Long before the famine claimed its final victim – deaths from smallpox, cholera, and malaria continued well into 1946, and violence poxed the province well into partition – Indian journalists, academics, and artists clamored to Bengal to bear witness to the spectral scene. Pioneering statistician P.C. Mahalanobis, then a professor at Presidency College, would later chart a course for independent India's development as an influential member of its Planning Commission. But in a grizzly season, he held fast to his disciplinary moorings: numbers mattered, he believed, and a full accounting of the horrors in Bengal would require statistical precision. Strolling past the silk cotton trees outside his office in Baker

---

[61] *Bengal Famine and Sind Merchants: Report of the Karachi Commercial Bodies' Famine Relief Committee for the Period Ending 31st December 1943* (Karachi: Karachi Indian Merchants' Association, 1944).

[62] M.R. Masani, *Your Food: A Study of the Problem of Food and Nutrition in India* (Bombay: Padma Publications for Tata Sons, 1944); M.R. Masani, *Why This Starvation?: Some Facts about Food* (Bombay: New Book Company, 1943). By war's end, Masani was explicitly tying the food crisis to the lack of a strong popular government. "Freedom Only Solution: Mr. M.R. Masani's View," *Times of India*, July 18, 1946.

[63] *The Servants of India Society Report for 1943–44* (Poona: Servants of India Society, 1944); *The Servants of India Society Report for 1944–45* (Poona: Servants of India Society, 1945).

[64] "The Hindustan Times Relief Fund," *Hindustan Times*, September 4, 1943.

[65] S.T. Thakore, *Statement of Account up to 31-12-43 of Bengal Relief Fund* (Nairobi: Bengal Relief Fund, 1944).

[66] Assistant Treasurer, Eastern Africa Indian National Congress, letter to Purshottamdas Thakurdas, April 28, 1944, Purshottamdas Thakurdas papers, folder 315, NMML.

36   Hungry Nation

Laboratory, Mahalanobis set out for the province's districts in 1944 to calculate the demographic particulars of the mounting death toll.[67]

Educated in Cambridge and London, elite nationalists and privileged expatriates often embarked upon national pilgrimages upon their return.[68] Arriving from South Africa in 1915, Mohandas Gandhi toured India at the advice of his mentor, Gopal Krishna Gokhale, who urged the activist to see the country's hinterlands with "his ears open but his mouth shut." Jawaharlal Nehru had returned to India three years prior. Raised in urban opulence, he had not so much as seen an Indian village; in 1920, the future Prime Minister's "wanderings among the *kisans*" showed him both the suffering and the resilience of the Indian peasantry. In a similar manner, the pilgrimages of India's Anglophone journalists to a hungry province helped tie famine victims and readers together across provincial boundaries. Accounts of districts blighted by corruption were marshaled as the grim evidence of misrule, and proof that a better society could only be ushered in by a representative national government.

Women journalists fueled by professional daring and revolutionary fervor took the lead in producing these accounts. Vasudha Chakravarty had delivered early reports on the plight of Bengal for *Independent India*; soon, a cadre of left-leaning women took up the charge in longer missives. Kalyani Bhattacharjee's 1944 *War against the People: A Sharp Analysis of the Causes of Famine in Bengal*, among the first.[69] Bhattacharjee had assumed the radical mantle of a sister imprisoned after attempting to shoot the Governor of Bengal years prior; in the famine, she presided over a major women-staffed relief group, the Chattri Sangha.[70] *War against the People* narrated the onset of the famine and skewered the complicity of India's Communists: a cartoon accompanying the short book depicted Party chair P.C. Joshi pouring Bengal's blood into a chalice held by a British officer. Yet Bhattacharjee reserved her greatest ire for the imperialists themselves. "The dead men, women and children of Bengal," she proclaimed, "make short work of the so-called democratic fairy tales of Churchill and Roosevelt."

---

[67] P.C. Mahalanobis, "The Bengal Famine: The Background and Basic Facts," July 25, 1946, IOR/L/I/1/1104.

[68] Manu Goswami has framed journeys like these as efforts to make "the nation appear natural." Goswami, *Producing India*, 1–2.

[69] Bhattacharjee and Kabir, *War against the People: A Sharp Analysis of the Causes of Famine in Bengal*. Later in the year, Bhattacharjee published a compilation of writings on the famine, Kalyani Bhattacharjee, ed., *Bengal Speaks!* (Calcutta: Servants of Bengal Society, 1944).

[70] Geraldine Hancock Forbes, *Women in Modern India*, New Cambridge History of India IV.2 (Cambridge: Cambridge University Press, 1996), 138–140, 211.

The Bengal Famine

That same year, Ela Sen's *Darkening Days: Being a Narrative of Famine-Stricken Bengal,* focused on the particular suffering of women during the famine, telling grizzly tales of girls sold to brothels with the hope of at least some food.[71] The young Bengali artist Zainul Abedin lent his famine sketches to the volume, and as Sen cast the famine as the obvious consequence of imperial rule, she pleaded for a reanimated national leadership that would "knit the hungry millions into one strong force that will demand of a corrupt government the death penalty for the hoarder, proper rationing and price control, and considerate planning to safeguard the future."

These women's accounts dovetailed with those produced by men who were also traveling through the blighted province.[72] Most prominent among them was T.G. Narayan, a veteran journalist with the *Hindu* who traveled from Madras to Calcutta and then to the "human misery" of the Bengal hinterlands.[73] Strolling through Calcutta's Maidan at the end of his pilgrimage, Narayan contrasted the peaceful green and the imposing Victoria Memorial with the graveyard that Bengal's districts had become. "The same crew, who had fouled [Bengal] against the shoals," he wrote, were "still on the bridge." The future was uncertain, but he knew that "the problem of famine [has] resolved itself finally into the power to order the destinies of the country." So long as Indians continued to be "denied the power to arrange our own affairs in a democratic manner," he concluded, "so long there would recur preventible economic disasters resulting in indescribable human wretchedness."

Poetic and visual accounts were essential in linking human suffering to the imperative of political transformation. By the mid 1940s, Sunil Janah was India's most celebrated photographer; a close friend of P.C. Joshi, he had become the photo editor for *People's Age,* the Communist Party daily, in 1943. Armed with a cheap Kodak Brownie and a ream of film, Janah had borne witness to the famine alongside cartoonist and fellow Communist Chittaprosad Bhattacharya; their photos and cartoons were printed in *People's Age* and distributed as postcards to raise funds for relief.[74]

---

[71] Ela Sen, *Darkening Days: Being a Narrative of Famine-Stricken Bengal, with Drawings from Life by Zainul Abedin* (Calcutta: Susil Gupta, 1944).

[72] The first monograph-length investigation of the origins of the famine appears to have been Santosh Kumar Chatterjee's *The Starving Millions* (Calcutta: M.A. Ashoka Library, 1944).

[73] T.G. Narayan, *Famine over Bengal* (Calcutta: Calcutta Book Company, 1944).

[74] Haresh Pandya, "Sunil Janah, Whose Photographs Chronicled India, Dies at 94," *New York Times,* July 9, 2012; Chittaprosad, *Hungry Bengal: A Tour through Midnapur District, by Chittaprosad, in November, 1943* (Bombay: New Age Printing Press, 1943).

Figure 2 The artist Chittaprosad Bhattacharya published his account of a voyage to famine-ravaged Midnapur district in November 1943 as *Hungry Bengal*, illustrating it with his harrowing sketches. Here, he depicts "the five corpses that I counted one morning in the short stretch of road." (Credit: DAG Modern / Chittaprosad / Hungry Bengal)

The Bengal Famine 39

Words on vellum and newsprint were no less powerful. The Bengali poet Kazi Nazrul Islam accused the imperialists of snatching "the morsel of food from thirty-three crores of mouths. Let their destruction be announced in letters written with my blood."[75] Hemango Biswas, a fellow Bengali bard, urged the Congress and League to unite to "expel these traitors from our land" in the name of ending famine.[76] Short stories and novels chronicled the ravaging of the province: Manik Bandyopadhyay wondered, in *Chiniye Khayeni Keno*, why Bengalis did not simply loot, concluding they were too depleted to do the same. In *Manwantar*, Tarasankar Bandyopadhyay imagined a free India where those responsible for famine would meet swift ends. Gopal Haldar's *Terasa Pancasa* portrayed a corrupt government eager to profiteer and willfully ignorant of the famine's toll.[77]

Writers and poets far from Bengal deployed the famine to exemplify India's woeful decline. Urdu poet Jigar Moradabadi, writing from his home village near Lucknow, was "far away, yet haunted by / cow dust time, the moonrise and dawns of Bengal / I can see them all: those who are dying."[78] Maithili writer Nagarjun imagined a grinding stone in Bengal so desolate that "for days and days, the rats, too, were miserable."[79] Kannada-language novelist R.S. Mugali linked the Bengal famine with other shortages in his novel *Anna*.[80] So many Progressive Writers had written on the famine that the young Urdu writer Ibrahim Jalees was able to assemble a major compilation of stories and poems in the aftermath of the movement's meeting in Hyderabad.[81]

For many Indian citizens, however, news of the famine came through film. K.A. Abbas would later become one of India's most celebrated directors and writers, known for his radical bent. But at the time of the famine, Abbas was not yet thirty, working as a publicist for the Bombay Talkies studio and a columnist for the Bombay *Chronicle* while trying to sell his first scripts. Unnerved by the news from Bengal, Abbas booked a ticket to Calcutta, aghast from the moment his train pulled up at Howrah

[75] Sisir Kumar Das, *A History of Indian Literature, 1911–1956, Struggle for Freedom: Triumph and Tragedy* (New Delhi: Sahitya Akademi, 1991), 321. One crore = ten million.
[76] Partha Sarathi Gupta, ed., "Bishan by Hemanga Biswas," in *Towards Freedom 1943–1944, Part III* (New Delhi: Indian Council of Historical Research, 1997), 2589.
[77] Srimanjari, "War, Famine, and Popular Perceptions in Bengali Literature, 1939–1945," in *Issues in Modern Indian History: For Sumit Sarkar*, ed. Biswamoy Pati (Mumbai: Popular Prakashan, 2000), 258–290.
[78] Jigar Moradabadi, "Bengal Famine (1943)," trans. Qurratulain Hyder.
[79] Nagarjun, "Famine and After," *Indian Literature* 30, no. 3 (119) (May 1, 1987): 27.
[80] R.S. Mugali, *Anna [Food]* (Dharwad: Manohar Grantha Mala, 1948).
[81] Ibrahim Jalees, *Bhooka Hai Bangal [Bengal Is Starving]* (Hyderabad: Nafees Academy, 1946).

station, where "emaciated refugees were sleeping in the shadow of the posh hotels and glittering shops of Chowringhee."[82]

Chased away by the stench of death, Abbas returned to Calcutta six months later in his new capacity as general secretary of the Indian People's Theatre Association, eager to see the production of *Nabanna* – the "New Harvest" – that the left-wing drama group had been staging.[83] Written by Bengali playwright Bijon Bhattacharya, the production culminated in a skeleton dancing to the wails of a singer that "Bengal was starving." Abbas brought the production back to Bombay, facilitating its staging in an open green next to the Charni Road train station. "The well-fed Bombay audience just gaped and wondered," one viewer recalled, "dumb-struck by this phenomenon that had hit Bombay like a tornado."[84] He set to work adapting the play for the screen.

The film that Abbas completed became *Dharti ke Lal* – "Sons of the Soil" – and it told the story a farmer driven to Calcutta during the famine after losing his grain and land to a usurious *mahajan*.[85] The farmer arrives in Calcutta alongside thousands of other refugees. The relief kitchens are wracked by communal strife, and families are driven apart by prostitution and crime. Yet hunger, a relief worker assures the farmer, not only crushes spirits but can also raise the people. News of the famine spreads throughout India, and as a chorus of schoolchildren proclaim that "Hindustan is our country," a new harvest is reaped, bigger than any previous one.

The crew and cast of *Dharti ke Lal* traveled to Calcutta to film, yet after filming two short streetscapes, the cast was detained and banished from the city by the military police. Returning home, the crew transformed the town of Dhule into the Bengal hinterlands: members of the Khandesh Kisan Sabha played Bengal's destituted peasants, and Ravi Shankar played sitar for the soundtrack. The film premiered at Bombay's Shree Sound Studios in 1946 before a second screening in Shimla, timed to coincide with the Cabinet Mission sent to negotiate India's transition to self-rule. Congressmen and Congresswomen flocked to the film, with the communist journalist Rajani Palme Dutt telling Abbas that the problem of India "would be solved if the twelve old men sitting there in the

---

[82] Khwaja Ahmad Abbas, *I Am Not an Island: An Experiment in Autobiography* (New Delhi: Vikas Publishing House, 1977), 264–275.
[83] Das, *History of Indian Literature, 1911–1956*, 171.
[84] Gul Bardhan, *Rhythm Incarnate: Tribute to Shanti Bardhan* (New Delhi: Abhinav Publications, 1992).
[85] Khwaja Ahmad Abbas, *Dharti ke Lal [Children of the Earth]* (Indian Progressive Theatre Association Pictures, 1946). The film drew heavily upon Krishna Chander's short story in Urdu, *Annadatta*.

The Bengal Famine   41

Viceregal Lodge had only come here to see this film and been confronted with the reality of India."

Throughout the war and the famine, Indians and sympathetic Britons in England had been drumming up support for self-rule. Indian sentiment was as marked by a fundamental unity of purpose, but nationalist politics were as rancorous in Britain as they were at home. The India League, the Indian Freedom Campaign, the Committee of Indian Congressmen, and Swaraj House all raised separate relief funds for Bengal, even as they came together to emphasize the paramount necessity of a national government in New Delhi.[86]

London's streets were blanketed with Indian pamphlets. In 1943, Nagendranath Gangulee published a major incendiary tract, *India's Destitute Millions Starving Today – Famine?* The physician and nutritional scientist had served dutifully on the Royal Commission on Indian Agriculture, but by the Depression, had signed on to the nationalist cause, and he asked the British public to recognize that only immediate independence would prevent the spread of famine.[87] V.K. Krishna Menon would later emerge as free India's most revered, and feared, statesman; as secretary of the India League, he authored a call for *Unity with India against Fascism*, which characterized the famine as "not just an incident in maladministration but a major crime."[88] Rajani Palme Dutt published a plan for post-famine agricultural reconstruction in India, predicated upon the notion that "food for all can only be achieved by the masses of the people of India themselves under the leadership of a Government of their own choice."[89] British allies of the Indian cause, from the socialist leader Ben Bradlee to the Labour parliamentarian Reginald Sorensen to the Quaker activist and Gandhi confidant Horace Alexander, all published their own fiery treatises on the plunder of Bengal.[90]

The effort to take stock of the famine in Bengal was assisted by those who had been part of Britain's own food administration. A new Ministry of Food, its administration cobbled together from the staff of the Food (Defense Plans) Department, had been established in the United Kingdom shortly before the war. The head of the Ministry, Henry French, had overseen the domestic issuance of ration cards and

---

[86] Nicholas J. Owen, *The British Left and India: Metropolitan Anti-Imperialism, 1885–1947* (Oxford: Oxford University Press, 2007), 269.

[87] Nagendranath Gangulee, *India's Destitute Millions Starving Today: Famine?* (London: Swaraj House, 1943).

[88] V.K. Krishna Menon, *Unity with India against Fascism* (London: The India League, 1943).

[89] Rajani Palme Dutt, *The Problem of India* (Toronto: Progress Books, 1943).

[90] Ben Bradlee, *India's Famine: The Facts* (London: The Communist Party, 1943); Reginald Sorensen, *Famine, Politics – and Mr. Amery* (London: The India League, 1944); Horace Alexander, "Famine Returns to India," *Contemporary Review*, January 1944.

42   Hungry Nation

the counting of backyard hens, purchasing sugar and wheat and whale oil for government stores and urging citizens to "serve just enough" and "use what is left." And in August 1944, Lord Amery, the Conservative Secretary of State for India, called upon French to help exculpate the colonial administration from responsibility for Bengal's suffering.

The provincial and colonial administration in Bengal had been scrambling to rewrite the story of the famine itself. The Muslim League ministry in Bengal had brought out a polished brochure which asked whether it had, in fact, done "all that was humanly possible to minimize suffering, reduce mortality and restore conditions as nearly approximating to normal as was possible in the extraordinary circumstances."[91] Touting its free kitchens, canteens, and orphanages, the brochure's author assured the reader that, in fact, it had. "Prejudiced critics," it warned, "shall not talk Bengal into a second famine." Bengal's new governor, Richard Casey, took to All India Radio to promise that, until self-rule came, the "government will be concerned with the problem of ensuring that the people of Bengal are fed."[92] Yet by bringing Britain's foremost food expert to India, and asking another senior bureaucrat to chair a major commission on the famine, Lord Amery was inadvertently demonstrating how Bengal had ruptured the imperial status quo ante.

French's host in India was B.R. Sen, India's new Director of Food, who had replaced the much-reviled civil servant J.P. Srivastava. Both Sen and Srivastava were members of the Indian Administrative Service, yet while Sen had done his best to procure relief, Srivastava had been lamentably tone-deaf. "Sometimes," he had mused in the Central Assembly in the midst of the famine, "I wonder whether we devoted sufficient attention in the past to the food problem of the country."[93] Traveling with Sen through Punjab, Bengal, and Bombay, French frequently clashed with the press.[94] In Delhi, he deflected questions about the comparative toll of the war in Britain and India.[95] At a press conference held in the Punjab Secretariat in Lahore, French grew angry at reporters who ignored his plea to avoid "political" subjects.[96] He returned to London to present his grim findings at the India Office: India, he declared, stood no chance at becoming self-sufficient in food in anything less than four or five years.

[91] Director of Public Information, Bengal Government, *Famine and the Government* (Alipore: Bengal Government Press, 1944).
[92] Richard Casey, "Governor of Bengal's Speech, All India Radio, Calcutta," July 10, 1944, IOR/L/I/1/1103.
[93] *India Food Situation 1943* (London: His Majesty's Stationery Office, 1943), 15.
[94] "British Food Expert to Tour India," *Times of India*, August 14, 1944.
[95] "Sir Henry French on Rationing," *Times of India*, August 19, 1944.
[96] "Sir Henry French's Advice," *Times of India*, September 19, 1944.

The Central Administration had done its best to manage an impossible situation and an obdurate provincial administration, and it bore little responsibility for the deaths in Bengal.[97] "Food control in the UK," he sighed, "is child's play compared with India."[98]

French's report drew less attention than the formation that same month of the Famine Inquiry Commission chaired by John Woodhead. The veteran civil servant, a friend of Lord Amery, had a knack for thorny issues: six years prior, he had been placed in charge of a commission to partition Palestine into Jewish and Arab states. In his newest role, Woodhead brought together a Hindu and Muslim representative, the nutrition expert W.R. Aykroyd, and the businessman and former deputy governor of the Reserve Bank of India Manilal Nanavati as representative of the trade. Upon the Commission's disbanding, Woodhead took it upon himself to destroy its voluminous proceedings of the interviews held *in camera*; Nanavati surreptitiously saved a copy of the rancorous transcripts. In one characteristic exchange, the secretary of the Calcutta Relief Committee, Jnananjan Niyogi, a longtime *Swadeshi* activist and Congress organizer, assailed the central government over its "wanton bungling." Britain could serve no role in the reconstruction of Indian agriculture, he declared. "Can this parental task be taken and performed by a foreign power? Emphatically – No!"[99]

The deliberations recorded in the transcripts that Nanavati stowed away evidence of great sensitivity to the man-made machinations which had helped produce famine. The emergent conclusions evidenced a nuanced reading of food availability and its decline, and set the stage for the careful analyses undertaken decades hence. Yet the political imperatives of the day won out in the published document. Even as the final version of the *Famine Enquiry Report*, published in April 1945, conceded the failure of New Delhi's price control policy and transportation efforts, it exonerated the imperial administration from graver wrongdoing; likewise, its estimate of 1.5 million famine deaths was far lower than the number of 3 or 4 million circulating widely at the time.[100] The nationalist response was indignant. The Calcutta journalist Kali Charan Ghosh,

---

[97] "Indian Food Situation: Sir Henry French's Visit to India," October 10, 1944, War Cabinet Secret W.P. (44) 562, UKNA.

[98] *Indian Information* 15, 618 (1944).

[99] Partha Sarathi Gupta, ed., "Central Government Indicted for Weakness of Its Basic Plan (before Aug. 1944)," in *Towards Freedom 1943–1944, Part II* (New Delhi: Indian Council of Historical Research, 1997), 1975–1976.

[100] Famine Enquiry Commission, *Report on Bengal* (New Delhi: Government of India Press, 1945). Final word on the famine came in 1948, with the publication of *Report Showing Action Taken by Central and Provincial Governments on the Recommendations Made by the Famine Inquiry Commission in Their Final Report* (Calcutta: Government of India Press, 1948).

44   Hungry Nation

who had covered the famine for the *Modern Review*, fulminated against the *Report*'s exculpation of British officialdom, who had cavorted with loyalist princes "when people had been dying in the millions."[101]

Two months after the publication of the *Report* the Congress leadership was released from wartime detention. The war in Europe had ended in May; before long, Labour would ascend to power in London in a landslide election. In less than ten days, the luminaries of India's nationalist struggle would meet in the imposing Viceregal Palace in Shimla in a first effort to negotiate a transfer of power.

Those who had spent the war in prison were to grapple quickly with the dramatic impact of the Bengal famine on Indian notions of just rule. The famine's victims and Indians across the country, a 1945 Kisan Sabha manifesto asserted, "were thrilled with a new hope when Mahatma Gandhi, Pandit Jawaharlal Nehru, Sardar Ballabhai Patel [sic] and Maulana Azad declared on their release that the famine stricken were the uppermost in their mind."[102] These leaders were quick to speak after years of silence: K.M. Munshi, later India's Food Minister, berated those who had "destroyed [India's] industry, drained away its resources, kept it under-developed, under-nourished, backward," and who had allowed a final, devastating famine.[103] "The British officer," he scowled, "claimed to be the *Mabaap* [mother-father] of the poor people of India. We have only to look at the result of the *Mabaap* rule to see what it has done."

The British claim to just rule and the promotion of welfare through food had advanced haltingly throughout the first decades of the twentieth century. Yet colonial administrators, aware the famine had brought concerns of sustenance to the fore, had scrambled to make a belated case. In July 1943, the Department of Food had assembled a Foodgrains Policy Committee, charging it with devising measures to increase food supplies.[104] Towards the end of the year, the government had enlisted the help of A.V. Hill, an economist at the Royal Society, to help develop a "food plan for India."[105] The Director of Food J.P. Srivastava, cheering these moves as proof of the colonial administration's good intentions, vowed that New Delhi's task was now

not only one of feeding four hundred million of our countrymen, but also of providing the supplies to do so for millions of small cultivators and seeing that

---

[101] Kali Charan Ghosh, "An Imperfect Report," *Modern Review*, August 1945, 107–109.

[102] Krishna Benode Roy, *Bengal Famine and Problems of Rehabilitation* (Calcutta: Bengal Provincial Kisan Sabha, 1945).

[103] Kanaiyalal Maneklal Munshi, *The Ruin That Britain Wrought* (Bombay: Padma Publications for Bharatiya Vidya Bhavan, 1946).

[104] Theodore Gregory, *Report of the Foodgrains Policy Committee, 1943* (New Delhi: Government of India Press, 1943).

[105] A.V. Hill, *A Food Plan for India* (London: Royal Institute of International Affairs, 1945).

The Bengal Famine 45

they pass without being hoarded to the public. Our task is not only to bring food supplies into the open market, but also to make them available quickly to every nook and corner in this vast country which cannot otherwise support itself.[106]

Stung by the belief that the British had starved Bengal, the Departments of Food and Agriculture drafted a new joint policy in 1945. Food would remain a provincial concern, their statement affirmed, but the Departments in Delhi would work to "promote the welfare of the people and to secure a progressive improvement of their standard of living. This includes the responsibility for providing enough food for all, sufficient in quantity and of requisite quality."[107] Publicists worked to communicate this new "Policy of Food for All," even as imperial bureaucrats worried about what they had unleashed by affirming this basic position. "It will be more modest and more realistic," a concerned official in the Department of Industries and Supplies wrote, "to say that Government intend to do its best, or to aim at providing enough food for all, etc., for that is as much as any Government can possibly say."[108]

Yet the imperatives of war, the global promise of equitable development, and India's own wartime struggles had made it hard for any government seeking legitimacy to offer any less. From his second-floor White House study, Franklin Roosevelt had promised an end to "freedom from want" four years prior. The pioneers of modernization theory in the United States and Europe were touting the need to bolster standards of living in the name of containing totalitarianism.[109] In Québec's stately Château Frontenac, delegates from thirty-four countries were coming together for the first meeting of the Food and Agriculture Organization (FAO), a team of Indian delegates among them.[110] An ambitious government brochure published while the FAO conference met linked the Departments of Food and Agriculture's new joint policy to the new possibilities and paradigms of modernization, planning, and development.[111] Just as the American government had harnessed collective human energy through the Tennessee Valley Authority, the administration in New Delhi

---

[106] Norman Angell, "The Indian Famine," *Far Eastern Survey* 13, no. 1 (January 12, 1944): 7–10.

[107] *A Statement of Agriculture and Food Policy in India* (New Delhi: Department of Agriculture and Department of Food, Government of India, 1945).

[108] "Policy of Agriculture and Food," 1945, Food – Policy – SCB-2401(1) / 1945, NAI.

[109] David Ekbladh, *The Great American Mission: Modernization and the Construction of an American World Order* (Princeton: Princeton University Press, 2010).

[110] Department of Agriculture, Government of India, *Report of the Indian Delegation to the United Nations Conference on Food and Agriculture at Québec City* (New Delhi: Government of India Press, 1946).

[111] *400 Millions to Be Fed* (New Delhi: Bureau of Public Information, Government of India, 1945).

was eager to demonstrate "the extent to which vast scale planning can produce and harvest those bumper crops of necessities and luxuries that spring up from the seeds of organized and controlled human endeavor."

British administrators had heeded the call of sympathetic Indian voices who had urged them to reform the moral orientation of their rule. At the dawn of the famine, one Indian economist had urged imperial planners to consider the "vast majority of our population [who] rarely drink milk, hardly eat meat or fruits or other expensive though nutritious items of diet." When the war was over, he declared, "economic planning in India must aim towards better distribution of national wealth."[112] Manilal Nanavati, coming off his stint with the Woodhead Commission, wrote that the "debacle" of the famine had proven the need for change in the realm of food. "If freedom from want is going to be the basis of the new economic order after the war," he wrote, "it is necessary to assure at least a bare minimum to India's teeming millions."[113]

Those less beholden to imperial objectives were freer to imagine what the lessons of Bengal held for free India's planning. The president of the nationalist All India Women's Conference, Kamaladevi Chattopadhyay, had urged members to envision what a free India's food plan might look like. "Only a careful development of its vast untapped wealth," she urged, "based on an economy designed to meet the needs of the people by a free Indian people's government, can aspire to overcome this dreadful scourge of perpetual famines."[114] An economist in Agra lamented the "absence of planning or control" in British India; agricultural progress could not be similarly hampered after self-rule.[115] Physicist Meghnad Saha, who had forwarded many plans for national development in the pages of his *Science and Culture* before the war, now felt that it was impossible to plan "unless we have a Government which has popular support and is composed of leaders in whom the people have confidence."[116]

The most prominent vision of a free, fed India came from Bombay, where seven industrialists and a lone economist gathered after the famine to draft a plan for India's economic development after independence. The Bombay Plan, as it came to be known, held that all Indian citizens

---

[112] A. Appadorai, *Democracy in India*, Oxford Pamphlets on Indian Affairs 5 (London: Oxford University Press, 1942).

[113] Manilal B. Nanavati and J.J. Anjaria, *The Indian Rural Problem* (Bombay: Indian Society of Agricultural Economics, 1944).

[114] "Kamaladevi Urges Women to Fight for Freedom," *Bombay Sentinel*, April 8, 1944.

[115] Baljit Singh, *Whither Agriculture in India? A Study of the Re-Organisation of Agricultural Planning in India* (Agra: N.R. Agrawal, 1945).

[116] David Arnold, *Science, Technology and Medicine in Colonial India* (Cambridge: Cambridge University Press, 2000), 209.

The Bengal Famine

would need to be guaranteed a daily quantum of 2800 calories. This was the number which underwrote their scheme to boost both industrial and agricultural output, with a priority on the former, since only the increased purchasing power born of industrialization would let Indians acquire the food they so desperately needed.[117] The Bombay Plan would be debated extensively, but moderate commentators lent it some cautious support. One 1944 book reflecting on the famine, part of a popular series on "contemporary topics," lauded the Plan as one good option among many being drafted in India which intended to render "the famines of the type of 1944 consigned for ever to the limbo of the past."[118]

In 1947, the forty-year-old writer Bhabani Bhattacharya published his first novel, an English language account of the famine which had so transformed India's political landscape. *So Many Hungers!* skewered the British administration, and the rapaciousness of men like M.A.H. Ispahani, who was caricatured as the venal director of Cheap Rice, Ltd. "This famine," Bhattacharya's narrator insists, "this brutal doom, was the fulfillment of alien rule." He asks his reader to imagine "two million Englishmen dying of hunger that was preventable, and the Government unaffected, uncensored, unrepentant, smug as ever! 'Quit India!' cried the two million dead of Bengal."[119]

In 1942, Indian nationalists had asked the British to quit India. But famine and death unleashed the year afterwards made the case that political declarations alone could not. Bengal would be forever changed by the famine. Its death toll aside, the famine poisoned provincial politics even further. The return of the Muslim League to power in Bengal in 1946 antagonized the opposition: the province's new Chief Minister was H.S. Suhrawardy, whose famine strategy Hindu Mahasabha members and others considered responsible for millions of deaths.[120] The party head saw in the famine a warning against the mounting Muslim demand for Pakistan: if a separate Muslim state had existed during the famine, he reasoned, its control of Bengal's arable land would have killed the whole of the population which had remained.[121]

---

[117] Purshottamdas Thakurdas et al., *A Plan of Economic Development for India* (Bombay: The Commercial Printing Press, 1944), 12–26. See P.S. Loknathan, "The Bombay Plan," *Foreign Affairs*, July 1945, 680–686; a socialist critique of the plan is M. Naidu, "The Bombay Plan," *Workers' International News* 5, no. 7 (December 1944): 1–4.

[118] M.S. Nata Rajan, *Famine in Retrospect* (Bombay: Padma Publications, 1944).

[119] Bhabani Bhattacharya, *So Many Hungers!* (London: V. Gollancz, 1947).

[120] Chatterji, *Bengal Divided*, 230.

[121] T.K. Dutt, *Hungry Bengal* (Lahore: Indian Printing Works, 1944). This claim was repeated in the Punjab; see Ayesha Jalal, *Self and Sovereignty: Individual and Community in South Asian Islam since 1850* (London: Routledge, 2002), 462.

48   Hungry Nation

Yet at a national level, famine had transformed India's political landscape, underscoring the need for self-rule to Indian citizens far away from its epicenter. Photographs and journalism and the affective bonds of charity tied Indians inextricably to Bengal and made its suffering their own; a provincial atrocity was turned, in the midst of war, into a national case against imperial rule. With the nationalist movement at its apogee, no publicity effort or overdue food scheme could convince disillusioned Indians of the munificence of a bankrupt administration.

Famine was, for Indian planners and citizens, the mandate for fundamental transformation – not merely a transition to self-rule, but the crafting of an economy and a polity that would be fundamentally different in its responsibility to citizens. Jawaharlal Nehru maintained that Bengal's dead "were vivid, frightful pictures of India as she is, suffering for generations past from a deep-seated organic disease which has eaten into her very vitals."[122] Only a fundamental recomposition of India's body politic would offer a cure. "There are still many people," the future Prime Minister wrote,

who can think only in terms of political percentages, of weightage, of balancing, of checks, of the preservation of privileged groups, of making new groups privileged, of preventing others from advancing because they themselves are not anxious to, or are incapable of, doing so, of vested interests, of avoiding major social and economic changes, of holding on to the present picture of India with only superficial alterations.

The famine would need to remind citizens, he wrote, of the need to fashion a fundamentally new India, and the Congress leadership seized quickly upon this mandate. In summer 1946, the party's National Planning Committee met in Bombay to draft up its first plans. A subcommittee comprising Nehru and the economists John Mathai and K.T. Shah affirmed that "the provision of adequate food" would be the item of highest priority in any scheme for post-war development.[123]

In the years surrounding independence, the memory of the famine was sutured to the mandate for a cohesive national government, and fundamental economic change. A popular 1947 Hindi pamphlet on India's food problem was dedicated to the victims of the Bengal famine: India's planners and citizens could redeem their deaths by ensuring, through

---

[122] Nehru, *The Discovery of India*, 535.
[123] K.T. Shah, *National Planning Committee: Priorities in Planning (Food, Education, Housing)* (Bombay: Vora & Co., 1946); A.M. Zaidi and S.G. Zaidi, eds., "Congress Working Committee, Bombay, March 12–15, 1946," in *The Encyclopaedia of Indian National Congress*, vol. 12: *A Fight to the Finish* (New Delhi: S. Chand / Indian Institute of Applied Political Research, 1981), 495–496.

The Bengal Famine   49

planning, that free India never saw a similar tragedy.[124] Three years after independence, Kasturba Lalwani, the author of a Hindi text on India's most pressing economic matters, recalled a foreign administration in New Delhi "snatching grains from the country's east. Black marketeers and former officials wrested control of the entire nation. The worst type of misbehavior the twentieth century has seen was carried out in the name of 'civilization.' And in the midst of that frenzied dance, the country's people were marked for death like so many pests."[125] For her, too, the promise of economic freedom was the promise of an end to famine wrought of foreign exploitation.

The Bengal famine galvanized an India increasingly linked by bonds of economy and affect alike. And it provided to planners and citizens the necessary, if horrific case for a strong, central, and independent government which stood to actualize the promises of economic transformation. The famine brought food to the center of Indian state-making at the moment of its actualization and saddled India's nationalist leadership with the obligation to succeed where the British had failed. In 1946, a gloomy but undaunted Harivansh Rai Bachchan had asked Indians to remember Bengal as they "realized the strength of hunger / the strength of your own daring and boldness." A year later, as the Union Jack fell across the country, Indians' boldness was no longer in question, but the strength of hunger would continue to animate their varied plans and dreams.

---

[124] Jain, *Hamari Roti ki Samasya [Our Food Problem]*.
[125] Kasturba Lalwani, *Bharat ki Arthik Samasyaye [India's Economic Problems]* (Ahmedabad: Navajivan Publishing House, 1950), 36.

2 Independent India of Plenty

Shamrao Krishnarao Kelavkar was far more comfortable in the courtroom and the boardroom than he was tilling in the fields. Trained as a barrister at Cambridge and called for the Bar by Gray's Inn, Kelavkar had returned to India to eke out a career in industry, touring the Middle East as a representative of Vissanji and Sons, a trading firm owed by independence-minded industrialists. Eventually, Kelavkar was drawn back to the law and to his native Kolhapur, where he was asked to build a small law college in the diminutive princely state, and subsequently, to serve as its Judicial Minister.

Kelavkar's retirement from service had coincided with the Bengal famine; as a lawyer and a businessman, he could see that the imperial government had thoroughly bungled matters. Sent by Kolhapur as a delegate to the All India Food Conference in late 1943, Kelavkar had pressed the case that food needed to be treated as a national issue, and more specifically, that provinces with surpluses and provinces with deficits would need to cooperate if India were to thrive after independence.[1]

Kolhapur state was, as it happened, a deficit state, and as independence passed, Kelavkar could not help but notice the enduring and pitiful sight of laborers who subsisted on *kanda bhakri* – onion and rice flour flatbread – or worse, rice and tamarind water. "Our government," he sighed, "does not seem ever to have made a proper, sufficient, and effective effort to tackle the problem of food."[2] This was the country's most pressing problem, Kelavkar felt, and the deficit most severely impeding India's economic progress. "An awakened and properly organized India," he wrote in a 1946 pamphlet, "will not only be capable of feeding properly her present, so-called overpopulation of 400 million, but a far larger number. All what is needed is that we must all become conscious that food – sufficient and proper food – is the birthright of every human being and we must all work for it."

---

[1] *Fourth All India Food Conference* (New Delhi: Government of India Press, 1944), 90–91.
[2] Shamrao Krishnarao Kelavkar, *Our Food Problem* (Kolhapur: Arya Bhanu Press, 1946).

Independent India of Plenty

Like many Indian citizens who wrote on the nation's food problem in the years surrounding, Kelavkar wanted his own assessments considered by the state and his fellow citizens. Free India's government, he wrote, should build research stations to develop better seeds for the people. Hydroelectric dams could provide peasants with power for cooking, freeing up cow dung which could then be used as fertilizer. Oilseeds and lentils, he contended, were more valuable as nutritious foods than as commercial products, and their export should accordingly be banned. Village propaganda schemes could teach people how to grow vegetables for food and shared profit. And Indians would cooperate by reversing their old food prejudices and becoming "meatatarians," allowing the government to purchase or build trawlers to dredge edible fish from the sea. Most importantly, after independence, every Indian would need to become "food-minded – not food-minded in the sense that we all become when we feel hungry, but food minded in the sense that the growth of more food must become an obsession with us."

Kelavkar was one of many Indians drafting up their own plans for plenty. While he brainstormed one route to prosperity, a Madurai physician was hard at work on his own pamphlet, which he would self-publish as *A Scheme of Collective Effort to Promote the Health and Well-Being of the People of India through Proper and Sufficient Food.*[3] M.V. Natesan had seen the deleterious effects of malnutrition in his own practice for years: since his days as a medical student in Madras, he had seen how Indians suffered from poor health, reduced "vivacity," diminished resistance to infectious disease, and an overall unconscionably high mortality rate. All this was known before, yet the famine in Bengal had underscored how truly precarious the well-being of India's citizens had become. Natesan had read the Bombay Plan authored by India's leading industrialists, but objected to it on the grounds that no one knew how long it would be until India would actually enjoy the freedom that was the program's precondition. Natesan offered a plan that he believed would work in free India, and equally well under prolonged British rule. And since India was not likely to adopt either "the Totalitarian system of Hitler or the Soviet system," this plan, Natesan declared, was optimally suited to Indian social and economic conditions.

The program would begin with the establishment of IDEAL – the "Indian Dietary Expansionists' Association Limited." This limited liability company would open dairy farms throughout India and entice investment through the promise of shared profits. IDEAL would pool

---

[3] M.V. Natesan, *A Scheme of Collective Effort to Promote the Health and Well-Being of the People of India through Proper and Sufficient Food* (Madurai: Sampath Press, 1944).

resources to allow "selective cultivation," and encourage "fair and wise" methods for marketing produce at affordable but remunerative rates. It would also establish communal kitchens across the country "where food suited to the physiological needs of that group or society shall be cooked under expert direction, and distributed to the people at as cheap a rate as possible." Families who bought shares in these kitchens would enjoy the benefits of more time and better food. The greatest advantage, of course, would be to "the Lady of the House," who, "relieved of the sickening routine of the kitchen ... will have more leisure time to educate herself, to relieve the husband of much of the management of the household, to look after her children's health and education, and to enable the more advanced ladies to take up social work or seek a lucrative employment and augment the family exchequer." Dr. Natesan had drafted up a brief form for prospective investors to fill out, sending a copy of the pamphlet and an application to Purshottamdas Thakurdas, the eminent industrialist who had helped author the Bombay Plan, and whom he saw as a potential backer for his scheme.

The plans that Kelavkar, Natesan, and others produced in the years surrounding independence speak to a moment when citizens came to see themselves as obligate participants in local and national efforts to stave off hunger. The tragedy of Bengal had brought India's food problem to public consciousness, and as independence neared, Indian citizens looked to the inchoate national government with the expectation that it would offer sustenance where the imperial administration had failed to do so. And in declaring their plans to be the necessary responses to nationalists' call for cooperation on the food front, they implicitly urged that their expertise be constituent of and considered in the march of state planning itself.

Yet the plans of citizens and politicians alike foundered against the difficulties posed by a wave of early food crises harkening back to the horrors of 1943. Worsening shortages prompted India's representatives to plea for food abroad, and the country's partition cleft the Republic of India of its most fertile land and saddled it with the burden of feeding new refugees. An ill-advised attempt to deregulate the food economy, discussed later in greater depth, raised the specter of hunger once again. And the planners of a renewed Grow More Food campaign struggled against the reality that it was difficult to do so on the modest funds allotted to the task.

Yet even as India's leadership wrestled with the prospect of famine which would undercut its political legitimacy, the moment between 1943 and the drafting of India's first Five-Year Plan in 1951 was a period of creative foment and the negotiation of expertise, as Indian citizens,

Independent India of Plenty

planners, and politicians advanced particular visions for how the food crisis would best be solved. Citizens saw themselves as fundamental interlocutors in a set debates rooted in the farmers' fields and in the offices of national and provincial-level bureaucrats. This divergence of ideas for how best to solve India's food problems – between administrators, citizens, and groups – hints at a fleeting moment of creative postcolonial planning. So, too, do plans like Kelavkar's and Natesan's, and even the more staid plans of state representatives, hint at the flourishing of participatory political schemes that in time would come to be replaced with technological solutions.

"There has been a steady improvement in the food situation throughout the country," a member of the Food Department declared confidently in India's Central Legislature in February 1945.[4] A joint plan issued by the Departments of Food and Agriculture seemed to be increasing procurement and production modestly. Prices of grain had fallen low enough to cheer consumers, but not so much as to depress production. A fledgling rationing system was nonetheless calming a panicked public. And the monopoly procurement of foodgrains that certain provinces had adopted seemed to be helping matters where it had been undertaken.

Yet the Food Department's optimism was short-lived. A poor winter harvest was compounded by a massive cyclone which destroyed fields across the Godavari-Krishna and Cauvery deltas in the South. Drought in Bombay and the Deccan and poor rains in the Punjab had yielded an anemic crop of wheat. In Madras, mill owners were intimidating peasants into selling their rice by spreading rumors of an incoming shipment of Burmese stock that would devastate prices.[5] Food riots broke out in the towns of Kanchipuram and Cheyyar, and the Food Department deployed propaganda vans to calm tensions.[6] The fallout from the panic in the South reached as far as Delhi, where Tamil refugees were setting up makeshift shelters under bridges.[7] In Bombay, a group of leftist writers had formed a Cultural Workers' Committee for Fighting Famine; other citizens bemoaned the diversion of their ration allotments to a group of hungry railmen who had gone on strike for the increase of theirs.[8]

---

[4] R.N. Chopra, *Evolution of Food Policy in India* (New Delhi: Macmillan, 1981), 46–47.

[5] Sumit Sarkar, ed., "Rice Ration Cut in Madras Province," in *Towards Freedom 1946* (New Delhi: Indian Council of Historical Research, 2007), 877–878.

[6] Sumit Sarkar, ed., "Political Capital Made out of Ration Cuts in Madras Province," in *Towards Freedom 1946* (New Delhi: Indian Council of Historical Research, 2007), 858–859.

[7] "South Indian Refugee Women," *Hindustan Times*, May 7, 1946.

[8] Sumit Sarkar, ed., "Cultural Workers' Committee for Fighting Famine," in *Towards Freedom 1946* (New Delhi: Indian Council of Historical Research, 2007), 862–863; "Inclusion of Millets, Gram and Maize in the Cereal Group Rations," March 1, 1946,

54 Hungry Nation

In February 1946, the popular Hindi newsweekly *Sansar* superimposed four photographs of Bengal famine victims over an oversized red question mark; below this gruesome tableau, Jawaharlal Nehru was quoted decrying a world where "one man dies of hunger, and another drowns in food."[9] Publications like these roiled an uneasy citizenry; before long, the country's north was seized by protests. In Lucknow, a "spectacular hunger march" saw 50,000 marchers overcome partisan rancor to hoist the flags of the Congress, the Muslim League, the Communist Party, and the Hindu Mahasabha together. Wearing rags, the marchers carried torn chapattis to demonstrate "the consequences of the cloth and food policies of an alien Government."[10] In Allahabad, a similar coalition met to the rallying cry of *roti ke liye ek ho* – "all are united for food."[11] Punjab had long enjoyed a substantial wheat surplus, but a temporary freeze on its private sale and the subsequent discovery of 400 bags of wheat slated for export led to a 3000-person riot.[12] The March revelation of 200 dead peasants on the streets of Calcutta stoked rumors that famine had returned to Bengal.

Members of the imperial cabinet in London were livid at what they perceived as inaction in New Delhi. The political cost of the Bengal famine had been devastating, and the breakdown of India's national food situation would spell disaster.[13] Yet as the Viceroy and the colonial government bucked London's demands to make rations stretch further, their actions were frustrating India's restless nationalists, as well. India had been allotted its own seat at the meeting of the United States' and United Kingdom's Combined Food Board in Washington, from which it was hoped some of the 4 million tons of grain it required would be obtained.[14] But the appointment of British food advisor Robert Hutchings as India's representative was a slap in the face to those who had hoped for a nationalist representative. Hutchings tried to canvass support from Congressmen

---

Food – Rationing – RP-1000/62/1946, NAI; Sumit Sarkar, ed., "Supply of Food Grains Getting Worse in Bombay Province," in *Towards Freedom 1946* (New Delhi: Indian Council of Historical Research, 2007), 866–867.

[9] *Sansar*, February 28, 1946.

[10] Sumit Sarkar, ed., "Lucknow Hunger-March," in *Towards Freedom 1946* (New Delhi: Indian Council of Historical Research, 2007), 855.

[11] Sumit Sarkar, ed., "Hunger March against Ration Cuts in Allahabad," in *Towards Freedom 1946* (New Delhi: Indian Council of Historical Research, 2007), 143–144.

[12] Sumit Sarkar, ed., "Demonstrations in the Punjab against Food Hoarders," in *Towards Freedom 1946* (New Delhi: Indian Council of Historical Research, 2007), 863.

[13] Secretary of State for India, "Cabinet Memo: Food Supplies, Indian Food Situation," April 28, 1946, IOR/L/E/5/75.

[14] Department of Information and Broadcasting, Government of India, "Telegram to Secretary of State for India," January 18, 1946, IOR/L/I/1/1104.

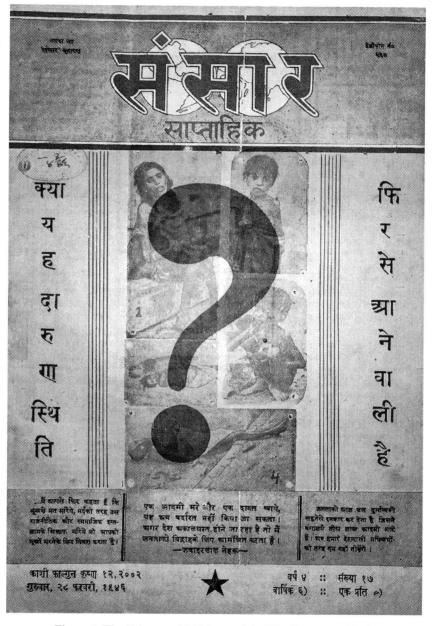

Figure 3 The February 1946 issue of the Hindi newsweekly *Sansar* asks whether famine will return to India, displaying photographs of victims of the Bengal famine. At bottom, Jawaharlal Nehru is quoted decrying a world where "one man dies of hunger, and another drowns in food." (Credit: author's collection)

56   Hungry Nation

but could not staunch the political fallout.[15] India, representatives of the Indian Merchants' Chamber declared, was still "being tied to the apron strings of His Majesty's Government," and even after contributing "men, money, and materials" to the war, the nation was being prevented from demanding its full requirements of grain.[16] Discontent spread to Indian parliamentarians in the Central Assembly: Muslim League representative Ziauddin Ahmad moved for the Food Department to be abolished altogether, and M.R. Masani moved to condemn the government for its failure to import sufficient foodgrains.[17]

In February, a recomposed team was announced, and J.P. Srivastava, loathed by nationalists for his misadministration in the Bengal famine, was asked to lead it. Hutchings continued to serve on the mission, but the colonial government had given the team an Indian look through the appointment of three Indian administrators – A. Ramaswami Mudaliar, another member of the Viceroy's Executive Council, Sonti Ramamurthy, Advisor to the Government of Madras, and A.D. Gorwala, Bombay's Commissioner of Civil Supplies.[18] Yet one frustrated administrator professed not to understand why the nationalist press "continue[d] to harp on the theme of a National government, the panacea for India's ills."[19]

Released from wartime detention, the Congress leadership was nonetheless precluded from participation in these negotiations, reduced to speechifying. "When there is a loaf of bread to share," Jawaharlal Nehru urged, "it must be eaten half and half by Punjabis and South Indians alike."[20] Gandhi, in February, outlined steps that officials and the public could take to meet the food crisis, including the minimizing of waste, the adoption of substitute food, the growing of crops on fallow land, and the elimination of the black market. The Viceroy agreed with these suggestions, but lamented that the public had only noticed Gandhi's call for an immediate recomposition of the Executive Council.[21] Gandhi declared,

---

[15] Department of Food, Government of India, "Telegram to Secretary of State for India," February 19, 1946, IOR/L/I/1/1104.

[16] Indian Merchants' Chamber, Bombay, "Telegram to Viceroy re: Food Situation in The Country," February 6, 1946, Indian Merchants' Chamber, Bombay papers, folder 821, NMML.

[17] Sumit Sarkar, ed., "Central Legislative Assembly Discussion on Food Shortages," in *Towards Freedom 1946* (New Delhi: Indian Council of Historical Research, 2007), 854–855.

[18] "India Food Mission: Sir J.P. Sriviastava Will Lead Delegation in U.S.," *Times of India*, February 14, 1946.

[19] Frederick William Pethick-Lawrence, "Draft Telegram to Government of India," February 8, 1946, IOR/L/I/1/1104.

[20] Department of Food, Government of India, "Telegram to Secretary of State for India."

[21] Archibald Percival Wavell, "Telegram to Secretary of State for India," February 14, 1946, IOR/L/I/1/1104.

Independent India of Plenty 57

in turn, that he would fight the foreign government on all fronts but food, but even on this matter, "we shall fight them if they betray callousness or contempt for reasoned public opinion."[22]

Gandhi renounced this pledge of cooperation at the end of March, urging Congress to refuse to join a food committee which was to be staffed by Jinnah, the Viceroy, and the Nawab of Bhopal, citing the continued absence of a national popular government.[23] The party's Working Committee met in Bombay instead to formulate a plan for growing and redistributing food in the present emergency and after independence.[24] The editors of the *Modern Review* cheered Congress' steadfastness. "The people are convinced," they wrote, "that food production will not increase, food waste will not cease, and food exports will not stop till a fully responsible National Government comes into being at the Centre."[25]

Arriving in Washington, the colonial delegation found that there was little grain forthcoming from the world's depleted coffers.[26] Khawaja Nazimuddin, the disgraced former Chief Minister of Bengal who had joined the mission, asked reporters how the world could claim a wheat shortage when there were so many wasted dinner rolls and slices of toast in the dining room of the Waldorf-Astoria.[27] Sonti Ramamurthy made India's case in the *Washington Post* and on the *CBS Country Journal Program*, declaring that it would be unjust to let 10 million Indians die when they had contributed so much to the war effort.[28] Girija Shankar Bajpai, India's representative at the United Nations, declared that without assistance, India would face another famine.[29] And in a meeting with President Truman, A. Ramaswami Mudaliar made his own desperate case for 2 million tons of cereal.[30]

---

[22] Information Services, Government of India, "Gandhi's 8-Fold Programme to Meet Food Crisis," February 26, 1946, IOR/L/I/1/1104, British Library; "Food Crisis: Gandhiji's Suggestions to Viceroy," *Forward*, March 15, 1946.

[23] Sumit Sarkar, ed., "Congress Unwilling to Join Food Council Proposed by Viceroy," in *Towards Freedom 1946* (New Delhi: Indian Council of Historical Research, 2007), 857; "Conversation with Chancellor of Chamber of Princes, H.H. of Bhopal," March 12, 1946, Political – Internal – 1(33) I.B., 1946(Secret)(B), NAI.

[24] Zaidi and Zaidi, "Congress Working Committee, Bombay, March 12–15, 1946."

[25] "Congress Food Policy," *Modern Review*, April 1946.

[26] *Report of the Special Meeting on Urgent Food Problem, Washington D.C., May 20–27, 1946* (Washington, DC: Food and Agriculture Organization of the United Nations, 1946).

[27] "Delegates from India Go Window Shopping Here," *New York Times*, March 13, 1946.

[28] Sonti Venkata Ramamurty, "10 Million Will Die – and Not Easily," *Washington Post*, March 17, 1946; Information Services, Government of India, "India's Appeal to USA: Broadcast by Leader of Food Delegation," March 22, 1946, IOR/L/I/1/1104.

[29] Information Services, Government of India, "Speech by Girja Shankar Bajpai, Agent General for India, at UNRRA Conference in Atlantic City," March 21, 1946, IOR/L/I/1/1104.

[30] "India's Food Envoy Hopeful of U.S. Aid," *New York Times*, May 21, 1946.

58   Hungry Nation

These representatives returned home unsure of what aid, if any, they would ultimately receive. Sonti Ramamurthy declared on All India Radio that a mission undertaken by Indian representatives marked "the end of the colonial economy," and that if and when aid did arrive, it would be distributed via the well-managed food administration that was the hallmark of a modern state.[31] Private groups declared their eagerness to help assist that administration: the All India Women's Committee called for regular "Food Days" to help promote awareness of women's role in facilitating the equitable distribution of food aid.[32]

But instead of immediate aid, India received a visit from a former American President. Herbert Hoover was sent by the United States in March 1946 to assess India's true food needs, and B.R. Sen was assigned to take him on an All India tour.[33] Hoover painted a grim portrait of India's global role in a farewell address on All India Radio. "The world," he reflected, "has become a vast involuntary experimental laboratory as to different levels of calories which the population are to have in their rations." Hoover's visit was followed by an "American Famine Mission" led by economist Theodore Schultz, a pioneering agricultural economist who would soon play host to Nehru during his first visit to the United States several years later.[34] The members of the mission, including Pearl Buck and the heads of the Council of Churches, and the Federation of Jewish Philanthropies, visited ration depots and procurement operations, and met with prominent members of the Congress and Muslim League. "No country in the world," Schultz reported, "with perhaps the exception of Russia, has gone so far in controlling basic food distribution." Schultz returned to the United States to urge that it send at least three-quarters of a million tons of wheat to India.

The delay of wheat from the United States had soured Indians on American designs, and nationalist bureaucrats replaced imperial ones, they looked to other sources of aid which might better suit the diplomatic needs of a new nation. A food mission was sent to Argentina in hopes of South American wheat.[35] Bureaucrats in London approached Soviet representatives to see if the wheat the USSR was sending to France could be

---

[31] Sumit Sarkar, ed., "Threat of Famine Because of India's War Effort," in *Towards Freedom 1946* (New Delhi: Indian Council of Historical Research, 2007), 865.

[32] "Food," *Bulletin of Indian Women's Movement*, July 1946.

[33] Herbert Hoover, "Broadcast to India on the Food Situation in India and Australia," April 30, 1946, IOR/L/I/1/1104, British Library; "Hoover in India," *Times of India*, April 23, 1946.

[34] Lilliam Smith et al., *India's Hunger: Report of the American Famine Mission to India* (New York: India Famine Emergency Committee, 1946).

[35] "Food Mission to Argentina," 1946, IOR/L/I/1/1104, British Library; "Indian Food Mission in Argentina," *Times of India*, August 13, 1946.

Independent India of Plenty   59

diverted to India instead.[36] An entreaty to Indonesia led to the shipment of half a million tons of rice.[37] And Ijaz Ahmad, a senior official in the Department of Food and later Pakistan's representative to the FAO, was sent on a remarkable mission to West Asia and Africa.[38] From Karachi, Ahmed traveled to Tehran, Alexandria, and Cairo, before a final audience with Emperor Haile Selassie of Ethiopia. His tour, however, was fruitless. "Whatever politicians of these countries may profess," Ahmad wrote, "there is no real sympathy with India in her food difficulty, and every country has her own interests in the forefront."

These largely unsuccessful ventures underscored to nationalist politicians India's pitiable agricultural state. "It is a tragic sight," Rajendra Prasad wrote, "to see India's representatives going from one end of the earth to another – literally from Persia to Peru – with the begging bowl in their hands for food which she ought to be able to produce."[39]

In August 1946, Robert Hutchings convened a final meeting of the imperial government's provincial food ministers. The colonial administration and its Indian successors, Hutchings declared in New Delhi, shared the same goal: "to prevent disaster for our people and to prevent suffering and starvation."[40] With independence in sight, Hutchings asked his Indian counterparts to believe that his administration, the biggest of its kind in the world, would work tirelessly to feed India's 400 million people until the foreign government's inevitable exit.

A month later, Hutchings ceded control of the Ministry to Rajendra Prasad. The Cabinet Mission which had arrived in India in May 1946 to discuss the logistics of British withdrawal had stalled over Jinnah's insistence on the "Pakistan demand"; the Muslim League's subsequent call for a "Direct Action Day" in August had unleashed mass rioting and slaughter in Calcutta. By September, a frustrated imperial government conceded the formation of an "interim government"; Congress accepted its invitation in September, and the Muslim League joined the transitional administration a month later. These political machinations played out while Indians contended with a worsening food crisis: a trickle of

---

[36] "Russia Has Food to Spare: Indian Mission Visit Suggested," *Hindustan Times*, May 31, 1946.
[37] M.O. Mathai, "Offer of Rice by the Indonesian P.M.," May 1946, M.O. Mathai papers, subject files, folder 12, NMML; "Java's Rice Offer to India," *Times of India*, May 20, 1946.
[38] "Report of Mr. Ijaz Ahmad, Director of Food Purchase," December 14, 1946, External Affairs – Middle East – 4(2)-ME, 1947, NAI.
[39] Chopra, *Evolution of Food Policy in India*, 50.
[40] Department of Food, Government of India, *Proceedings of the All India Food Ministers' Conference Held in New Delhi on 9th and 10th August 1946* (Simla: Government of India Press, 1946), 85.

60   Hungry Nation

American grain had arrived through Bombay's Alexandra Port throughout the summer on decommissioned Liberty warships, but most Indians shared the assessment of that city's Trade Union Committee of the "food situation in the country which, instead of improving, is deteriorating day by day."[41]

Rajendra Prasad's appointment as Food Minister meant that India's precarious food situation was now in the hands of its future rulers. His first address to the Ministry had a populist air: Prasad declared that the new government's "approach to all agricultural problems should also be in the interest of the poor peasant, as he needs the utmost assistance in all form." Abundance alone would not be enough: citizens and their new government would need to work to ensure nutritious food for all, as well.[42] Prasad repeated a call for shared sacrifice on All India Radio several weeks later. "Each one of us," he declared, "must examine our little store and spare what he can out of it, even at inconvenience to himself. Those who have very large stocks, either as producers or traders, must realize the seriousness of the situation and produce them for pooling for the common good." While the current situation was bleak, Prasad spoke with optimism. "Our people," he concluded, "have a knack of getting through calamities which may well break others."[43]

The ascent of the interim government cheered the departing imperial administrators, now tasked with overseeing a transition to self-rule. Bombay's Minister of Civil Supplies admitted that the province was facing a major food deficit, but declared that "there is no cause for despondency now that the Interim Government are functioning at the Center."[44] When the United Kingdom's Ministry of Food proposed diverting to London a shipment of Turkish wheat destined for India, the Secretary of State for India intervened, warning that such a move "would be likely to color the atmosphere attending the closing days of British rule in India."[45]

The International Emergency Food Council's pledge of half a million tons of rice to India – its largest-ever package – came as a boon to nationalist planners, but also underscored the need for real plans.[46] Jawaharlal

---

[41] "Wheat Shipments from America," July 25, 1946, IOR/L/I/1/1104; Sumit Sarkar, ed., "Bombay Provincial TUC Resolution on the Food Situation," in *Towards Freedom 1946* (New Delhi: Indian Council of Historical Research, 2007), 880–881.

[42] "India's Food Member Urges All Out Effort," *News from India*, September 3, 1946, IOR/L/E/8/7236.

[43] Rajendra Prasad, "Broadcast on the Food Position," September 23, 1946, IOR/L/I/1/1104.

[44] "Bombay's Food Deficit of 225,000 Tons," *Times of India*, September 12, 1946.

[45] Secretary of State for India, "Distribution of Ministry of Food's Wheat Purchases in Turkey," January 4, 1947, IOR/L/E/5/75.

[46] "410,000 Tons of Rice to India," *Times of India*, January 13, 1947.

Nehru addressed the Indian Science Congress gathered in Delhi at the New Year, asking India's researchers to place their talents in the service of the nation's food problem. "For a hungry man or hungry woman," Nehru said, "truth has little meaning. He wants food."[47] In the Food Ministry, Prasad and his assistants began devising a "Five-Year Plan to Free India from Hunger." Investment in the plan for 11.5 percent increased annual production, the Minister declared, would come from all invested parties: in any scheme, a third of funding would come from New Delhi, a third from any involved province, and a third would come from the farmers directly impacted by the scheme.[48]

Yet objections to Prasad's first plan came quickly. The *Eastern Economist* declared that the Food Minister's was "just the war-time Grow-More-Food campaign to be revived and re-invigorated under the auspices of the Interim Government."[49] Without a commitment to intensive production with chemical fertilizers in areas with sufficient water and irrigation – precisely the commitment that India's government would make fifteen years later – this plan was unlikely to get India nearer its goal of half a billion individuals fed by 1970. The Indian Merchants' Chamber worried that their role in trade was being neglected in the plan; its members petitioned the Food Ministry to "preserve the principle of utilizing the normal channels of trade in all the stages of the work."[50] Further discontent came from India's communists: *People's Age* warned that 300 million Indians stood on the brink of famine, and the Interim Government's plan did nothing to induce urgent assistance from the American and Argentinian governments, which "prefer to feed grain to animals or burn it rather than give to the starving people."[51] In May, rationing officers in Lucknow str1ked to protest delayed shipments of food from New Delhi.[52] A week after these protests, 3000 villagers outside Baroda descended upon a rationing depot to demand food, looting 80 tons of wheat before the police swarmed in.[53]

Incidents like these stoked worry among India's representatives abroad. Labor economist N.G. Abhyankar, India's new delegate to the International Emergency Food Council, warned that Indians would

[47] "Science Must Serve India's Hungry Masses," *Bombay Chronicle*, January 4, 1947.
[48] "No Fear of Famine in India," *Bombay Chronicle*, January 14, 1947.
[49] "The New Food Plan," *Eastern Economist*, January 24, 1947, 180–181.
[50] A.C. Ramalingam, "Setting up of a Rice Food Board at Delhi," January 16, 1947, Indian Merchants' Chamber, Bombay papers, folder 830, NMML.
[51] Prem Sagar Gupta, "Three Crores May Go Hungry This Year!," *People's Age*, May 4, 1947.
[52] "Rationing Officials to Strike," *Vartman*, May 4, 1947.
[53] "Attack on Rationing Store," *Vartman*, May 27, 1947.

62   Hungry Nation

"rebel" against the country's fledgling rationing system if grain supplies were not increased.[54] India's outgoing imperial administrators were similarly anxious. In May 1947, the newly appointed Secretary of State for India wrote to London to warn that food, more than any other issue, stood to disrupt the course of an orderly departure.[55] "India has scraped by tight corners before," he wrote, but the atmosphere of political tension would exacerbate the effects of any shortage. "It is greatly to our interest," the Secretary of State wrote, "that food should as little as possible increase the difficulties of the next few months; anything like a repetition of the 1943 famine would be likely both to jeopardize our whole policy and to provoke severe criticism of His Majesty's Government in press and Parliament." The Viceroy and others sought to minimize supply disruptions that nationalists could read uncharitably. When the United Kingdom's Minister of Food once again urged a redirection of Indian wheat imports to Britain, the Viceroy insisted that London

> consider the matter mainly from the political angle. It is important to our interests that the orderly transfer of power should not be jeopardized by a food breakdown and it would be unfortunate if the closing days of our responsibility for the good government of India coincided with another famine, particularly if we had done nothing to help prevent it.[56]

On the morning of August 15, India's tricolor was raised across the length and breadth of what had become the Indian Union. Some hours after Jawaharlal Nehru announced the arrival of India's "tryst with destiny," Rajendra Prasad arrived at the leafy campus of the Indian Council of Agricultural Research to proclaim that the chief task facing free India would be "to conquer that dread evil – hunger."[57] Dairymen announced that free milk would be given away on Uttar Pradesh's Vidhan railway line to celebrate hopes of new abundance.[58] Yet the optimism of the day was marbled with fear. Partition had cleaved India's most arable provinces, Bengal and Punjab, into two, and the most fertile districts of each were now across the border in Pakistan. India was cleaved of 18 percent of its population, and left with only 69 percent of its irrigated land, as well as nearly all of India's traditional famine regions.[59] *People's Age*, ever dour, was apoplectic. Independence had arrived, it declared, but

---

[54] "Indian Delegate Warns IEFC," *Reuters Indian Service*, May 26, 1947, IOR/L/E/8/7236.
[55] William Francis Hare, "The Food Situation in India," May 19, 1947, IOR/L/E/5/75.
[56] Cabinet Memo, June 18, 1947, IOR/L/E/5/75.
[57] "Flag Hoisting Ceremony at the Indian Council of Agricultural Research."
[58] "Milk to be Given Away Free," *Vartman*, August 15, 1947.
[59] Chopra, *Evolution of Food Policy in India*, 52.

Independent India of Plenty 63

India's "whole agrarian economy is on the way to a complete collapse."[60] Gandhi's dramatic fast at independence, the *Economist* declared, was ironic given that "for many millions of Mr. Gandhi's fellow-countrymen, however, fasting to-day is involuntary, and is likely in the near future to overshadow all other problems of India."[61] India's Department of Information and Broadcasting grimly asked the press for help in staving off food riots. "India's political freedom," officials warned in a telegram to editors, "must not be allowed to prove illusory by a complete collapse on her food front."[62]

A collapse did seem imminent. Hindi newspapers were declaring the impending depletion of food supplies in front-page headlines.[63] Ten days after independence, Rajendra Prasad reached out to V.K. Krishna Menon, now India's representative in London, to ask him to press the case for food.[64] Given that "a breakdown of rationing is inevitable at any time after the 15th September," Prasad wrote, a few diverted shipments from British government purchases in Iraq "may just save the situation till our own position begins to ease as a result of the new crop."[65]

India, however, could not count on British largesses, particularly after the United Kingdom's efforts to commandeer imports destined for the subcontinent. The Food Ministry dispatched its own food mission to Iraq and Iran, yet its deputy secretary, H.L. Khanna, was dismayed to find that Iran was only willing to trade grains for usurious quantities of textiles, and jute in particular.[66] There was little interest in the raw Khandasari sugar India was offering, and Khanna lamented the steely Iranians who were "exploiting the present world food position to the utmost." Iraqi negotiators were more willing to part with surplus wheat, but the passage of a legislative ban on its export soured the deal. Dejected, India launched another hopeful mission to the first World Food Council Meeting of the FAO in hopes of garnering international support.[67] Kamaladevi Chattopadhyay surveyed these missions with

[60] Prem Sagar Gupta, "Reconstruct India: Break the Shackles of Imperialist-Feudal Economy!," *People's Age*, August 15, 1947.
[61] "Politics and Food in India," *Economist*, August 16, 1947.
[62] Department of Information and Broadcasting, Government of India, "Guidance for Food Publicity."
[63] "India's Food Situation Perilous," *Vartman*, September 28, 1947.
[64] Rajendra Prasad, letter to the Indian High Commissioner, London, August 25, 1947, External Affairs – Overseas – V – 7(73)-O.S.(V), 1947 (Secret), NAI.
[65] "Opening of Emergency Food Ration Shops," October 3, 1947, Agriculture – Rationing – RP 1020/66, NAI.
[66] "Deputation of H.L. Khanna to Iraq and Iran," 1947, External Affairs – Iran and Afghanistan – 2(2)-IA, 1947 (Secret), NAI.
[67] "India's Food Delegate," *Times of India*, October 25, 1947.

64   Hungry Nation

dismay, declaring in the *Modern Review* that "it is morally and materially undermining for a nation to have to build her food front on imports. It merely serves to emphasize our own weaknesses, for it is most disheartening for a country like India, with her enormous resources, to indefinitely plead for mercy at others' doors."[68]

The most visible yet inaccessible grains, however, were those which lay across India's new borders. Pakistan's food surpluses and broad tracts of arable land tantalized Indian bureaucrats, who seethed at their new neighbor's unwillingness to continue shipping grains to New Delhi. Preparing for independence, the Export Committee of the Partition Council had decided that until March 1948 the new dominions of India and Pakistan should "give or receive supplies of controlled commodities as if there had been no partition."[69] Yet India's Food Ministry groused in a November memo that no foodgrains had been shipped to India since independence – an absence that Pakistani officials blamed on their own rationing requirements, difficulties in transportation, and the "complete chaos ruling in Punjab." A delegation of Pakistani officials arrived in New Delhi in late 1947 to ask for payment for the 32,000 tons of wheat that New Delhi had borrowed from provinces now in Pakistan. Pakistan's post-independence procurement efforts, its representatives asserted, necessitated these withheld funds; accordingly, unable to procure Pakistan's withheld shipments did not constitute a breach of faith. Vishnu Sahay, a senior Ministry of Food official, brokered a compromise that involved sending wheat and barley in exchange for rice. Yet this ad hoc solution did nothing to facilitate any further transfer of cash or grain.

Refugees moved quicker than gunny sacks. As bureaucrats negotiated, millions of migrants were streaming across new borders, contending with not only violence and death, but the abandonment of their agricultural livelihoods.[70] India's new Military Evacuation Organization sought to provide refugees with food, sometimes even before they arrived in one of the thirty odd camps established for their rehabilitation. The Indian Air Force airdropped food to caravans crossing the border, and on one occasion, delivered 280 maunds of chapattis baked by volunteers in Delhi to feed a stranded convoy.[71] India's central and provincial governments

[68] Kamaladevi Chattopadhyay, "The Food Problem," *Modern Review*, November 1947, 357–360.
[69] B.R. Patel, "Foodgrain Quotas to Pakistan," November 27, 1947, External Affairs – Overseas – V – 5(3)-O.S.(V), 1947, NAI.
[70] On refugees and state-building, see Ian Talbot, "Punjabi Refugees' Rehabilitation and the Indian State: Discourses, Denials and Dissonances," *Modern Asian Studies* 45, Special Issue 1 (2011): 109–130; and Zamindar, *The Long Partition*.
[71] *Millions on the Move: The Aftermath of Partition* (New Delhi: Publications Division, Ministry of Information and Broadcasting, Government of India, 1949), 12; Yasmin

Independent India of Plenty   65

split the significant cost of feeding refugees – 400,000 of them, according to the Food Ministry. At Kurukshetra, the largest camp, nearly 100,000 refugees received 1538 tons of wheat, 20 tons of sugar, and 2 tons of salt from government stores.[72] Where state institutions faltered, citizens occasionally came to refugees' assistance: after a fire tore through Delhi's Kingsway refugee camp and displaced 10,000 residents, citizens in the capital cooked food for the twice-homeless, serving them "meals under dim moonlight."[73]

Tales of generosity were outweighed, however, by the complaints of refugees who protested their meager rations. Refugees from East Pakistan who arrived at Calcutta's Sealdah station were fed austerely on puffed rice and jaggery, with the province and private charities splitting the bill. "There," the *Amrita Bazar Patrika* contended, "ends the responsibility of the Government."[74] One refugee in a Gujarat camp declared that he and his compatriots were "eating stuff which we used to throw away in Pakistan for the birds to eat."[75] Dalits wrote to B.R. Ambedkar to contend that the promise of rations was meaningless if they were not even let into camps on account of caste.[76] Delhi's Executive Council fielded numerous petitions from Muslim refugees asserting discrimination by the camp shopkeepers tasked with feeding them.[77]

A month after partition, Mahatma Gandhi eschewed police protection to tour the camps around Delhi's Jama Masjid, fielding the complaints of some of the 30,000 refugees bemoaning widespread hunger.[78] Refugees elsewhere declared that the flour, lentils, and jaggery promised by camp managers rarely materialized.[79] Jairamdas Daulatram toured Bombay refugee camps with characteristic tone-deafness, lecturing an elderly woman who had asked for heartier rations on the severity of India's import crisis. Elsewhere, Daulatram begged refugees to call off the food *satyagraha* that they had planned, awkwardly held a "rickety

---

Khan, *The Great Partition: The Making of India and Pakistan* (New Haven: Yale University Press, 2007), 162.

[72] Press Information Bureau, Government of India, "Political Freedom and Battle against Hunger," August 15, 1948, IOR/L/E/8/7230.

[73] "Delhi Refugee Camp Fire," *Times of India*, May 27, 1948.

[74] Bashabi Fraser, *Bengal Partition Stories: An Unclosed Chapter* (New York: Anthem Press, 2000), 29.

[75] Ramachandra Guha, *India after Gandhi: The History of the World's Largest Democracy* (New York: Ecco, 2007), 91.

[76] Urvashi Butalia, *The Other Side of Silence: Voices from the Partition of India* (Durham: Duke University Press, 2000), 239–240.

[77] Zamindar, *The Long Partition*, 250.

[78] "Mahatma Tours Delhi Refugee Camps: Muslims Narrate Tale of Woe," *Times of India*, September 13, 1947.

[79] "More Rations for Refugees," *Times of India*, May 11, 1948.

child" proffered as proof of poor rations, and found his motorcade blocked by refugees demanding transfer to a better-managed camp.[80] (Nutrition researchers were also surveying those rickety children and scraggy adults, having realized that camps were ideal sites to conduct studies on malnutrition.[81])

The sharing of costs between center and provinces meant that administrators at all levels felt the need to alleviate the burden that refugees exerted upon treasuries and granaries. In January 1948, the Diwan of Baroda wrote to New Delhi to assert that the provision of food had made refugees idle and demoralized; refugees were clamoring for more supplies, but the Dewan asked for permission to slash them.[82] The Diwan's complaint presaged severe cuts in food expenditure: the following year, Bombay's government drafted a plan to reduce the number of refugees eligible for free rations from 195,000 to 40,000; by August, the province had stopped feeding refugees altogether, sending those asking for supplies to Madh Island to work in exchange for daily rations.[83] Refugees creatively protested these reductions: in February 1949, 500 Dalit refugees from Sindh went on hunger strike in an effort to bring back free rations in place of paid ones, tying their cards in a bundle and displaying it on a lamppost in protest.[84]

The plight of refugees was dire. But in India's northwest, a farsighted administrator was leveraging the arrival of refugees to plan for prosperity. The partition of Punjab had deprived the province of its most fertile regions, including the well-irrigated "Canal Colonies," and refugees who had once occupied 67 lakh acres of land were arriving in a province with only 47 lakh acres of more barren tracts.[85] New arrivals in East Punjab argued that their hereditary villages should be reassembled brick-by-brick, and big landlords argued that the size of their old plots be maintained. The problem of land redistribution was solved by the newly appointed Director General of Rehabilitation, Tarlok Singh.

---

[80] "Rehabilitation of Refugees," *Times of India*, July 19, 1948; "Rise above Narrow Interest," *Times of India*, December 13, 1948.

[81] "Training Classes in Practical Nutrition Work to Be Held at the IRFA," 1947, Gujarat States Agency – 571, 1947, NAI.

[82] Diwan of Baroda, letter to the Secretary of the Government of India, Ministry of States, January 30, 1948, Ministry of States – General – 23(1)-G(R), 1948, NAI; "Note on Free Rations to Refugees in Baroda," 1949, Ministry of States – General – 2(22)/G(R), NAI.

[83] "No More Free Rations for Non-Destitutes," *Times of India*, August 24, 1949.

[84] "Hunger Strike by Refugees," *Times of India*, February 15, 1949; "Harijans Call off Hunger Strike," *Times of India*, February 17, 1949.

[85] M.S. Randhawa, *Out of the Ashes: An Account of the Rehabilitation of Refugees from West Pakistan in Rural Areas of East Punjab* (Chandigarh: Public Relations Department, Punjab, 1954), 93. One lakh = one hundred thousand.

Independent India of Plenty 67

Singh proposed the establishment of the "standard acre," a unit of land defined not by its size, but by its productive capacity for food – in this case, around 380 pounds of rice. This metric allowed Singh to oversee a quarter million refugee allotments across Punjab, where the state offered loans for food, seed, bulls, fodder, and tractors.[86] In two decades, these lands would be the proving grounds for India's Green Revolution.

However expensive India's refugees were to feed, their food needs represented only a fraction of India's 700,000 to 800,000 ton food deficit.[87] The author of a self-published treatise on India's nutrition needs dedicated his 1947 work "to the starving millions of India, whose silent tears and sorrows have deeply moved our thinkers to-day."[88] Dwarkanath Chatterjee declared that he was happy that his book had been written at "a time when there is a universal cry for more and more food." Yet it was uncertain how that cry would be translated into concrete plans.

India's first year of independence saw New Delhi embarking upon what one economist would decry shortly thereafter as "the most disastrous and costly experiment [undertaken] by the Government."[89] Urged on by Mohandas Gandhi and India's most influential businessmen and traders, India's Foodgrains Policy Committee called for the removal of controls on India's food procurement and sales, allowing for a short-lived free market experiment. Lamented by economists, this decontrol effort, discussed extensively in Chapter 4, was massively unsuccessful, leading to unchecked inflation of food prices. The assassination of Mohandas Gandhi allowed New Delhi to roll back this experiment, reintroducing food control in hopes of a "gradual reduction of foodgrains prices to a reasonable level" by the end of the following year.[90]

The failed experiment underscored the need for ambitious planning to yoke together a disparate program of imports, distribution, reclamation, and research. As the Food Ministry began reviving "the old machinery of procurement and rationing [which] had virtually gone to pieces," an unprecedented 4.5 million tons of grains streamed into Indian ports soiled with the "ancient and heavily weevilled residue of previous unloadings."[91]

---

[86] Gyanesh Kudaisya and Tan Tai Yong, *The Aftermath of Partition in South Asia* (London: Routledge, 2002), 123–139.

[87] Ram Gopal Agrawal, *Price Controls in India since 1947* (New Delhi, 1956), 22.

[88] Dwarkanath Chatterjee, *Food and Nutrition in India* (Calcutta: D.N. Chatterjee, 1947).

[89] N.V. Sovani, *Post War Inflation in India: A Survey*, Gokhale Institute Studies 21 (Poona: Gokhale Institute of Politics and Economics, 1949), 54.

[90] Ministry of Food, Government of India, "Letter 619/34 to All Provincial Governments and Administrations and States; All Regional Food Commissioners," September 25, 1948, Indian Merchants' Chamber, Bombay papers, folder 672, NMML.

[91] "Food Facts and Fancies," *Economic Weekly*, January 22, 1949; "Food Needs of India for 1949," *Times of India*, January 22, 1949; Derry, Airgram #2631, December 8, 1948,

68   Hungry Nation

Further inland, India's new reclamation schemes were creaking to life, most notably, the clearing of wastelands in Uttar Pradesh's Terai region.[92] The FAO's first ever grant saw stubborn *kans* grass yanked from the lands of the Indo-Gangetic Plain.[93] Major damming schemes – most notably, the Damodar Valley Project – saw soil darken with water.[94] And the country's agricultural institutions, under new leadership, were undertaking ambitious new schemes of basic research. Observers could – and did – challenge the degree to which India had a food deficit, yet all conceded in the end that it did. A retired agricultural commissioner self-published a short pamphlet *Is Our Country Really in Deficit of Food?* to run the numbers for himself, conceding that this was indeed the case.[95]

With food prices sky-high, the subject of Indians' increased ire was the Food Minister, Jairamdas Daulatram, who was censured, by Parliament for his administrative failures, with some legislators calling for the Prime Minister to take over the vital ministry on an emergency basis.[96] The anger was palpable: the *Economic Weekly* declared the attack on Daulatram fiercer than any "ever directed against any other Ministry at the Centre."[97] The cartoonist K. Shankar Pillai, whose pen left few politicians unscathed, lampooned the corpulent Food Minister incessantly, depicting him touting improbable figures of agricultural growth to a famine victim, or feasting on sweets at the inauguration of a land reclamation scheme.[98]

As provinces drained their coffers and borrowed from the central government's to stave off shortages, onlookers urged other administrators to take the lead in the absence of greater leadership in the Food Ministry. "Food and Agriculture can never become a Central subject," Britain's commercial advisor concluded, "unless provincial autonomy practically

---

RG 469 / UD 237 / Box 42 / India Comm. Food 1950 April 1951, USNA; Office of the Adviser in India to the Central Commercial Committee, Report #16, February 1949, DO/133/108, UKNA.

[92] M.S. Randhawa, *A History of Agriculture in India*, vol. 4: *1947–1981* (New Delhi: Indian Council of Agricultural Research, 1986), 51–60; Eric A. Strahorn, *An Environmental History of Postcolonial North India: The Himalayan Tarai in Uttar Pradesh and Uttaranchal* (New York: Peter Lang, 2009).

[93] *More from Mother Earth* (New Delhi: Publications Division, Ministry of Information and Broadcasting, Government of India, 1951).

[94] Randhawa, *A History of Agriculture in India*, vol. 4: *1947–1981*: 73–76; on the Damodar Valley Project, see Klingensmith, *One Valley and a Thousand*.

[95] Indubhusan Chatterji, *Is Our Country Really in Deficit of Food?* (Calcutta, 1951).

[96] Loy W. Henderson, Airgram #3299, March 9, 1949, RG 469 / UD 237 / Box 42 / India Agriculture, USNA.

[97] "Mobilisation against Hunger," *Economic Weekly*, February 26, 1949, 4, 24.

[98] "Give Us This Day Our Daily Bread! [Cartoon]," *Shankar's Weekly*, January 10, 1949; "The Glorious Morrow! [Cartoon]," *Shankar's Weekly*, January 23, 1949.

Independent India of Plenty   69

disappears. But a really strong Minister is certainly needed to harden his heart and slash the exorbitant food bills presented by the provinces."[99] The Cabinet's Economic Committee had begun to raise concerns over India's depleted dollar resources – identifying food imports as the major culprit.[100] It was this external pressure that helped forge early, if fleeting consensus between the Ministries of Food and Agriculture, both headed by Daulatram but manned by separate staff. In March and April 1949, India's national leaders began to tout the imperative of ending imports via increased production and procurement. In an address to businessmen, Jawaharlal Nehru set a target date, declaring that

the very ease with which we have been able to get foodstuffs from abroad has rather prevented us from facing the [food] problem properly. I think we should think in terms of not getting any food at all from abroad after a certain period – let us put it at two years, I should not add a day more, and just make up our mind that we shall live on the food that we produce after two years or die in the attempt.[101]

A week later, C. Rajagopalachari, then India's Governor-General, echoed the imperative, casting food imports as "the greatest shame we can inflict on our motherland."[102]

The plan that the Prime Minister advanced at the executive level was a new version of the Grow More Food campaign, just as skeptical onlookers had suggested Rajendra Prasad's 1946 plan had been. Its wartime antecedent, announced in April 1942, had emphasized a shift from cash to food crops, intensive cultivation through better irrigation, seeds, manures, and practices, and the urgent reclamation of unused wastelands. The Foodgrains Policy Committee of 1947 had concluded that these goals had been pursued only half-heartedly, recommending that they be advanced more aggressively, with the aim of a 10 million ton increase in annual production.[103] With command of the food market reestablished, the other instruments of the 1947 plan were reanimated with the hopes of self-sufficiency in food within two years.

The disagreements which ensued concerning the feasibility of that goal revealed major fissures between the Food and Agriculture Ministries,

---

[99] Office of the Adviser in India to the Central Commercial Committee, Report #16.
[100] "Cabinet Concern over Dollars," *Economic Weekly*, March 5, 1949.
[101] Jawaharlal Nehru, "We Should Pull Together [New Delhi, March 4, 1949]," in *Independence and After: A Collection of Speeches* (New York: Day, 1950), 193–195.
[102] C. Rajagopalachari, "The Food Problem [All India Radio, July 6, 1949]," in *Speeches of C. Rajagopalachari, Governor-General of India: June 1948 – January 1950* (New Delhi: Superintendent, Governor-General's Press, 1950), 251.
[103] B.M. Bhatia, *India's Food Problem and Policy since Independence* (Bombay: Somaiya Publications, 1970), 57.

70   Hungry Nation

and the ways in which bureaucrats in each could call upon international expertise. "Though they share one Minister," a British observer noted, "the ministries are situated two miles apart, and their approach to the common problem about as wide apart, too."[104] Officials in the Agriculture wing had pressed for the two-year timeframe, reaching out to former FAO Director Lord John Boyd-Orr to come to India to give his blessing. But Food Ministry officials, by contrast, had rallied behind the more conservative estimates of sitting FAO Director Norris Dodd that India would only realistically be able to reduce food imports to 1.5 million tons annually.

Nehru clearly sided with the ambitious estimates of the Agriculture Ministry. The Prime Minister invited Boyd-Orr to speak from his residence to urge Indians to adopt a "war-like psychology" in their pursuit of self-sufficiency.[105] On June 29, he addressed the nation directly on All India Radio, pleading for popular cooperation "in a mighty drive for food production." The Government of India, he declared, would soon appoint a "Food Controller" to oversee the project of achieving self-sufficiency by 1951.[106] The United Kingdom's High Commissioner in Delhi lauded Nehru for dedicating his first substantive radio address to the nation on the food crisis. "The Indian government," the Commissioner wrote, "and Pandit Nehru in particular are at last beginning to turn their attention to the very serious economic problems which now face the country."[107]

Nehru marginalized the increasingly unpopular Food Minister, Jairamdas Daulatram.[108] In July, without having consulted with Daulatram, the Prime Minister's Secretariat designated senior ICS officer R.K. Patil "Commissioner for Food Production." One Delhi observer noted that Patil's appointment as "de facto minister for agriculture" would be a good change from the officials who had only offered "promises, pep talks, broadcasts, and high-sounding exhortations."[109] Yet Patil did not enjoy more capital than his peers. The new Commissioner for Food Production wrote to provincial governments in August to emphasize

the psychological approach to this question. Half our battle on the food front will have been won if we succeed in making the people realize that there is a food

---

[104] Office of the Adviser in India to the Central Commercial Committee, Report #18, April 1949, DO/133/108, UKNA.

[105] "Food Expert in Bombay," *Times of India*, April 16, 1949; "Boyd Orr Suggests War-Like Psychology Needed," *Times of India*, May 2, 1949.

[106] "Need for All-Out Food Drive," *Times of India*, June 30, 1949; "Nehru's Broadcast," *Indian Express*, July 1, 1949.

[107] UK High Commissioner, New Delhi, opdom #26, June 30, 1949, IOR/L/E/8/7237.

[108] "Food Front," *Times of India*, July 1, 1949; "India's Food Problem: Pandit Nehru's Appeal," *Commerce*, July 9, 1949.

[109] "Delhi Letter: Immense Responsibility Awaits Food Production Commission," July 16, 1949, IOR/L/E/8/7230.

Independent India of Plenty

problem, that it is of a very emergent nature, that it will have to be tackled on a war footing, and that a failure on the food front would mean very serious consequences to us, as a nation.

He urged provinces to adopt legislation to induce greater production and to encourage producers to put stocks on the market.[110] With Patil at the helm, the revived Grow More Food campaign enjoyed widespread public attention throughout the summer and fall of 1949. The Prime Minister urged newspapers to publicize the campaign, though *Shankar's Weekly* wondered if the press should avoid printing portraits of the rotund Jairamdas Daulatram for fear that readers might blame him personally for India's food deficit.[111] Touring cinema vans were sent around the country to show films like *Grow More Food, Kisan,* or *Abundant Harvest.*[112] Provincial food ministers urged city-dwellers to plant window gardens and adopt substitute foods, and traveled to the countryside to demonstrate compost-making.[113] The nation's government-employed gardeners were ordered to "utilize their entire spare time, during working hours, for the cultivation of food crops and vegetables in Government bungalows."[114]

Commercial interests capitalized upon the ubiquity of these messages: Ferguson Tractors advertised their powerful tractors as the best way to "farm better, farm faster" in the name of the Grow More Food campaign.[115] A manufacturer of electric pumps declared that the "National Emergency of the Day" could only be addressed with the sort of irrigation that its high-capacity pumping sets could provide.[116] The Jayabharat Insurance Company reminded citizens that as they worked to grow more food, so too should Indian citizens grow their capital through a wise life insurance policy investment.[117] Politicians' proclamations continued unabated. In August, Nehru delivered a second major radio address in Hindi. "No one," he said, "can afford to ignore the basic problem of food." He urged citizens to grow vegetables and grains at home,

---

[110] R.K. Patil, letter no. F.1–42/49-GMF, August 6, 1949, Rajputana Agency – Political – P-245, 1949 – Food Conference, NAI.

[111] "Newspapers and Grow More Food," *Times of India*, July 4, 1949; "The Editor's Dilemma [Cartoon]," *Shankar's Weekly*, July 10, 1949.

[112] M.S. Randhawa and U.N. Chatterjee, *Developing Village India: Studies in Village Problems* (Bombay: Orient Longman, 1951), 92–96.

[113] "Minister at Work," *Bombay Chronicle*, September 8, 1949.

[114] "Grow More Food Campaign: Employment of CPWD Malies," October 22, 1949, Home – Public – 51/355/49, NAI; "Another Move in Food Drive," *Bombay Chronicle*, September 21, 1949.

[115] "Farm Better, Farm Faster [Advertisement]," *Times of India*, August 30, 1949.

[116] "National Emergency of the Day: Grow More Food [Advertisement]," *Times of India*, September 10, 1949.

[117] "You Can Grow More Food But Can You Grow More Money? [Advertisement]," *Shankar's Weekly*, October 29, 1950.

Figure 4 The Grow More Food campaign of 1949 reanimated the strategies and publicity efforts of its wartime antecedent. This film, *Grow More Food*, was directed by A. Bhaskar Rao and produced by Ezra Mir for the Department of Information and Broadcasting. Urging Indians to take up "kitchen gardening," it depicts the expenses of purchasing food from the trader against a backdrop of scarcity. The husband's skepticism about the kitchen garden his wife plants is overcome by the beautiful eggplant it yields. (Credit: Films Division, Ministry of Information and Broadcasting, Government of India)

Independent India of Plenty   73

and implored Congress workers to go to villages to help them produce more effectively.[118]

Yet the Grow More Food campaign was more bark than bite: without greater investment in inputs, it was folly to hope that exhortations would win the day. "It is difficult," a British observer wrote, "to imagine a peasant producing a grain more food under the encouragement of a town-bred politician whose only acquaintance with the plough or tractor has been for the benefit of the Publicity Department's photographer."[119] That observer might have been referring to the photographs published in newspapers of R.K. Patil who, in calling for the establishment of a "land army" of trained workers to explain new cultivation techniques, had been taken to some fields in Khandesh district to "show" peasants how to weed.[120] The *Eastern Economist* observed that "mere radio talks by the Prime Minister and the Governor-General, too, are not enough: for one thing, radios are few and far between."[121] Even as officials continued to insist upon self-sufficiency by 1951, the British commercial advisor in India estimated that India would still fall short by at least a million tons.[122] The Prime Minister's own negotiation stance betrayed his own uncertainty: as Nehru prepared for his first visit to the United States, the exchange of food for Indian rare earth minerals was to be a major item of the agenda.[123] "All of Delhi except the Prime Minister," the Commercial Advisor declared wryly, "now seems to be quite certain that the target of self-sufficiency in food by the end of 1951 will have to be lifted."[124]

Ganesh Narain Somani had been a longtime advisor to the royal family of Jaipur. But the ascension of the state to the Republic of India had left Somani with time to ponder the state of the nation's affairs. In 1949, Somani composed a series of letters to the Prime Minister in response to the call to grow more food. The epistolary booklet that he compiled came with a unique price tag: the reader's vow to produce his or her own food.[125]

---

[118] Jawaharlal Nehru, "Grow More Food [August 7, 1949]" (All India Radio, August 7, 1949), *Selected Works of Jawaharlal Nehru (Second Series)*, 70 vols. (New Delhi: Jawaharlal Nehru Memorial Fund, 1984–2017), vol. 12, 74–75. Henceforth *SWJN*.

[119] Office of the Adviser in India to the Central Commercial Committee, Report #22, August 1949, DO/133/108, UKNA.

[120] "Food Commissioner Pleads for a Land Army of Trained Workers," *Bombay Chronicle*, September 8, 1949.

[121] "War Footing for Food," *Eastern Economist*, July 8, 1949, 43–44.

[122] Office of the Adviser in India to the Central Commercial Committee, Report #23 September 27, 1949, DO/133/108, UKNA.

[123] "The Wheat Deal," *Economic Weekly*, November 5, 1949.

[124] Office of the Adviser in India to the Central Commercial Committee, Report #24, October 1949, DO/133/108, UKNA.

[125] G.N. Somani, *An Observation on the Food Production Drive of the Hon'ble Prime Minister Pandit Jawahar Lal Nehru* (Jaipur: The Manoranjan Press, 1949).

74   Hungry Nation

The hearts of India's leaders, Somani knew, were in the right place. They shared his belief that, above all else, it was self-sufficiency in food that would "make India free, independent, prosperous, economically supreme and peace-maker of the world." Yet most of these men were too removed from the soil to know what was truly required. "Panditji," Somani wrote of Nehru, "seems to have little experience of the village life and of the farmers." India's governmental officers were skilled at making theoretical plans, but little else.

One thing alone was needed. "Please arrange to legislate," Somani wrote to the Prime Minister, "that every adult Indian high and low, rich or poor, from Governor-General to a common man, be bound to cultivate himself or have cultivated under his eyes an average area of land that be assigned to him by the Agricultural officer or Revenue officer of his circle." Even the lowliest pot-thrower or leatherworker could help make agricultural implements; beggars could be "bound down to take agriculture," and Congressmen "now doing no constructive work except making useless demonstrations," should remake themselves as farmers. "Until this is done," Somani concluded, "India can not survive and must pass in to the hands of foreigners again. No begging of food after 1951, is a dream. Without this specific and effective piece of legislation, your speeches and broad-cast have no meaning."

The Grow More Food campaign was faltering, but Nehru and others continued to speechify. The Prime Minister spoke to a hundred food officials in Delhi in November 1949 to reaffirm the goal of freedom from imports by 1951. "Whatever happens," the Prime Minister asserted, "whether there is a cyclone or an earthquake, we are determined to stick to the target date."[126] Food officials reviewed the quantities of grain which had been shipped to India from the United States, the Soviet Union, Argentina, Morocco, Yugoslavia, Egypt, and Iran, as well as the abundant complaints from consumers about the quality of imported grains. They looked to state efforts to procure and distribute foodgrains, to manage prices, and how officials in their own department were working to advance collaboration with the Ministry of Agriculture. And under no small pressure from the top down, they concluded that the goal of self-sufficiency could indeed be achieved by 1951.[127]

---

[126] "India Determined to Stick to Date of 1951," *Times of India*, November 29, 1949.
[127] "Report of the Ministry of Food during the Year 1949 and the Policy and Proposals for 1950," 1950, Ministry of States – Kashmir – 16(15)-K, 1950, NAI; "Proposals for Increased Food Production," *Times of India*, November 30, 1949.

Outside observers were no longer checking their skepticism. "The more doubt that is cast on the possibility" of self-sufficiency, one British observer noted, "the more insistent become Mr. Patil and the Prime Minister that it must and shall be attained."[128] American officials shared this doubt: a much hoped-for wheat deal was on the verge of failure, and one embassy employee asserted in a memorandum that admonishments to grow more food were fruitless in the absence of efforts to "assure the adoption of improved agricultural techniques by the peasant-cultivators [and] give them the concrete evidence of the government's concern in their welfare."[129] Parliamentarian Frank Anthony took Nehru to task for his "unjustified optimism" on the food front.[130] And Shankar could be counted upon for his trenchant take: a cartoon of maligned Food Minister Jairamdas Daulatram watching in pleasure as the Food Commissioner, R.K. Patil, moved around in a fruitless rain dance.[131]

Daulatram, long-sidelined, was finally pushed aside in early 1950, replaced with a new Food Minister, Kanaiyalal Maneklal Munshi, who established a new Foodgrains Procurement Committee to survey procurement and distribution efforts.[132] Convinced that the Food Ministry was plagued by rampant corruption, Munshi filed a request with the Home Ministry's Intelligence Branch to investigate suspect officials in Bombay.[133] Yet Munshi's initial burst of energy was overwhelmed by a worsening crisis. Hopes for an American wheat deal had now fully collapsed, and officials wondered if a smaller food gift might be offered in compensation – even in the form of malt, which American ambassador Loy Henderson characterized in a letter to Munshi as a "product normally fed to animals, wanted here to feed human beings who cannot afford wheat or rice."[134] Famine conditions were appearing throughout the country and Munshi took to the radio to assure the public that, even though the food situation was worsening, government would not let starvation deaths occur – while denying rumors that babies and children

---

[128] Office of the Adviser in India to the Central Commercial Committee, Report #25, November 1949, DO/133/108, UKNA.
[129] Jerome B. Cohen, "India's Deteriorating Food Situation," January 10, 1951, RG 59 / 54D341 / Box 14 / Food, General Correspondence, 1951, USNA.
[130] UK High Commissioner, New Delhi, opdom #3, February 16, 1950, IOR/L/E/8/7237.
[131] "Foodprints [Cartoon]," Shankar's Weekly, December 4, 1949.
[132] M. Thirumala Rao, Report of the Foodgrains Procurement Committee, 1950 (New Delhi: Government of India Press, 1950).
[133] "Complaint from K.M. Munshi Regarding Corruption," 1950, Home – Police – II – 25/ 7/50, NAI.
[134] Office of the Adviser in India to the Central Commercial Committee, Report #27, January 1950, DO/133/108, UKNA; Loy W. Henderson, Telegram #61, July 11, 1950, RG 469 / UD 237 / Box 42 / India Comm. Food 1950 April 1951, USNA.

76   Hungry Nation

were being sold into slavery in exchange for food and that villagers in Bihar and Madras were living on tree bark and leaves.[135] Nehru spoke afterwards on All India Radio to admit that the prognosis was not as rosy as he had once hoped: natural calamities had hampered production, inflation wrought by the Korean War had empowered hoarders, and refugees were streaming into Bengal owing to conflict in East Pakistan. Yet Nehru assured Indians that government would "still adhere to the pledge we have taken to be self-sufficient by 1951."[136]

With India's worst scarcity crisis since independence on the horizon, these claims seemed more and more far-fetched. "There must be something in the air of New Delhi," a *Commerce* columnist wrote,

which goes to the head of the Ministers and makes them see rosy dreams. There should be no objection to their indulgence in these dreams, so long as they, in their more sober moments, let the people know the real position, however grim it might be, and prepare for it, instead of trying to grow millions of tons of additional foodgrains on paper and trying to feed the people on these phantom foodgrains.[137]

Writers at *Indian Finance* pronounced that, for New Delhi, "the possible consequences of food self-sufficiency were so clear and appealing that it did not bother in the least either about the conditions necessary for attaining it or the date by which it can be reasonably expected to be attained, if it were really feasible."[138] The committee tasked with reviewing the results of the Grow More Food campaign admitted that it had "not fully achieved the results expected of it, as it has not aroused enthusiasm in the countryside."[139] But the coup de grâce was the confidential report that five Food Ministry analysts delivered to K.M. Munshi, confirming with all available data that self-sufficiency by 1951 was unequivocally a pipe dream.[140]

New Delhi could not simply will food into existence, and by 1950, it was evident that self-rule alone had not delivered upon the promise of food for all. Distancing themselves from the pledges made in the wake

[135] "Government Will Not Let Starvation Deaths Occur," *Times of India*, July 21, 1950; "Munshi Says Adequate Stocks of Grain in Bihar and Madras," *Times of India*, August 15, 1950.
[136] "Speech by Mr. Nehru re: India's Food Shortage," August 30, 1950, RG 59 / 54D341 / Box 14 / Food, 1950, USNA.
[137] Rover, "Off the Record," *Commerce*, August 12, 1950, IOR/L/E/8/7230.
[138] "Clibe Street Gossip," *Indian Finance*, September 9, 1950, IOR/L/E/8/7230.
[139] V.T. Krishnamachari, *Report of the Grow More Food Enquiry Committee* (New Delhi: Ministry of Food and Agriculture, Government of India, 1952), 68.
[140] Office of the Senior UK Trade Commissioner, note to Under Secretary, Commercial Relations and Exports Department, Board of Trade, August 31, 1950, IOR/L/E/8/7237.

Independent India of Plenty

of the Bengal famine, India's politicians were growing more cautious in what they would offer citizens. Indian bureaucrats qualified earlier promises, urging citizens to remold their diets and the expectations that they had of the struggling nation. They experimented with different paradigms for rationing and procurement, diluting loftier promises through the vagaries of bureaucratic administration. And before the widespread embrace of new agricultural technologies and models, they sutured the question of food to the equally thorny issue of land and its use. Accordingly, the years between the Bengal famine and the drafting and adoption of India's first Five-Year Plan in 1951 must be seen as a time of great creative foment with regard to the nation's seemingly intractable food problem. As many planners struggled to set a course for abundance with a minimum of capital output, other legislators, technical experts, and citizens from disparate backgrounds reminded them of the promises made in the final years of the struggle for self-rule.

This dynamic was immediately evident in the debates of India's Constituent Assembly, which met in eleven sessions between December 1946 and January 1950 to draft India's constitution. Over the course of many meetings, representatives debated what to borrow and what to disregard from the administrative structure of the colonial state, and what fundamental rights the Republic of India would afford its citizens.[141] Jawaharlal Nehru made his aims clear in the opening session of the debates, urging delegates to "free India through a new constitution to feed the starving people and clothe naked masses and to give every Indian fullest opportunity to develop himself according to his capacity."[142] C. Rajagopalachari declared that a successful assembly would usher in an India which "will have not only enough food to feed its teeming millions but will once again have become a land flowing with rivers of milk."[143] Indians, Haryanvi lawyer Thakurdas Bhargava reminded delegates, must "hang our head in shame when we find that we have to import cereals from outside."[144]

The memory of the Bengal famine hung heavily over the debates. One of the most quickly settled matters concerned the colonial Government of India Act of 1935, which had made food a provincial concern, rather than a national one. It was through this split, Oriya legislator

---

[141] Granville Austin, *The Indian Constitution: Cornerstone of a Nation* (New Delhi: Oxford University Press, 1999).

[142] J. Nehru, January 22, 1947. Citations here are to speaker and date; the full text of the debates are widely available online, and published as *Constituent Assembly Debates: Official Report* (New Delhi: Lok Sabha Secretariat, 1967).

[143] C. Rajagopalachari, August 15, 1947.

[144] T. Bhargava, November 24, 1948 [in Hindi].

78   Hungry Nation

Bhubanananda Das recalled, that "India was robbed of her food and the result was that 50 to 75 lakhs of people died in Bengal of famine and starvation ... That was the social security and social justice that the Government of India Act gave us."[145] Gujarati businessman G.L. Mehta articulated an emerging consensus that food be a subject delegated to the central government. "The food question," he declared, "the whole question of price control, the whole question of rationing – all these require development and organization on an All India basis."[146] Kashmiri politicians H.N. Kunzru affirmed that "if there is anything today that requires to be dealt with by the National Government, it is questions relating to food and agriculture."[147]

Yet the delegate's commitment to a federal structure precluded the adoption of agriculture and food as central subjects that could be organized and arranged in Delhi. A "directive principle of state policy" was added to the document, but spoke more to an ascendant cow protection lobby than questions of welfare, asking the government "to organise agriculture and animal husbandry on modern and scientific lines and [take] steps for preserving and improving the breeds, and prohibiting the slaughter, of cows and calves and other milch and draught cattle." But agriculture was added to the list of subjects which fell to the responsibilities of India's provinces, and later, to its states. New Delhi could make laws, in other words, but it would be up to provinces' departments themselves to implement them.

Delegates who had hoped for greater state control, let alone those who had lobbied for a more explicit right to food in the constitution, were crestfallen by the document's restraint. Tamil representative M. Ananthasayanam, reviewing a draft version, expressed the consternation that certain delegates felt.[148] "Where is a single word in the Constitution that a man shall be fed and clothed by the State?" he asked. "Is there a single word in the Constitution that imposes on the future Governments the obligation to see that nobody in India dies of starvation?" Upon reviewing the preamble to India's constitution, Andhra lawyer T. Prakasam expressed his optimism "that everything would follow in regular course and bring out a Constitution that will give food and cloth to the millions of our people and also give education and protection to all the people of the land." But he and others who hoped for the articulation

[145] B. Das, July 30, 1947.
[146] G.L. Mehta, August 21, 1947.
[147] H.N. Kunzru, August 25, 1947.
[148] M. Ananthasayanam Ayyangar, November 9, 1948.

Independent India of Plenty

of more concrete socioeconomic rights were in the end disappointed by the document's shortcomings.

Independence had confronted planners and citizens with stark choices about India's future development. Mohandas Gandhi had rallied Indians to the cause of mass nationalism through saintly charisma and political savvy. Since the 1909 publication of his tract *Hind Swaraj, or Indian Home Rule*, he had developed a progressively fiercer critique of Western civilization and the modern nation-state. And over thousands of pages of writing and countless speeches and prayer meetings, Gandhi had proposed independent India as an amalgamation of self-sustaining village republics responsible for their own production and consumption.

Yet much of the mainstream Congress leadership subscribed to a very different vision of national development. Inspired by modernizing projects in the Soviet Union, the United States, and elsewhere, Jawaharlal Nehru and those in the Congress left looked to the promise of scale and science in service of the nation. Better fertilizers, seeds, and implements could yoke more food from the earth. Peasants' lots would improve, and in time fewer Indians would need to farm as industrialization brought greater wealth to a modernizing India. There was much modern in Gandhi's "traditional" village republic, and Nehruvian modernization relied upon fallacious visions of a static society. But as planners, citizens, and experts envisioned how India might attain self-sufficiency by 1951 or any other date, they drew upon different aspects of these competing models, and advanced their own idiosyncratic readings of Indian state and society.

India's "Gandhian economists" braided together the task of reconstructing the rural economy with the project of uplifting the village and the self.[149] Indian citizens, they averred, would only be capable of producing enough for their own requirements if they reoriented themselves towards the collective goals of their communities, and shed both statist approaches and liberal impulses borrowed from the West. K.N. Vaswani, an academic and confidant of Gandhi, contended that the Bengal famine had demonstrated "the close dependence of different parts of India on one another, in matters economic, even in matters of food, the basic necessity of life."[150] But the solution of the food problem had as much to do with moral transformation as economic reform. "The Indian masses," he wrote, "need not have the intoxicating wine of an ever-rising standard of living; wants multiplying without end and without aim."

---

[149] Ajit K. Dasgupta, *Gandhi's Economic Thought* (London: Routledge, 1996).
[150] Khushiram Nebhraj Vaswani, *Planning for a New India* (Lahore: Dewan's Publications, 1946), 26–27.

80   Hungry Nation

J.C. Kumarappa was a Christian, Columbia-trained economist who had similarly thrown in his lot with Gandhi. Having coined the term "Gandhian economics" himself, Kumarappa had been charged with constructing rural economic policy from the Mahatma's hazier prescriptions, carrying the torch long after Gandhi's death. India's food shortage in colonial times, he contended, came from the inequity of the imperial economy. "But the present phenomenon," he wrote, "is one which we have brought on ourselves, and we are unable to get rid of it because of our incapacity to think without being influenced by vested interests."[151]

The siren call of Western modernization, Kumarappa felt, was leading the new state to excess and folly, exemplified in costly projects like its massive dams. These large projects required foreign capital, were showier than small, village-based schemes, and were being built in search of pride as much as results. "If," he proposed, "we have to concentrate our efforts on works that may not attract world attention, that would not need the bigger dam in the world, that would not be a wonder of the world, are we prepared to work away on great many details that will ultimately produce the required results?" This fundamentally spiritual task was "the first hurdle that the country has to cross after obtaining independence. Shall we prove worthy or shall we be found wanting?" Kumarappa envisioned a state which would primarily offer advice on which plants to crop for a balanced diet, and which might also offer prices to producers to encourage them to produce very slightly above their needs. If the Republic of India were serious about feeding itself, it would ensure that "the Prime Minister himself should be a cultivator and take up the portfolio of agriculture" – a barb at Nehru, whose familiarity with farming implements came primarily through staging photo opportunities.

More steely economists felt that in any planning, it was essential to determine whether India's food deficit stemmed from colonial maladministration or real defects in India's soil. The principal of Baroda's Pratapsinha College of Commerce and Economics felt that independent India's agriculture had been only temporarily stunted by the effects of war and decolonization. When these aftershocks lifted, the Republic's campaigns would lead to a glut of production and a drop in prices, and India would then have to decide how to transition into a modern, industrialized agricultural economy.[152]

---

[151] Joseph Cornelius Kumarappa, *Our Food Problem* (Wardha: All India Village Industries Association, 1949), 1–2.

[152] Vasudeo Yeshwant Kolhatkar, *Reconstruction of Indian Agriculture* (Bombay: Popular Book Depot, 1946).

Independent India of Plenty

81

Most others were less rosy, suggesting that India's food predicament stemmed from land which had been bad to begin with and which had grown worse under colonial rule. The chair of the Economics Department at Dharmendrasinhji College in Rajkot reminded his readers that "the cries of food that we hear around us ... is not a problem created because of the war."[153] The 63 million Indians who remained hungry – this estimate drawn from Radhakamal Mukerjee's calculations – could only be fed through large-scale projects based upon "the Tennessee Valley Authority example," bringing more land under cultivation and increasing yield through better irrigation.

An economics professor in Poona declared that India's "uninformed and conservative" citizens would need to shed deeply held beliefs about their land and its quality if agricultural schemes were to flourish.[154] It was only a lower population in the past and traditional complacency that had allowed Indians of earlier centuries to believe that theirs was a land blessed with fertile soil. At freedom, he wrote, "We [cannot] accept the hackneyed statement that the land in *Aryawart* (India) is the best in the world and that it is *suvarn bhumi* (golden land)." India's land was, in fact, poor and profoundly depleted; and only irrigation, manuring, and the improvement of seed and soil would facilitate its betterment. Economist Kasturba Lalwani, in a Hindi tome on the nation's most pressing economic problems, likewise asserted that India's land was much worse than earlier estimates had held: even by the most optimistic calculations, planners and peasants would need five or ten years, not two, to yield enough for all.[155]

Partition had made all these calculations more urgent and vexing. In 1947 a professor of agricultural economics in Agra undertook a major study of the quality of India's soil and possible remedies for it – but published it with a slip declaring that most of his calculations were off owing to the split of the nation.[156] Another economist at the University of Bombay waited until 1950 to publish the book he had readied before partition. While pleased that "the advent of Independence [had] led to an effort to bring about a social and economic revolution in the country or to evolve a Welfare State," India's worsening agricultural predicament was far harder to assess in the wake of its division.[157]

---

[153] R.V. Rao, *Our Economic Problems* (Lahore: Lion Press, 1946).

[154] P.C. Patil, *Food Problem in India in General and Kolhapur State in Particular* (Poona: V.H. Barve, 1948), iii.

[155] Lalwani, *Bharat ki Arthik Samasyaye [India's Economic Problems]*, 40.

[156] Baljit Singh, *Population and Food Planning in India* (Bombay: Hind Kitabs, 1947).

[157] C.N. Vakil, *Economic Consequences of Divided India* (Bombay: Vora & Co., 1950).

82   Hungry Nation

Modernist thought and economic logic held similar sway over businessmen eager to forward profitable plans for plenty. B.L. Jalan, President of the Marwari Chamber of Commerce, drew upon studies like these to produce his own treatise on the *Food Problem in India*, whose suggestions presaged many of those which would be taken up years later by votaries of the Green Revolution.[158] No exhortation to grow more food, he felt, would match substantive investment undertaken by the state and private producers in tandem. This partnership could bring uncultivated land under the plough, increase the percentage of double-cropped lands and India's yield per acre, and supply irrigation facilities, fertilizers, storage houses, and better agricultural implements. Most importantly, the state could promise a procurement bonus to cultivators to induce them to undertake these improvements, boosting "the National interests at large," as well as the "economic status of the cultivators."

Even mystics could find themselves swept up in the promise of modernization, like the Keralan-born priest Anthony Elenjimittam who published an imaginative short novel, *Hindustan Hamara [Our India]*, on India's second anniversary.[159] Two acquaintances, Bharat and Fatima, tour the country to debate the pressing issues of the age. They travel together from Shillong to Calcutta, then split, one heading towards Madras, and the other towards Delhi, before meeting again in Benares. Bharat has traveled with the aim of discovering if India has enough food. "There is enough," he concludes, "and more. To feed the famished, shriveled and sunken bellies of India's millions, we need adopt scientific agriculture, scientific manuring, and introduce collective farming as in the Soviet Union." Fatima agrees. "I have given serious thought for years to the two systems of thought," she says, "that of a mechanized and rooted society and the go-back-to-the-village gospel of men like John Ruskin, Leo Tolstoi, W. Thoreau, and Mahatma Gandhi." But the antiquarian schemes, she concludes, are "out of place in a progressing India, determined to survive the chaos and confusion of the present century."

There were also those who simply asked Indian administrators to pay less attention to theorists and more to men and women of the soil. Neither modernists nor traditionalists, these citizens asked bureaucrats to consider the problem of food shortage from the perspective of India's hungry and its cultivators. In the small Madras village of Konerirajapuram, a cultivator named V. Ramiah published a short treatise, *Independent India of Plenty*, detailing in unorthodox but mellifluous English how India "should feed

---

[158] B.L. Jalan, *Food Problem in India* (1951).

[159] Anthony Elenjimittam, *Hindustan Hamara, Or, Our India* (Calcutta: Orient Book Co., 1949), 72–74.

about 400 million human beings, as well as at least about 100 million living beings, such as elephants, camels, horses, cows, goats, sheep, pigs, fowls, and birds of plains and forests of air. Should also be exported!!!"[160] Towards this end, Ramiah urged the national government to ban "all luxuries like motor cars, wrist watches, gaudy dresses, shaping a man's personality to that of a foreigner, smoking, alcoholic addictions, gambling, racing, wastefully wasting time and money in clubs, card and chess-playing and cricketing ... All the energies of Indian population will concentrate to make India plenty."

The essential problem, Ramiah claimed, was that India's cultivators were primarily lower castes, who had been driven away from agriculture by the lure of city life and the unattractiveness of the village. "The coolies working in the harbor, railway, and other industries," he claimed, "Kothwal-chavadi-basket-bearers and rickshaw-wallahs were all originally cultivators, who have chosen other walks of life, taste something of the anglicized civilization of the day, and they do taste it now." If the new state wished to lure them back to the village, it would need to ensure that its agencies understood village life and the problems of cultivation. India's ministers would need to be honest with themselves, observing "whether the laborers plough the lands with the same ploughs as the Agricultural Department advocate ... Let the same Ministers and Editors go to Madras Kothwal-Chavadi, observe the best varieties of vegetables [and ask] and what relief or help the government should give farmers to produce more and enjoy profits of such productions." It was humble and curious ministers, not ideologues or politicians, whose partnership with cultivators would revitalize the nation's agriculture.

Several weeks before independence, a Hindi pamphlet-writer, Jagdishchandra Jain, published a short text on what he and countless other citizens saw as the most pressing challenge to the new state.[161] *Our Food Problem*, dedicated to the victims of the Bengal famine, held that nothing else was as important as the task of feeding free India.[162] "Wherever you go these days," he wrote, "everyone speaks constantly of food." Indian citizens anywhere repeated the same complaints: "War ended years ago, Congress runs the country, yet there's no end in sight to rationing. You must keep your ration card safe, since if you were to

---

[160] V. Ramiah, *Independent India of Plenty: What Congress Government Ought to Do* (Madras: Andhra Publishing House, 1946).

[161] See Mahendranatha Pande, *Bhojana Hi Amrta Hai [Only Food Is Truth]* (Allahabad: Mahendra Rasayanasala, 1946); Jyotirmayi Thakur, *Aahar aur Aarogya [Diet and Health]* (Varanasi: Sahitya-Sevak Karyalay, 1948); *Hindustan ka Zar'ai Mas'alah [India's Agrarian Problems]* (Bombay: Communist Party of India, 1950).

[162] Jain, *Hamari Roti ki Samasya [Our Food Problem]*, iv.

84   Hungry Nation

lose it by mistake, you would have no option but to starve." Every Indian who saw his rationed sugar run out by the fifth day, or couldn't find *dal* to cook, knew that "food is not only a problem of the farmer's field, but a problem worldwide, and one which the common man must approach seriously."

India was not alone: all around the world, different countries were undertaking their own experiments in the name of food, and some of them might be adapted to Indian conditions before long. Rumors had circulated about English farmers sowing their fields with airplanes: a 20-acre plot, it was said, had been planted in just two hours. In Russia, shared farming was said to be yielding strong results, and might be tried in India, too. But India might differ, in some ways, in how responsive its government would be to its people's food needs. When the peasant leader N.G. Ranga had called attention to ration shops in Madras, empty for six months, Rajendra Prasad had vowed action. Until independence, Jain concluded, "we blamed the British for matters. But now we know that they are soon to leave. And we have full faith that our people-loving government will reach out to farmers, increase the country's production through beneficial projects, and by distributing grain justly, increase the prosperity of our people."

Hampered by a crisis whose severity outweighed their expectations, India's political leadership made scant progress on the food problem in the first several years of independence. In the closing days of imperial rule, international representatives had struggled to bring in sufficient imports while taking the reins of the state's administrative machinery. Partition had strained India's resources further, and the ill-fated decision to decontrol food had brought India perilously close to tragedy. A feeble Food Minister had seen his authority usurped by the Prime Minister, and the administrator who had been brought in to undermine him had simply repeated the mantra of self-sufficiency while reanimating a toothless production campaign.

Yet if a national government was not a panacea to India's economic woes, and the independent nation was no more able than its colonial predecessor to eke plenty from the earth, food had nonetheless emerged as one of the most central and visible tests of the free nation's legitimacy. Legislators tussled over how matters of food and agriculture would be handled by the state, economists and agronomists advanced competing schemes for better production, and citizens drew up their own schemes for diagnosing and remedying India's precarious food deficit, asking that their expertise be heard and incorporated in the process of planning. The expansive schemes that S.K. Kelavkar had drafted up in 1946 had not come to fruition. By 1951, India was not, as he had hoped, "capable of feeding properly her present, so-called overpopulation of 400 million." Yet Indians and their representatives had become deeply aware "that food – sufficient and proper food – is the birthright of every human being and we must all work for it." In the decade that followed, the nature of this work would continue to serve as a site of potent contestation.

3 Self-Help Which Ennobles a Nation

India's hopes of self-sufficiency in food seemed a quixotic fantasy in the bleak summer of 1950.[1] While politicians clung publically to aspirational targets, India's representatives were steadily increasing their requests for food aid from the United States: from 2.5 million tons, the Food Ministry's estimates rose to 4 million, before being raised once again to an alarming 6 million tons.[2]

K.M. Munshi, named Jairamdas Daulatram's replacement as Food Minister in the beginning of 1950, was an unpromising candidate in whom to place hopes of reform. A former advocate at the Bombay High Court, Munshi was known primarily for his Gujarati novels and religious writing, as well as his founding of the Bharatiya Vidya Bhavan, a nominally apolitical cultural organization with a decidedly Hindu nationalist bent.[3] While R.K. Patil had used his pulpit to advance the fruitless Grow More Food campaign, Munshi had instead drilled down on a tree-planting campaign suffused with religious bombast. As lower-level officials in the Food Ministry were fretting over missed targets, Munshi urged Bombay businessmen to plant trees "in your compound, in your native place, in holy Banaras, in Mathura, in Delhi, where the Father of the Nation was cremated, or in Somnath, where there are nine square miles of land ready for the plantation of trees and the boring of wells."[4] If the Minister's "propaganda techniques are bad," the *Economic Weekly* had grumbled, "his economics is worse still."[5]

---

[1] An earlier version of this argument appears as Benjamin Siegel, "'Self-Help Which Ennobles a Nation': Development, Citizenship, and the Obligations of Eating in India's Austerity Years," *Modern Asian Studies* 50, no. 3 (2015): 1–44.

[2] Merrill, *Bread and the Ballot*, 61.

[3] Christophe Jaffrelot, *The Hindu Nationalist Movement and Indian Politics, 1925 to the 1990s: Strategies of Identity-Building, Implantation and Mobilisation (with Special Reference to Central India)* (London: Hurst & Co., 1996), 84–85.

[4] "Reception to Food Minister," *Times of India*, May 24, 1950.

[5] "Delhi's Hobby Horse," *Economic Weekly*, May 27, 1950, 505–506.

Yet by summer, Munshi could no longer ignore the rumors emanating from Bihar. Across the blighted province, rural citizens were said to be subsisting on jute leaves; in poorer villages, tree branches were being ground into sawdust to pad empty stomachs.[6] Traveling to rural districts, Munshi dismissed the whispers of a new famine that would rival Bengal's seven years earlier, and he repeated a call that he and other politicians had issued since independence. In order for India to avoid famine, Munshi declared, Indians would need to transform their diets, eschewing the wheat and rice that kept the country wedded to the import of foreign grain. Women, Munshi noted, should take the lead on this front, observing one day a week as a cereal-less day, and helping their families wean themselves from an expensive diet subsidized by foreign exchange. Only then, Munshi held, would India be fed and free, and rid of the food controls loathed by most Indians.

Munshi's tone-deaf exhortation met a hostile reception. Hearing word of the familiar call for Indians to change their diets, a *Times of India* editorial sarcastically wondered if the starvation deaths in Bihar were the victims' "own fault, because they refuse to change their food habits, [and refuse] to eat grass and leaves?" Was it right, the journalist wondered, "that the Biharis should die in this unpatriotic manner when their ears should be attuned to Ministerial sermons?" The nation could learn much from Bihar, the author continued, by adopting Tuesday as a day for all Indians to have meals of jute leafs. These fasts in the name of economic self-reliance would "prepare the stomach for the remaining five cereal-less days of the week." *Shankar's Weekly*, a regular and withering critic of government food policy, ran a caricature of a smug K.M. Munshi surveying skeletal Biharis as they gnawed on trees, clutching a proclamation to "eat more vegetables."[7]

The heady promises of plenty made by India's nationalists in the wake of the Bengal famine had amounted to little in the first years of independence. Frustrated by land and cultivators that would not yield more on command, India's political leadership, assisted by civic organizations and a network of women's groups, sought to transform what, how, and how much Indians ate. Drawing upon a wartime antecedent, global ideologies of population and land management, and an ethos of austerity imbued with the power to actualize economic self-reliance, the new state urged citizens to give up rice and wheat, whose imports sapped the nation of the foreign currency needed to forward a plan of industrial development. In place of these staples, India's new citizens were asked to

---

[6] "Jute Leaf Days," *Times of India*, July 29, 1950.
[7] "Quick Results! [Cartoon]," *Shankar's Weekly*, August 6, 1950.

88   Hungry Nation

adopt "substitute" and "subsidiary" foods – including bananas, groundnuts, tapioca, yams, beets, and carrots – and give up a meal or more each week to conserve India's scant reserve of grains. And as Indian planners awaited the possibility of more fundamental agricultural advance and agrarian reform, they looked to food technology and the promise of "artificial rice" as a means of making up for India's perennial food deficit. India's women, as anchors of the household – and therefore, the nation – were tasked with facilitating these dietary transformations, and were saddled with the blame when these modernist projects failed.

These projects did not replace the more orthodox plans for abundance. India's food control and rationing apparatus continued to serve as a locus for managing and imagining the nation's food economy. The contentious project of land reform animated major contestations over the proper relationship between tiller, soil, and food. And new schemes of field research and experimentation marched forward, inching towards the fundamental transformations that would remake Indian agriculture in the 1960s. Even as early as 1951, India's new Planning Commission would come to exert greater authority over national development, and state representatives would transfer a lesser share of the burden of national development onto its citizens. But for a key period immediately after independence, India's national leadership placed greater faith in its ability to tie citizens' practices and sentiments to the reconstruction of a self-reliant national economy, seeing in changed diets and artificial foodstuffs the possibility of renegotiating the terms of postcolonial citizenship and development itself. Indian citizens were being asked to embrace notions of rights contingent upon the completion of duties, helping to actualize the economic self-reliance representing "real," and not merely formal, independence.[8]

In a letter to the nation's Chief Ministers shortly after independence, Jawaharlal Nehru asserted that India's new citizens would "have to feel that they are partners in the great enterprise of running the State machine … sharers in both the benefits and obligations."[9] This twinning of rights and obligations was born of India's late colonial experience, and the emergence of a communitarian notion of citizenship wherein a citizen's rights derive from the completion of responsibilities to one's co-citizens and the nation – rather than a libertarian model wherein rights exist

---

[8] Lloyd I. Rudolph and Susanne Hoeber Rudolph, *In Pursuit of Lakshmi: The Political Economy of the Indian State* (Chicago: University of Chicago Press, 1987), 1011.

[9] W.H. Morris-Jones, "Shaping the Post-Imperial State: Nehru's Letters to Chief Ministers," in *Imperialism and the State in the Third World: Essays in Honour of Professor Kenneth Robinson*, ed. Michael Twaddle (London: British Academic Press, 1992), 233.

Self-Help Which Ennobles a Nation   89

without attached and inherent responsibilities.[10] Colonial administrators like William Lee-Warner had helped advance this model, and Indian jurists like Srinivasa Shastri had furthered it.[11] While secular thinkers like Nehru relied upon more worldly rationales, state representatives like K.M. Munshi were quick to adopt religious or ethical idioms, drawing from precepts like that in the Bhagavad-Gita which suggested the right to perform a duty, but rejected a right to the fruit of that action.[12]

The people of independent India were indeed "infantile citizens" in need of "state tutelage and protection in order to realize the potentials of citizenship," offered rights only conditionally by the new nation-state.[13] Yet the category of citizenship itself in early independent India drew creatively upon preexisting social and economic debates, and carried with it an increased appeal to "public service," virtue, and the maintenance of national order.[14] These appeals were increasingly linked to larger questions of national development.[15] And it was in the state's campaigns for dietary transformation that the connections between the responsibilities of citizenship and the burden of national development were made most explicit.

In practical terms, India's mid-century efforts to remake its citizens' diets drew inspiration from a broad range of late colonial antecedents, from the rise of population as a global and a colonial problem to the

[10] Upendra Baxi, "The Justice of Human Rights in Indian Constitutionalism," in *Political Ideas in Modern India: Thematic Explorations*, ed. V.R. Mehta and Thomas Pantham (New Delhi: Sage Publications, 2006), 263–284.

[11] Niraja Gopal Jayal, *Citizenship and Its Discontents: An Indian History* (Cambridge, MA: Harvard University Press, 2013), 109–135. See also Amba Datt Pant, *Bharatiya Savidhan tatha Nagarikta [The Indian Constitution and Citizenship]* (Allahabad: Central Book Depot, 1959), particularly 97–117.

[12] On postcolonial thought and the concept of abnegation, see Leela Gandhi, *The Common Cause: Postcolonial Ethics and the Practice of Democracy, 1900–1955* (Chicago: University of Chicago Press, 2014).

[13] Roy, *Beyond Belief*, 20.

[14] See Dipesh Chakrabarty, "'In the Name of Politics': Democracy and the Power of the Multitude in India," *Public Culture* 19, no. 1 (2007): 35–57; William Gould, "From Subjects to Citizens? Rationing, Refugees and the Publicity of Corruption over Independence in UP," *Modern Asian Studies* 45, Special Issue 1 (2011): 33–56; Eleanor Newbigin, "Personal Law and Citizenship in India's Transition to Independence," *Modern Asian Studies* 45, Special Issue 1 (2011): 32. On the complex genealogy of postcolonial citizenship, see also Joya Chatterji, "South Asian Histories of Citizenship, 1946–1970," *The Historical Journal* 55, no. 4 (2012): 1049–1071.

[15] Stuart Corbridge, *Seeing the State: Governance and Governmentality in India* (Cambridge: Cambridge University Press, 2005), 52. Anand Pandian suggests that rural citizens, in particular, have since independence been identified as "subjects of development, [who] must submit themselves to an order of power identifying their own nature as a problem." Anand Pandian, "Devoted to Development: Moral Progress, Ethical Work, and Divine Favor in South India," *Anthropological Theory* 8, no. 2 (June 1, 2008): 159.

90   Hungry Nation

idioms of nationalist planning and wartime experiments in food policy. In the closing decades of the nineteenth century, Indian economic thinkers had transformed India's pervasive hunger from a Malthusian inevitability into a trenchant critique of colonial rule. Yet as famine and hunger emerged as political concerns – threatening colonial administrators not only with death and disease, but with shocks to labor and revenue collection – these administrators began to abstract the idea of India's "population" as a problem of governance. Questions of population growth underwrote broader national planning schemes in food and other matters, reaching a dramatic crescendo in the forced sterilization schemes of the Emergency era.[16] These earlier developments, however, dovetailed with a broader, global perception of the world's population and its anticipated "overpopulation": in the first decades of the twentieth century, experts across the world began to interlink the planetary problems of "land, migration, territory, soil, density, emptiness, arability, colonization, and settlement."[17]

The questions of land, populations, and their diets, health and productive capacity for labor grew increasingly interconnected in the colonial context through the new idiom of nutrition.[18] The founding of the Nutrition Research Laboratories in Coonoor and the subsequent publication of India's first nutrition textbooks demonstrated how the

[16] On family planning during the Emergency and its antecedents, see Matthew Connelly, "Population Control in India: Prologue to the Emergency Period," *Population and Development Review* 32, no. 4 (December 1, 2006): 629–667; and Rebecca Jane Williams, "Storming the Citadels of Poverty: Family Planning under the Emergency in India, 1975–1977," *The Journal of Asian Studies* 73, no. 2 (May 2014): 471–492. More broadly, see Rebecca Jane Williams, "Revisiting the Khanna Study: Population and Development in India, 1953–1960" (Ph.D. diss., University of Warwick, 2013). Yet long before this era, the interlinked nature of food and population was perceived acutely by Indian economic thinkers in the 1930s, as evidenced in Gyan Chand, *India's Teeming Millions: A Contribution to the Study of the Indian Population Problem* (London: G. Allen & Unwin, 1939); D.G. Karve, *Poverty and Population in India* (London: H. Milford, Oxford University Press, 1936); Bhalchandra Trimbak Ranadive and C.N. Vakil, *Population Problem of India*, Studies in Indian Economics 4 (Calcutta: Longmans, Green and Co., 1930); and P.K. Wattal, *Population Problem in India* (Bombay: Bennet Coleman, 1934). Independence would see a proliferation of publications tying the two problems together in a national context, particularly in the writing of the Indian demographer Sripati Chandrasekhar. See Omprakash, *Hamari Khurak aur Aabadi ki Samasya [Our Food and Population Problem]*; Singh, *Population and Food Planning in India*; S. Chandrasekhar, *Hungry People and Empty Lands: An Essay on Population Problems and International Tensions* (London: G. Allen & Unwin, 1954).
[17] Alison Bashford, "Nation, Empire, Globe: The Spaces of Population Debate in the Interwar Years," *Comparative Studies in Society and History* 49, no. 1 (January 1, 2007): 173–174.
[18] Ludden, "The 'Discovery' of Malnutrition"; Worboys, "The Discovery of Colonial Malnutrition between the Wars."

Self-Help Which Ennobles a Nation

legitimacy of colonial sovereignty had grown sutured to the improvement of lands and human health. Village surveys like those undertaken in 1933 by John Megaw, director of the Indian Medical Service, helped quantify the percentage of Indians said to be malnourished – 61 percent, by his account.[19] Studies like American anthropologist and missionary Charlotte Viall Wiser's influential five-year survey of food habits in a United Provinces village suggested how Indians' putatively fixed habits – a colonial bogey since at least the turn of the twentieth century – might be rebuilt along scientific lines.[20]

Nutrition animated new understandings of the Indian economy, and the need for "national food planning" in the name of self-sufficiency.[21] As Indians began to perceive the nation as a body whose national development would be predicated upon "morally and physically healthy citizens," they looked to the promise of "reconstruction" to restore that body to health.[22] This project would not only facilitate food production to meet India's growing needs, but would repair the structural defects of India's food economy: beyond problems of production, the nation's food stores were further lessened by a deficient transportation system, and poor storage facilities which condemned supplies to rot and consumption by rodents and insects. Gandhian thinkers further decried the waste of industrial food practices, from the milling of rice to the manufacture of *vanaspati* (vegetable oil) – but they and modernist planners alike agreed that nearly 10 percent of India's food was wasted annually.[23]

---

[19] Megaw, *Public Health Aspects of Village Life in India*.

[20] "Note on the Work of the Nutrition Research Laboratories, Coonoor," 1940, Mysore Residency – Mysore Residency Bangalore – 598-D, 1940, NAI; Robert McCarrison, *Food: A Primer for Use in Schools, Colleges, Welfare Centres, Boy Scout and Girl Guide Organizations, Etc., in India* (Madras: Macmillan, 1928); Charlotte Viall Wiser, *The Foods of a Hindu Village of North India*, 2nd edn., Bureau of Statistics and Economic Research, United Provinces (Allahabad: Superintendent, Printing and Stationery, United Provinces, 1937), 115–116.

[21] Sunil S. Amrith and Patricia Clavin, "Feeding the World: Connecting Europe and Asia, 1930–1945," *Past & Present* 218, no. suppl 8 (2013): 38.

[22] Zachariah, "Uses of Scientific Argument." The project of reconstruction as a palliative to India's economic stagnation had been clearly articulated as early as 1920, with the publication of engineer Mokshagundam Visvesvaraya's *Reconstructing India*; fourteen years later, his *Planned Economy for India* forwarded a plan for increasing the productivity of Indian agriculture. Mokshagundam Visvesvaraya, *Reconstructing India* (London: P.S. King & Son, 1920); Mokshagundam Visvesvaraya, *Planned Economy for India* (Bangalore: Bangalore Press, 1934).

[23] Kumarappa, *Our Food Problem*, 3–4; Masani, *Your Food: A Study of the Problem of Food and Nutrition in India*, 66; Singh, *Population and Food Planning in India*, 85–88. On rice milling, see David Arnold, "Technology and Well-Being," in *Everyday Technology: Machines and the Making of India's Modernity* (Chicago: University of Chicago Press, 2013), 121–147.

92   Hungry Nation

The imperatives of national food planning were most powerfully expressed by Radhakamal Mukerjee, the Lucknow-based polymath who tied together the concerns of population, land use, and food planning in a series of influential publications in the 1930s and early 1940s, most notably his 1938 *Food Planning for Four Hundred Millions*.[24] Among his proposals was a forceful call to promote "a mixed diet based on several staples" in place of rice and wheat, promoting beans, pulses, and edible roots as salutary for national health, and invaluable "insurance against the shortage of staples."[25] Mukerjee's holistic understanding of India's food problem echoed throughout vernacular texts: one of the most widely used economics textbooks in Urdu, written by a lecturer at the Jamia Osmania in Hyderabad, framed the problem of agricultural rehabilitation in the face of an expanding population as the greatest economic challenge facing the nation.[26]

India's nationalist planners and its incipient institutions were increasingly echoing the call for a transformed diet: in 1935, physicist Meghnad Saha began publishing *Science and Culture* under the aegis of the National Institute of Science, establishing a journal which emerged as a primary vehicle for debates over the future course of national reconstruction.[27] In an early issue, Subhas Chandra Bose submitted to the journal a list of key questions about national planning, asking whether it would be desirable to plan a national diet for India.[28] The question of a "standard diet" did not presuppose the flattening of culture in the name of national unity, but it did animate discussions over systematic agricultural planning with India's food needs in mind. When the Congress Working Committee, headed by Jawaharlal Nehru, met that same year to formalize a plan of national reconstruction, it recommended that such planning

---

[24] Mukerjee, *Food Planning for Four Hundred Millions*.

[25] Radhakamal Mukerjee, *The Food Supply*, Oxford Pamphlets on Indian Affairs 8 (London: Oxford University Press, 1942).

[26] Muhammad Nasir Ali, *Hindustan ke Ma'ashi Masa'il*, 2nd edn. (Hyderabad: Idarah-yi Ma'ashiyat, 1945).

[27] Deepak Kumar, "Reconstructing India: Disunity in the Science and Technology for Development Discourse, 1900–1947," *Osiris* 15 (January 1, 2000): 241–257; Abha Sur, "Scientism and Social Justice: Meghnad Saha's Critique of the State of Science in India," *Historical Studies in the Physical and Biological Sciences* 33, no. 1 (2002): 87–105.

[28] Subhas Chandra Bose, "Some Problems of Nation-Building," *Science and Culture* 1, no. 5 (October 1935): 258. *Science and Culture* explored the potentialities of such a transformation in its pages, delivering a broadly affirmative response at a Science News Association meeting in August 1938. "Improvement of National Diet," *Science and Culture* 2, no. 2 (August 1936): 95–96; D. Dutta Majumder, "Subhas Chandra and National Planning," *Janata: A Journal of Democratic Socialism* 47, no. 2 (February 23, 1992): 11–17.

Self-Help Which Ennobles a Nation

be coordinated with the new Central Nutrition Board.[29] Yet Congress' planning agenda was interrupted in 1939, when Britain's declaration of war against Germany on behalf of India led to the party's mass resignation from its provincial ministries.

The experience of the Bengal famine of 1943 underscored the fundamental insecurity of diets deriving their weight from cereal staples, and the need to fashion a national diet more resilient to inevitable disruptions. In the wake of famine, India's colonial administrators relinquished moral authority over the food question, leaving nationalists with a potent claim to legitimacy. Yet those nationalists took many cues from the colonial government's embrace of austerity, and adopted a potent set of economic paradigms linking individual behavior to national outcomes. In the face of nationalist ferment, the British government relied increasingly upon the putatively neutral idioms of economics to express wartime imperatives.[30] And it was under the auspices of the Permanent Economic Advisor to the Government of India, Sir Theodore Gregory, that the transformation of individual consumption was formally sutured to the promise of national strength.

Gregory, a confidant of John Maynard Keynes, had served in this position since 1938, exerting a heavy influence over India's wartime economic planning.[31] His 1941 treatise, "Problem of Personal Economy in War-Time," posited an intensified connection between individual behavior and macroeconomic outcomes during wartime: even if India's scarcity conditions allowed for only minimal reduction of consumption, Gregory asserted, guidance, exhortation, and "sumptuary legislation" were well-suited to Indian economic and cultural contexts.[32] Gregory's oversight of many food committees suggests his influence on later state projects. As Chair of the 1943 Foodgrains Policy Committee, Gregory moderated a dispute between Debi Prasad Khaitan, a Calcutta jute merchant representing the Indian Chamber of Commerce, and W.H. Kirby, Rationing Advisor to the Government of India.[33] To Khaitan's suggestion that, in the new Calcutta rationing scheme, individuals be granted some mechanism for choosing their preferred grain, Kirby and Gregory affirmed the

---

[29] Jawaharlal Nehru, *Report of the National Planning Committee, 1938* (New Delhi: Indian Institute of Applied Political Research, 1988), 154.

[30] Zachariah, *Developing India*, 97.

[31] Theodore Gregory, *India on the Eve of the Third Five-Year Plan* (Calcutta: Thacker Spink, 1961).

[32] Theodore Gregory, "Problems of Personal Economy in War Time," February 13, 1941, MSS Eur D1163.

[33] "Foodgrains Policy Committee: Evidence of W.H. Kirby on Rationing," July 26, 1943, IOR/L/E/8/7236.

94   Hungry Nation

notion that choice should be "entirely subsidiary" to "keeping the people off the starvation point." The notion that preference should be subsumed to national ends would grow increasingly important as nationalist food planners took control of policy-making bodies.

Wartime events would bring this notion to new prominence in the Food Department. The fall of Burma in 1942 prompted a memorandum within the department suggesting that the public should be encouraged to replace rice with other grains, since a preponderance of India's rice stores were alleged to come from Burmese imports.[34] By early 1944, Delhi's Lady Irwin College, the premier institution of home economics in India, had been tasked with planning wheat and *kambu* [pearl millet] dishes for South India's "habitual rice-eaters"; in Hyderabad, a thousand people were reported to have attended a cooking demonstration at the War Services Exhibition.[35] The import of Australian wheat in September led the Madras government to add wheat in place of some of its rice ration, with a "wheat propaganda officer" appointed to help popularize its use. And along the Malabar coast, ninety-three public and private "Civic Restaurants" were set up to showcase new recipes. Yet the alleged beneficiaries of these schemes chafed at the notion that their diets were composed of interchangeable calories. Bombay's nationalist *Free Press Journal* decried its citizens' "being made to swallow barley" in place of regular grains.[36] "Who are the people whose food is barley," it groused, "and for whose benefit was this barley ordered?" Rationing officers had looked favorably upon the deployment of wheat and tapioca in India's South.[37] But in Cochin, famine relief workers with experience in distribution noted that tapioca could only be deployed in dire emergencies to pad "those parts of the stomach which the ration is not enough to fill."[38]

Indians' putatively unchangeable dietary preferences – particularly those of rice-eaters – were occasionally used to exculpate colonial officials for its late colonial failings. Beverly Nichols' *Verdict on India*, a popular apology for British rule in India, recounted a train ride spent with an Indian officer in the Food Administration in the wake of the 1943

---

[34] "Recommendation of the Central Food Advisory Council," July 1944, Food – Policy – R-1008/39/1944, NAI.

[35] "General Circulars Issued by the Food Department," 1944, External Affairs – War Progs., Nos. 59(49)-W, 1944 Secret, NAI.

[36] "In Defence of the Wild Grass-Seed," *Free Press Journal*, January 7, 1944. The continuing effort to foist barley upon Bombay's rice-eaters was a source of enduring frustration; see "Barley Again for Bombay?," *Bombay Chronicle*, January 22, 1947.

[37] Aubrey Dibdin, "Diary of a Tour of Inspection of Food Supplies and Rationing in India," 1945, MSS Eur D907.

[38] K.G. Sivaswamy, J. Ananta Bhat, and Tadepally Shankara Shastry, *Famine, Rationing and Food Policy in Cochin* (Royapettah, Madras: Servindia Kerala Relief Centre, 1946).

famine. "Food," Nichols recounted the officer declaring, in an exoneration of British famine policy "means [rice], and nothing else. It doesn't mean meat, nor fish nor eggs nor potatoes; it doesn't mean corn, nor millet, nor even *bajri* [pearl millet] which bears many resemblances to rice ... If you gave [Bengalis] anything else, most of them wouldn't know what to do with it."[39] Yet in the final years of colonial rule, the Department of Food increasingly touted the possibility of Indian dietary reform. In late 1944, W.R. Aykroyd, Director of the Nutrition Research Laboratories since 1935, noted that wartime efforts had "shown that it is possible to exercise a considerable degree of control over the diet of the people," and that popular canteens staffed by women might be useful in promoting "socially inferior" grains in peacetime.[40]

Ground-level administrators debated the quantity of millets, maize, or other grains which could be substituted in rations before courting public disaffection.[41] But so, too, did they follow the example of the Madras Food Department, which in early 1946 appointed a permanent public relations officer charged with a press, radio, poster, pamphlet, and cinema campaign designed to explain rationing and austerity schemes, and to popularize unfamiliar foods in the hungry south.[42] These eleventh-hour campaigns hinted at the more ambitious reengineering of citizenship and diets in tandem that India's nationalist leadership would soon attempt.

The Indian National Congress' post-war ascension to power saw a fundamental transformation in the orientation of development planning. The nationalist leadership, prior to the war, had "intended to accomplish what they had critiqued the colonial state for not being able to do, i.e., to bring about the benefits of material progress through scientific means to be shared equitably among all citizens."[43] Yet its post-war assumption of centralized state power saw the Congress "[lose] sight of the vision of eradicating poverty, morbidity, and illiteracy that had inspired the debates on national development in the colonial era": the "instruments" of national development came to enjoy primacy over its "idioms,"

---

[39] Beverley Nichols, *Verdict on India* (New York: Harcourt, Brace and Co., 1944), 203.
[40] W.R. Aykroyd, *Notes on Food and Nutrition Policy in India* (New Delhi: Government of India Press, 1944). On Aykroyd's career in India, see Kenneth J. Carpenter, "The Work of Wallace Aykroyd: International Nutritionist and Author," *The Journal of Nutrition* 137, no. 4 (April 1, 2007): 873–878. One of Aykroyd's most important younger colleagues in Coonoor was M.S. Swaminathan.
[41] "Inclusion of Millets, Gram and Maize in the Cereal Group Rations."
[42] H.K. Matthews, letter to F.W. Brock, April 12, 1946, IOR/L/I/1/1104.
[43] Medha Kudaisya, "'A Mighty Adventure': Institutionalising the Idea of Planning in Postcolonial India, 1947–60," *Modern Asian Studies* 43, no. 4 (October 2008): 940.

96   Hungry Nation

drawing greater inspiration from colonial bodies like the Department of Planning and rather than Congress' National Planning Committee.[44]

Famine in Bengal and enduring post-war shortages had underscored the calls for a transformed national diet: the National Planning Committee, meeting in 1945 and 1946, affirmed that wartime experiences had "woken up Government to its wider sphere of duty: [meeting] the food requirements of the people."[45] Another subcommittee on national priorities, chaired by Jawaharlal Nehru, affirmed that in "any well-conceived plan of national Development, the provision of adequate food must be the most important item with the highest priority."[46] Yet as the incipient government forwarded the imperatives of economic self-reliance, shifting the object of development from human welfare to national autarky, it looked increasingly to citizens themselves to undertake the burden of that task.

As nutritionists and economists continued to draft plans for the reconstruction of India's food economy and national diet, customers voiced resentment at the substitutes for wheat and rice which continued to appear in their rations.[47] India's Bureau of Public Administration, recognizing "the difficulty of persuading the people to consume [coarse] grains such as maize and barley," suggested that shops appeal to consumers' sense of national sacrifice when distributing them.[48] The Congress leadership increasingly framed the food crisis as a matter best solved through individual or household-level action, affirming in a December 1945 meeting that "everyone should realize his personal duty [regarding food] and perform it to the best of his ability, believing that if everyone acted likewise India will be able to surmount all difficulties with courage and confidence and be able to save thousands of poor lives."[49] A Congress Working Committee meeting in March 1946 contended that the responsibility for conserving scarce foodstuffs fell at the level of the household.

Simultaneously, Indian scientists were envisioning new technologies by which individuals and households might actualize their duty to conserve. Addressing the 1946 Indian Science Congress in Bangalore, the agricultural scientist M. Afzal Husain called for the establishment of

---

[44] Bose, "Instruments and Idioms of Colonial and National Development," 52–53.

[45] S.S. Sokhey, "Planning for a New India: Food of the People," in *Report of the Sub-Committee on National Health*, ed. K.T. Shah, National Planning Committee Series (Bombay: Vora & Co., 1948), 135–139.

[46] Shah, *National Planning Committee: Priorities in Planning (Food, Education, Housing)*.

[47] Gopal Chandra Pattanayak, *Planned Diet for India* (Allahabad: Kitabistan, 1946).

[48] Government of India, "Draft Reply," December 9, 1946, IOR/L/E/8/7236.

[49] Zaidi and Zaidi, "Congress Working Committee, Bombay, March 12–15, 1946."

a "National Institute of Food Technology" to incubate synthetic food-stuffs: beyond promoting the consumption of yeasts, tapioca, and tubers, reducing cereal consumption and freeing land for valuable cash crops, the institute would promote "synthetic rice" to free India from the ravages of Malthusian logic.[50] Later in the year, the chair of the Indian Institute of Sciences' biotechnology department, V. Subrahmanyan, wrote to the Ministry of Food to propose that a new Food Conservation Board include in its mandate the promotion of "less commonly used food materials" like groundnuts, soybeans, sweet potato, and tapioca.[51] A year later, the scientist would publish an extensive article in *Science and Culture* outlining his plan for an organization in New Delhi that would undertake this task.[52] The journal's editors responded approvingly, contending that "that which appears to be a strange method of getting food today may become the usual method tomorrow."[53]

Indian industrialists, eager to free the Indian economy from imports and increase its citizens' purchasing power, asserted a distinct influence over the nation's economic arrangements. Two of the authors of the "Bombay Plan," the textile magnate Lala Shri Ram and industrialist Purshottamdas Thakurdas, quickly assumed control of two major food planning bodies.[54] Shri Ram, who would soon be placed in charge of the subsidiary food campaign, reached out to representatives of the Ministry of Agriculture's Grow More Food campaign in June 1947.[55] Predicting the agricultural losses of partition, Shri Ram encouraged the Ministry to promote the production of potatoes, yams, beets, carrots, and tapioca. The Indian consumer should "turn to maize, bananas, and date palms, and above all, grow food in every free area of land. [Not] doing so should be considered an unpatriotic act." Rajendra Prasad soon appointed a Foodgrains Policy Committee with Thakurdas as its chair. Thakurdas – who had previously chaired Bombay's Provincial Food and Commodity Advisory Board and the Foodgrains Policy Committee of 1943 – echoed

[50] M. Afzal Husain, "Food Problem of India (1946, Bangalore)," in *The Shaping of Indian Science: 1914–1947*, ed. K. Kasturirangan (Hyderabad: Universities Press, 2003), 548–571.
[51] "Correspondence with Prof. Subramaniam re: Formation of Food Conversation Board at the Centre," 1946, Mysore Residency – Mysore Residency Bangalore – 25(8)-W, 1946, NAI.
[52] V. Subrahmanyan, "A Practical Approach to the Food Problem in India," *Science and Culture* 13, no. 6 (December 1947): 213–218.
[53] "Food," *Science and Culture* 13, no. 6 (December 1947): 211–213.
[54] Thakurdas et al., *A Plan of Economic Development for India*; see also Vivek Chibber, *Locked in Place: State-Building and Capitalist Industrialization in India, 1940–1970* (Princeton: Princeton University Press, 2003), 85–109.
[55] "Note by Sir Shri Ram Containing Suggestions for Meeting the Food Shortage in India," 1947, Agriculture – G.M.F. – 8–152/47 – G.M.F., NAI.

98   Hungry Nation

Shri Ram in recommending the inclusion of subsidiary foods in rations to lessen the demand for cereals.[56]

The recommendation of these industrialists prompted loud objections. Bombay's Supply Commissioner wrote to the Committee to protest, noting that "bananas, sweet potatoes, carrots, turnips are *supplementary* and not *substitute* foods."[57] P.C. Joshi, general secretary of the Communist Party, lambasted the "reactionary recommendations of the [committee] dominated by representatives of Big Business and rich growers," which had eschewed discussion of agrarian reform.[58] Yet objections like these were soon drowned out by state representatives who increasingly linked the question of diet to citizens' responsibility for national unity and development. In March 1947, Rajendra Prasad presided over a "Food and Nutrition Exhibition" in Delhi, showcasing alternatives to wheat and rice through lectures, films, and cooking demonstrations to female guests.[59] In December 1948, the Ministry of Information and Broadcasting requested media outlets to join the campaign for changed diets, appealing "to the upper class people to avoid and discourage all activities involving waste of food, and to urge on them the need for a minimum use of cereals in their diet, [enabling] the less rich classes to get more cereals."[60]

In the months after independence, Nehru and the Congress' left-leaning modernizers' national food planning schemes had been assailed by Mohandas Gandhi, who, with the support of influential businessmen, successfully campaigned against food controls. Yet Gandhians and modernists found common ground in asking citizens to steward the project of self-sufficiency in food. Decrying the "centralization of foodstuffs" in an October 1947 prayer meeting, Gandhi asked citizens to grow food at home and undertake regular fasts. "If the whole nation realized the beauty of [religious] partial self-denial," he contended, "India would more than cover the deficit caused by the voluntary deprivation of foreign aid ... If many must die of starvation, let us at least earn the credit of having done our best in the way of self-help, which ennobles a nation."[61]

---

[56] Purshottamdas Thakurdas, *Final Report, Foodgrains Policy Committee, 1947* (New Delhi: Government of India Press, 1948).

[57] V.S. Patvardhan, *Food Control in Bombay Province, 1939–1949* (Poona: D.R. Gadgil, 1958), 128.

[58] Letter from P.C. Joshi to Rajendra Prasad, October 25, 1947, reprinted in Communist Party of India, *India's Food Crisis: Analysis and Solution: Memo of the Communist Party of India to the Government of the Indian Union* (Bombay: People's Publishing House, 1947).

[59] "Food and Nutrition Exhibitions," 1947, Home – Public – 157/47, NAI.

[60] Ministry of Information and Broadcasting, Government of India, "Directive on Food Publicity," December 9, 1948, Home – Public – 51/469/48-Public, NAI.

[61] M.K. Gandhi, "The Problem of Food [6 October 1947]," in Mohandas K. Gandhi, *Delhi Diary* (Ahmedabad: Navajivan Publishing House, 1948), 65–68.

Votaries of village-centered models of India's economic reconstruction would lose out to the modernizing vision of the Nehruvian state. But on the food front, Jawaharlal Nehru and other bureaucrats would frequently use the Gandhian language of self-reliance, denial, and cooperation to express the imperatives of state-driven development.[62] As Prime Minister, Jawaharlal Nehru's endorsement was materially and symbolically essential in the campaign for Indians to practice austerity and transform their food habits. In public, Nehru cast these tasks as fundamental responsibilities of postcolonial citizenship, framing personal transformation and individual responsibility as a critical instrument for national development.[63] Privately, Nehru brooded over the nation's foundering agricultural schemes and Indians' unwillingness to cooperate with these plans in what Judith Brown had described as the Prime Minister's characteristic "exasperated paternalism."[64]

The Prime Minister's support underwrote new scientific initiatives: the Council of Scientific and Industrial Research had called, at independence, for a laboratory to advance food technology in the service of the nation, and Subrahmanyan was tasked with establishing it on land donated by the Mysore government.[65] Nehru inaugurated the All India Institute of Food Technology in late 1948. "We are eating wrong things," Nehru declared in his address, "and we are eating too much of them."[66] Nehru exhorted the Institute to help India conserve foodstuffs by developing "new types of composite foods which will be useful in times of emergency."[67] The veteran Congressman C. Rajagopalachari – long a foe of centralized planning on Gandhian grounds – would later defy the Prime Minister by unilaterally removing food controls in 1951, as Chief Minister of Madras. But at the inauguration, the then-Governor-General

---

[62] As Ornit Shani notes, the new state "was able to appropriate aspects of the Gandhian citizenship notion and its political vocabulary as a means of justifying some key policies of resource allocations. This gave Indian governments a mantle of legitimacy and the ability to resist contestation and dissent in the early formative decades." Ornit Shani, "Gandhi, Citizenship and the Resilience of Indian Nationhood," *Citizenship Studies* 15, no. 6–7 (October 2011): 661.

[63] On Nehru's modernizing philosophy, see Bhikhu Parekh, "Nehru and the National Philosophy of India," *Economic and Political Weekly* 26, no. 1 (January 5, 1991): 35–39, 41, 43, 45–48.

[64] Judith M. Brown, *Nehru: A Political Life* (New Haven: Yale University Press, 2003), 192.

[65] D.P. Burma and Maharani Chakravorty, eds., *History of Science, Philosophy, and Culture in Indian Civilization*, vol. 13, part 2: *From Physiology and Chemistry to Biochemistry* (New Delhi: Centre for Studies in Civilizations, 2010).

[66] Bose, *His Majesty's Opponent*, 125.

[67] "Importance of Food Technology (December 29, 1948)," in Jawaharlal Nehru, *Jawaharlal Nehru on Science and Society: A Collection of His Writings and Speeches*, ed. Baldev Singh (New Delhi: Nehru Memorial Museum and Library, 1988), 70–71.

100   Hungry Nation

of India echoed the Prime Minister in a second address. "If the cow or the goat," Rajagopalachari asked, "can build her own body and make and give beautiful milk out of the simple grass or leaves she eats, why should man with all the science available to him relegate grass and leaves to the realm of inedible things?"[68]

Returning to Delhi, Nehru directed the Ministry of Food and Agriculture in February 1949 to examine whether Delhi's open spaces – including the length of New Delhi's imposing Rajpath, in particular – could be used to plant food crops, as an example of the importance of citizens growing their own food.[69] On the same day, inaugurating a planned township several hours from Delhi, the Prime Minister reported that he had begun subsisting on a mixture of wheat and sweet potato flower, urging citizens to emulate his example. "The people," he warned, "should understand their duties and responsibilities … in making the motherland great. They talk of rights and privileges – and forget all about duties."[70] Nehru's timing was not incidental: privately, the Prime Minister was lamenting the failure of the Grow More Food campaign, complaining about Food Minister Jairamdas Daulatram's mediocre performance in a letter to C. Rajagopalachari, and urging a redoubling of the effort to promote new foods as staples.[71] Addressing the Federation of Indian Chambers of Commerce and Industry, Nehru estimated that the 10 percent food deficit India faced in a bad year could be compensated for only through increased output, more land, or inducing Indians to changing their food habits *en masse*.[72]

Several days after John Boyd-Orr's visit to Teen Murti as an "expert witness" in the tussle between the Ministries of Food and Agriculture, Nehru delivered an address on All India Radio, insisting that "there must be no waste and there must be no feasting while we fight for every ounce of food."[73] Nehru repeated the call in several addresses over the following weeks, exhorting every Indian to think of herself as a "soldier on the food front," planting food crops and stamping out waste.[74] Media across

---

[68] C. Rajagopalachari, "Inaugural Speech at the Central Food Technological Research Institute, Mysore," October 21, 1950, C. Rajagopalachari papers (V), Speeches and Writing, folder 11, NMML.

[69] Jawaharlal Nehru, "Utilisation of Land: Note to Food and Agriculture Ministry, 6 February 1949," in *SWJN* vol. 9, 70.

[70] Jawaharlal Nehru, "Self-Sufficiency in Food," *SWJN* vol. 9, 70.

[71] Jawaharlal Nehru, letter to C. Rajagopalachari, *SWJN* vol. 9, 71–72.

[72] Nehru, "We Should Pull Together [A Speech Delivered at the Meeting of the Federation of Indian Chambers of Commerce and Industry (22nd Annual Session), New Delhi, March 4, 1949]."

[73] "Need for All-Out Food Drive: Pandit Nehru's Call to Nation."

[74] "Popularise Grow Food Campaign," *Times of India*, July 4, 1949; "Sober Rejoicing Throughout India," *Times of India*, August 17, 1949.

Self-Help Which Ennobles a Nation 101

the political spectrum rallied behind the Prime Minister's suggestions.[75] Nehru wrote to India's Chief Ministers in the summer of 1949 to encourage them to replace the rice or wheat in their province's rations with a substitute starch once a week, and to grow subsidiary foods on their estates.[76] Nehru did so himself in July, having the lawns of his residence planted with groundnut, millet, maize, and sweet potatoes, in addition to bananas, tapioca, bitter gourd, and aubergines – harking back to the Second World War, when the Viceroy and several governors and princes replanted their own estates as vegetable gardens.[77] Indira Gandhi gave tours to visitors, and Nehru proudly proclaimed that his household was free of rice, subsisting instead upon sweet potato.[78]

Aware of the impropriety of public feasting in the face of widespread shortage, India's food ministers met in Delhi in August 1949 to discuss the imposition of new food austerity measures. Extending wartime legislation, the Ministry of Food enacted a uniform, national "Guest Control Order" structuring the types and quantity of food legally permissible at gatherings, allowing for unlimited attendees at events where non-rationed food would be served, and capping the number at twenty-five for those serving wheat or rice.[79] (Provincial governments, however, balked at the enforcement of these rules, and even ministerial gatherings saw them flouted.[80])

These enforcement failures did little to shake Nehru from his belief in the possibilities of remaking Indian notions of national responsibility through dietary transformations. Britain's High Commissioner

---

[75] "Nehru's Broadcast"; "India's Food Problem: Pandit Nehru's Appeal."

[76] Jawaharlal Nehru, letter dated July 1, 1949, in Jawaharlal Nehru, *Letters to Chief Ministers, 1947–1964*, vol. 1 (New Delhi: Jawaharlal Nehru Memorial Fund; distributed by Oxford University Press, 1985), 400–401. In August, Nehru wrote to R.K. Patil, then Food Commissioner, to see if Teen Murti could be supplied with planters for growing food. Jawaharlal Nehru, File No 31(71)/49-PMS, *SWJN* vol. 13, 75.

[77] Among other booklets issued, see *Vegetable Growing in the Delhi Province*, 2nd edn., ICAR Booklet 5 (New Delhi: Imperial Council of Agricultural Research, 1946).

[78] "Compound Lawns Become Farm," *Times of India*, July 25, 1949.

[79] Ministry of Food, Government of India, "Food Policy – Austerity Measures – Guest Control," November 1, 1949, Home – Public – 51/373/49, NAI. On guest control orders, see Hayden S. Kantor, "'A Dead Letter of the Statute Book': The Strange Bureaucratic Life of the Bihar Food Economy and Guest Control Order, 1950–1954," *South Asian History and Culture* 7, no. 3 (July 2, 2016): 239–257.

[80] Unable and often unwilling to undertake the burden of monitoring transgressions, particularly as the decontrol of foodgrains outpaced the Order's withdrawal, individual states began to flaunt these regulations, forwarding alternate Guest Control Orders at the provincial levels or sometimes discarding them altogether. Within several years, the Order had been effectively withdrawn throughout the country. "Food Austerity Measures," 1957, Agriculture – Basic Plan – 86(1)57 BP II, NAI; "Food Austerity Measures Adopted by the Assam Government," July 12, 1952, Food – Basic Plan – BP.II/1085(36)/50, NAI.

102   Hungry Nation

reported on these campaigns with anxiety, worrying that directives like Nehru's were inadequate palliatives for India's serious food problem.[81] Yet Nehru expressed a deepening commitment to the notion that Indians must remold their diets in the name of national development. In a letter to Jairamdas Daulatram in late October, Nehru encouraged the Food Minister to cut out rice from the rations allotted to wheat-eating areas. "We must take this risk in regard to rice," Nehru wrote, "and I believe that the country would be prepared for it, if only we set about it in right earnest and tell them what we are doing and what we expect them to do. If certain pinch is felt here and there, we need not be afraid."[82] When West Bengal's Chief Minister, B.C. Roy, wrote to Nehru to appeal for increased provision of foodgrains, the Prime Minister tied his support to a demand that Roy persuade Bengalis to change their food habits. "It is dangerous," Nehru warned, suggesting that Bengalis might take to tapioca, "for us to be subservient to a particular type of food which may not be available tomorrow. We live on the verge of a world war, and no one knows what will happen."[83] Implicit in Nehru's order was the notion that adherence to regional tastes was an impediment to forging the type of citizenship that would forge national unity through national self-reliance.

State-driven efforts to transform diets through an appeal to the responsibilities of citizenship were matched by a parallel effort from civil society. In September 1949, a group of Indian leaders, including representatives of the Congress, the Constituent Assembly, the All India Harijan Sevak Sangh, the Servants of India Society, the All India Refugee Association, the All India Women's Conference, the All India Hindu Mahasabha, and the All India Anglo-Indian Association, signed their support for the "Miss a Meal Movement." The movement's organizer was Jag Parvesh Chandra, a Lahore refugee and Delhi politician.[84] The group asked Indians to pledge to give up one meal a week, contributing the grains saved to a national fund, and in so doing, foster "the national habit of uniting and striving jointly at a time of crisis and emergency."[85]

Rajendra Prasad and Rajkumari Amrit Kaur – a founder of the All India Women's Conference, and independent India's new Health Minister – gave early support, prompting bureaucrats and politicians nationwide to

---

[81] UK High Commissioner, New Delhi, opdom #26.
[82] Jawaharlal Nehru, letter to Jairamdas Daulatram, October 3, 1949, *SWJN* vol. 13, 82–83.
[83] Jawaharlal Nehru, letter to B.C. Roy, July 13, 1950, *SWJN* vol. 14, 218.
[84] Jag Parvesh Chandra, *Miss a Meal Movement: An Experiment in Voluntary Errors and National Co-Operation* (New Delhi: Constitution House, 1949).
[85] "Miss a Meal a Week: Leader's Appeal," *Indian Express*, September 12, 1949.

Self-Help Which Ennobles a Nation   103

affirm their own approval.[86] The Governor of Punjab's pledge of drawing only six days' rations was followed by the Bombay premiere's announcement that he would be skipping two meals a week; Bengal's Minister of Civil Supplies declared that he had given up rice altogether.[87] Citizens were urged to make food pledges, like that asked of non-cultivators in Bombay to "reduce my consumption of food grains by using non-cereal foods and to avoid wastage of food in the kitchen and on the table."[88] Ration shops in Uttar Pradesh began to stock pledge forms, and representatives of Government godowns announced that they would reduce grain supply to stores in proportion to the number of pledges received.[89]

In early 1950, Chandra spoke about the movement to a gathering of businessmen and bureaucrats in Hyderabad, estimating that the movement would make up for 7 percent of India's estimated 10 percent total food deficit, saving approximately 400 crore rupees each year – "the total sum of the amount spent by the nation on 52 meals a year."[90] Yet more than killing the black market and freeing India from the yoke of foreign imports, missing a meal would

train you in the art of self-discipline, for control of the palate, as Gandhiji taught us, was the basis of self-discipline[.] A country become a great nation, when the people living in that country are not just human beings but think, behave, and act like true citizens, ready to discharge their duties willingly and gladly. A true citizen is he who thinks more of his duties and less of his rights; for in the final analysis, rights flow from duties well performed. Rights divorced from the performance of duties, is a contradiction in terms and a mockery of democracy.

Chandra's speech neatly linked the project of dietary transformation to the reimagination of rights in postcolonial India. Yet his

---

[86] "Miss a Meal Movement: Dr. Prasad's Support," *Sunday Indian Express*, November 4, 1949; "Miss a Meal a Week: Health Minister's Call," *Times of India*, November 19, 1949.

[87] Governor of East Punjab, letter to Jag Parvesh Chandra, December 21, 1949, Jag Parvesh Chandra papers, subject files, folder 2, NMML; "Bombay Premier Sets an Example," *Sunday Indian Express*, December 21, 1949; Prafulla Chandra Sen, letter to Jag Parvesh Chandra, November 18, 1949, Jag Parvesh papers, subject files, folder 2, NMML.

[88] "Making Citizens Food-Conscious," *Times of India*, November 23, 1949. Elsewhere, the pledge involved a promise to miss Friday lunch, "leave my plate clean of leavings," and return extra ration cards to the ration depot. B.P. Pathak, letter to Jag Parvesh Chandra, December 16, 1949, Jag Parvesh Chandra papers, subject files, folder 2, NMML. The choice of Friday as a preferred fast day appears to have been influenced by Gandhi's assassination on a Friday four years prior. "Miss a Meal Movement Explained," *Sunday Indian Express*, December 26, 1949.

[89] "Miss a Meal Per Week," *Times of India*, November 6, 1949. The movement also inspired poems, essays, and other creative ventures designed at garnering support. One Lucknow resident composed a short doggerel on the movement: "Men sacrifice in times of need / In every way have shown this deed / Stop a meal in a fortnight please / Save your Country, roll your sleeve / Make in daily meal this sure / Eat less rice or rice no more / Ask your people waste no food / Love your Country love your food." S. Asghar Ali, letter to B.G. Kher, December 21, 1949, Jag Parvesh Chandra papers, subject files, folder 2, NMML.

[90] Jag Parvesh Chandra, "Untitled Speech Delivered at Hyderabad," 1949, Jag Parvesh Chandra papers, subject files, folder 2, NMML.

104   Hungry Nation

movement was not infrequently lambasted as misguided and ineffectual. One former prince wrote to Chandra to gripe that "out of the 300 and odd millions [in India], His Highness thinks not more than one million could profitably miss a meal. The other 300 million are so undernourished that they should get an extra meal and not miss a meal."[91] Orissa's Law Minister concurred that "more than half of the population do not get two meals a day ... To such a population I feel diffident to suggest the campaign of fasting."[92] Yet the ethos resonated in official publicity. Addressing the nation over All India Radio on the food crisis and the perils of foreign aid, Nehru urged Indians to take up the Movement's signature act. "Each one of us," he enjoined, "should demonstrate active sympathy and desire to help by giving up one meal a week."[93] Nehru proposed sending surplus foodgrains to famine victims, and the Ministry of Food began to devise mechanisms for collecting and distributing them.[94]

As public institutions and representatives of civil society urged an austerity ethos, the Central Food Technological Research Institute and the government's Subsidiary Food Production Committee worked to provide the institutional and scientific mechanisms for the transformation of Indian diets. In early 1949, as scarcity loomed once more, the Ministry of Health had inquired of provincial governments whether banana roots were eaten by the poor in their respective provinces, looking to promote them in daily diets and scarcity crises alike.[95] The Ministry of Food examined a similar proposal to distribute imported Iraqi dates in place of rationed cereals.[96] These schemes grew more concrete with the creation of the Subsidiary Food Production Committee, chaired by industrialist Lala Shri Ram, and staffed by the senior Madras bureaucrat Sonti Ramamurthy and the Secretary of the Ministry of Food. Shri Ram reported directly to Rajendra Prasad, and asserted "that meeting the

---

[91] Unsigned letter to Jag Parvesh Chandra, January 6, 1950, Jag Parvesh Chandra papers, subject files, folder 2, NMML.

[92] Nityanand Kanungo, letter to Jag Parvesh Chandra, November 16, 1949, Jag Parvesh papers, subject files, folder 2, NMML.

[93] Jawaharlal Nehru, "Broadcast to the Nation, New Delhi, 1 May 1951," in *SWJN* vol. 16 (part 1), 39–42.

[94] Jawaharlal Nehru, letter to Food Secretary, Ministry of Food, New Delhi, May 2, 1951, in *SWJN* vol. 16 (part 1), 43–44.

[95] "Banana Roots as Human Food," June 25, 1949, Rajputana Agency – Political – Food – P-183, NAI.

[96] "Exploration of Possibility of Utilizing Dates from Iraq to Rations," February 9, 1949, Food – Basic Plan – BP-201(96)/49, NAI. The proposal appears to have only been accepted in 1951, when dates were distributed in ration packages in Uttar Pradesh and Bihar; see "Dates Given Away in Bihar," *Aaj*, February 12, 1951; "Distribution of Dates," *Aaj*, February 15, 1951.

Self-Help Which Ennobles a Nation

shortage of food is not merely the business of the Governments but of the 330 million people of the country."[97] Taking as its mandate the promotion of bananas, sweet potatoes, tapioca, groundnut flour, and synthetic cereals, the Committee met throughout the following year, building upon the work of the 1947 Foodgrains Policy Committee. The Committee's report posited that a "substantial reduction in the consumption of cereals in this country" could be effected through the production and consumption of alternate foodstuffs, beginning by appointing Development Officers to foster the expansion of each crop.[98]

The campaign offered, at least in theory, the possibility of feeding more citizens at no cost to the state. And as one British intelligence officer reported, the "attempt to persuade the public to change their diet by eating more 'substitute' foods like potatoes and sweet potatoes is discernible in all statements by government officials about food self-sufficiency."[99] One such statement came from Governor-General C. Rajagopalachari, who called in a radio address for a "fanatical zeal" for the food campaign. "The fashion must be set," he said, "for greater consumption of *ragi*, *cholam*, maize and millet … Like jail-going, hobnobbing with outcastes, spinning, [and] wearing Gandhi-caps, millet food must be made a patriotic high class fashion."[100] In August 1949, Shri Ram petitioned India's provincial food members to embrace the campaign, through publicity and by bringing subsidiary foods into the ration as soon as production targets were met.[101] The Ministry of Food similarly asked provincial ministries to consider distributing subsidiary foods in place of wheat and rice, requesting rationing administrations to estimate "how far [their] increased consumption can be popularized."[102] By the end of the year, a glut of bananas and sweet potatoes were being made available at cooperative stores and ration shops in Bombay Province; in the new guest control and public austerity measures enacted across India

---

[97] Valmiki Choudhary, ed., "Letter from Shri Ram to Rajendra Prasad, 20 May 1949," in *Dr. Rajendra Prasad: Correspondence and Select Documents*, vol. 11 (New Delhi: Allied Publishers, 1988), 69. Later, Shri Ram would pressure Prasad into planting banana shrubs and sweet potato vines at his Delhi residence. Valmiki Choudhary, ed., "Letter from Shri Ram to Rajendra Prasad, 17 September 1949," in *Dr. Rajendra Prasad: Correspondence and Select Documents*, vol. 11 (New Delhi: Allied Publishers, 1988), 160.

[98] No copies of the final report appear to exist in print; a résumé is "Summary of Conclusions of the Subsidiary Food Production Committee (1950)," in *Reports of the Estimates Committee 1960–61* (New Delhi: Lok Sabha Secretariat, 1961), 70–72.

[99] Bombay Weekly Political Report #21/49, May 1949, IOR/L/E/8/7230.

[100] Rajagopalachari, "The Food Problem [All India Radio, July 6, 1949]."

[101] Letter from the Ministry of Food, 1949, Agriculture – Rationing – RP-1084(14)/54, NAI.

[102] "Banana Roots as Human Food."

106   Hungry Nation

the following year, subsidiary foods would continue to be permitted in unlimited quantities.[103]

Encouraged by the drive for subsidiary and substitute foods, the Central Food Technological Research Institute revived earlier, futuristic proposals for an ersatz grain to replace rice and wheat. The Institute's director, V. Subrahmanyan, had pledged to underwrite Nehru's promise of food self-sufficiency by 1951, promising that a quarter of the nation's grain consumption could be replaced by that date with sweet potatoes or tapioca.[104] "Artificial rice" would be a key component of that campaign. As early as 1945, the nationalist agricultural scientist M. Afzal Husain had postulated that since "chemists have produced rayon, nylon, [and] plastics," there should "be no reason why they cannot produce artificial rice from tuber starch."[105] And a decade earlier, Sonti Ramamurthy of the Subsidiary Food Production Committee had witnessed a Travancore Maharaja importing tapioca into the state during the war. The schoolchildren fed on tapioca alone, Ramamurty recalled, were "rickety," but the civil servant continued to tout the possibility of a rice substitute based on tapioca supplemented with groundnut flour for protein.[106] In 1948, Ramamurty had contracted a manufacturing firm in Coimbatore to formulate a prototype, and on the Subsidiary Food Production Committee, he took charge of the "artificial rice" project, while Lala Shri Ram steered the production of "a flour mixed from tapioca and wheat flour to make chapattis in North India." Publicly declaring his intent to manufacture a substitute cereal that would satisfy "the psychology of people accustomed to eat cereals," Ramamurty asked the CFTRI's V. Subrahmanyan to undertake pilot trials for the rice in Kerala.[107] A pilot plant was established in Mysore, and the Committee set to work formulating distribution plans for South and North India.[108]

The project captured the imagination of the bureaucrats whose more staid agricultural schemes were stagnating. In April 1951, Rajendra Prasad sampled chapattis and halva made from tapioca in the CFTRI laboratories.[109] In the summer, Subrahmanyan was called to speak to

[103] "Subsidiary Foods Output," *Times of India*, December 29, 1949; "Concurrence of the Central Government to the Withdrawal of Food Austerity Measures," July 1950, Agriculture – Rationing – RP 1085/26/50, NAI.
[104] "Achieving Self-Sufficiency in Food by 1951: Mysore Research Body's Proposals," *Times of India*, July 1, 1950.
[105] Husain, "Food Problem of India (1946, Bangalore)," 569.
[106] Sonti Venkata Ramamurty, *Looking across Fifty Years* (Bombay: Popular Prakashan, 1964), 117.
[107] "Difficulty in Ending Food Imports," *Times of India*, May 16, 1949.
[108] Ramamurty, *Looking across Fifty Years*, 149.
[109] Valmiki Choudhary, ed., "Notes on Mysore Tour," in *Dr. Rajendra Prasad: Correspondence and Select Documents*, vol. Presidency Period (New Delhi: Allied Publishers, 1984), 198–200.

Self-Help Which Ennobles a Nation 107

ministers in Travancore-Cochin about the possibility of scaling up consumption of synthetic rice.[110] In Delhi, one minister surprised colleagues with the announcement that the rice they had eaten at lunch was in fact the CFTRI's ersatz version.[111] "The grains that we now make are round," V. Subrahmanyan proclaimed at the pilot plant in Mysore, but "we can make beautiful, white rice-shaped grains which can satisfy even the most fastidious consumers."[112]

Fastidiousness aside, Indian consumers took poorly to these ersatz grains, evidencing scant demand. An early, critical assessment from Madras pointed to the reluctance of producers to switch to tapioca from proven cash crops, and the dim potential for the "dietetic habits of a nation [to] be altered by propaganda, persuasion or fiat."[113] The conclusion was not unwarranted. Artificial rice was deployed to a small famine in Southern India in 1952, but there was little interest outside of famine conditions.[114] The first artificial rice factory in Trivandrum was shuttered shortly after its inauguration.[115] Save for a small number of famine victims in Rayalaseema, producers in Mysore, and enthusiastic bureaucrats in Delhi, few Indians ever tasted the much-touted artificial rice.[116] Before production could be adequately scaled up, the state had grown reluctant to ask citizens to reimagine their rights, their responsibilities, and their diets in tandem.[117]

---

[110] B.S. Bawa, "From a Deficit to a Surplus State," *The Punjab Farmer* 3, no. 2 (June 1951): 58.

[111] "Synthetic Rice and Curds," *Times of India*, October 7, 1952.

[112] V. Subramanyam, "Planning for Food Emergency," in *Food and Population and Development of Food Industries in India* (Mysore: Central Food Technological Research Institute, 1952), 133. The CFTRI's efforts gained the attention of observers overseas; "Two Other Artificial Products: Synthetic Rice and Milk," in *Indian Horizons*, vol. 1 (New Delhi: Indian Council for Cultural Relations, 1952), 340–341. V. Subrahmanyan and M. Swaminathan published an optimistic early report in *Nature*, touting the promise that artificial rice held to obviate India's food problem. V. Subramanyam et al., "Rice Substitutes," *Nature* 174 (1954): 199–201.

[113] Balasubrahmanya Natarajan, *Food and Agriculture in Madras State* (Madras: Director of Information and Publicity, Government of Madras, 1951), 125–127.

[114] "Centre to Open Research Units in Villages," *Times of India*, May 29, 1953.

[115] E. Ikkanda Warrier oral history transcript, November 13, 1970, NMML.

[116] In 1957, Jawaharlal Nehru wrote to the Directory of India's Council of Scientific and Industrial Research, to ask what had happened to the project. Informed that no production was taking place, Nehru testily brought up the issue of the project's seeming failure several days later with Food and Agriculture Minister A.P. Jain. The last mention of the artificial rice project seems to have come in 1960, when administrators in Kerala constituted a propaganda team to promote it before an unceremonious disbanding in 1960. Jawaharlal Nehru, letter to M.S. Thacker, May 28, 1957, *SWJN* vol. 38, 112; letter to A.P. Jain, June 2, 1957, *SWJN* vol. 38, 115; *Administration Report of the Civil Supplies Department for the Year 1961–62* (Trivandrum: Civil Supplies Department, Government of Kerala, 1962), 14.

[117] The CFTRI nonetheless played an important role in the development of India's modern food processing and preservation industries. In 1951, a government work looked

108   Hungry Nation

As male bureaucrats and scientists forwarded the twinned imperatives of austerity and alternate foodstuffs, Indian women, the "anchors of the household," were saddled with the burden of remolding the diets of their husbands and children, and in so doing, recasting the relationship between the household and the nation.

Colonial planners and nationalist organizations had cast women as essential agents of India's national development, interweaving the aims of household health and national well-being.[118] One of the earliest primers on "domestic science" in India linked the promulgation of the field to the advancement of national health and hygiene.[119] W.R. Aykroyd would nonetheless lament, a decade later, that "the women of India have not yet been enlisted in the campaign for improved nutrition"; the National Planning Committee's 1938 sub-committee on "woman's role in planned economy" suggested that women would play a key role in constructing a national diet after independence.[120] During the Bengal famine, the left-wing Mahila Atmaraksha Samiti – the "Women's Self-Defense League" – had affirmed repeatedly that women's duties towards the nation were split between self-defense and the provision of food.[121] The connection between the maintenance of the home and the uplift of the nation grew more explicit after independence. Social worker Rameshwari Nehru would write, shortly after independence, that "the home is the foundation on which the structure of society is built," and that its improvement would ultimately underwrite national development.[122]

expectantly to the CFTRI for its projects for "the processing of coarse grain to render it acceptable to rice eaters ... and new and improved methods of processing pulses without affecting their nutritive value."Yet over the next several decades, the Institute's work was dedicated to more mundane matters of canning, preservation, and the prevention of adulteration *Progress of Science* (New Delhi: Publications Division, Ministry of Information and Broadcasting, Government of India, 1951); *Abstracts of CFTRI Papers* (Mysore: Central Food Technological Research Institute, 1966).

[118] On the intersections of nationalism and domesticity in colonial India, see Mary Hancock, "Gendering the Modern: Women and Home Science in British India," in *Gender, Sexuality and Colonial Modernities*, ed. Antoinette M. Burton (London: Routledge, 1999), 148–160; Mary Hancock, "Home Science and the Nationalization of Domesticity in Colonial India," *Modern Asian Studies* 35, no. 4 (2001): 871–903; and Judith E. Walsh, *Domesticity in Colonial India: What Women Learned When Men Gave Them Advice* (Lanham, MD: Rowman & Littlefield Publishers, 2004). More broadly, see Durba Ghosh, "Gender and Colonialism: Expansion or Marginalization?," *The Historical Journal* 47, no. 3 (September 1, 2004): 737–755; and Tanika Sarkar, *Hindu Wife, Hindu Nation: Community, Religion, and Cultural Nationalism* (Bloomington: Indiana University Press, 2001).

[119] Mabel A. Needham, *Domestic Science for High Schools in India* (Bombay: Oxford University Press, 1929).

[120] Aykroyd, *Notes on Food and Nutrition Policy in India*; K.T. Shah, *Woman's Role in Planned Economy: Report of the Sub-Committee*, National Planning Committee Series (Bombay: Vora & Co., 1947).

[121] Forbes, *Women in Modern India*, 210–211.

[122] Rameshwari Nehru, *Gandhi Is My Star: Speeches and Writings* (Patna: Pustakbhandar, 1950).

The All India Women's Conference, well-connected to the mainstream Congress leadership, emerged as the dominant voice of nationalist women after independence.[123] One of the Conference's Presidents would declare that "our aim is to make the woman a healthy and useful member of society; a good mother, self-reliant, and a responsible citizen conscious of her rights and responsibilities."[124] Those rights and responsibilities quickly converged around the provision of food to the home and the nation. In 1946, the AIWC declared that the fourteenth of every month was to be designated a "Special Food Day," tasking each chapter with teaching its members "the duty of the people to cooperate" in the tasks of avoiding waste and using substitute foods.[125] A second resolution in 1949 saw the AIWC ask its members to begin growing substitute foods in kitchen gardens; soon, the group organized mobile demonstrations and canteens to promote the same.[126] One member asserted that the conservation of food and the promotion of new foodstuffs "is a work suited primarily to the genius of women. Let it not be said that women have failed in a task of such supreme national importance."[127]

Yet even as the AIWC affirmed, through its initiatives, the state's contention that "women, more than men, could effectively help Government in the solution of [the] food problem," India's bureaucrats assigned to women the burden of failure for their modernist schemes.[128] Nehru was particularly damning in his twinning of female agency and the food crisis. Visiting the Gujarati village of Gandhinagar, he contended that women should not complain about grain shortages, but instead, "carry on with what they get." Noting India's expenditure on food imports, he asserted that it had been women's desire for sugar which had forced the government to purchase it from abroad; their propensity for black market purchases of rationed commodities had further undermined government food control efforts.[129] The failure of women to upkeep the new imperatives of postcolonial citizenship was seen as underwriting India's continued dependence.

AIWC members nonetheless continued to view their efforts as instrumental in modeling domestic solutions to the food crisis. In July 1949, a

---

[123] Jawaharlal Nehru nonetheless complained in 1936 that the AIWC was "superficial" since it did nothing to examine the "root causes" of the social issues it championed. Forbes, *Women in Modern India*, 81.

[124] All India Women's Conference, Cultural Section, *Education of Women in Modern India* (Anudh: Anudh Publishing Trust, 1946).

[125] "Food," *Bulletin of Indian Women's Movement*, July 1946.

[126] "Resolutions Passed at the Meeting of the Standing Committee of the AIWC at Bombay, August 1949," *Roshni*, September 1949.

[127] Kitty Shiva Rao, "Grow More and Eat Wisely," *Roshni*, September 1949.

[128] "Housewives Can Help Change Food Habits," *Times of India*, September 9, 1949.

[129] "Carry on with Food You Get," *Times of India*, September 20, 1950.

110   Hungry Nation

month after Jawaharlal Nehru delivered a series of speeches on citizenship and the food problem on All India Radio, Indira Gandhi convened a meeting that led to the formation of the Women's Food Committee, Delhi, seeking to popularize subsidiary foods among women.[130] In Bombay, Lilavati Munshi, outgoing AIWC president and wife of Food Minister K.M. Munshi, organized several state-funded substitute food exhibitions.[131] A year later, in the wake of the Subsidiary Food Production Committee's report, the Ministry of Food announced that it would be turning over the task of substitute food promotion to a new All India Women's Council for Supplementary Foods, funded by the Ministries of Food and Agriculture and comprising "representatives of All India Women's Organizations and prominent women active in public, social and Parliamentary life."[132]

The Council soon organized a series of exhibitions in Bombay and Delhi demonstrating recipes without rice and wheat. Rajendra Prasad inaugurated the Delhi exhibition, where Lilavati Munshi contended that the nation's food problem "had baffled the greatest of our men," but that women would no doubt find a solution, given that "it is their province to handle food."[133] The Council's first booklet, touting substitute foods costing eight annas or less, was soon supplemented by an ambitious two-volume cookbook.[134] And after two initial schemes for cafeterias in Bombay fell through, the Council opened the Annapoorna restaurant in Delhi in January 1951. India's "most democratic restaurant" was staffed by women and served a buffet of substitute foods, quickly becoming an important political pilgrimage site. Beyond "thousands of middle class and poor customers," the cafeteria drew a steady stream of parliamentarians and diplomats, in addition to catering the 1951 Indian National Congress in Delhi. Appealing to women as the "food ministers" of their own households, the AIWC continued to expand the Annapoorna chain nationwide, establishing thirty-two branches by 1955.[135]

---

[130] "Popularising Subsidiary Foods," *Times of India*, July 30, 1949.

[131] "Subsidiary Foods Education," *Roshni*, November 1949.

[132] Ministry of Food, Government of India, "All India Women's Council for Supplementary Foods: Measures for Increased Production and Consumption," August 5, 1950, IOR/L/E/88/8698.

[133] "Supplementary Food," *Times of India*, December 4, 1950. See also Rajendra Prasad, "The Food Problem (Speech delivered in Hindi at the opening of the Food Exhibition at the Town Hall, Delhi, on December 1, 1950), in Verinder Grover, *Political Thinkers of Modern India*, vol. 23: *Dr. Rajendra Prasad* (New Delhi: Deep & Deep Publications, 1993), 488–490.

[134] A.R. Vyas, "Annapoorna: India's Democratic Restaurants," *March of India* 4, no. 2 (December 1951): 29–31; All India Women's Food Council, *Annapurna Recipes of Supplementary Foods*, 2 vols. (New Delhi: All India Women's Food Council, 1951).

[135] *The Fourth Annual Meeting of the All India Women's Food Council, West Bengal Branch, 1954–55* (Calcutta: All India Women's Food Council, 1955).

Figure 5 Indian politician Uma Nehru and Lilavati Munshi, wife of Food Minister K.M. Munshi, oversee cooking and nutrition classes at the Annapoorna restaurant in Delhi, September 1951. (Credit: Photo Division, Ministry of Information and Broadcasting, Government of India)

Even as the state continued to fund and subsidize the AIWC and its Annapoorna chain of restaurants, the nation's bureaucratic leadership continued to saddle women with the blame for Indian households' putative inability or unwillingness to change their food habits. As late as the mid 1950s, Nehru was proclaiming that on the matter of food, "women will justify themselves [sic] not so much by making demands but by the part they play in the building up of new India."[136] If rights in postcolonial India stemmed only from the proper completion of duties, that compact was expected even more acutely of the nation's women.

Against the backdrop of a worsening food crisis, and India's continued inability to meet the targets of the renewed Grow More Food campaign, legislators, writers, and satirists inveighed against the calls to miss meals and transform diets, their objections an implicit rejection of the new

[136] Jawaharlal Nehru, "Food Problem and the Role of Women," *SWJN* vol. 40, 276.

112   Hungry Nation

state's transferal of developmental responsibilities. These critiques linked substitute foods to the historical deprivations of famine, and rejected the modernist notion that, in the name of nation-building, one calorie might be just as readily taken as another.[137]

The earliest, most trenchant critiques came from the Communist Party of India, which accused the Congress of promoting subsidiary foods and austerity at the expense of real agrarian reform. *People's Age* reported frequently upon the callous statements of India's food officials. A 1948 report lambasted the Foodgrains Policy Committee's emphasis on substitute foods, and took Jairamdas Daulatram to task for asking a group of villagers, as they waited outside a ration depot, "why after getting political freedom they have made themselves slaves of taste."[138] Two years later, as scarcity broke out nationwide, a Party circular doubled down on these charges. "They advise the starving people to 'miss a meal a week,'" it read, "who are not getting even one full meal a day!"[139] These partisan critiques soon dovetailed with a broader assault on India's food ministers and bureaucrats, like the jabs at K.M. Munshi which appeared in the *Times of India* and *Shankar's Weekly*.

Increasingly, legislators and politicians voiced their own objections to the state's quixotic projects. Later in 1950, Madras parliamentarian and physician A.L. Mudaliar – later director of the World Health Organization – deplored that "when such suggestions are made to people who miss not only a meal in a week, but a meal every day, and who have neither vegetables nor anything else to consume, we ask: 'What is the competence of the honorable Minister for Food to give such advice?'"[140] An internal Ministry of Agriculture review assessed India's various guest control orders as ineffective as they were unpopular, useful "mainly for the psychological value."[141] Nehru's estranged secretary, M.O. Mathai, would recall the Prime Minister's faith in the Subsidiary

---

[137] Various jungle roots, yams, sago palm, and other foodstuffs, for instance, were common famine foods among the Mizos, when rats, a "preferred" scarcity staple, was unavailable. Sajal Nag, "Bamboo, Rats and Famines: Famine Relief and Perceptions of British Paternalism in the Mizo Hills," in *India's Environmental History: Colonialism, Modernity, and the Nation*, ed. Mahesh Rangarajan and K. Sivaramakrishnan, vol. 2. (Ranikhet: Permanent Black, 2012), 389–399.

[138] "You Are Slaves of Taste! Food Minister Admonishes Starving Kisans of South," *People's Age*, June 6, 1948.

[139] Communist Party of India, "The Catastrophic Food Situation and Our Tasks" August 10, 1950, 1950.91, P.C. Joshi Archives on Contemporary History.

[140] A.L. Mudaliar, "On the Governor's Address (4th August 1950)," in *Searchlight on Council Debates: Speeches of Sir A.L. Mudaliar in the Madras Legislative Council* (Bombay: Orient Longmans, 1960), 167.

[141] Ministry of Agriculture, "Austerity Measures: Guest Control Order," Agriculture – Basic Plan – 86(1)/57 BP II, NAI.

Self-Help Which Ennobles a Nation

Food Production Committee as akin to a "drowning man clutching at a straw."[142] And C. Rajagopalachari drafted a private memorandum in January 1952 decrying state efforts to manage the minutiae of food production and consumption as an affront to personal liberty and a source of India's enduring hunger – presaging his unilateral lifting of food controls in Madras six months later.[143] Assessments from overseas were no more sympathetic. "The tragedy," an *Eastern World* correspondent wrote of the Miss a Meal campaign, "is that millions of Indians have no choice of forgoing a meal, but are savagely dieted by poverty."[144] Implicit in these rejections lurked the notion that India's efforts to remake personal practice and sentiment represented the desperate campaigns of a weak state unable to actualize the promise of sustenance which had animated the nationalist struggle.

The announcement of India's First Five-Year Plan at the end of 1951 saw an assertive revision of India's agricultural planning. The Prime Minister had fended off internal political challenges from Sardar Patel and Purshottamdas Tandon – conservative voices whose antipathy towards socialist planning may have rendered the transformation of Indian citizenship, rather than that of agrarian structure, a more palatable shared goal. Beyond an emphasis on industrial development, the Plan concentrated on the coordinated transformation of rural India's social and economic conditions, affirming food production as a primary national goal. "Unless the food problem is handled satisfactorily," the Plan held, "economic conditions in the country will not be stable enough to permit the implementation of the plan." Its overwhelming focus on increasing agricultural output rendered the goal of transforming Indian diets a "valuable supplement to the food supply."[145]

Yet the campaign to remold citizens' diets and their relationship to the state in consort never fully receded from the national conversation. In years of higher agricultural production, when imports waned, the discussion of subsidiary foods, ersatz foodstuffs, and austerity receded from the limelight – only to reemerge forcefully at moments of crisis. It was often industrialists and businessmen who continued to press for these ends. A year

---

[142] M.O. Mathai, *My Days with Nehru* (New Delhi: Vikas Publishing House, 1979).

[143] C. Rajagopalachari, "Amateurish Experiments and Imperial Food Production: An Article," January 1952, C. Rajagopalachari papers (VI to XI), Speeches and Writing, folder 114, NMML.

[144] J.F. Stirling, "The Background to Famine," *Eastern World* 5, no. 12 (December 1951): 14.

[145] Planning Commission, Government of India, *The First Five-Year Plan: A Draft Outline* (New Delhi: Government of India Press, 1951), 67. For an analysis, see Francine R. Frankel, *India's Political Economy, 1947–2004: The Gradual Revolution* (New Delhi: Oxford University Press, 2005), 94–106.

114   Hungry Nation

after the publication of the First Five-Year Plan, the Andhra Chamber of Commerce heard the state's outgoing Industrial and Development Commissioner outline a scheme for a private subsidiary foods lobby.[146] He, like the industrialists who had spearheaded the first subsidiary foods campaigns, was likely motivated by the aim of freeing up agricultural land used for cereals for the increased cultivation of exportable goods.

Officials joined industrialists in reviving the language of citizenship, rights, and responsibility to urge dietary transformations at moments of crisis. The 1957 Foodgrains Enquiry Committee, chaired by Ashok Mehta in the wake of a failed monsoon, lamented the turn away from subsidiary foods, which the economist held was "an unfortunate result of the feeling that our food problem [was] purely transitory."[147] Mehta urged the Ministry of Food and Agriculture to establish a new department to promote the production and consumption of substitute foods. In June, a new Congress resolution reaffirmed the need for their consumption; the year afterwards, Lala Shri Ram would resurface to urge the creation of a "Ministry for Non-Cereal Foods" – proposals which earned the praise of the *Eastern Economist*.[148] By the end of 1957, the Prime Minister had revived the language of personal transformation, exhorting Indians to "change your food habits in accordance with the needs of the country."[149] Nehru's "exasperated paternalism" remained in evidence. "I am very worried," the Prime Minister declared as the crisis continued,

about this habit which seems to be growing of everybody asking somebody else to feed him, [of] everybody going to the State Government and saying, give us this, give us that ... Somehow, mind [sic] has become so perverted that we must have so much rice, and not take the other things which are better than rice, and in fact prefer starvation. I do not understand it.[150]

Indians' failure to remake their diets, Nehru proposed, was a fundamental defect in their understanding of rights and responsibilities.

The most iconic revival of the campaign came in the mid 1960s, with the breakout of war with Pakistan presaging India's most significant

---

[146] "Suggestions for Solving the Food Program by Shri V. Ramakrishna," 1952, Agriculture – G.M.F. – 10–5/52-GMF(Eng), NAI.

[147] Ministry of Food and Agriculture, Government of India, *Report of the Foodgrains Enquiry Committee, November 1957* (New Delhi: Government of India Press, 1957), 103.

[148] "AICC Resolution on Food Production (June 1 and 2, 1957)," in Sunil Guha, *India's Food Problem* (New Delhi: Indian National Congress, 1957), 15; "A Plea for Non-Cereal Foods," *Eastern Economist*, August 15, 1958, 218.

[149] Jawaharlal Nehru, "Yoga and Food Habits: Speech while Inaugurating the Annual Celebrations of Vishwayatan Yogashram, New Delhi, 17 November 1957," *SWJN* vol. 40, 251.

[150] Jawaharlal Nehru, "India and the World: Press Conference, 2 January 1958," *SWJN* vol. 41, 798.

Self-Help Which Ennobles a Nation 115

food crisis since independence in the form of the Bihar famine. The new Prime Minister, Lal Bahadur Shastri, took up the call to "miss a meal" once more. Newspapers echoed Shastri's call, at rallies, for weekly "dinnerless days," with the new slogan "*Jai jawan, jai kisan*"– "Long live the soldier and the farmer" – braiding together the aims of food and national defense.[151] Congress rallied behind the Prime Minister, asking party workers to go door-to-door in support of a new food austerity campaign.[152] The Federation of Indian Chambers of Commerce and Industry urged its members to refrain from receptions or dinner parties for the duration of the war, mooting a proposal to grow sweet potatoes in vacant factory lots.[153] And as war ended, the central government sponsored a conservation campaign showing two chapattis separated from a third. "Every third chappati you eat," it proclaimed, "is made from imported wheat. Let's not eat it."[154]

"Adversity," education minister Maulana Azad stated on India's first anniversary, "is part of this independence package. The government needs courageous citizens. We have to lift burdens like strong, real men."[155] An analogous advertisement for a major bank ran a month after India's independence, carrying the words of a nationalist financier, T.A. Pai, who would later become first president of the Food Corporation of India. "No food minister can give us food," Pai wrote, "and no finance minister can give us economic stability and independence, unless and until every man and woman in the country helps them."[156]

The language of adversity, austerity, and sacrifice suffused public institutions and public speech throughout India's early independent years, structuring the efforts of state institutions and national leaders to remake

---

[151] "The Threat of Famine," *Time* 86, no. 23 (December 3, 1965): 52. A discussion of the symbology of Shastri's call, and its representation in visual media, is "Yogendra Rastogi: Visualizing Modernity," in Christopher Pinney, *Photos of the Gods: The Printed Image and Political Struggle in India* (London: Reaktion, 2004), 168–174.

[152] "Congress Working Committee, New Delhi, November 7, 1965," in A.M. Zaidi, ed., *INC: The Glorious Tradition. Texts of the Resolutions Passed by the INC, the AICC and the CWC* (New Delhi: Indian Institute of Applied Political Research, 1989), 495–497. The movement also enjoyed a revival in the form of new support from India's trading community, which embraced the conceit of voluntary self-regulation in food consumption as an alternative to federal and provincial legislation. See Ambalal Kilachand, letter to Mr. Dhirajlal Maganlal, President, Indian Merchants Chamber, July 28, 1964, Indian Merchants' Chamber, Bombay papers, folder 797, NMML; and Ambalal Kilachand, letter to C.L. Gheevala, August 14, 1964, Indian Merchants' Chamber, Bombay papers, folder 797, NMML.

[153] L.N. Birla, letter to G.L. Bansal, October 28, 1965, Indian Merchants' Chamber, Bombay papers, folder 800, NMML.

[154] "Every Third Chappati [Advertisement in Save Food for Self-Sufficiency campaign]," c. 1965–66.

[155] Roy, *Beyond Belief*, 105.

[156] "Canara Industrial & King Syndicate, Limited [Advertisement]," *Indian Express*, October 7, 1947.

Figure 6 Government publicity campaign reminding Indian citizens that "Every third chappati you eat is made from imported wheat," c. 1965–1966. (Credit: Ministry of Information and Broadcasting, Government of India)

Self-Help Which Ennobles a Nation   117

Indian diets. This ethos built upon a diverse range of late colonial ante-cedents, from the international Malthusian debates over population, land, and people and the economic writing of early Indian nationalists to the colonial language of nutrition and the schemes for reconstruction proposed by Indian planners.[157] Independence brought the nationalist concerns of human welfare and the amelioration of India's agriculture to the fore of national planning efforts, but the need to forward a plan of economic self-reliance and free up resources for industrial develop-ment saw India's leadership transferring the burden of food planning to citizens themselves, appealing to the qualities of virtue, shared burden, and sacrifice sutured to notions of postcolonial citizenship. In the years between independence and the First Five-Year Plan, in particular, that leadership could frame enduring scarcity as an incomplete assumption of the obligations of citizenship. "If you cannot give up your sugar, your wheat or your rice for a while," Nehru contended in an emblematic par-liamentary debate in 1950, "then the biggest army will not be able to protect you, because you lack inner strength."[158]

The government of early independent India, Sunil Khilnani has argued, "was transformed from a distant, alien object into one that aspired to infiltrate the everyday lives of Indians ... The state thus etched itself into the imagination of Indians in a way that no previous political agency had ever done."[159] The campaign to remake Indian diets exemplified this transformation, and the ways in which a state initially unable to actual-ize fundamental social and economic change attempted to restructure the sentiments and behavior of its citizens themselves, casting them as a fundamental obligation of postcolonial citizenship. Over the next dec-ade, India's postcolonial leadership would grow more confident in the state's ability to undertake fundamental structural reform, and the 1950s were a high water mark in the state's "romance with developmental planning."[160] The remaking of diets, however, remained a convenient idiom for a state at moments of scarcity and developmental uncertainty.

By the time the technological advances of the Green Revolution began to take root in India in the form of the "new agricultural strategy" of

---

[157] Undoubtedly, it also harkened back to the idioms of *Swadeshi* nationalism, which, Manu Goswami notes, "radicalized and generalized the nationalist critique of colonial-ism on multiple, overlapping sociocultural terrains and in a deeply passionate idiom of autonomy, self-reliance, and sacrifice." Goswami, *Producing India*, 243.

[158] Jawaharlal Nehru, "The Growth of Violence: Speech in Reply to a Debate on Foreign Affairs in Parliament, New Delhi, December 7, 1950," in *Jawaharlal Nehru's Speeches*, vol. 2, 3rd edn. (New Delhi: Publications Division, Ministry of Information and Broadcasting, Government of India, 1963), 259–273.

[159] Khilnani, *The Idea of India*, 41.

[160] Kudaisya, "A Mighty Adventure."

118   Hungry Nation

the mid 1960s, the focus of development planning had wholly shifted. If, in the earliest years of independence, the new state had looked to citizenship as an opportune site for transformation in the name of development, the relative inattentiveness of the state to the agrarian unrest and concentration of incomes wrought by the Green Revolution spoke to a paradigm of development that had become radically disjunct from questions of citizenship and shared sacrifice. The connection between citizenship and agricultural development would be left, in years to come, to representatives of the "new farmers' movements" whose populist narrative suggested that earlier nation-building efforts had been inimical to agrarian citizenship.[161] For a crucial period, however, India's public institutions and figures asked citizens to reimagine their relationship to the new state and their co-citizens, saddling Indians, and women in particular, to steward the transformations that would help realize the goal of national self-reliance. As India's institutions and politicians charged citizens themselves with responsibility for their own sustenance, so, too, it charged them with the burden of the nation's development.

---

[161] See Tom Brass, ed., *New Farmers' Movements in India* (Ilford: Frank Cass, 1995); Akhil Gupta, "Agrarian Populism in the Development of a Modern Nation (India)," in *International Development and the Social Sciences*, ed. Frederick Cooper and Randall Packard (Berkeley: University of California Press, 1997), 320–344.

4 The Common Hunger of the Country: Merchants and Markets in Plenty and Want

In August 1951, Kondidasu Appalaswamy's lawyer arrived at the Madras High Court, ready to make a creative case for his client, jailed on grounds of preventative detention.[1] It was a grave injustice, the lawyer argued, that a "leading citizen" was languishing behind bars. While Appalaswamy might have been guilty of the unjust smuggling charges, it could not be argued that he had done a disservice to his community. Holding him in jail on grounds that he might sell rice again was, according to the lawyer, a ludicrous charge.

It had been hard for the authorities to ignore the hundreds of citizens of East Godavari district flocking to the tiny hamlet of Payakaraopeta, where Appalaswamy and his nephew presided over the operations of the Sri Ganeswara Rice and Oil Mills. They came with baskets on their heads and on boats, by bull-cart and even by train, leaving wet paddy behind in exchange for handfuls of coins and bills. When the police raided Sri Ganeswara on the morning of June 6, they found 280 sacks of rice above what Appalaswamy was legally entitled to purchase. The unrepentant proprietor had been taken away in cuffs, and the officers cheered the arrest of East Godavari's most flagrant black marketeer.

Under the Madras Foodgrains Control Order, one of many wartime laws extended after independence, Appalaswamy held a license to purchase, process, and sell rice to authorized dealers in neighboring Visakhapatnam district. But even in this unrationed district, it was only those dealers who could sell rice to consumers. These restrictions were not only odious to Appalaswamy's business instinct, but to his libertarian understanding of the new state itself. His lawyer conceded that there were certain essential undertakings that only India's government could manage – the construction of railways and the provision of electricity, for example. But with so many competent food dealers, purchasers, and

---

[1] Somasundaram Mack, *Kondidasu Appalaswamy vs. Unknown*, All India Reporter (Madras 1951).

119

processors working in India, Appalaswamy considered it unjust to frame the regulation of food markets as an essential government service.

The smuggler's argument, if not his actions, would have been applauded by the late Mohandas Gandhi, who had inveighed tirelessly against food controls in the final months of his life. But the position was summarily dismissed by an incensed judge, who reminded the petitioner that "the Food Department, and a vast system of food control, have come into existence for the specific purpose of providing food of the community on an equitable and rationed basis, with a view to seeing that so far as humanly possible, no deficit areas perish from starvation." This mandate was baked into the very fabric of the state itself, and if Appalaswamy was the "leading citizen" that he claimed to be, it was imperative that he be made an example. "Our courts," the judge wrote, "are today cluttered as never before in their history with masses of cases against comparatively small persons for violating food control laws and regulations." Seeing East Godavari's worst rice smuggler molder behind bars would no doubt dissuade them from similar offenses.

The case of an unrepentant rice runner posed no legal conundrum to the Madras High Court judge who presided over it. But Appalaswamy's claim that food provision fell beyond the mandate of the state tapped into an insistent, alternate vision of commercial life in independent India. Since the Second World War, bureaucrats had cast the regulation of food markets as the appropriate purview of government – a paradigm readily adopted by India's mainstream nationalists as they wove idioms of welfare into the functioning of the state. Yet this vision was assailed by traders, classical liberals, and citizens frustrated by regulatory ingress, all operating under the shadow of Mahatma Gandhi and his belief that regulated markets made a mockery of independent India's claim to self-rule. As American grain underwrote a sprawling network of semi-public ration shops, frustrated traders and dealers battled proposals for full state trading and courted the support of politicians sympathetic to the ends of free markets, all protesting the purported stymieing of India's commercial life. And as the nation lurched towards the new agricultural strategy that would radically reconfigure urban–rural relations, these traders and their allies worked to thwart and then capture the new state agency meant to regulate them.

These actors were tapping into divergent visions of what independence and the promise of sustenance would mean for market players, and what limits a state would place on commercial life in the name of welfare. The unsatisfactory resolution of these conflicts cleared space for a strategy predicated upon technological change, leaving unsettled the critical questions of how citizen, trader, and producer were to interact in the markets of independent India.

The Common Hunger of the Country 121

Bombay was the first of India's cities to be rationed.[2] The municipal government had declared March 8, 1943 a public holiday to allow its residents to pick up the ration cards now required of them.[3] 1.7 million citizens had been divided into two groups – ordinary citizens and industrial workers, the latter entitled to 50 percent more grain – who would in three weeks' time be required to pick up wheat, rice, pearl millet, and sorghum at one of 800 authorized shops.

Citizens' groups in Bombay had mobilized to demand rationing that would ensure the sustenance of a worried population: residents of the city had taken note of a first national Foodgrains Control Order passed in May 1942, which prevented the movement of grains between provinces. As the tragic consequences of wartime regulations like these grew clear through news of Bengal's suffering, Bombay's citizens appealed for more substantive support than the city's ineffectual grain shops and their interminable lines could guarantee. The leadership of the Bombay Committee of the Communist Party had called for ration cards that would entitle bearers to a fixed quantity of grain based on the number of family members.[4] The All Indian Muslim Chamber of Commerce and Industry joined the call, followed by the city's butchers, who threatened to halt the city's supply of meat if ration cards were not issued.[5]

City officials and commercial groups collaborated on Bombay's first rationing scheme. Shops selected by the Bombay Grain Dealers' Association, the Muslim Grain Merchants' Association, and an Ismaili merchant association would dole out grain alongside stores run by cooperative organizations and "communal and public institutions." Industrial workers were asked to pick up their increased rations at their mills, railway stations, and factories, though these workers petitioned for a provision to pick up their grains closer to home. By November, one of Bombay's English representatives in the Central Legislative Assembly could contend, if aspirationally, that "the coolies employed by my company, my own personal servants, my co-Directors,

---

[2] On provincial rationing undertakings, see *A Short Memorandum on Food Control during the War in Bihar* (Patna: Government of Bihar, 1944); Henry Knight, *Food Administration in India, 1939–1947* (Palo Alto: Stanford University Press, 1954); Patvardhan, *Food Control in Bombay Province, 1939–1949*; Debidas Ray, *Food Administration in East India: 1939–54* (Santiniketan: Agro-Economic Research Centre, Visva-Bharati, 1958); and Sudhir Kumar Rudra, *Rationing of Foodgrains in the United Provinces during World War II*, Department of Economics and Statistics, U.P. Bulletin 4 (Allahabad: United Provinces Department of Economics and Statistics, 1946).
[3] "Final Touches to Rationing Plans," *Times of India*, March 4, 1943.
[4] "Food Committees," *Times of India*, January 2, 1943.
[5] "City Butchers on Strike: Demand for Grain Shops," *Times of India*, January 9, 1943.

122 Hungry Nation

myself and my staff eat sugar and grain all purchased from precisely the same source."[6]

As Calcutta starved, Bombay's rationing encouraged those advocating for greater government intervention in food markets. Concerned administrators urged New Delhi to follow the lead of Bombay and smaller towns which had undertaken pilot rationing schemes. Srischandra Nandy, Maharaja of Cossimbazar, used his bully pulpit as an independent MLA to ask the central government to "inspire public confidence and enthusiasm by assuming full responsibility for distribution of foodstuffs through rationing."[7] Theodore Gregory, economic advisor to the government of India, echoed the call for rationing across India in his capacity as chair of the June 1943 Foodgrains Policy Committee.[8]

Others objected to what they perceived as government meddling. The British Indian Association, a group of landlords and industrialists, suggested that the Indian producer, "unhampered by the spirit of sacrifices for collective interests," would ultimately baffle "any scheme of supply of sufficient food stuffs."[9] In September, a letter was intercepted in Quetta on its way from Kaniguram, the stronghold of the Pushtun Burki tribe. "The government," Mullah Fazl Din had written to an associate in Baluchistan, "now tells us to buy sugar and tea with permits. I say that nothing should be controlled for the [members of our clan], whether it is sugar or tea or any other thing."[10]

Protests like these did not halt the advance of rationing schemes: by July, the project of controlling food in India's towns and cities had begun in earnest. New Delhi recruited W.H. Kirby, a former Karachi grain merchant turned rationing advisor in Britain, to head India's own efforts. Kirby undertook an exploratory tour of all existing rationing systems, and recommended that India's government implement a "comprehensive, efficient, coupon/card food rationing scheme," undertaken in tandem with full food control, even if insecure supplies meant that implementation would be difficult.[11] Against the backdrop of a worsening situation in Bengal, the first standard manual for food control and rationing was published in 1944, with the aim of securing "the conservation of stocks,

---

[6] Partha Sarathi Gupta, ed., "Motion Regarding the Food Situation – Debate in the Central Legislative Assembly – November 1943," in *Towards Freedom 1943–1944, Part II* (New Delhi: Indian Council of Historical Research, 1997), 1908–1955.

[7] Srischandra Nandy, *Rationale of Food Crisis: A Plea for Rationing* (Calcutta: Cossimbazar House, 1943).

[8] Gregory, *Report of the Foodgrains Policy Committee, 1943*.

[9] P.N. Singh Roy, *Food Policy in India* (Calcutta: British Indian Association, 1943).

[10] "Intercept of Letter from Quetta," 1943, External Affairs – Frontier – 648-F, 1943, NAI.

[11] W.H. Kirby, "Report on Food Rationing in India," July 25, 1943, IOR/L/E/8/7236.

The Common Hunger of the Country

the creation of confidence by the assurance of regular supplies, the enabling of all sections of the people to obtain their essential foods at reasonable controlled prices, and the elimination of privilege for the wealthy or unscrupulous."[12]

Skeptical onlookers worried that the process of implementation would be hampered by shopkeepers' and traders' footdragging and poor management. All India Trade Union Congress leader B.T. Ranadive assailed shops which had been "farmed out to dishonest individuals who whisk away the meagre supplies into the black market."[13] Kirby fretted privately about provinces where the will to implement seemed to be lacking, the general standard of licensed shopkeepers was low, and quality of available foodgrains quite poor.[14] There was reason to worry: Bombay's *Free Press Journal* lambasted the unhusked barley appearing in that city's wheat rations, and the *Eastern Economist* took note of the "chaff, bran, stones, dirt or even injurious matter, such as glass" appearing in Delhi's rations, declaring them routinely "unfit for human consumption."[15]

Administrators nonetheless touted the sprawling food control infrastructure taking shape across the country. In April 1944, Kirby spoke on the BBC, declaring that "the fundamental principles governing food rationing in India are the same as for any country – namely that rationing provides a yardstick for measuring consumption, and guarantees an equal quantity of essential foods in short supply to everyone, at a controlled price which everyone should be able to afford."[16] The villain in Kirby's story was the Indian food trader. When the government enacted a Price Control Order, Kirby suggested,

the goods immediately disappear. [But] who makes them disappear? Not the Government, not the consumer, but that type of merchant whose object in life is to attempt to profit by the misfortunes of others. In a food rationing scheme such malpractices will cease, and profiteers will be dealt with in a manner commensurate with their crimes against their fellow beings.

Posters in Indian towns and cities echoed Kirby's suspicion, urging citizens to "act as an inspector" and turn in dealers who overcharged,

---

[12] *A Manual on the Organisation of Food Control and Rationing* (Simla: Government of India Press, 1944), 1.

[13] Ranadive, *Food in Bombay Province*.

[14] W.H. Kirby, letter to R.H. Hutchings, March 31, 1944, IOR/L/E/8/7236.

[15] "In Defence of the Wild Grass-Seed"; "Rationing and Quality Standards," *Eastern Economist*, September 8, 1944.

[16] W.H. Kirby, "Broadcast Talk on Food Control and Rationing in India," April 1944, IOR/L/I/1/1103.

124 Hungry Nation

refused to sell, or refused to give a receipt.[17] More prosaically, an Indian Civil Service administrator delivered five All India Radio addresses from Lucknow on the use of the rationing card, ostensibly motivated by "recently having to initiate my wife into the mysteries of total rationing of foodgrains."[18]

In January 1945, Aubrey Dibdin of the India Office's Economic and Overseas Department was sent on a tour to evaluate the implementation of rationing and food control in India.[19] Landing in Karachi, Dibdin marveled at the quantity of rations available to the consumer; in Bombay, he praised the children sent to pick up rations from "girl and women clerks" overseeing massive card indices. In India's southwest, Dibdin watched children traveling with brass pots, coconut shells, and repurposed fruit tins to collect grains, milk, tapioca, and plantains; in neighboring Madras, village officers made ad hoc assessments of community needs. The undertaking was "grubby and does not show well in the shop window," Dibdin concluded, "but the whole immense machinery works."

That immense machinery was not, however, working everywhere. On the morning of August 25, 1946, life in the town of Karnal, 80 miles from Delhi, ground to a standstill. A *hartal* had been called the day prior, and as day broke, the stores and offices of this prosperous agricultural town in the Punjab remained shuttered. A 6000-person strike in a town of 25,000 was "unprecedented in the history of the town for the last 25 years," even in the tumultuous years of war and anti-colonial agitation.[20] "All persons young and old," a scribe wrote, "irrespective of caste, color, and creed," had come together for a single cause: the introduction of wheat rationing in the Punjab needed to be called off.

Even Karnal's women had come out to protest the odious plan: collectors would soon confiscate all but a six-week supply of wheat, doling out ration cards which could be presented for fixed quantities of grain. The scheme represented an inexcusable incursion on the economic life of the village. It had been acceptable to ration sugar, kerosene, oil, and cloth. But this was Karnal's staple grain, and soon, farmers would have to "go begging for bad and mixed wheat from month to month." These

---

[17] "Instructions for the Enforcement of the Hoarding and Profiteering Prevention Ordinance, 1943," 1943, Purshottamdas Thakurdas papers, folder 294, NMML.

[18] J.D. Banks, "Control Measures" (Lucknow, December 28, 1945), "Control Measures" (Lucknow, January 31, 1946), "Control Measures" (Lucknow, February 25, 1946), "Your Ration Card" (Lucknow, August 19, 1946), and "Food Shortage and Rationing" (Lucknow, December 23, 1946), MSS Eur D919.

[19] Dibdin, "Diary of a Tour of Inspection of Food Supplies and Rationing in India."

[20] "Deputation of Residents of Karnal to the Food Minister," 1946, Food – Rationing – RT-1032/7/1946, NAI.

The Common Hunger of the Country 125

agriculturalists would have been happy, they declared, to sell grain to hungry Bengal at a cut rate, but the government's plan was profiteering plain and simple. "Grain," the scribe recorded, "can be procured more by the good will and cooperation of the people than by the introduction of wheat rationing in the teeth of public opposition."

When the meeting ended, those few Karnal residents who could sign their name did so. Those who could not dipped their thumbs in a pot of ink, rolling prints on threadbare paper. Six thousand men and women, Hindus, Muslims, and some Christians, left a hundred pages of thumbprints, before addressing the petition to Food Minister Rajendra Prasad, soon to become India's president, and sending it to his office in Delhi.

Freedom was nearing – but India's godowns were nearly as depleted as her balance sheets, and the ascendant nationalist government was doubling down upon efforts to control the food economy. The promise of a ration card had been a heady inducement to India's urban poor. Yet the tangle of restrictions and forms and lines that ensued was loathsome to other citizens, who chafed and petitioned for the dismantling of food control. "Controls," the *Eastern Economist* sympathized in October 1945, "are at best necessary evils, and they become mere atrocities once the emergency which justified them has ceased to exist."[21]

In their last days in office, jittery about what had transpired in Bengal and what might occur after their departure, India's administrators were insistent that controls continue, even when supplies could not be assured.[22] "Price control, procurement, and rationing represent facets of a single policy," W.H. Kirby averred in October 1945. "To decontrol until visible supplies are available – and are known to be available by the public as a whole – is to court disaster."[23] This sort of disaster would be even more damning were it to transpire as Indian representatives were clamoring for food assistance overseas.[24] Despite food control's unpopularity among traders, farmers, and the middle classes, a reduction of rationing commitments would court political disaster. Citizens rebelled when rations were padded with unpopular grains.[25] And laborers showed no eagerness to give up rations: in March 1946, 20,000 electric, mill,

[21] *Eastern Economist*, August 24, 1945.
[22] "Policy of Agriculture and Food."
[23] Bureau of Public Information, Government of India, "Necessity for Food Control Measures," October 5, 1945, IOR/L/E/8/7236.
[24] Information Services, Government of India, "India's Appeal to USA"; Press Information Bureau, Government of India, "India Not Getting Her Due Share of Allocations," May 23, 1946, IOR/L/I/1/1104.
[25] "Inclusion of Millets, Gram and Maize in the Cereal Group Rations."

126   Hungry Nation

coal, and railway workers in Calcutta went on strike to protest a cut to their quantum.[26]

As nationalists took over India's provincial ministries, they stood to inherit one of the largest public administrations of any sort in the world. "No country in the world," Theodore Schultz wrote in the wake of a June visit to India, "with perhaps the exception of Russia, has gone so far in controlling basic food distribution."[27] Even as it vexed certain segments of the public, the rationing and food control regime – which provided grains to nearly 150 million of India's 400 million citizens – was the pride of many administrators.[28] "On the eve of Partition," a Punjabi Civil Service member would recall, "we had men in every market of Punjab." With every major town rationed, he contended, the food administration "was an organization that breathed. If you stabbed it in the belly, or even on the toe, it was adequately geared to react with both feeling and knowledge and did so with the whole body – like a single person."[29] S.K. Rudra, economic advisor to the United Provinces government, remembered in 1946 that when the idea of rationing grains had been proposed just four years earlier, it had been "somewhat of an academic idea." Yet now, a robust food control system had forced Indians, "physically and ideologically, [to] share the common hunger of the country."[30]

Rajendra Prasad, Food Minister in the interim government, defended the administration against petitions like that which had arrived from Karnal. He spoke in the Central Assembly in November 1946 over the cries of legislators who alleged mounting corruption and inedible supplies.[31] Yet the rationing system, he declared, would continue into independence, despite the hardship it caused certain communities. "Our people," Prasad declared, "are used to suffering and they know how to face such difficulties because they have done it in the past."

Those difficulties would continue as rations were slashed across India, and the Indian delegate to the International Emergency Food Council in Washington warned that Indians would soon "rebel" against a rationing system that provided inadequate supplies and restricted free market

---

[26] "One and a Half Lakh Workers Strike," *People's Age*, March 31, 1946.
[27] Chopra, *Evolution of Food Policy in India*, 49.
[28] Press Information Bureau, Government of India, "Extension of Rationing," November 1, 1946, IOR/L/I/1/1104. Chopra, *Evolution of Food Policy in India*, 47, gives a slightly lower estimate of 54 million under statutory rationing and 90 million under other forms of public distribution.
[29] Chopra, *Evolution of Food Policy in India*, 81.
[30] Rudra, *Rationing of Foodgrains in the United Provinces*.
[31] Press Information Bureau, Government of India, "Dr. Rajendra Prasad's Speech in the Central Assembly," November 4, 1946, IOR/L/I/1/1104.

The Common Hunger of the Country   127

purchases.[32] Administrators debated proposals for how to ensure that civil servants would continue to receive their promised rations during partition, worried that a government unable to feed its own employees would be able to do little else.[33] And when independence and partition came at the stroke of midnight on August 15, 1947, food riots broke out across the country, and the Department of Information and Broadcasting urged bureaucrats to stick to the theme that "India's political freedom must not be allowed to prove illusory by a complete collapse on her food front."[34]

Mohandas Gandhi sat on the cool stone floor where his body would soon lie in state. The Mahatma had called Keralan economist John Mathai to the palatial Birla House for a meeting in late 1947, asking Mathai and a colleague to explain the economic logic behind food controls. Gandhi was uninterested, however, in hearing them out. He interrupted the two men to expound for a half hour on his moral case against food regulation, "putting out with much earnestness the dishonesty, corruption and greed which control had brought about and his determination to do everything in his power to put a stop to it."[35]

Now a renunciant from public life, Gandhi spent his final living months inveighing against food control, inviting experts to make their case at prayer meetings before bludgeoning them into silence.[36] "When this control is removed," Gandhi proclaimed at one gathering, "the nation will breathe free. It will have the right to make mistakes."[37] Food controls, the Mahatma contended in a November 1947 meeting, "give rise to fraud, suppression of truth, intensification of the black-market and to artificial scarcity. [It] unmans the people and deprives them of initiative; it undoes the teaching of self-help they have been learning for a generation."[38] Gandhi contended that if control were removed, India's shortage would end within twenty-four hours, since housewives would not allow "a single grain to be spoiled and wasted" under free trade.[39] Now, Gandhi threw his weight behind the recommendations of the Foodgrains Policy Committee. Chaired by financier Purshottamdas Thakurdas, packed with industrialists, and urged by the Indian Merchants' Chamber

---

[32] "Indian Delegate Warns IEFC."
[33] "Opening of Emergency Food Ration Shops," October 1947, Food – Rationing – RT-1020/66/1947, NAI.
[34] Department of Information and Broadcasting, Government of India, "Guidance for Food Publicity."
[35] Agrawal, *Price Controls in India since 1947*, 22.
[36] Chopra, *Evolution of Food Policy in India*, 55.
[37] Mohandas K. Gandhi, *Harijan*, December 21, 1947, 477.
[38] Agrawal, *Price Controls in India since 1947*, 22.
[39] Mohandas K. Gandhi, *Food Shortage and Agriculture* (Ahmedabad: Navajivan Publishing House, 1949), 49, 55.

128   Hungry Nation

to allow private trade "to play their proper role in this sphere of activities," the Committee urged New Delhi to remove controls and rationing immediately.[40]

Decontrol flew in the face of most economic counsel. The harvest of 1946 had been poor, the nation was facing an 800,000 ton deficit, and hoarding was on the rise.[41] A British commercial observer in Delhi noted widespread dissatisfaction with controls but cautioned against their dismantling. "It is not clear," he wrote, "how you operate a system in which food is imported by Central Government but rationing is abandoned."[42] Hindi newspapers buzzed with rumors that decontrol was imminent, yet their prediction of a new policy by the end of 1948 was a year off.[43] In December 1947, Rajendra Prasad spoke in Parliament to announce the withdrawal of "all official rationing and control schemes as soon as might be possible." Corruption, black-marketing, and a flowering of fake ration cards, he declared, had hastened this day – but if the experiment failed, the food administration would double down and "eliminate trade altogether."[44]

Food administrators, labor activists, and those reliant upon rations were aghast. A debate on decontrol at Bombay University, presided over by the mayor, descended into a clash between trade unionists and businessmen.[45] The All India Trade Union Congress filled a Bombay *maidan* with protesters to mark an "Anti-Decontrol Day," and the president of the local unit asserted that removing controls to root out corruption was "like setting a house on fire because rats were a nuisance inside the house."[46] The All India Women's Conference's Madras chapter passed a resolution condemning the decision, and the sober *Tata Quarterly* warned that, should another famine break out, the government would be guilty of having dismantled the administration needed to combat it.[47] Bombay's former Civil Supplies Commissioner, A.D. Gorwala, remembered the days of endless queues before rationing, "when stocks poured into shops never seemed to be able to meet the demand, when the atmosphere was full of tumult and unrest and policemen with *lathis* could scarcely keep

---

[40] A.C. Ramalingam, letter to Secretary, Foodgrains Policy Committee, October 15, 1947, Indian Merchants' Chamber, Bombay papers, folder 800, NMML.

[41] B.R. Tomlinson, *The Economy of Modern India, 1860–1970* (Cambridge: Cambridge University Press, 1993), 162.

[42] L.D. Walsh Atkins, letter to N.E. Young, December 11, 1947, IOR/L/E/8/7236.

[43] "AICC Proposal for Immediate Lifting of Controls," *Vartman*, November 18, 1947; "All Control to Be Lifted by End of 1948," *Vartman*, November 24, 1947.

[44] Terence Shone, "India's Revised Food Policy," December 11, 1947, IOR/L/E/8/7236.

[45] "Decontrol Policy Attacked in Bombay," *Times of India*, December 20, 1947.

[46] "Anti-Decontrol Day in City," *Times of India*, January 5, 1948.

[47] "Women in Conference," *Times of India*, January 3, 1948; *Tata Quarterly*, January 1948.

The Common Hunger of the Country 129

the peace, when reports used to come in of the looting of *mofussil* grain shops." No one, he declared, "should want to take the risk of seeing such days again."[48]

Yet the decision to decontrol was a rare glimmer of hope for Gandhi in the despondent weeks before his death. As decontrol was announced, the Mahatma urged growers and traders to "disarm the suspicion" that the decision would lead to skyrocketing prices.[49] Hindi papers reported erroneously that he would leave his seclusion in Birla House to tour Kanpur, Calcutta, and Bombay to make the case against hoarding in person.[50] In January, he scolded a friend who had expressed concern over black-marketing in the pages of *Harijan*. "You still write as if you had a slave mind," Gandhi snapped. "The shooting up of prices by reason of decontrol does not frighten me. If we have many Sharks and we do not know how to combat them, we shall deserve to be eaten up by them."[51] Nineteen days later, Gandhi was assassinated on the grounds of Birla House.

Yet Gandhi's imprimatur had cheered the middle-class consumers who reveled in the felt freedoms of decontrol. "We are happy," a Gujarati villager wrote, "that controls have gone, and bless Mahatma Gandhi for his courage in demanding it from Government. May the Rationing Department, with all its files, circulars, and statistics, rest in peace."[52] In its publicity campaigns, New Delhi concurred: a celebratory pamphlet issued on the first anniversary of independence lauded Gandhi's "ceaseless campaign against food controls, and his persistent efforts to instill in us the lesson of self-reliance in food." With that lesson learned, it had been possible to dismantle restrictions on food. "War against food scarcity is still on," the pamphlet concluded, "but there cannot be a return to the old tactics of rigid control."[53]

One resident of the Maharashtrian town of Dombivli was less certain.[54] Throughout the spring, each time he visited a store, shopkeepers warned C.E. Mathai to expect higher rice prices. He recalled spending 25 rupees a month for his family of five during rationing. But three months into decontrol, his monthly bill was more than twice that. Mathai's was not the only food bill inching upwards: in deficit areas, prices of wheat and

---

[48] A.D. Gorwala, "Dangers of Food Derationing," *Times of India*, January 11, 1948.
[49] Mohandas K. Gandhi, *Harijan*, November 30, 1947.
[50] "Gandhi to Visit Kanpur to Stop Black-Marketing," *Vartman*, December 11, 1947.
[51] Mohandas K. Gandhi, *Harijan*, January 11, 1948.
[52] J.G. Christian, "Decontrol," *Times of India*, January 17, 1948.
[53] Press Information Bureau, Government of India, "Political Freedom and Battle against Hunger / Planned Withdrawal from Controls / Difficulties of Transition Period."
[54] C.E. Mathai, "Decontrol," *Times of India*, April 8, 1948.

rice had soared to nearly 250 percent of their controlled prices.[55] The International Monetary Fund, surveying the rising costs of foodgrains that summer, urged India to change course.[56] It had not even been a year since decontrol, but individual provinces began to act: Uttar Pradesh was the first to announce, in August, that it was bringing back controls.[57] New Delhi followed suit the following month: an anti-inflationary committee debated the merits of reintroducing rationing and control before a conference of provincial Food Ministers overwhelmingly agreed upon it.[58] It was a dramatic volte-face from what one agricultural economist called "the most disastrous and costly experiment" in independent India's short history.[59]

The reconstituted food administration was notably more restrictive than its predecessor, assuming full control over major foodgrains, preventing their movement in between provinces, and requiring licenses for any dealing in food.[60] The decontrol experiment had been short-lived, but it had been damning enough for the government to now thoroughly repudiate. The Press Information Bureau issued detailed directions for how provinces might best publicize a swift policy reversal, offering assistance to the Food Ministry in staging publicity films.[61] "All controls," a Food Ministry official declared on All India Radio in May 1949, "are annoying. Food controls annoy all the more, as food is something which touches us very intimately. Control on food walks right into the home and affects our life from day to day – in fact twice or thrice a day."[62] But citizens would need only to remember those skyrocketing prices to steady themselves. Controls, he concluded, "must be put up with as the soldier puts up with the discipline of the Army. To my mind this is a really small price to pay for our economic freedom."

R.L. Gupta's calm assurances on All India Radio belied the chaos of a sprawling system chugging back to life. As the first province to institute rationing six years earlier, Bombay had the thickest network of

---

[55] Agrawal, *Price Controls in India since 1947*, 24; see also Tomlinson, *The Economy of Modern India, 1860–1970*, 163.
[56] J.J. Anjaria, "A Review of Wartime Price Controls in India and the Consequences of Recent Decontrol," May 31, 1948, RD-634, International Monetary Fund.
[57] "UP Returns to Food Control," *Eastern Economist*, August 6, 1948, 6.
[58] "Reimposition of Food Control," *Times of India*, September 13, 1948; Ministry of Food, Government of India, letter 619/34.
[59] Sovani, *Post War Inflation in India: A Survey*, 54.
[60] Bhatia, *India's Food Problem*, 39.
[61] Ministry of Information and Broadcasting, Government of India, "Directive on Food Publicity."
[62] Press Information Bureau, Government of India, "Food Secretary's Broadcast on Ministry's Policy," May 9, 1949, IOR/L/E/8/7230.

The Common Hunger of the Country 131

administrators and dealers to rely upon. Provincial administrators had moved slowly to implement decontrol in the first place, asking decommissioned collectors to report on stocks, prices, health, and migration.[63] As prices had soared, old ration shops had been turned into relief shops. When the restoration of food control was announced, these shops were converted into formal rationing outlets once again. Provincial officials prohibited the movement of grain between village, banned the sale of grain to anyone but government agents, and gave collectors the authority to search homes and shops for hoarded grains. Yet even Bombay's eager controllers could not ferret out enough grain to meet rationing requirements. The situation was far direr elsewhere in provinces where administrators lacked the will to recontrol.

The central government's new plan called for a major expansion of rationing commitments.[64] New Delhi suggested the convening of "local advisory committees" to give rationing shops a varnish of popular participation. But these committees were likely never constituted, and citizens griped over how regulations hampered trade and did little to lessen pangs of hunger. In Madhya Pradesh, a Ministry of Food official noticed that there was "really no strict enforcement of rationing," while in Punjab, a coterie of frustrated food merchants complained that not a single dealer among them had been able to get the interstate export permit needed to ship chickpeas to the South.[65] In Delhi, *Eastern Economist* staff calculated the costs of food rationing and control with alarm, noting that this ineffectual undertaking represented the fourth largest item of national expenditure.[66] "There is point," they concluded, "in guaranteeing to the poor man the rationed allowance of grain at a controlled price so as to make him independent of the extractions of unscrupulous dealers. We see little point, however, in making the occasion one for charity on a petty scale which does him little good, but collectively does us plenty of harm."

In public, administrators doubled down on the contention that there was no alternative to food control. India's Constitution, ratified in 1951, reaffirmed the aspiration of becoming a "welfare state," and the draft First Five-Year Plan affirmed that "the equitable distribution of foodgrains

---

[63] Patvardhan, *Food Control in Bombay Province, 1939–1949*, 136.
[64] P.C. Bansil, *India's Food Resources and Population: A Historical and Analytical Study* (Bombay: Vora & Co., 1958), 47.
[65] S.K. Sen, letter to the Director of Food Supplies, Madhya Bharat Government, June 25, 1948, Ministry of States – Labour & Agriculture – 1(58)-L, 1949 (Secret), NAI; Indian Merchants' Chamber, Bombay, "Movement of Bengal Gram," 1948, Indian Merchants' Chamber, Bombay papers, folder 782, NMML.
[66] "The High Cost of India's Food Policy," *Eastern Economist*, March 4, 1949, 352–353.

132   Hungry Nation

among different sections of the population at reasonable prices" was to be "the Government's first duty in the economic field."[67] Referencing the 1948 decontrol fiasco, planners declared that there was "no room for any proposal or experiment which detracts from this responsibility or exposes the economy to risk or uncertainty."

There was much to worry about on the food front. The Grow More Food campaign was struggling, and India would soon find itself appealing for 2 million tons of American food aid. Even as they recognized continued public discontent, India's bureaucrats insisted throughout 1950 that rationing and control would continue. In a major speech on the food situation in late August, the Prime Minister declared that, in spite of complaints, there was no question of decontrol in any foreseeable future.[68] In December 1951, state food ministers meeting in Bombay declared that "any theoretical consideration of control or decontrol is out of question in the context of the present situation."[69] Visiting the Andhra Chamber of Commerce after it had petitioned for the abolition of controls, Food Minister K.M. Munshi rejected the notion outright. "I cannot for the life of me see how food control can be lifted at present," he declared. "I cannot envisage it without a shudder."[70]

Yet even amidst worsening shortages throughout 1950 and 1951, the mounting discontent was hard to ignore. Producers in Bombay state were refusing to sell to government collectors.[71] State administrators were complaining that imported grains were being regularly diverted, threatening to abandon controls unilaterally if supplies were not forthcoming.[72] By August 1950, Madras commissioners were reporting that food rationing had broken down completely in some districts, where villagers were surviving on tree bark and launching intermittent raids of depleted ration shops.[73] The Communist Party exhorted citizens to "unearth and seize the hoards" held at rationing depots, taking what was rightfully theirs from a government whose leaders had "no right to exist if they cannot supply to the starving people."[74] Defending controls at a

---

[67] Planning Commission, Government of India, *The First Five-Year Plan: A Draft Outline*, 69.
[68] Office of the Senior United Kingdom Trade Commissioner, note to Under Secretary, Commercial Relations and Exports Department, Board of Trade.
[69] "Food Policy and Basic Plan for 1951," 1951, Agriculture – Basic Plan – BP-301(1)/51, NAI.
[70] "Food Decontrol May Lead to Inflation," *Times of India*, July 7, 1950.
[71] "Food Controls in Bombay: No Change Likely," *Times of India*, February 28, 1950.
[72] UK High Commissioner in India, opdom #3, February 16, 1950, IOR/L/E/8/7227.
[73] "Madras Fortnightly Report #19/50," September 1950, IOR/L/E/8/7230.
[74] Communist Party of India, "Catastrophic Food Situation and Our Tasks."

The Common Hunger of the Country 133

meeting of Bihari peasants in February 1951, Rajendra Prasad watched in horror as the meeting descended into a stampede.[75]

Underneath a patina of unity, India's bureaucracy was riven by dissent. The Foodgrains Procurement Committee that met in 1950 worried that inconsistent implementation and sudden reversals had severely hampered efforts to regulate the food economy. India's food administrators, the Committee summarized, "do not know exactly what they wish to achieve. It is necessary to remedy this state of affairs. Whether it is control or decontrol, partial or whole, this must be based on a plan understood, accepted and enforced throughout the country."[76] R.P. Noronha, a Madhya Pradesh civil servant with vast experience in food administration, appended a litany of objections to the report, suggesting that whatever the economic merits of control, they were less important than the political implications of extending control in the face of popular unease. "Intensification of controls," he wrote,

particularly in self-sufficient or surplus areas, leads to a progressive stiffening of opposition. It is all very well to say that politics should be kept aloof from food, but in a democracy politics cannot be kept aloof from any subject that affects the interests of the people. If the people oppose a particular course of action, that course must ultimately fail. [C]onsent to stringent measures can be obtained in times of stress and for temporary periods; it can never be obtained indefinitely.[77]

Soon, one of Nehru's own ministers would withdraw his own consent. On June 6, 1952, C. Rajagopalachari, then Chief Minister of Madras, addressed the struggling farmers and frustrated citizens of his state on All India Radio.[78] "You may now take your grains to any place, anywhere," the seventy-four-year-old Congressman proclaimed, "and sell it as you like to anyone, anywhere – and no one shall interfere with you in any way. There is no need to hide and walk under cover, as if you did not own what you possessed. You are free and can dispose, as you choose, of what is yours." Farmers and consumers in Madras would henceforth enjoy full freedom of movement and trade, and the state would transform ration shops into "fair price shops," while holding on to the half-million tons of rice in its supply chain as an emergency buffer. At a press conference the day afterwards, Rajagopalachari touted the benefits to production and commerce that his decision would herald.[79] Free "from the harassments of control," farmers would produce more and consumers would flock

[75] "Dr. Prasad Defends Food Controls," *Times of India*, February 27, 1951.
[76] Rao, *Report of the Foodgrains Procurement Committee, 1950.*
[77] Chopra, *Evolution of Food Policy in India*, 156–160.
[78] "Statutory Rationing in Madras Ends," *Times of India*, June 7, 1952.
[79] "Decontrol Based on Intuition," *Times of India*, June 8, 1952.

Figure 7 Customers purchase wheat at a "fair price shop" in Delhi, 1959. (Credit: Photo Division, Ministry of Information and Broadcasting, Government of India)

to free market grain purchases, eventually obviating the new fair price shops. Hotels and restaurants, too, would be free to dispense of the burdensome restrictions on what and how much could be served and when. "Everything," Rajagopalachari declared, "will be unlimited hereafter."

In Delhi, Nehru fumed at Rajagopalachari's insubordination. The Prime Minister tried to make the best of matters in a letter to N.V. Gadgil, the Minister of Public Works.[80] "We have not changed our basic policy of controls at all," he deadpanned. "Rajaji has rather emphasized one aspect of it, while we would have liked some other aspects to be emphasized."

Tussles between administrators and center-state wrangling would soon prove less important than two sprawling pieces of legislation that hovered over the lives of traders and consumers. In 1955 and 1956, struggling to fill warehouses, New Delhi extended one piece of domestic food legislation and negotiated another international agreement that would weigh heavily upon merchants and citizens. The first was the Essential

---

[80] Jawaharlal Nehru, letter to N.V. Gadgil, June 9, 1954, in *SWJN* vol. 18, 68–69.

The Common Hunger of the Country 135

Commodities Act, a revived wartime statute that gave the central government a new tool for the regulation of food markets.[81] The second was Public Law 480, the "food for peace" deal signed with the United States that ensured that grain depots and fair price shops would be stocked with grain from the American Midwest. In tandem, these two acts worked to thwart hoarders and stave off shortages, but frustrated traders who asked what role commerce was to play in the public life of a free nation.

In the midst of war, India's Central Legislature had pushed through the Defense of India Act, with a critical subsection giving the state widespread "control in respect of certain commodities essential for human beings." In 1946, this authority over the production, transportation, and distribution of those commodities was extended as the Essential Supplies (Temporary Powers) Ordinance. When these powers were set to lapse in 1955, New Delhi affirmed them on a permanent basis as the Essential Committees Act. Food was not the only commodity controlled by the legislation – cattle fodder, coal, automotive parts, textiles, drugs, iron, steel, paper, and petroleum were similarly regulated – but the preponderance of cases brought under the Act were related to the exchange of foodstuffs. Under the Act, the central government could require the licensing of food shops or producers, force fallow land to be brought under cultivation, prevent food from being moved across state lines or overseas, and compel individuals to dislodge their stocks.[82]

Citizens had often challenged the temporary iteration of the Ordinance, occasionally prevailing against the state. In 1954, India's Supreme Court heard the appeal case of Nath Mal and Mitha Mal, two licensed grain dealers whose millet had been commandeered, with only half the market rate paid as restitution.[83] Nath and Mal argued that this seizure represented a violation of the right "to practice any profession, or to carry on any occupation, trade or business," and the Court concurred. "No dealer," Chief Justice Mehar Chand Mahajan wrote, "will be prepared to buy foodgrains at the market price when he knows that he is exposed to the risk of his stocks being freezed any moment." Nath and Mal's victory

[81] On the regulation of markets viz the Act, see Rohit De, "'Commodities Must Be Controlled': Economic Crimes and Market Discipline in India (1939–1955)," *International Journal of Law in Context* 10, no. 3 (September 2014): 277–294. See also M.S. Ansari, R.P. Kataria, and S.K.A. Naqvi, *M.S. Ansari's Commentary on the Essential Commodities Act, 1955* (Jodhpur: Unique Law Publishers, 2011); and Sarjoo Prasad et al., *Sarjoo Prasad's Commentaries on Essential Commodities Act, 1955* (Allahabad: Law Publishers, 1980).
[82] See Lawrence F. Ebb's essay on comparative interstate commerce legislation, "Interstate Barriers in India and American Constitutional Experience," *Stanford Law Review* 11, no. 1 (1958): 37–93.
[83] G. Hasan, *State of Rajasthan vs. Nath Mal and Mitha Mal* (Supreme Court of India 1954).

136 Hungry Nation

was an uncommon one: more often, courts affirmed the state's claim to broaden powers in the interests of rooting out the hoarder and the black marketeer, who, according to two experts on the Act, should be "considered an enemy No. 1 who insidiously stabs his country-men in the back." The state was on the side of right, Bhawani Lal and Harbans Lal Mital declared, to go after these "flinty-hearted, short-sighted worshippers of Mammon [who] want to make extra profits at the expense of their country, at a time when it is faced with a grave situation."[84]

In April 1956, a year after the passage of the Essential Commodities Act on a permanent basis, New Delhi signed its first agreement with the United States under the two-year-old Agricultural Trade Development and Assistance Act, more popularly known as Public Law 480. India's administrators had signed the three-year agreement for 3.1 million tons of wheat and 190,000 tons of rice with the aim of building up a strong buffer stock: in Parliament, India's new food minister A.P. Jain proudly trumpeted his intent to build a reserve of a million tons of wheat and rice alike.[85] Yet no such buffer materialized, and while the 63.41 million tons of wheat that India would import under the aegis of P.L. 480 over the next fifteen years kept shops stocked, it simultaneously hampered agricultural production and handcuffed India to American foreign policy aims.[86]

P.L. 480 made it possible for Nehru to avoid the political costs of extracting food from India's reluctant peasants, but the arrangement masked real deficits: the 1966 Foodgrains Policy would later conclude that imports "cloak[ed] a situation that was essentially grave."[87] The legislation stoked accusations from left and right that India was being held hostage to American interests. "Washington," an Indian Communist would allege in 1965, "is using food as an additional lever to pressurize us into surrendering Kashmir to Pakistan."[88] It opened up avenues for pork barrel legislation like the import of 30,000 tons of American maize for the Indian starch industry.[89] It would ultimately do little to ameliorate India's food deficits,

---

[84] Bhawani Lal and Harbans Lal Mital, *The Law of Essential Supplies* (New Delhi: Federal Law Depot, 1951), introduction.

[85] "Nation's Food Situation Described," *US Foreign Broadcast Information Service Daily Reports*, April 11, 1956.

[86] B.R. Shenoy, *P.L. 480 Aid and India's Food Problem* (New Delhi: Affiliated East-West Press, 1974), 35.

[87] *Report of the Foodgrains Policy Committee, 1966* (New Delhi: Ministry of Food and Agriculture and Ministry of Community Development and Cooperation, Government of India, 1966).

[88] S.C. Gupta, *Freedom from Foreign Food: Pernicious Effects of PL480* (New Delhi: Blitz National Forum, 1965), 5.

[89] "Import of 30 Thousand Tons of Maize from USA under PL480," July 1959, Food – Basic Plan – 135(37)/59-BP.III, NAI.

The Common Hunger of the Country

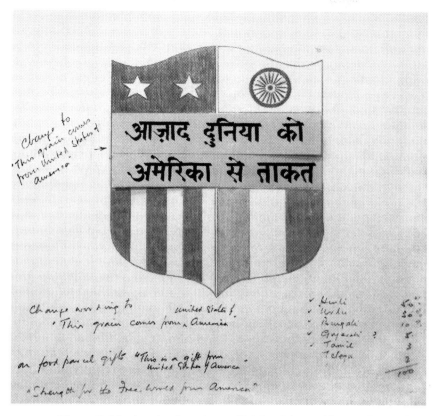

Figure 8 Mockup by American officials of the emblem to be used on grains distributed in India under Public Law 480. In the margins, an official has put forth different options and has given suggested breakdowns of the languages in which this emblem should be printed. The Hindi version reads "Strength from America to the Free World." (Credit: United States National Archives, College Park, Maryland)

and from its passage, it convinced Indian merchants and traders of the state's insistence upon stamping out commercial life.[90]

Since the Second World War, Indian grain traders had worried that the state would move to take over the whole of the food trade. There was merit to their fears: proposals had swirled as early as 1944 that the state should either compete with wholesalers to drive down prices, or

[90] Shenoy, *P.L. 480 Aid and India's Food Problem*, 245–246.

138   Hungry Nation

"socialize" the trade altogether.[91] In 1955, the Calcutta Employers' Association published a booklet detailing and then assailing state experiments in foodgrains trading, concluding that state efforts were twice as wasteful and half as efficient as those of the private sector.[92]

By early 1957, foodgrain traders and dealers had some cause for worry. P.C. Mahalanobis, architect of India's Second Five-Year Plan, was eager to see the trade nationalized in order to move savings in agriculture to other purposes.[93] By contrast, the new Food Minister, A.P. Jain, was no proponent of state trading: his political base was comprised of Uttar Pradesh's landlords and traders, and Jain watched in exasperation as Indian bureaucrats returned from China with breathless reports of what agricultural collectivization could allegedly achieve.[94] Yet three years into his tenure, Jain learned that nearly all of the P.L. 480 imports were needed for current consumption, rather than building up his proposed buffer stock.[95] "It does seem a cruel joke," the *Economic Weekly* opined, "to talk about a welfare state, when men cannot buy food because they have not the money to pay for it."[96]

Three groups met to propose measures to combat the shortages. The National Development Council, steered by the Prime Minister, fielded multiple proposals, including C. Subramaniam's proposal for minimum prices to producers that he would resurrect as Agriculture Minister nearly a decade later.[97] Blocks away, the Planning Commission met in Yojana Bhavan to discuss similar proposals. Finally, Jain himself oversaw the deliberations of the Foodgrains Enquiry Committee. Concerned, the businessmen of the Indian Merchants' Chamber petitioned the Committee to resist the temptation to recontrol the food economy or enact state trading in foodgrains. India, the Chamber's Secretary reminded Committee members, had ample evidence "of the attendant evils and the distortion which the system of control is likely to give rise to in the economy."[98] The Planning Commission and most of the

---

[91] Natesan, *Scheme of Collective Effort.*

[92] *State Trading in Food* (Calcutta: Employers' Association, 1955).

[93] Ashutosh Varshney, *Democracy, Development, and the Countryside: Urban-Rural Struggles in India* (Cambridge: Cambridge University Press, 1998), 39.

[94] See Chapter 5.

[95] B.B. Ghosh, "Import of Wheat and Rice from USA," April 30, 1957, Food – Policy – FIMP-110/61/I/57, NAI.

[96] Flibbertigibbet, "Yield to the Night ... and Hear the Shriek of Hunger," *Economic Weekly,* September 14, 1957, 1179–1180.

[97] Jawaharlal Nehru, "Role of the National Development Council I," June 3, 1957, *SWJN* vol. 38, 49–53.

[98] Secretary, Indian Merchants' Chamber, Bombay, letter to Secretary of the Foodgrains Enquiry Committee, September 9, 1957, Indian Merchants' Chamber, Bombay papers, folder 790, NMML.

The Common Hunger of the Country

members of the Foodgrains Enquiry Committee were unmoved. "Until there is social control over the wholesale trade," the Committee's majority resolved, "we shall not be in a position to bring about stabilization of foodgrains prices. Our policy should therefore be that of progressive and planned socialization of the wholesale trade in foodgrains."[99]

Yet Jain, unwilling to antagonize his base in Uttar Pradesh and sympathetic to traders' interests elsewhere, resisted a proposal for a creation of a Foodgrains Stabilization Organization.[100] Jain directed his Food Ministry to undertake lesser measures, including the creation of self-sufficient food zones for the movement of rice and wheat and the supply of major population centers with imported grains. A large volume of commercial imports from Australia, and the first wheat surpluses arriving under P.L. 480 underwrote the distribution of wheat; rice procured from Burma, Cambodia, and Thailand went to consumers via a network of fair price shops, government-licensed foodgrain dealers, and cooperatives. At the end of the year, as foreign exchange dwindled, the Food Ministry began procuring on its own account, first in Andhra Pradesh, Mysore, and Orissa, and then in Punjab, Assam, and West Bengal.

Jain had contorted himself to placate traders, but merchants were nonetheless antagonized by these new strategies. The Bombay government's Food Advisory Committee found its year-end meetings flooded with foodgrain dealers seeking exemptions from the new restrictions on moving foodgrains into the city.[101] K.C. Jatia, President of the M.B. Flour Mills Association in Calcutta, declared that the restrictions on grain imports from the South had destroyed the city's flour milling business.[102] The Andhra Produce Exports Association beseeched its customers to "agitate with your provincial Government, individually as well as collectively, for the import of cheaper Andhra rice, which were [sic] hitherto imported in bulk" before the imposition of zonal restrictions.[103] And in December 1957, the Hotel Owners' Conference met in Bombay to protest new restrictions on rice dishes in restaurants.[104] "These restrictions,"

---

[99] Ministry of Food and Agriculture, Government of India, *Report of the Foodgrains Enquiry Committee, November 1957*, 12.

[100] Frankel, *India's Political Economy*, 143–147.

[101] "Minutes of First Meeting of the Food Advisory Committee," November 16, 1957, Indian Merchants' Chamber, Bombay papers, folder 791, NMML.

[102] "Speech of Shri K.C. Jatia, President of the M.B. Flour Mills Association," November 14, 1957, Food – Basic Plan – 105(95)/57-BP.III, NAI.

[103] Andhra Produce Exporters Association, Vijayavada, "Formation of Southern Zone for Rice," November 19, 1957, Indian Merchants' Chamber, Bombay papers, folder 790, NMML.

[104] "Resolutions Protesting Restrictions on the Service of Rice," December 27, 1957, Indian Merchants' Chamber, Bombay papers, folder 790, NMML.

140   Hungry Nation

a Poona restaurant owner declared, "will not only paralyze the catering trade but also deprive thousands and lakhs of homeless people in cities of their indispensable food being rice, as they are entirely dependent on the catering establishments for their meals."

Over the howls of traders, A.P. Jain would become a reluctant protagonist in another push for state trading. In November 1958, the Prime Minister listened to Finance Minister T.T. Krishnamachari warn the National Development Council that a reduction of the Second Five-Year Plan budget was inevitable, and that further deficit financing would be inadvisable unless there was an assurance of increased agricultural production and lower food prices.[105] Nehru, sensing an opportunity, suggested that the Council adopt the recent recommendations of the Planning Commission: an intensified push for agricultural cooperatives, and the undertaking of state trading in foodgrains.

India's left responded enthusiastically to the Council's two-stage plan, which called for the licensure and fixing of prices of all wholesale foodgrain dealers, followed by the establishment of a state-sponsored trading corporation. P.C. Joshi reminded the Communist Party that only land reform could truly solve India's food crisis, but he saw the plan for state trading as an essential move to "save the mass of poor people from the tyranny of ever-increasing food prices."[106] The Jana Sangh, with a growing base among urban merchants, objected vociferously, claiming that nationalization would put 30,000 wholesale and 3 million retail vendors out of business.[107] These considerations were all obviated by A.P. Jain's stonewalling: forced to propose the scheme in the Lok Sabha in April, the Minister then delayed and professed confusion about the workings of the plan – a move that the *Economic Weekly* equated with "extending an invitation to speculators to help themselves, and to the producers to hang on to their stock."[108] Unable to stomach a position so wholly offensive to his own beliefs about the market, A.P. Jain summarily tendered his resignation.

The push for state trading had failed, but the continuing restrictions on the movement and sale of grains continued to flummox merchants and mendicants alike. In June 1959, a frustrated renunciant from the town of Nashik wrote to the Ministry of Food and Agriculture to ask for

---

[105] Frankel, *India's Political Economy*, 171.

[106] P.C. Joshi, "Note on the Struggle for a Correct Food Policy," 1958, 1958.27A, P.C. Joshi Archives on Contemporary History.

[107] Bruce Desmond Graham, *Hindu Nationalism and Indian Politics: The Origins and Development of the Bharatiya Jana Sangh* (Cambridge: Cambridge University Press, 1990), 191.

[108] "Food Precept – and Practice," *Economic Weekly*, August 29, 1959, 1.

The Common Hunger of the Country 141

an exemption from the ban on the private transport of grains between states.[109] In his national preaching tours, Swami Sudarsanacharya Mahanth had secured a legion of pledges of rice from devotees, promising that he would use the grains to feed pilgrims at the Kumbh Mela pilgrimage in Allahabad. The officers reviewing the case wondered whether the pilgrims' expectation of *purya*, or religious merit which "will stand them in good stead when they leave this world for the next," was sufficient to permit the swami to transport 100 maunds of rice from Andhra Pradesh and 50 maunds of wheat from Rajasthan and Madhya Pradesh. Three months later, the head priest of the Shreshtha Seva Ashram wrote to the Ministry to ask for a similar exemption. Twice a year, he declared, "hundreds of Devotees come for spiritual elevation to mitigate their miseries and the sorrows of this worldly life," and all of them were to be fed simple meals made of ingredients donated by wealthier devotees. This practice was against the Ministry's restrictions, but the abbot asked for an exemption that would obviate the "great hardship [which] is experienced in coming out of this devotional need."

These holy men received exemptions, or referrals to local agencies. But as they chafed, they joined merchants and traders who continued to seethe at the suppression of trade. "We appreciate your agreement with America," the head of the Shree Laxmi Pulse Rice and Roller Flour Mills in Gujarat wrote to the Ministry, "for supply of Huge quantity of Wheat." Yet the import of processed grains had destroyed the market for the mill's chief product.[110] The Indian Grain Dealers' Federation petitioned unmoved Food Ministry officials for the exemption of "petty dealers" from the district licensing requirements on different grains, whose complexity had hamstrung their trade.[111]

Yet distressed petitions like these belied the fact that the new Food Minister, S.K. Patil, would be even less inclined than his predecessor to regulate food markets. Jawaharlal Nehru, his authority diminished in the wake of the Nagpur resolution, discussed later, had replaced one state party boss with another. Patil was an unusual candidate for the Ministry: seven years earlier, as President of the Bombay Pradesh Congress Committee, Patil had urged Congressmen to agitate against food regulation and control, declaring himself an "unrepentant champion

[109] "Permission to Movement of Donated Wheat and Rice for Free Feeding at Kumbahmela, Allahabad," 1959, Food – Policy – 210(BOM)(1)/59-Py.II, NAI.

[110] Head, Shree Laxmi Pulse Rice and Roller Flour Mills, letter to Food and Agriculture Minister, New Delhi, December 16, 1960, Indian Merchants' Chamber, Bombay papers, folder 793, NMML.

[111] "Exemption of Dealing in Quantity Below Hundred Maunds," 1961, Agriculture – Policy – 205(MAH) (2)61.PY-II, NAI.

142   Hungry Nation

of the open market system."[112] Assuming control of the Ministry of Food and Agriculture, a position which he declared "a graveyard for many ministers who were cleverer and more imaginative than I," Patil declared that he should like to be "90 per cent Agriculture Minister and only 10 per cent Food Minister."[113]

Where A.P. Jain had proffered false compliance, S.K. Patil actively resisted the top-down push for further regulation, rejecting even the most limited efforts to license wholesale traders, set minimum procurement prices, or concede to the state the power to acquire stocks in emergencies. In food, Patil declared, "a free economy must come into being."[114] Speaking to the Andhra Pradesh Federation of Chambers of Commerce and Industry, Patil gushed over the "wonderful and unprecedented manner" in which traders, farmers, and consumers had restrained themselves, reassuring them that "there is no need to tighten your belts."[115]

Patil's breezy optimism confounded even the most tepid supporters of state intervention. "Shri Patil generally chooses to dismiss with a shrug" the gravity of the food situation, the *Economic Weekly* opined in 1962, flouting his Cabinet colleagues' directives and placing his "abiding faith in the businessman's sense of national duty."[116] The faith was misplaced: in the absence of greater regulation and more rigorous procurement, India's godowns were stocked wholly with American grains imported under P.L. 480, and its small state buffer stores were almost entirely exhausted by the end of 1963.[117] As the Planning Commission, with Nehru's endorsement, forwarded a plan to build up those stores through state procurement and trading, Patil headed to the United States with a limited mandate to request more P.L. 480 imports. He returned to India with a dramatically expanded agreement; the price of insubordination was the Prime Minister's demand for his resignation.

The traders who had luxuriated in Patil's embrace had little to celebrate in his successor, Swaran Singh. After two subordinates who had bucked the push for state trading, Jawaharlal Nehru needed a compliant Minister, and Singh's weak power base among the Sikhs of Punjab made him a logical choice. When the party's Bhubaneswar Resolution of 1963 doubled down on the goal of socialized agriculture, with new price

---

[112] "Mr. Patil Condemns Food Policy," *Times of India*, May 25, 1952.

[113] "Mr. Patil Denounces Food Hoarder," *Times of India*, September 13, 1959.

[114] "State Trading in Food Grains as Short-Term Policy," *Times of India*, September 1, 1959.

[115] "Easy Availability of Food Grains," *Times of India*, January 2, 1963.

[116] "Patil on Food," *Economic Weekly*, November 24, 1962, 1800–1802.

[117] "Foundation Laid for Talks on New P.L. 480 Agreement," *Times of India*, June 25, 1963; Frankel, *India's Political Economy*, 174, 226–230.

The Common Hunger of the Country

controls and the nationalization of the 43,000 rice mills as a key demand, Singh fell into line. At a February 1964 conference, Singh announced a rigorous foodgrain dealers' licensing order, informing state agriculture ministers that they should anticipate a renewed push to regulate private traders.[118]

Alarmed, representatives of India's foodgrains trade sprung into action. M.H. Hasham Premji, head of a successful oil and grain company named Wipro and president of the Federation of All India Foodgrain Dealers' Associations, led the charge against Singh, decrying the Ministry's apparent goal of "denying employment to nearly 600,000 to 700,000 licensed foodgrains traders and their immediate employers and their dependents, numbering in all 6 to 7 million people, who have been in this vital trade for generations."[119] A brochure published by the Federation decried the "witch-hunters in the so-called abuses of private trading [who] have come out with the dogmatic assertion that only by the elimination of the merchant and taking over the foodgrains trade by the States can the basic dilemma can be resolved."[120]

As Singh pressed forward, the Indian Merchants' Chamber fought back. Food stocks were continuing to diminish in the summer of 1964, but the Chamber issued a statement to exonerate traders and decry the restrictions on interstate food commerce.[121] The president of the Chamber, introducing M.R. Masani to a meeting of Bombay's Commerce Graduates' Association, contended that "trade channels, by and large, have functioned effectively and with due sense of responsibility. It is therefore painful to see that spokesmen of Government, from time to time, trying to pass the blame for the current 'food shortage' on to the trade."[122] The efforts of the trade to stymie regulation frustrated the Food Minister, but delighted his reluctant predecessor, licking his wounds in political exile. It had proven impossible to regulate the trade as Nehru and others so wished: just as Patil had predicted, the position was a graveyard.

The dignified serenity of Jawaharlal Nehru's flower-covered body masked the vicious jostling of the Congressmen who arrived at his

---

[118] Frankel, *India's Political Economy*, 235.

[119] "Press Statement by Shri M.H. Hasham Premji," April 6, 1964, Indian Merchants' Chamber, Bombay papers, folder 798, NMML.

[120] M.H. Hasham Premji and Bhani Ram Gupta, *India's Food Problem: Its Complex Nature* (New Delhi: Federation of All Indian Foodgrain Dealers' Associations, 1964).

[121] Indian Merchants' Chamber, Bombay, "Food Situation X-Rayed," *M.P. Chronicle*, July 30, 1964, Indian Merchants' Chamber, Bombay papers, folder 797, NMML.

[122] "Observation of Shri Dhirajlal Maganlal," August 6, 1964, Indian Merchants' Chamber, Bombay, NMML.

144   Hungry Nation

residence to pay their respects. Within six weeks, External Affairs Minister Lal Bahadur Shastri had won out over Finance Minister Morarji Desai as Prime Minister, a victory that cheered onlookers at the United States Embassy, who considered Shastri "more pragmatic, more parochial than Nehru; less ideological, less theoretical-minded."[123] The consensus among American diplomats was that S.K. Patil would be asked to reassume the Food Ministry. But when longtime Shastri booster Sanjiva Reddy was named Minister of Industry and Commerce, the veteran Madras bureaucrat C. Subramaniam, who was said to be lobbying for that position, was given the Food and Agriculture Ministry as a consolation.[124]

Shastri had inherited from Nehru a full-blown food crisis, and his party was deeply divided over the question of how to regulate food markets, if at all. The enforcement of existing controls had atrophied: the number of cases brought against hoarders and unlicensed traders had plummeted, and convictions were rare.[125] The new Food Minister was doubling down on his belief that major investment in food production could stave off recurrent crisis, but the nation found itself contending with the urgency of plummeting food stocks. Grain depots had begun to run dry in the weeks after Nehru's death; by the time Shastri had assembled his cabinet, trade union leaders and Hindu extremists were threatening violence against grain dealers, and the alarmed US ambassador, Chester Bowles, announced a doubling of grain shipments in hopes of calming matters.[126] Yet neither this announcement, nor President Sarvepalli Radhakrishnan's declaration that food prices were once again India's "great menace," could prevent Indian citizens from rising up. In Bombay, a Communist-led food demonstration against soaring prices saw 700 people arrested, including 200 women carrying babies. Two weeks of peaceful demonstration in Calcutta ended when a group of protesters seized a convoy for its cargo of rice.[127] A riot broke out when ration-card holders outside Varanasi were informed that local wheat stock had been depleted, only to notice grain being ferreted secretly from the depot.[128] In Akkalkot, Maharashtra, police fought off a mob descending

[123] "Lal Bahadur Shastri," June 9, 1964, RG 59 / 5254 / Box 5 / Lal Bahadur Shastri, USNA.
[124] Benjamin H. Read, "India Under Shastri Government," June 2, 1964, RG 59 / 5254 / Box 5 / Lal Bahadur Shastri, USNA; L.D. Heck, "Memorandum of Conversation between Dr. S. Gopal and Mr. L. Douglas," June 18, 1964, RG 59 / 5254 / Box 5 / Lal Bahadur Shastri, USNA.
[125] Frankel, *India's Political Economy*, 262.
[126] "India Periled by Famine after Nehru Death," *Boston Globe*, July 31, 1964.
[127] "India Places Controls on Grain in Effort to Stop Speculation," *New York Times*, July 28, 1964.
[128] "One Speared to Death," *Times of India*, July 25, 1964.

The Common Hunger of the Country

upon the town's grain shops.[129] Provincial police forces undertook raids on traders' homes and godowns to unearth hidden stocks, while leftist parties alleged that Shastri and the rest of the new Congress regime were too beholden to traders and big farmers to take meaningful action.[130] The public trials of traders suspected of profiteering did little to dampen unrest, nor did they stifle the grim joke heard in Delhi circles that had Nehru lived through the summer, the misadministration of the food crisis would certainly have killed him.[131] "Indians," the *New York Times* reported, "will remember 1964 as the year that Nehru died and the food shortage began."[132]

Punctual and taciturn, the new Food and Agriculture Minister had earned a reputation as a diligent and occasionally creative administrator. As Madras' Minister of Finance, C. Subramaniam had weighed in on the question of state trading at a Congress confab in Ooty in 1959, professing empathy with India's farmers and frustration with mendacious traders.[133] He had asked the new Prime Minister to allow him to continue working as Minister for Steel, Heavy Industry, and Mines, in hopes of completing a major reorganization of India's steel industry, yet accepted the new position that he joked was "the Waterloo of many former ministers."[134]

Bitter at his own sacking five years prior, A.P. Jain heaped contempt upon the "young and virile" Subramaniam, scoffing at his promise to stamp out profiteering.[135] Yet observant farmers looked to Subramaniam's proven administrative competence with hope. While the Ministry was, *Food and Farming* agreed, "a graveyard of reputations," for once "the gloom peddlers are going to be proved wrong. Mr. Subramaniam has got the guts to face the challenges of the assignment."[136]

The Planning Commission, presenting Subramaniam with data demonstrating three years of stagnant food production, blamed a "farmer–trader axis" for the summer's crisis, urging tightened regulation, new price controls, and expanded state procurement. Three predecessors had

---

[129] "Grain Shops in Akalkot Looted," *Times of India*, September 30, 1964.

[130] "Food, Please," *Economist*, August 8, 1964.

[131] Michael Brecher, "Transition in India," *International Journal* 20, no. 1 (1964): 85–89.

[132] Thomas F. Brady, "India: The Year of Hunger and Ideological Changes," *New York Times*, January 18, 1965.

[133] C. Subramaniam, "Land and Food: Problems of Implementation of Congress Party Policy," in *Ooty Seminar: Papers Discussed* (New Delhi: All India Congress Committee, 1959), 128–140.

[134] C. Subramaniam, *The New Strategy in Indian Agriculture: The First Decade and After* (New Delhi: Vikas Publishing House, 1979), 2.

[135] Ajit Prasad Jain, "Our Food," July 30, 1964, Ajit Prasad Jain papers, NMML.

[136] K. Balakrishnan Nair, "Mr. C. Subramaniam's Challenging Task," *Food and Farming* 16, no. 6 (June 1964).

146　Hungry Nation

been unwilling or unable to undertake similar reform. But Subramaniam, primarily interested in increasing production, proposed a twist: the establishment of a food trading organization that would not monopolize trade, but compete directly with dealers.[137]

With characteristic prevarication, the Prime Minister delegated the decision to an expert committee headed by his chief secretary, L.K. Jha, a former finance secretary and head of the Indian Civil Service. Production, the committee agreed, was key to a real solution, but good price incentives played a part in inducing production. Where earlier Ministers of Food and Agriculture had recommended procurement prices so low that they posed little competition to private retailers, the Jha Committee recommended that the state become a real player in the foodgrains market.[138] Subramaniam, energized, spent the summer shopping the idea of an organization along these lines at a Chief Ministers' Conference in Delhi and then in the Cabinet, where he built up enough support to convince the Prime Minister.[139]

Traders' resistance, a worsening crisis, and Shastri's fecklessness set the proposal on the back burner. S.K. Patil's unauthorized extension of the last P.L. 480 agreement was bringing in massive quantities of grains, but little was appearing in shops.[140] A dock worker strike in Kerala was holding up the arrival of 2000 tons of Pakistani rice and 10,000 tons of American wheat.[141] In October, having barely survived a vote of no confidence, the Prime Minister decided to abandon temporarily the push for a competitive trading organization, asking his Chief Ministers to hold summary trials of suspected hoarders and cede to New Delhi the power to commandeer stocks from recalcitrant traders. State Ministers rejected Shastri's gambit, conceding nothing save for the cordoning off of the starving state of Kerala. Humiliated, the Prime Minister tried once more at the Congress meeting in Guntur two weeks later, calling for an ordinance under the Essential Commodities Act that would allow for unappealable trials of suspected hoarders, the ability to seize stocks, and the designation of at least one magistrate in every Indian district for food-related prosecutions. The Prime Minister was rebuffed again.[142] The *Times of India* urged Shastri to buck up and combat the "growing

---

[137] Frankel, *India's Political Economy*, 256–258.

[138] L.K. Jha, *Report of the Jha Committee on Foodgrains Prices for 1964–65 Season* (New Delhi: Ministry of Food and Agriculture, Government of India, 1968).

[139] "Cabinet Meeting: Foodgrains Corporation of India," 1965, Cabinet Secretariat – Executive Council Office – 37(6)-CF, 1964, NAI.

[140] "Aide-Memoire," November 23, 1964, RG 59 / 5254 / Box 1 / P.L. 480 Food for Peace Program, USNA.

[141] "Food-Ration Test Falters in India," *New York Times*, November 8, 1964.

[142] Frankel, *India's Political Economy*, 258–262.

The Common Hunger of the Country 147

impression that a few Chief Ministers can effectively prevent the adoption of a national food policy."[143] Yet the only thing that Shastri could manage was a compromise agreement wherein surplus states would procure 2 million tons of extra rice – meeting minimum commitments but undertaking no new ones – and doubling down on anti-hoarding laws that had been left unenforced.

The compromise averted crisis, but did little to temper traders' excess. Two years on, only 6000 dealers had been prosecuted for hoarding, and convictions were obtained in only half of these cases. Merchants nonetheless responded with indignation. C. Subramaniam, meeting with the Indian Merchants' Chamber, heard members' complaints that

the foodgrains trade, which have considerable experience in the matter of handling foodgrains in circumstances favorable or otherwise, has never been consulted by the Government in formulating food policies. On the other hand, it has become the fashion of the day to make them villain of the piece when the Government finds that their controls are ineffective measures in a situation of short supply.[144]

Meeting with the Madurai-Ramnad Chamber of Commerce, Subramaniam fielded further invectives. "The dealers in foodgrains," its members resolved,

are as much citizens of India as anyone else who point their accusing finger at them. They are born and bred in India and they are no wit less patriotic than other citizens. [If] the Government doubts the integrity of the trade in its assurance of Co-operation with the Government, it is desirable that the Government take over the entire trade of foodgrains and free the trade from suspicion. And the trade will be very happy to wish them joy of it.[145]

After much delay, the Lok Sabha passed the Food Corporation Act in December 1964, urged on by C. Subramaniam. The Corporation would work as a purchasing body: states would set their own targets of surplus grains, delegating purchases to registered dealers, millers, and cooperatives, or to the Corporation's agents themselves.[146] The FCI

---

[143] "Inexcusable," *Times of India*, November 10, 1964.

[144] "Points for Discussion with Shri C. Subramaniam," 1964, Indian Merchants' Chamber, Bombay papers, folder 797, NMML.

[145] V.P.R. Gangaram Dorairaj, and M. Dhanasekarapandian, "Memorandum Presented to Shri C. Subramaniam," November 1, 1964, Indian Merchants' Chamber, Bombay papers, folder 799, NMML.

[146] Food Corporation of India, *Review of Activities since Inception* (New Delhi: Food Corporation of India, 1967); Chopra, *Evolution of Food Policy in India*, 112. See also *Five Years with the Grain Man: A Review (1965–1970)* (New Delhi: Food Corporation of India, 1971); *Inauguration, January 14, 1965: The Food Corporation of India* (Madras: Food Corporation of India, 1965); and *The Flood of the Golden Grain* (New Delhi: Food Corporation of India, 1972).

148   Hungry Nation

would compete with traders and not supplant them, but it would enjoy a monopoly over the shipment of foodgrains by rail, circumventing the interstate restrictions which had so frustrated private traders.

Inaugurating the Corporation in Madras, Subramaniam thanked the members of the "farming community" who had offered suggestions and the commodity credit team from the United States which had proffered further assistance. The Minister declared the FCI to be rooted in private sector paradigms suitable for trade, but lambasted the merchants who had stonewalled instead of offering insight. "It is a matter of regret to me," he declared, "that the trading community, as a whole, did make hay while the sun of scarcity shone, and ignored their social function in preference to their immediate individual gains."

A week after the establishment of the Corporation, Congress president K. Kamaraj urged the nation's traders and merchants, in the name of advancing a welfare state, "to play their patriotic part in the nation's well-being, and [to] subordinate their profit motive to the nobler sentiments of national service."[147] Yet the exhortation to patriotism did little to stop India's grain traders from rallying against this final incursion upon their trade. The Madurai-Ramnad Chamber of Commerce, representing the interests of traders in the South, had resigned itself to the formation of the Corporation, but resolved that "private trade should not be discriminated against in the matter of either purchase or transport, and care should be taken that the Food Trading Corporation does not become a monopolist concern."[148] The president of the Gujarat Vepari Mahamandal held that the Corporation's monopoly on rail transport was a fatal affront to "the working of trade channels which have been serving the community since generations."[149] The Federation of All India Foodgrain Dealers' Associations lodged a formal petition to abolish the FCI, and the Jana Sangh urged that traders be compensated for the establishment of the Corporation with the complete lifting of all other food restrictions.

The outbreak of war with Pakistan saw the Prime Minister exhorting merchants to fall into line. Shastri spoke in Hindi to a massive crowd at New Delhi's Ramlila Maidan, declaring that in war, "traders must hold the price-line. The traders and dealers can be of great help and service in this hour. If they guarantee price stability, the other tasks that are before

---

[147] K. Kamaraj, *Presidential Address: Indian National Congress 69th Session, Durgapur, West Bengal, 9th January 1965* (New Delhi: All India Congress Committee, 1965).

[148] V.P.R. Gangaram Dorairaj, letter to Secretary, Indian Merchants' Chamber, November 10, 1964, Indian Merchants' Chamber, Bombay papers, folder 799, NMML.

[149] Vepari Mahamandal and Rohit C. Mehta, letter to C. Subramaniam, January 29, 1965, Indian Merchants' Chamber, Bombay papers, folder 799, NMML.

The Common Hunger of the Country 149

us today can be carried out without unnecessary complications."[150] He repeated the call on All India Radio, declaring that "a great responsibility devolves" on traders and merchants at a moment of national crisis.[151] M.H. Hasham Premji declared that traders would "enhance their reputation by distributing in such a manner that an atmosphere of faith and confidence could continue to prevail among the government, dealers, and consumers."[152] But his support came sutured to a demand: if dealers expelled "unsocial elements" from their midst, the government would need to withdraw all pending lawsuits against dealers and appoint an advisory committee of traders across levels to weigh in on the FCI's operations. Privately, Premji penned an angry letter to C. Subramaniam, reminding him that the state was asking for cooperation not a year after working for the "complete elimination of the wholesale trade."[153]

The most plaintive complaint came from the president of the Birmitrapur Merchants' Association of Sundargarh, Orissa, who reported that the delayed licensure of the region's foodgrain traders in the wake of the FCI's establishment was leading to starvation.[154] "The people are assured by our government," he wrote,

that they are the Citizens of Socialistic Pattern of Society, and are breathing in the Democratic atmosphere. But in reality, there is no Democracy at all. The people, specially the business Community, is the victim of the Dictator-like Government Officials. They are not ready to facilitate the business Community to handle the business. By all means, they are losing the business.

Long before the emergence of nationalist politics, Indian businessmen had circulated the nation and the world, linking the smallest towns in India to the circulation of global capital.[155] The transformations wrought by the colonial economy, in turn, transformed the worlds of Indian artisans, businessmen, and merchants, rendering them more connected and more visible.[156] Colonial observers, vexed by the unknowability of

[150] D.R. Mankekar, *Lal Bahadur: A Political Biography* (Bombay: Popular Prakashan, 1965), 163–164.
[151] *The Meaning of Self-Reliance* (New Delhi: Publications Division, Ministry of Information and Broadcasting, Government of India, 1965).
[152] M.H. Hasham Premji, letter to the Prime Minister, November 13, 1965, Indian Merchants' Chamber, Bombay papers, folder 800, NMML.
[153] M.H. Hasham Premji, letter to A.L. Dias, August 31, 1965, Indian Merchants' Chamber, Bombay papers, folder 800, NMML.
[154] Birmitrapur Merchants' Association (Sundargarh), "Problem of Food Stuffs and Pitiable Condition of Business Community," August 25, 1965, Indian Merchants' Chamber, Bombay papers, folder 800, NMML.
[155] Parthasarathi, *The Transition to a Colonial Economy Weavers, Merchants, and Kings in South India, 1720–1800*.
[156] Claude Markovits, *Merchants, Traders, Entrepreneurs: Indian Business in the Colonial Era* (Basingstoke: Palgrave Macmillan, 2008); Claude Markovits, *Indian Business and*

150   Hungry Nation

"vernacular" capitalism, developed commercial and contract laws to regulate the market, casting it as a novel object of governance and seeing in it a new commercial public.[157] In the twentieth century, the workings of nationalist politics and economics sutured abstracted notions of the Indian economy and the market to the nation itself.[158] Markets and the state were, in many ways, produced together.

Independence, however, brought with it a new set of concerns related to the role of markets and merchants, particularly in the realm of food, where nationalists had made some of their most potent claims to self-rule. The regulation of India's food markets followed closely the pattern set in other nations: wartime exigency saw the emergence of rationing schemes and controlled markets, placating the urban poor but antagonizing many other sectors of society.[159] Yet in India, wartime regulation extended well beyond the war itself, evolving into a byzantine and much-loathed system for managing recurrent scarcity. The market discipline that colonial regulators and Indian planners had hoped for never emerged, and much of the postcolonial Indian economy was managed in a state of permanent emergency.[160]

It was against this backdrop that India's left-leaning politicians and bureaucrats sought to regulate the food market in the name of scarcity, while merchants and their allies, claiming the liberal mantle of Mohandas Gandhi himself, argued against the continued and increasingly restrictive management of India's food economy. It was through these contestations that Indian citizens played out major debates as to the nature of the postcolonial Indian economy. Poor citizens could rally for rations while their middle-class peers chaffed at interminable lines and bewildering regulations, producers longed to see marketing infrastructure that would

Nationalist Politics, 1931–1939: The Indigenous Capitalist Class and the Rise of the Congress Party (Cambridge: Cambridge University Press, 1985); Douglas E. Haynes, *Small Town Capitalism in Western India: Artisans, Merchants and the Making of the Informal Economy, 1870–1960* (Cambridge: Cambridge University Press, 2012).

[157] Birla, *Stages of Capital*; U. Kalpagam, "Colonial Governmentality and the 'Economy,'" *Economy and Society* 29, no. 3 (January 2000): 418–438.

[158] Goswami, *Producing India*.

[159] On wartime rationing internationally, see Keith Allen, "Sharing Scarcity: Bread Rationing and the First World War in Berlin, 1914–1923," *Journal of Social History* 32, no. 2 (1998): 371–393; Amy Bentley, *Eating for Victory: Food Rationing and the Politics of Domesticity* (Urbana: University of Illinois Press, 1998); Collingham, *The Taste of War*; William Moskoff, *The Bread of Affliction: The Food Supply in the USSR during World War II* (Cambridge: Cambridge University Press, 1990); Orit Rozin, "The Austerity Policy and the Rule of Law: Relations between Government and Public in Fledgling Israel," *Journal of Modern Jewish Studies* 4, no. 3 (2005): 273–290; and Ina Zweiniger-Bargielowska, *Austerity in Britain: Rationing, Controls, and Consumption, 1939–1955* (Oxford: Oxford University Press, 2000).

[160] De, "'Commodities Must Be Controlled.'"

connect them to consumers, and traders bucked regulation and courted political allies as they protested the "elimination" of their trade. The wrangling that ultimately gave way to the Food Corporation of India – a largely ineffectual trading organization – represented in large measure the end of a paradigm that saw the food economy as one that might be managed on an emergency basis. These transformations, the end of a potent era of land reform, the emergence of new agricultural technologies, and the resurrection of maligned paradigms of growth in India, represented a critical shift in how citizens and planners would conceptualize and address India's enduring food crisis.

5   All the Disabilities Which Peasant and Land Can Suffer

In 1950, two students in Varanasi came together in the days after their matriculation exams to write a short play in the "Indian mold."[1] An English play, they declared, was usually sustained by bloodshed. But the best Indian playwrights of the day, by contrast, "wrote beautifully on welfare-related subjects," the matters of greatest importance to the new nation.

The *Zamindar-Kisan Natak* – the "Landlord-Peasant Drama" – was written in straightforward Hindi, save for the comedic role afforded to a Bhojpuri-speaking jester. Before the curtain rises, a director consults onstage with one of the play's dancers. "Independence is here at last," he proclaims, "and yet the country's masters keep on exploiting through their own twisted logic and rules." The naïve director wonders what religious epic might suit the vexing economic and social conditions of a newly independent nation, proposing various mythical kings and saints. The dancer rejects each of these suggestions with a good-natured laugh. Instead, he suggests, their troupe should rehearse "a drama staged for the welfare of the country." There is one subject, he adds, that every Indian would know about: the struggle between tenants and their landlords – between those who produce food and those merely seeking their cut.

The ensuing drama centers on Ramdas, a poor farmer and Congress supporter who laments the disparity between "those with cars and those with horse-carts." The object of his ire is Lalaji, the village *zamindar* whose money never runs out, and who lives off the labor of his poor tenants. Ramdas is devastated that after independence, the lot of India's hungry peasants is still no better than that of the mangy buffaloes who roam the nearby fields. Yet he is stirred from self-pity by the exhortations of his wife, Sukhiya, who urges Ramdas to make a new organization to help farmers resist the collection of rent. In a newly independent India, she declares, "no oppressors' injustice can stand up to a unified

---

[1] Jhunnilal Prasad Kesari Phabhat and Gaurishankar Prasad Gupta, *Zamindar-Kisan Natak [A Peasant-Landlord Drama]* (Varanasi: Bindeśvagi Prasāda Bukselara, 1950).

152

Figure 9 The cover of the *Zamindar-Kisan Natak [Landlord-Peasant Drama]*, a short Hindi-language play on land reform written by two students in Varanasi in 1950. (Credit: University of Chicago Library)

organization." Sukhiya is ultimately proven correct. "I don't understand what's happened to our people," Lalaji mutters from the opulence of his stately residence, as the peasants withhold their rent. Yet ultimately, watching the tenants unite to produce more, Lalaji capitulates, setting aside a substantive share of his vast wealth for the peasants' organization.

The students' drama spoke to the revolutionary hope that independence had birthed. India's struggle for self-rule, from its earliest moments, was inextricably connected to the struggle for land.[2] And as food emerged as a central locus for questions of nation-building, citizens and planners drew upon earlier struggles over land as they balanced the production of sufficient food against the equitable distribution and proper use of arable land. Peasants like the imaginary Ramdas and his peers clamored for plots of fertile land to plant and sow independently, and an end to the landlordism that kept them in fetters. Yet agronomists and leftist planners, inspired by the apparent success of experiments in China and the Soviet Union, maintained that only the large-scale pooling of land and the collectivization of Indian agriculture would lead to abundance. All the while, conservative votaries of India's so-called "middle peasantry" insisted that the liquidation of hereditary *zamindari* estates was eroding the social stability needed to actualize any plan of agrarian improvement.

As the struggles of India's peasantry were braided into the nationalist project, land reform was imbued with new salience. For a decade and a half after independence, left-leaning planners saw the equitable distribution of land as a key imperative for the new state, even as their efforts were overshadowed by the more populist *bhoodan* movement led by a Gandhian mendicant. And as the project of land reform staggered forward, those same left-leaning planners sought to convince citizens that cooperative or collective agriculture along Chinese or Soviet lines would produce food most effectively upon reclaimed lands, antagonizing wealthy peasants, free-market liberals, and conservative elements within the ruling Congress Party. The ensuing political struggle quashed leftists' hopes for collaborative agriculture, and paved the way for an alternate vision of abundance rooted in technical advances and the concentration of inputs.

Since the earliest days of colonial rule, those who studied Indian agriculture saw in land the defects of nature, ownership, and use stymieing greater production. Colonial bureaucrats had implemented the Permanent Settlement in 1792 in hopes that secure tenures would induce owners to improve their holdings; over the subsequent century

---

[2] Sanjoy Chakravorty, *The Price of Land: Acquisition, Conflict, Consequence* (New Delhi: Oxford University Press, 2013).

The Disabilities Which Peasant and Land Can Suffer   155

and a half, agronomists, administrators, and collectors had all searched for patterns of land use that would bring more crops to larger, global markets.[3] The structure of India's agrarian holdings was seen as deficient in two divergent regards. On the one hand, *zamindars* and other titular land-holders prioritized the extraction of rent over the improvement of agricultural lands. Yet a parallel critique on grounds of productivity held that India's land holdings were too fractured to cultivate efficiently.

At independence, the popular struggle for land would take on new meaning. But the debates and contours of landlord abolition in the first two decades of independence drew robustly upon the idioms of the *kisan*, or peasant, movements of earlier decades, and a longer set of debates over the proper use and distribution of India's productive lands.[4] Concerned with the amelioration of their own distress, regional peasant organizations had agitated for reform from the 1920s onward, tussling with the Congress over its supposed urban bias and urging the formation of parties to represent their own particular needs.[5] Under the leadership of N.G. Ranga, the All India Kisan Sabha pressed for the abolition of *zamindari* without compensation; by the 1940s, the group had become a formidable competitor to the Congress in the Indian countryside, where contestations over land frequently eclipsed the broader national struggle.[6]

Despite fierce internecine competition, the Kisan Sabha and the Congress Party forged a shared understanding of India's agrarian crisis during the Great Depression. The Congress leadership, drawing liberally upon Kisan Sabha analysis, saw India's agricultural predicament as one rooted in landlordism and the extraction of rent. And as the Bengal famine brought the questions of rural production, credit, and sustenance to

---

[3] Ranajit Guha, *A Rule of Property for Bengal: An Essay on the Idea of Permanent Settlement* (Paris: Mouton, 1963).

[4] On land reform in India, see Ronald J. Herring, *Land to the Tiller: The Political Economy of Agrarian Reform in South Asia* (New Haven: Yale University Press, 1983). An excellent provincial study is Walter C. Neale, *Economic Change in Rural India: Land Tenure and Reform in Uttar Pradesh, 1800–1955* (New Haven: Yale University Press, 1962). The classic journalistic account is Kusum Nair, *Blossoms in the Dust: The Human Element in Indian Development* (London: G. Duckworth, 1961). See also Daniel Thorner, *The Agrarian Prospect in India: Five Lectures on Land Reform Delivered in 1955 at the Delhi School of Economics* (Columbia, MO: South Asia Books, 1976). D.A. Low situates Indian land reform efforts in the context of a global turn towards the same in *The Egalitarian Moment: Asia and Africa, 1950–1980* (Cambridge: Cambridge University Press, 1996).

[5] See, for example, Omkaranth, *Kisan Shreni Sajaga Ho! [For the Peasants' Class Consciousness]* (Allahabad: Harṣadeva, Bhāratī Bhavana, 1934).

[6] The AIKS consistently lobbied the Congress to sever ties with the large landholders bankrolling its mainstream leadership. See Frankel, *India's Political Economy*, 55; and M. Abdullah Rasul, *A History of the All India Kisan Sabha* (Calcutta: National Book Agency, 1974).

156   Hungry Nation

national consciousness, the Kisan Sabha braided together the goals of land reform and the bolstering of the national granary. It was India's "outmoded land-tenure under the system of landlordism," a 1947 Kisan Sabha manifesto declared, which facilitated hoarding, encouraged black-marketing, and kept peasants from increased productivity.[7]

Peasant activists of the 1930s and 1940s saw in independence the possibility of a free nation whose citizenry, regardless of background, would reorient itself towards more equitable landholding. The earliest critiques of the 1930s saw the case against *zamindari* made in economic and legalistic terms, with hereditary landholding cast as a violation of proper administration, and a burdensome constraint on agricultural productivity.[8] With independence looming, a sense emerged that self-rule would inevitably be accompanied by a shattering of the extant rural order. Even landholders, the Andhra Pradesh Congress Committee declared somewhat improbably in 1938, could agree that the "welfare of the peasants ought to be the chief concern of the *zamindar*."[9] Less partial observers were unconvinced that landlords would so readily betray their own self-interest. "The past has been so kind to the landlord," civil servant Malcolm Darling dryly observed in 1930, "that he cannot believe that the future may be harsh."[10]

A parallel vision accompanied these hopes for economic and legal reform: independence would not only usher in an improved administrative order, but a more just social order, as well. The *kisan*, or peasant-cultivator, was identified by activists as the bulwark of Indian civilization itself. Peasants, poems, and treatises asserted, were constituted differently than the landlords who oversaw their toil, and the urban Indians who knew little of agriculture.[11] This notion of difference underwrote political action: the peasant leader Charan Singh would enjoy a year-long stint as Prime Minister four decades after the heyday of Kisan Sabha mobilization, skewering India's aim of industrial development as inimical to the agrarian character of the country.[12] But this vision dated back at least

---

[7] "Kisan Sabha's Blue-Print for the Solution of the Food Problem," *People's Age*, June 15, 1947.

[8] Dvijadas Datta, *Landlordism in India*, Taraporevala's Indian Economic Series (Bombay: Taraporevala, 1931).

[9] *Hundred and Thirty Six Years under Zamindaries: Being the Report of the A.P.C.C. Regarding the Conditions of Zamin Ryots with Concrete Proposals* (Masulipatam: Andhra Provincial Congress Committee, 1938), 9–10.

[10] Malcolm Darling, *Rusticus Loquitur; or: The Old Light and the New in the Punjab Village* (Oxford: Oxford University Press, 1930), 335.

[11] Shad Malihabadi, *Sudharak Traikt [A Tract of Improvement]* (Lucknow: Rama Shankar, 1939).

[12] On Charan Singh, see Paul R. Brass, *An Indian Political Life: Charan Singh and Congress Politics, 1937 to 1961* (New Delhi: Sage Publications, 2011); Paul R. Brass, *An Indian Political Life: Charan Singh and Congress Politics, 1967–1987* (New Delhi: Sage

The Disabilities Which Peasant and Land Can Suffer

as far as the late 1930s, when, as a newly elected member of the United Provinces Assembly, Singh had proposed a 50 percent quota in public administration for the sons of farmers. Such a representation, he argued, would ensure that the agrarian character of Indian society was represented in its political institutions. "The social philosophy of a member of the non-agricultural, urban classes," he explained, presaging an argument he would make decades later, "is entirely different from that of a person elongating to the agricultural rural classes."[13]

Peasant leaders like Singh, N.G. Ranga, and Swami Sahajanand Saraswati began to conceptualize the *kisan raj* – rule of peasants, diversely conceptualized – that would emerge as the dominant social order in independent India.[14] Drawing to varying degrees upon socialist thought and the heuristics of Gandhian *Swaraj*, the idea of a *kisan raj* might first have been used by Ranga in an address to the Second Andhra Ryot's Conference, where he declared the aim of the *kisan* movement to be *kisan raj* itself.[15] The term gained traction throughout the decade as *kisan* politicians sketched out what a rule of peasant-farmers freed from *zamindari* might resemble. "Congress struggles," K.D. Paliwal, a socialist politician from Agra would frequently proclaim during anti-rent campaigns late in the decade, "would usher in *Swaraj*, which means *Kisan raj*, when *kisans* will have the power to dismiss officials from *thanedar* to Governor."[16] Yet if the *kisan* was a peasant somewhere between a landless tenant and a large *zamindar*, his exact position was and would remain undefined. This ambiguity would have major consequences on the course of land reform, and India's search for abundance.

Publications, 2014); and Terence Byres, "Charan Singh, 1902–1987: An Appreciation," *Journal of Peasant Studies* 15, no. 2 (1988): 139–189. See this book's conclusion.

[13] Christophe Jaffrelot, "The Rise of the Other Backward Classes in the Hindi Belt," *The Journal of Asian Studies* 59, no. 1 (February 1, 2000): 91.

[14] Swami Sahajanand Saraswati's stirring manifesto for the *kisan* and the agricultural laborer was published in the early 1940s as *Khet Mazdoor*, and outlines the aims of the struggle for peasant rights; see Sahajanand Saraswati, *Sahajanand on Agricultural Labour and the Rural Poor: An Edited Translation of Khet Mazdoor*, trans. Walter Hauser (New Delhi: Manohar Publishers and Distributors, 1994). See also Saraswati's short account of the Kisan movement itself, Sahajanand Saraswati, *Kisan Sabha Ke Samsara [The World of the Kisan Sabha]* (Allahabad: New Literature, 1947); as well as N.G. Ranga's, *Revolutionary Peasants* (New Delhi: Amrit Book Co., 1949).

[15] Lalan Prasad Sinha, *The Left-Wing in India, 1919–47* (Muzaffarpur: New Publishers, 1965), 303.

[16] Zoya Hassan, "Congress in Aligarh District, 1930–1946: Problems of Political Mobilization," in *Congress and Indian Nationalism: The Pre-Independence Phase*, ed. Richard Sisson and Stanley A. Wolpert (Berkeley: University of California Press, 1988), 336. See Paliwal's later publication, in Hindi, Krishna Dutt Paliwal, *Kisan Raj [Peasants' Rule]* (Agra: Ramprasad and Sons Prakashan, 1945).

As independence neared, the question of what to do with lands if and when they were seized from their hereditary owners grew more pressing, tied increasingly to the question of food production. The mainstream Congress leadership could not affirm the insurrectionist language of India's socialists, who declared that "every peasant uprising strikes terror into the hearts of the *Zamindars* and the bourgeoisie!"[17] Yet they could embrace visions like that of the General Secretary of the Bengal Provincial Muslim League, writing in 1940. "The interest of the peasants shall be protected and all rents shall be standardized and all forms of iniquitous impositions and levies shall be abolished," Abul Hashim wrote. "Permanent Zamindary settlement shall be forthwith abolished and agriculture rescued from being an uneconomic occupation."[18]

There was scant consensus as to how agriculture would be "rescued." Would estates seized from landlords be distributed to the landless to cultivate as individual proprietors? Or would collective and cooperative farming, as many Congress leftists hoped, be the policy to usher in social equity and greater productivity alike? Jawaharlal Nehru was contending as early as the 1940s that "cooperatives are the one and only way for agriculture in India."[19] Yet those closer to the soil sensed that buy-in from former landlords would be necessary. "Joint management," the influential ICS officer Tarlok Singh wrote in 1945, was a better option than collective farming, "since through it, we may hope to work through and with the help of peasant owners [to] make the village economy efficient and progressive."[20]

The question would in time split the party. But in spite of discord, the Congress moved to build momentum: shortly after the formation of the interim government in November 1946, the Congress formed an Agrarian Reforms Committee, tasking it with planning the course of land reform in independent India. Rajendra Prasad appointed a disparate group of members to the Committee: Gandhian economist J.C. Kumarappa was appointed as chair, while agricultural economist M.L. Dantwala and the All India Kisan Congress' N.G. Ranga were asked to make "recommendations about agrarian reforms rising out of the abolition of *zamindari* system."[21] Asked to consider the best ways of increasing agricultural output and bettering the lot of India's landless peasants, the

---

[17] Naidu, "The Bombay Plan."

[18] Andrew Sartori, *Liberalism in Empire: An Alternative History* (Berkeley: University of California Press, 2014).

[19] Gunnar Myrdal, *Asian Drama: An Inquiry into the Poverty of Nations* (New York: Twentieth Century Fund, 1968), 1347.

[20] Tarlok Singh, *Poverty and Social Change: A Study in the Economic Reorganisation of Indian Rural Society* (London: Longmans, Green & Co., 1945), 96.

[21] *Report of the Congress Agrarian Reforms Committee*, 2nd edn. (New Delhi: All India Congress Committee, 1951), 4.

The Committee spent a year and a half on exploratory visits to villages across the new nation.

The Committee's conclusions, released in July 1949, were radical by any measure.[22] Full-fledged capitalist agriculture, it admitted, could actualize the greatest possible yield of food and other crops. Yet the mechanization that such agriculture would entail would in turn make landless peasants wage-earners. Collective farming that deprived peasants of their own livelihood was similarly unacceptable. Rather, on reclaimed lands, two types of farming should prevail. Where holdings were smaller than a "basic" size, defined as unable to provide food and livelihood for a family of five, they would be pooled into jointly managed, cooperative farms. For holdings between this and a more "optimum" size, peasant-proprietorship would be recommended, but only as an intermediate stage en route to the establishment of cooperative farming as the dominant pattern for agricultural production in India.

The Committee's report satisfied the Congress left, who ignored N.G. Ranga's blistering note of dissent, which alleged that the rights of *kisans* were being abrogated. A perplexed agricultural economist from Allahabad University, writing in the *Economic Weekly*, wondered what the Committee meant

when it says that agricultural policy should be so framed as to provide an opportunity for the development of the farmer's personality? Does the latter need the mental climate of unfettered private enterprise for its full flowering? Or can the farmer's personality still develop when he is told to do this and that and is forbidden to do certain other things?[23]

Nonetheless, committed to the abolition of *zamindari*, and the elimination of "all intermediaries between the State and the toiler," independent India's government set to work actualizing these ends through law. Communists and socialists, in the lead-up to *zamindari* legislation, touted the victories of *kisans* over the landed order, demonstrating how the Kisan Sabha and other groups would be giving "all fallow land to agricultural laborers and poor peasants in order to help meet the growing food crisis."[24] The plight of India's landless and their rehabilitation was chronicled in films like Bimal Roy's 1952 *Do Bigha Zameen* ("Two Acres of Land") and a flurry of vernacular novels on land reform, from

---

[22] Francine Frankel characterizes this report as "the most threatening document ever drafted by an official committee of the Congress party with respect to the property interests of the landed castes." Frankel, *India's Political Economy*, 68–70.

[23] Ved Prakash Sharma, "Congress Agrarian Reforms Committee – A Critique," *Economic Weekly*, January 7, 1950, 9–11.

[24] "Andhra Kisans Score Victory over Zamindars," *People's Age*, July 13, 1947.

160   Hungry Nation

Nagarjun's Hindi-language *Balchanama* to Tarasankar Bandyopadhyay's Bengali novel *Kalindi*.[25]

The abolition of intermediaries was identified as the most urgent reform to be undertaken by the new state. Tenancy reform and the amelioration of landholding conditions was identified as a secondary concern. And the intertwined projects of land consolidation and the establishment of land ceilings animated a later strand of postcolonial reform efforts. The Indian constitution, in designating land a state subject, allowed for a plurality of legislative processes and outcomes which differed greatly by region. Unsurprisingly, the dominant castes which controlled provincial legislatures – such as the Jats in Uttar Pradesh, led by Charan Singh – forwarded legislation that sounded revolutionary and was in practice far less so. Propertied interests challenged land reform legislation by appealing to the new constitution's protection of fundamental rights, until the passage of the first amendment protected estate acquisition explicitly.[26] Even with this protection, however, *zamindari* abolition was frequently subverted in practice, with landlords frequently redistributing estates among family members or claiming lands for "self-cultivation" to avoid surrendering estates.

In the decade following independence, the task of abolishing formal intermediaries would be largely accomplished, even as the other projects languished. A decade after independence, all but five states – Gujarat, Kerala, Orissa, Assam, and Uttar Pradesh – would pass comprehensive legislation to abolish intermediaries. This work would largely eliminate the *zamindari* class, and by best estimates, benefit around 20 to 25 million tenant households. Yet the reform would do little to change tenures or revenue systems. The high hopes for land reform as a palliative to India's economic woes quickly foundered on the grittier shores of political contestation.[27]

As land reform lumbered forward, two political developments gave left-leaning planners a mandate to act more decisively: the sweeping victory of the Congress Party in India's first free elections, and the establishment of a Planning Commission charged with planning the course of

---

[25] Bimal Kumar Roy, *Do Bigha Zameen [Two Bighas of Land]* (Bimal Roy Productions, 1953); Nagarjun, *Balacanama [Novel]* (New Delhi: Vani Prakasana, 2009); Tarasankar Bandyopadhyay, *Kalindi [Novel]* (Calcutta: Janvan Prakashan, 1951). Phanishwar Nath Renu's well-known *Parti Parikatha*, a fictionalized account of *zamindari* abolition in a remote Bihari village, was published in Hindi in 1957; a recent translation is Phanishwar Nath Renu, *Tale of a Wasteland: An English Rendering of Parti Parikatha*, trans. Madhusudan Thakur (New Delhi: Global Vision Press, 2012).

[26] H.C.L. Merillat, "Abstract of Law and Land Reform in India," *Law & Society Review* 3, no. 2/3 (November 1, 1968): 295–297.

[27] Tomlinson, *The Economy of Modern India, 1860–1970*, 191–192.

national development. The elections of 1951 and 1952 saw a host of challenges to Congress dominance, with abundant capital to be made on its inability to provide abundance in place of want. Congress defended itself against charges that it had betrayed the promise of plenty: one pre-election brochure published by the Ministry of Food and Agriculture asserted that, even if unsuccessful, the Congress' efforts to attain self-sufficiency by 1951 had certainly "enriched the soil" and set the stage for future growth.[28] British observers noticed that Congress was being pummeled over food failures in Andhra Pradesh, Travancore-Cochin, and Malabar.[29] Communists assailed a "tottering" Congress which had failed on its promise of food, and India's socialists declared in their manifesto that the Congress had been derelict in providing "at least the minimum necessary food to all its citizens."[30] From abroad, *Pravda*'s Indian correspondent reported, with characteristic hyperbole, that "a mighty wave of demonstrations and meetings has swept through the country. Not only in the cities, but also in the villages, people have carried placards saying: 'A vote for the Congress Party is a vote for hunger.'"[31] Yet the Congress' ultimate success gave the party a mandate to advance the course of national planning.

The instrument for this planning was the powerful Planning Commission, endowed with the Prime Minister's personal authority. Towards the end of 1949, Jawaharlal Nehru had renewed his call for a Planning Commission that would direct the state's plans for economic development. Its establishment was not a given: the conservative stalwart Sardar Patel had labored to prevent its formation, and even after the Congress Working Committee had accepted it in principle, Patel lobbied to lessen its mandate to reduce economic disparity and the "anti-social concentration of wealth."[32]

As the Planning Commission's members worked to forward a plan for national development, a minority vision came briefly into view before quickly receding. A draft outline for a first Five-Year Plan, released in late 1950, assigned close to half of India's planning budget to agriculture, while affirming that the new state's goal would be to transform

---

[28] Ministry of Food and Agriculture, Government of India and Ministry of Information and Broadcasting, Government of India, *Towards Self-Sufficiency* (New Delhi: Publications Division, Ministry of Information and Broadcasting, Government of India, 1951).

[29] C.V. Martin, "Andhra Goes Communist," February 16, 1952, DO/133/114, UKNA; W.H. Young, "The Indian Elections," February 20, 1952, DO/133/114, UKNA.

[30] Communist Party of India, *Draft Programme of the Communist Party of India* (Bombay: New Age Printing Press, 1951); Madhu Limaye, *Food for All* (Bombay: Socialist Party, 1951).

[31] S. Borzenko, "On Elections in India," *Pravda*, February 22, 1952, CDRP 8:4.

[32] Frankel, *India's Political Economy*, 84–85.

162   Hungry Nation

"the character of Indian agriculture from substance farming to economic farming."[33] Reclaimed land would need to be pooled into larger units more conducive to modern farming techniques, and the ultimate goal, as the Agrarian Reforms Committee had declared, would be voluntary cooperative village management. The establishment of land ceilings was ruled out on grounds that it would risk lowering food production, and provisions for irrigation and chemical fertilizers would be made to larger land owners who could be expected to make good use of these inputs. In short, the draft Plan prioritized productivity in the name of abundance, eschewing the imperatives of equity that Nehru and left-wing planners might have wanted. This plan hinted quite explicitly at a paradigm in Indian agricultural planning that would ascend to prominence in the middle of the next decade.

A power struggle within the Congress, however, returned the advantage to left-wing planners extolling equity before growth. A conservative faction within the Congress, operating with the tacit support of Sardar Patel, had pushed to elect Purshottamdas Tandon as president, cheered by his opposition to secularism, socialism, and centralized planning. After an unstable six-month reign characterized by fierce politicking, the death of Sardar Patel impelled Nehru to intervene on behalf of J.B. Kripalani, a stalwart proponent of left-wing social reform and state-driven development.[34] As the Congress left reasserted its dominance, the final Five-Year Plan abandoned the brief, earlier impulse to prioritize productivity above equity, suggesting that shared uplift and parity among producers should be a paramount goal. The final draft reaffirmed the Agrarian Reforms Committee's commitment to land ceilings and redistribution. M.L. Dantwala, defending the final plan in the *Far Eastern Economist*, contended that land reform was the necessary precondition to technological advance. "In some quarters," he asserted, "it is argued that the most pressing need for technical measures is to increase production. [But] this argument betrays ignorance of the psychology of production, for the peasant has little incentive to increase his output unless by doing so he can hope to raise himself out of the stark poverty which he has known for generations."[35] Claims like these did little to encourage onlookers: the United States' Office of Intelligence Research in New Delhi produced a dispirited report on the Plan, suggesting that even if

---

[33] Planning Commission, Government of India, *The First Five-Year Plan: A Draft Outline*.
[34] Frankel, *India's Political Economy*, 86–100.
[35] M.L. Dantwala, "India's Progress in Agrarian Reforms," *Far Eastern Survey* 19, no. 22 (December 20, 1950): 239–244.

The Disabilities Which Peasant and Land Can Suffer   163

all its agricultural targets were met, India would still suffer the burden of pervasive hunger.[36]

The new decade's most resonant campaign for land reform, however, owed little to Congress machinations in Delhi: far from the capital, an unlikely leader's mission was suggesting both the populist appeal of land reform, and the material obstacles to its implementation. Six months before the elections of 1951, the restive Telugu-speaking Telangana district of Hyderabad was gripped by baleful violence. Villagers spurred on by Communist rhetoric were rising up to demand cultivable lands from the *zamindars* gripping to their hereditary estates. From Wardha, halfway across the country, a fifty-six-year-old renunciant, Vinoba Bhave, heard of the troubles in Telangana and set off on foot towards their epicenter.[37]

Bhave, who was living in Gandhi's ashram, had been one of his most cherished disciples: the Mahatma had selected him as the first "individual *satyagrahi*" in the civil disobedience campaign of 1940.[38] Clad in *khadi* robes and acetate eyeglasses, Bhave embodied the saintly air of his assassinated mentor.[39] He arrived in the village of Pochempelli on April 18, as low-caste laborers were threatening rebellion to acquire land for cultivation. Bhave, as mediator, persuaded a large landlord, Ramachandra Reddy, to donate 100 acres to the laborers, initiating what would become known as the *bhoodan*, or "land-gift" movement.

After fifty days in Telangana, Bhave had collected 12,000 acres to distribute to the landless; returning to his ashram, he an invitation from the Prime Minister to discuss *bhoodan* with the Planning Commission. Bhave accepted, but eschewed the plane sent to transport him in favor of a two-month journey to the capital on foot. Walking through archways of mango leaves erected by exhilarated villagers, Bhave collected pledges

---

[36] Jerome B. Cohen, *The Impact of the Indian Five-Year Plan on Foodgrain Availabilities* (South Asia Branch, Division of Research for Near East, South Asia, and Africa, Office of Intelligence Research, November 30, 1951), RG 59 / 54D341 / Box 14 / Food, General Correspondence, 1951, USNA.

[37] For narratives and speeches attributed to Vinoba Bhave himself, see Acharya Vinoba Bhave, *From Bhoodan to Gramdan* (Tanjore: Sarvodaya Prachuralaya, 1957); and Vinoba Bhave, *Democratic Values and the Practice of Citizenship: Selections from the Addresses of Vinoba Bhave, 1951–1960* (Rajghat, Kashi [Varanasi]: Akhil Bharat Sarva Seva Sangh Prakashan, 1962). Three contemporary accounts are T.K. Oommen, *Charisma, Stability, and Change: An Analysis of Bhoodan-Gramdan Movement in India* (New Delhi: Thompson Press, 1972); Tarkeshwar Prasad Singh, *Bhoodan and Gramdan in Orissa: A Social Scientist's Analysis (the First Inter-Disciplinary Study of India's Famous Land Gift Movement)* (Rajghat, Kashi [Varanasi]: Akhil Bharat Sarva Seva Sangh Prakashan, 1973); and Hallam Tennyson, *India's Walking Saint: The Story of Vinoba Bhave* (Garden City, NY: Doubleday, 1955).

[38] "Mr. Vinoba Bhave Sent to Jail," *Times of India*, October 22, 1940.

[39] On the "saintly idiom" in Indian politics, see W.H. Morris-Jones, "India's Political Idioms," in *Modern India: An Interpretive Anthology* (London: Macmillan, 1971).

164 Hungry Nation

for another 17,000 acres of land en route to Delhi.[40] Arriving in the capital, Bhave held court for eleven days near the site of Gandhi's cremation; Rajendra Prasad came to his tent to pledge land from his own estate to the movement, and Nehru and members of the Planning Commission arrived to discuss how *bhoodan* might be used to remedy India's problems of food and agriculture.[41] Bhave had upbraided communist organizers in Telangana, yet even the prominent CPI leader Ajoy Ghosh made a pilgrimage to the encampment for lengthy conversations. Inviting *Acharya* Bhave to Delhi, Nehru had hoped to co-opt his spiritual appeal into central government planning. But the ascetic would prove less pliant than the Prime Minister had desired. Like his mentor, Bhave disavowed the notion that the state should be involved in voluntary village uplift, and he insisted that his program of land-giving would be tainted if braided into government schemes. He fled Delhi having granted nothing, keener to collect pledges than parry with politicians.

In the months to come, Bhave would secure promises of 300,000 acres from landlords in Uttar Pradesh, and 400,000 in Bihar. His creed grew more ambitious: Bhave asked landowners to think of India's landless as their sons, distributing their plots evenly among them. When the residents of the tribal village of Koraput, Orissa, voluntarily pooled their lands together in 1955, Bhave declared that *Gramdan*, "village donation," would pave the way for cooperative farming, and eventually, the actualization of *Gramraj*, or full village self-rule, a vision harkening back to the rural economics of J.C. Kumarappa. Adherents of the movement came to refer to themselves as the Sarvodaya Samaj – the "Uplift Army" – and announced that theirs was a voluntary cooperative venture, in contrast to the forced collectivization which had taken place in China and which they feared left-wing planners in Delhi were contemplating.[42]

By 1957, 1734 villages had pledged themselves in principle to collective rule and the abnegation of individual property.[43] Affiliates saw the Sarvodaya movement as the most radical step Indian citizens could take on their own accord to remedy the maladies of agricultural underproduction and unequal land holding. Farsighted representatives like Jayaprakash Narayan, who had signed on to the movement in its earliest days, saw in *bhoodan* the possibility of an end to India's food crisis. "Our work does not end with [*bhoodan*]," Narayan asserted in 1953. "Those

---

[40] S.K., "The Land Gift Movement in India: Vinoba Bhave and His Achievement," *The World Today* 14, no. 11 (November 1, 1958): 487–495; "A Man on Foot," *Time* 61, no. 19 (May 11, 1953): 34–39.

[41] "Acharya Bhave in Delhi," *Times of India*, November 15, 1951.

[42] *Sarvodaya Yojana [Planning Sarvodaya]* (New Delhi: Sasta Sahitya Mandal, 1953).

[43] "1,734 Villages Donated," *Times of India*, January 1, 1957.

The Disabilities Which Peasant and Land Can Suffer 165

who will be receiving lands will have to be provided with agricultural implements."[44] The interlinked project of *sampattidan* – wealth giving – would eventually provide ploughs, bullocks, seeds, and irrigation tools to poor agriculturalists.

Aware of its populist resonance, Congressmen continued to seek to appropriate the idioms of *bhoodan* in their own planning. In 1957, Shriman Narayan declared that in agriculture, there was "no fundamental difference between the ideologies of the Congress, Socialism, and Sarvodaya." He was mistaken: there was a large and widening gap. Bhave rejected Nehru's efforts to use donated lands for state-managed cooperative farming, and in 1957, the Prime Minister was rebuffed in his efforts to link the government's Community Development programs to *bhoodan*; Bhave rejected the alliance on the grounds that it would represent an effective end to the movement's bottom-up approach.[45] *Bhoodan's* focus on voluntary redistribution was inherently at odds with state schemes for land reform. "It is true that [land reform laws] should be made," Jayaprakash Narayan had declared in 1953, "but without the people's support a law is not worth the paper on which it is written."[46]

Yet the Congress' inability to link itself to Vinoba Bhave's populist campaign was of little ultimate consequence, given the poor material results of the movement. The 5 million acres pledged by April 1958 was only a tenth of Bhave's original goal of 50 million; only 800,000 of those acres were actually distributed to landless cultivators.[47] Bhave's devotees would tout the gains in productivity seen on donated lands, contending that village food scarcity would be overcome through cooperation that ensued in the wake of donations.[48] More objective assessments suggested outcomes similar to those actualized by legal land reform projects: the quality of lands given under *bhoodan* was poor, and holdings in "Gramdanized" villages were little different than they had been status quo ante.[49] *Bhoodan's* effects on the Indian psyche may have been salutary; they were undoubtedly less so for India's agricultural productivity.

---

[44] Jayaprakash Narayan, "Intervention in the Debate on General Secretary's Report, Betul, 16 June 1953," in *Jayaprakash Narayan: Selected Works*, ed. Bimal Prasad, vol. 6 (New Delhi: Manohar Publishers and Distributors, 2006), 343–354.

[45] Frankel, *India's Political Economy*, 106–107; S.K., "The Land Gift Movement in India."

[46] Jayaprakash Narayan, "Address at a Public Meeting Regarding Bhoodan Yagna, Secunderabad, 17 May 1953," in *Jayaprakash Narayan: Selected Works*, ed. Bimal Prasad, vol. 6 (New Delhi: Manohar Publishers and Distributors, 2006), 338–340.

[47] S.K., "The Land Gift Movement in India."

[48] See the figures for a *bhoodan* village given in Raghavendra Nath Misra, *Bhoodan Movement in India: An Economic Assessment* (New Delhi: S. Chand & Co., 1972), 150–151.

[49] Myrdal, *Asian Drama*, 1321–1323.

166   Hungry Nation

As *bhoodan* continued to "[wend] its humanizing way in and out of India's villages, blessing beneficiaries and donors alike," India's national leadership continued to weigh the proper balance between social equity and agricultural productivity.[50] One camp continued to prioritize equity and social reform over growth. "Before we aspire to produce sufficient grains for consumption of the vast Indian population," Congress organizer Devi Singh Chauhan wrote, "the real cultivator should have the certainty and confidence that the land he cultivates is his own. Then only he can produce more."[51] As the Planning Commission's Panel on Land Reforms gathered to prepare for the Second Five-Year Plan, its members cleaved to a similar vision of the primacy of land reform. "Other things being equal," they wrote, "a personally cultivated holding is likely to yield more than one cultivated through hired labour." In time, a "hard-working, contented, and prosperous peasantry working on the land" would not only produce more food, but enjoy increased purchasing power for industrial goods.[52]

Yet these were far from consensus views. In 1952, Community Development organizer S.K. Dey disputed the Planning Commission's assumption that equitable distribution and maximum productivity were compatible aims. "In our current circumstances," he wrote, "this is patently untrue. Equity in distribution can have material significance only when there is substance to distribute. Our overriding need is effecting an increase in that substance."[53] Even P.C. Mahalanobis was said to be dismissing the notion of agrarian reforms as an essential prerequisite for increased production in his drafting of the Second Five-Year Plan.[54] These doubts had more extreme echoes beyond the Congress. India's ascendant right-wing was suggesting that land reform was inimicable to agricultural production: the right-wing Jana Sangh declared the entire project of agrarian reform to be a bogey, averring that self-sufficiency in food would not require land reform, but the replacement of chemical fertilizers with bovine excreta and the use of bullocks in place of expensive tractors.[55]

---

[50] T.N. Singh, ed., *Handbook for Congressmen* (New Delhi: All India Congress Committee, 1957).
[51] Devi Singh Chauhan, "Task of Agrarian Reforms," in *Souvenir, 58th Plenary Session, A.I.C.C. 1953, Nanal Nagar*, 1953.
[52] Tomlinson, *The Economy of Modern India, 1860–1970*, 192.
[53] Frank J. Moore, "Land Reform and Social Justice in India," *Far Eastern Survey* 24, no. 8 (August 1, 1955): 124.
[54] Somnath Lahiri, "Agrarian Reforms Not of Decisive Significance," *New Age*, June 19, 1955.
[55] Bharatiya Jana Sangh, *Election Manifesto 1957* (New Delhi: Bharatiya Jana Sangh, 1957).

Besieged landlords began raising their voices against the seizure of their lands, casting them as affronts not only to their livelihoods, but to the shared goals of sustenance. By the time one of these landlords, P.P. Ananthanarayana Aiyar, saw it fit to petition the Prime Minister, he had been retired as a college professor for nearly two decades.[56] After service at the University of Rangoon and a brief stint with the Burma government, Aiyar had retired to his home village in Kerala to reinvent himself in retirement as an agriculturalist. "It may be somewhat odd," he wrote to the Prime Minister, "that a retired College Professor should turn a farmer – but I can claim to have made good." As the owner of a modest plot of land, Aiyar rented out parcels to a small cadre of agricultural laborers. Seeing himself as a munificent landlord interested in the amelioration of India's food crisis, Aiyar claimed to be making small investments in improved techniques. The Congress' claim that it had almost finished the project of land reform, Aiyar declared, was belied by the public drive against landlords in Kerala. Two years ago the Communists had swept to power in the wake of "virulent propaganda in the vernacular press against the land owning classes generally." The landlord, Aiyar lamented, was portrayed "as the one class responsible for the ills of the land."

Aiyar admitted that he had evicted a few tenants: "the have-nots, the unsocial elements of society," and those who had refused to pay their rent. But now, new legislation was promising evicted tenants a return to their holdings and forgiveness of unpaid rent. The new Kerala Agrarian Relations Bill, proposing a ceiling holding of 15 acres for any landowner, seemed to evidence the state's determination to starve itself. With Kerala's landlord classes painted "in the darkest of hues," owners like Aiyar had little incentive to produce food. The courts and public opinion alike were prejudiced against landowners like him, and Aiyar could feel the "damper to the farmers' enthusiasm to grow more food." Aiyar asked Nehru to recognize this mounting danger to India's quest for increased food production, and to intervene appropriately. A declaration of support for landlords, he wrote, would "deliver confidence and strength to the large farming community that will reflect in increased agricultural production in the land. The land owners and agricultural associations [will] then launch on their own a drive for the cent per cent increase in agricultural production that we all look forward to."

Nehru, eyes gleaming with plans for cooperative farms and collectivization, would have been an unlikely supporter of Kerala's landlords. But Aiyar's sentiment was echoed by landlords elsewhere, who lamented their

[56] P.P. Ananthanarayana Aiyar, letter to Jawaharlal Nehru, October 31, 1958, C. Rajagopalachari papers (V to XI), Subject Files, folder 69, NMML.

168   Hungry Nation

decline and appealed to the role that would ostensibly play in the nation's quest for food. Pioneering journalist Kusum Nair left New Delhi in 1958 to undertake a year-long trip across the length and breath of India to survey the progress of land reform – a subject which was unavoidable in conversations in the capital, and which was animating sharp debates in every corner of the country.[57]

In Andhra Pradesh's Trichur district, Nair met with the landlord of a large estate who declared that land reforms were destroying India. The *harijans* who once guarded his land, too large to map completely, were now stealing his coconuts instead. If land ceilings were finally imposed, "so-called cultivators with only 15 acres of land will have neither the interest nor the capacity to make the necessary investment to produce more." Many of the poor farmers whom Nair consulted were equally bearish on land reforms, seeing them as futile. In Guntur district, Nair met with Hanumanthu, a poor farmer who cultivated a single acre plot of *bajra* [pearl millet] after his other land had been confiscated to repay a debt left by his deceased father. "We have no work and no food and you ask me about land reforms," Hanumanthu lamented. "For the last four months I have been living on only one meal a day of *bajra*."When Hanumanthu refused to speak further, a school teacher stepped in to explain that already, all land available had been distributed voluntarily among family members to avoid losing their collective plot.

Sita Ram Goel enjoyed the convert's zeal. A Marxist in his student days, Goel had grown sickened by the Soviet experiment and Nehru's obsequiousness towards it. The group that he founded in 1952, the Society for Defence of Freedom in Asia, was worried about many things, but most urgently by the troubling events taking place across the Himalayas. Goel had personally authored all the books in the Society's "Communist Slave-Empire Series." No installment was particularly subtle, but *China Is Red with Peasants' Blood*, published in 1953, offered the most unequivocal warning.[58]

It was the heyday of "Hindi-Chini-bhai-bhai," the notion that Indians and Chinese were Asian "brothers." In the name of fraternal cooperation and *panchsheel* – the shared values of mutual respect, non-aggression, non-intervention, equality, and peaceful coexistence – Nehru had lent his support to the People's Republic of China over the Republic of Taiwan in the United Nations, and had refused to condemn the 1950 invasion of Tibet. All this was repugnant to Sita Ram Goel. But no Indian

---

[57] Nair, *Blossoms in the Dust*.
[58] Ram Sita Goel, *China Is Red with Peasants' Blood* (Calcutta: Society for Defence of Freedom, 1953).

adulation of the People's Republic was as troubling as the way in which Congress' planners seemed to be ogling Chinese agrarian collectivization. Dedicating his manifesto to India's peasants "with a prayer that they should escape the doom which parasitic and self-righteous bookworms and politicians of the cities plan for them," Goel lambasted the notion that Chinese collectivization was any kinder than its Soviet predecessor. "The rice we import from Red China," he declared, chronicling the plight of those forced onto collective farms, "is stained with the blood of the Chinese peasants."

Goel, an unabashed Hindu nationalist, was wrong about many things. But he was correct in his belief that India's planners, by the mid 1950s, were seeing in China a riveting model for agrarian reform. China was not the first foreign influence on collaborative agriculture in India. In the early 1950s, India had sent government officials to Israel to receive training in cooperative farming on small *moshavim*.[59] The United States had sent advisors on cooperative credit to India, hopeful that this venture might stave off more radical turns.[60] But before the Sino-Indian war torpedoed the lure of *panchsheel*, and the curtains were pulled back upon China's devastating mid-decade famine, it was the People's Republic that seemed to offer by example the most promising solution for the twinned problems of land reform and agricultural productivity.

China's luster had grown over the course of the decade. New Delhi had appealed to Peking for intermittent food aid in the early 1950s, signing a major agreement on rice imports in May 1952.[61] By 1954, rumors of remarkable agricultural growth had trickled across the border: agricultural land, it was said, had been reorganized into cooperative and collective farms, providing abundant rice to a hungry peasantry. By 1955, Indian planners had begun to investigate. An Indian Trade Union delegation returned from a Chinese sojourn to report on 60,000 bustling producers' cooperatives. B.L. Sahney, a senior Ministry of Food official, went to China to settle outstanding debts from the earlier rice imports, coming back with reports of warehouses brimming with rice. Late in the same year, the Planning Commission invited agricultural economist Chen Han-seng to speak on China's agricultural successes, nodding

---

[59] "Introducing Cooperative Farming in India: Four Officers Studying Progress in Israel," *Times of India*, May 19, 1953.

[60] John J. Wilkey, *Farm Planning and Cooperative Credit* (New Delhi: Division of Cooperation, Ministry of Agriculture, Government of India, 1957). RG 469 / P 161 A / Box 7 / India Agriculture Reports, Jun–Dec 1957, USNA.

[61] Frankel, *India's Political Economy*, 139–142; B.L. Sahney, Report Submitted by Shri B.L. Sahney on the Food Agreement with China, External Affairs – Far East Asia – 3(19)-FEA, 1955(Secret), NAI.

170   Hungry Nation

approvingly at his estimate that Chinese cultivators were anticipating a
35 to 40 percent increase in production over the next five years.

Tempted to see things for themselves, two competing missions set off
for China the following year.[62] The Planning Commission designated
R.K. Patil as head of a Delegation on Agrarian Cooperatives, while
the Ministry of Food and Agriculture, locked in their dispute with the
Planning Commission over agricultural targets, launched its own mission. The dueling legations went on similar tours of producers' cooperatives and cooperative farms in the summer of 1956, and both missions
returned home with glowing reports of China's new cooperatives, where
peasants were reclaiming wastelands, constructing roads, irrigating
canals, and digging wells, having increased foodgrain output by 15 to
30 percent over three years. Members of both missions agreed that the
Second Five-Year Plan should set a goal of 10,000 cooperative farms in
India, and the Planning Commission took the unusual step of releasing
their report in Hindi in hopes of reaching a wider audience.[63]

The enthusiasm of leftists could not entirely mute dissent. Two
frustrated members of the Planning Commission delegation to China
reached out to the United States Embassy with their fears that planners
were heading down a dangerous path, prompting a rare meeting between
R.K. Patil and American diplomatic staff.[64] But Nehru was euphoric to
be given evidence that massive growth in foodgrain production could be
had without a major increase in capital investment. Over several years,
the Prime Minister had grown ever more confident in pushing his party
towards the left, famously committing India to a "socialistic pattern of
society where the principle means of production are under social ownership or control" at the Congress meeting at Avadi in 1955.[65] A year prior,
he had declared that India had "no other choice but cooperative farming"; these Chinese missions gave him the support he needed.[66] Writing

---

[62] *Report of the Indian Delegation to China on Agricultural Planning and Techniques* (New
Delhi: Ministry of Food and Agriculture, Government of India, 1956); R.K. Patil,
Report of the Indian Delegation to China on Agrarian Cooperatives (New Delhi: Planning
Commission, Government of India, 1957).

[63] A.K. Patil, ed., *Chini mein Krishi-Sahkari-Sansthayaen ke Aadhyayanarth Gaye Bharatiya
Pratinidhi Mandal ka Report [Agricultural Cooperatives in China]* (New Delhi: Yojana
Ayog, Bharat Sarkar, 1957).

[64] R.K. Patil, "Observations by Shri R.K. Patil, Leader of the Delegation on the Minutes
of Dissent by Shri B.J. Patel and Shri P.N. Rana," 1956, RG 469 / P 279 / Box 1 / Div
Affairs Agriculture, USNA.

[65] Indian National Congress, *Resolutions [of the] Indian National Congress Sixtieth Session,
Satyamurthinagar, Avadi, Madras, 21st to 23rd January 1955* (New Delhi: All India
Congress Committee, 1955).

[66] Low, *The Egalitarian Moment*, 23–24.

his Chief Ministers in August 1956, the Prime Minister asserted that China's "millions of cooperative farms" had not required an increase in fertilizer input, thus conserving funds for industrial development. "They are succeeding in increasing their agricultural production at a faster pace than we can," he reported. "Surely, it should not be beyond our powers to do something that China can do."

Nehru's assertiveness dovetailed with that of a galvanized Congress left. P.C. Mahalanobis, had already been taking stock of the Chinese example; a year later, he would travel to the People's Republic at Zhou Enlai's invitation. Mahalanobis had been frustrated by the realization that the government could exert strong pressure on the industrial sector's small set of key players, but not in agriculture, where there were millions of individual actors scattered across thousands of villages. The two missions' reports and Nehru's exaltation of cooperative farms emboldened Mahalanobis to set higher agricultural targets in the Second Five-Year Plan than many state planners had previously believed possible. In October 1956, under pressure from Nehru, Food Minister A.P. Jain agreed to deliver a comprehensive plan for cooperative farming in India.[67] And early the following year, Congress president Gulzarilal Nanda declared that the process of land reform in India would lead ultimately to cooperative farming and "co-operative village management."[68]

Rhapsodic leftists in the Congress might have done well to heed the quiet concern of Sunil Guha, a party economist and longtime student of India's food program. "As in all democratic countries," Guha wrote in 1957, taking stock of the delegations to China, "the [Indian] peasant is a firm believer in his proprietary right. Hence any attempt at collectivization on the Russian model, which does away with the individual peasant's economic autonomy, is bound to meet the peasant's emotional resistance from the very start."[69] Within two years, the left would meet that resistance and its explosive results head-on.

Indian citizens and planners had shown interest in the possibilities of pooling agricultural resources since the heyday of the cooperative movement in the 1920s and 1930s. In the earliest years of independence, vernacular visions of plenty had often appealed to the apparent success of experiments overseas. *Aaj*, a widely circulated Hindi daily printed in Benares, reported breathlessly on the possibilities of cooperative and collective farming in a 1951 dispatch. When Russia had faced its own food

---

[67] "Cooperative Farming: National Plan Is Being Prepared," *Times of India*, October 24, 1956.

[68] Gulzar Lal Nanda, *Progress of Land Reforms in India* (New Delhi: All India Congress Committee, 1957).

[69] Guha, *India's Food Problem*, 36.

problem, it reported, it used the "power of law" to "create gigantic farms the size of two to four villages, uniting all of their agricultural land."[70]

Yet as Nehru and the Congress left moved to introduce collective farming at the end of the decade, there were no more than a handful of experiments in India itself that planners could cite as domestic precedent. A group of agricultural economists cautioned as much in a 1958 preparatory report. "There are no genuine cooperative farming societies" in India, they concluded, "whose working can be helpful in deriving any guidance or inspiration." All existing societies were highly specialized – cooperative farms for displaced people, army veterans, or tribal citizens being induced to farming – and provided little data into the possibilities of widespread collective farming now being considered.[71] Economists had tried to compile some of that data, but had concluded that the project was politically untenable. A group at Delhi Polytechnic had suggested that collective farming could mean that "obsolete and primitive methods of agriculture will be replaced by up-to-date and modern methods [and] farmers will get accustomed to enjoy a decent standard of living which will provide them with a balanced diet," but that group farming was ultimately a political non-starter.[72] Another working group at Delhi University's Department of Economics had suggested, presciently, that even if group farming had the potential for success on the food front, political transformations would ultimately lose out to advances in "techniques, irrigation, crop patterns, and prices."[73]

In 1958, agricultural economist Daniel Thorner, who had long provided sage counsel to the Planning Commission, toured the Indian countryside to observe the progress of land reform, keenly aware of the top-down push for collective farming.[74] "The pressure for such group farming," he reported, "does not spring from India's villages. It is rather a policy laid down in New Delhi. The village strong have not asked for joint farms; they do not intend to surrender control of part or all of their land in favor of their tenants, crop sharers, or poorer neighbors." Kusum Nair similarly reported on an Uttar Pradesh village where poor farmers had seen their lands pooled in accordance with that state's five-year-old

---

[70] "Let's Get Farming!," *Aaj*, January or February 1951.

[71] *Progress Evaluation Report about Cooperative Farming* (New Delhi: Government of India, 1958).

[72] Shiv Chand and A.H. Kapoor, *Land and Agriculture of India: An Agronomic Study* (New Delhi: Metropolitan Book Co., 1959).

[73] Raj Krishna, "Agrarian Reform in India: The Debate on Ceilings," *Economic Development and Cultural Change* 7, no. 3 (April 1, 1959): 302–317.

[74] Daniel Thorner, *Prospects for Cooperation in Indian Agriculture* (Paris: L'École des hautes études, 1960).

The Disabilities Which Peasant and Land Can Suffer 173

Consolidation of Holdings Act. "Why," one farmer asked, "has consolidation been done against our will – compulsorily? We all know, now that *chakbandi* [consolidation] has been done, the next step will be to take away our lands. *Russibundi* will come here." The farmer was interrupted by a friend worried by another rumor. "We hear," he added, "the government will take away our lands and make hotels for us where we will be given our meals."[75]

The villagers' fears were closer than they might have realized. In October 1958, Jawaharlal Nehru convened and personally oversaw a committee to plan for India's agricultural development; in January, the Congress Working Committee met at Nagpur to endorse a "Resolution on Agrarian Organizational Pattern."[76] The resolution called for the completion of all remaining land reforms and the introduction of land ceilings, by year's end. Rather than turning over confiscated land to individuals, it would be given over to village *panchayats* for the establishment of "cooperative joint farming." The Nagpur resolution affirmed nothing beyond what had already been incorporated into the Second Five-Year Plan and the program of the National Development Council. Yet Nehru's push for cooperative farming was among the worst political miscalculations of his career.[77] At Nagpur, there had been little concordance as to the wisdom of such a push: a sympathetic agricultural economist in attendance had warned that proponents of cooperative agriculture must work to convince citizens "without the blandishments or the iron fist of Government. Involuntary co-operation is slavery, dishonest co-operation is a negation of the principle itself."[78] A British diplomat cabled to London to contend that Nagpur's push had little chance of succeeding among a peasantry "much more interested in the improvement of local crops" than in ideologically minded undertakings.[79] The *Times of India* illustrated Nehru's obduracy with a caricature of the Prime Minister proudly displaying the resolution to a room of muzzled Congressmen.[80]

---

[75] Nair, *Blossoms in the Dust*, 75.

[76] Frankel, *India's Political Economy*, 161–165.

[77] The Democratic Research Service, an anti-socialist advocacy group founded by M.R. Masani, released a thorough compendium of writing and speeches related to the Nagpur resolution and its aftermath. *Co-Operative Farming: The Great Debate between Jawaharlal Nehru, C Rajagopalachari, Jayprakash Narayan, K.M. Munshi, M.R. Masani, N.G. Ranga, Shirman Narayan, Frank Moraes, and Others* (Bombay: Democratic Research Service, 1959).

[78] S.V. Ayyar, "The Food Problem in India To-Day," in *The Indian National Congress, 64th Session, Nagpur, Souvenir* (Reception Committee, Indian National Congress, 1959), B-68.

[79] Malcolm MacDonald, "The Congress Party and Its Nagpur Session," February 27, 1959, DO 201/10, UKNA.

[80] "Now I Can Proceed without Fear of Contradiction [Cartoon]," *Times of India*, March 18, 1959.

174   Hungry Nation

The Prime Minister had repeatedly declared that cooperative farming would be voluntary, and would not truncate private property rights. But a conservative bloc of classical liberals, free-market advocates, and votaries of the middle peasantry responded with insurrectionary zeal. Erstwhile Food Minister K.M. Munshi characterized the bill as a prelude to despotism. Peasant leader Charan Singh – who had expressed his hesitation about the very project of *zamindari* abolition since independence – proclaimed that if the Nagpur resolution were implemented, India's proud peasantry would be reduced to wage laborers.[81] "These Sino-socialist minded planners," N.G. Ranga added, "have no compunction to plan for the communisation of all *kisans* – landed and landless – into a miserable status of a wage slavery under the so-called elected bosses of cooperative farms."[82] All declared that cooperative farming would do nothing to ameliorate India's vexing food crisis.

It was M.R. Masani, then an independent MLA from Ranchi East district, who took up the cudgel in Parliament.[83] The former socialist and one-time Bombay mayor had drifted rightwards since the war, and in February 1959, he lambasted in the Lok Sabha Congress' "adventures in the field of agrarian legislation," vowing "unrelenting opposition to the proposals for joint farming in place of the traditional Indian method of peasant family farming." Cooperative credit was acceptable to Masani and his allies, as well as voluntary collaboration, yet "collective farming of the Soviet-China model" represented an assault on personal property and freedom and had no place in India. If Nagpur went forward, "the same conditions will recur here as happened in Russia. You will have chaos, you will have a catastrophic drop in food production – and you cannot let the country starve."

Amidst the political imbroglio of 1959, a frustrated Punjabi farmer sent a short manifesto to C. Rajagopalachari.[84] B. Sharma had sent similar missives before – to the Planning Commission, to A.P. Jain, and even to the Prime Minister himself. But he believed that Rajagopalachari would be more sympathetic to his mimeographed essay. Having consulted "hundreds of articles written by eminent writers, scholars and experts on Land Reforms, Ceilings on Land Holdings and Cooperative

---

[81] Low, *The Egalitarian Moment*, 24. On Singh's hesitance to endorse *zamindari* abolition, see Charan Singh, *Abolition of Zamindari, Two Alternatives* (Allahabad: Kitabistan, 1947), iv.

[82] *Co-Operative Farming*, 27.

[83] M.R. Masani, *Dangers of the Co-Operative Farming* (Nidubrolu: Peasant Protest Committee, 1959).

[84] B. Sharma, letter to C. Rajagopalachari, June 8, 1959, C. Rajagopalachari papers (VI to XI), Subject Files, folder 69, NMML.

The Disabilities Which Peasant and Land Can Suffer 175

Farming etc.," Sharma reported with regret that "none has tried to read the mind of the farmer and reproduce the same." Sharma concluded his treatise on the problems in Indian agriculture with the idea that the Indian farmer had little confidence in the government. This, in turn, had precluded him from developing the "daring to do" that was required to produce more food. He thanked Rajagopalachari, in closing, for the campaign he had just launched on behalf of the Indian farmer.

At the beginning of the year, the conservative thinkers convening in Bombay salons for meetings of the Forum for Free Enterprise sensed that Nehru was about to embark upon a dangerous experiment. M.R. Masani, N.G. Ranga, Rajagopalachari, and others had invited Japan's ambassador to India to speak at the Forum on land reform there, in hopes of exploring a more agreeable model than those offered by China or the Soviet Union.[85] Thinkers at conservative institutions like Calcutta's Institute of Political and Social Studies met in the spring to chart the failures of the Chinese and Soviet examples, contending that there were only a few global cooperative farms, largely in Mexico and Israel, which merited the first word.[86] These groups inveighed against a Prime Minister who continued to assert that joint farming was the only feasible means by which India could increase its food production and achieve real rural uplift.[87]

The Congress Party could not stand the mounting centrifugal conflict. In early June, the All India Agricultural Federation, a lobbying group run by wealthy peasants, met in Madras to moot the forming of a conservative opposition to the Congress.[88] C. Rajagopalachari, whose antipathy towards Nehru's food and agriculture policies stretched back to his unilateral decontrol of food in Madras in 1951, called for a preparatory meeting in Ahmedabad in August.[89] The new party, Rajagopalachari declared, would be called Swatantra – "Culture" – and it "would stand for the freedom of the men on farm, the freedom of the farm and of the family, and against totalitarianism's attack on the freedom of the individual." N.G. Ranga quickly decamped from the Congress to join, as did a suite of parliamentarians from other parties. Swatantra's platform

[85] C. Rajagopalachari, "Text of Speech on 'Land Reforms in Japan' Delivered by His Excellency Dr. Shiroshi Nasu, Japanese Ambassador in India," December 1958, C. Rajagopalachari (VI to XI), Speeches and Writings by Others, folder 20, NMML.
[86] Balraj Puri, *Cooperative Farming: A Critique* (Calcutta: Institute of Political and Social Studies, 1959), 17.
[87] "Nehru Defends Joint Farming," *Times of India*, March 29, 1959.
[88] Sadhna Sharma, ed., "Andhra Pradesh," in *States Politics in India* (New Delhi: Mittal Publications, 1995), 63.
[89] Swatantra Party, *Preparatory Convention, Bombay, August 1959* (Bombay: Popular Book Depot, 1959).

176 Hungry Nation

did not revolve solely around agriculture but used the threat of collectivization to inveigh against what its leadership saw as the larger menace of Nehruvian "statism."[90] Yet its core constituency was India's wealthy peasantry, and the party vowed to fight state interference in agriculture and to support the "the self-employed peasant proprietor who is interested in obtaining, and equipped to obtain, the highest yield from his land."[91]

Few of the Prime Minister's miscalculations had been as dramatic as his failure to anticipate the popular and political blowback from the Nagpur resolution.[92] Developments across the border worsened matters. China's springtime suppression of the revolt in Tibet and the subsequent flight of the Dalai Lama to India ushered in distrust of all things Chinese. By May, Nehru was showing signs of retreat, sponsoring a bill that would promote "service cooperatives" for credit and implements instead of fully cooperative farms; a month later, a plan to train Congress volunteers in the establishment of these service cooperatives was scrapped. And over the summer, the Congress wrestled with the contested role of state trading in foodgrains – a debate which led to A.P. Jain's resignation in August.

The failure of the Nagpur resolution and its explosive aftermath led to quiet reassessments within the Congress. A planning seminar was held in the hill station town of Ooty, and C. Subramaniam was asked to prepare a brief on the Nagpur debacle and the way forward.[93] Long seen as ministerial material by local and foreign observers, Subramaniam had been rumored as the top candidate for Food and Agriculture Minister as early as 1954, though lost out to A.P. Jain; in the summer of 1959, he was seen as a promising candidate for Congress president.[94] Subramaniam, who would soon reemerge as the key strategist of India's "new agricultural strategy," gave a subtle account of Congress' failure. Indian peasants, he contended, had no faith that collective farms could work "without the compulsions of a totalitarian state." There was a place for state trading in

[90] Howard L. Erdman, *The Swatantra Party and Indian Conservatism* (Cambridge: Cambridge University Press, 1967), 63.

[91] *To Prosperity through Freedom: The Swatantra Party's Statement of Policy Adopted at the National Convention in Patna on March 19 and 20 1960*, Swatantra Series no. 3 (Bombay: Swatantra Party, 1960), 15.

[92] The Nagpur resolution's "revolutionary possibilities," Lloyd and Susanne Rudolph note, "seem to have dawned on Congress members only after it had been introduced." Rudolph and Rudolph, *In Pursuit of Lakshmi*, 316–318.

[93] Subramaniam, "Land and Food: Problems of Implementation of Congress Party Policy."

[94] H.G. Josif, "Possible Cabinet Changes in India," November 24, 1954, RG 59 / D 373 / Box 3 / Memo File, 1954, USNA; Stanley A. Kochanek, *The Congress Party of India: The Dynamics of a One-Party Democracy* (Princeton: Princeton University Press, 1968), 66.

foodgrains, he contended, yet Congress needed to recognize that Indian citizens were "allergic to the idea of 'Joint-Farming Co-operatives,' and that it is a sound and healthy national instinct which has given rise to this allergy." Land reform, carried out incorrectly, was worse than non-action. "It will diminish food production; it will aggravate the present disorders in the marketing of foodgrains; it will add greatly to the difficulties of mobilizing resources necessary for planned development."

Diehards within the party continued to seek out more agreeable models for cooperative farming. At the turn of the year, the Ministry of Community Development and Cooperation sponsored a six-week junket to view cooperative farms in Israel and Yugoslavia.[95] Yet most within the Congress realized that the Nagpur folly had been a severe blow to the Congress' authority and its plans for a political solution to the country's food problem.

As Congress sought a different way forward, the 1962 elections loomed as a referendum on the party's performance during the Nagpur debacle. In the lead-up to them, Swatantra continued to gain traction among free-market liberals and independent cultivators heartened by the new party's castigation of "the ruling party, which has failed singularly to deal with the food problem."[96] The Jana Sangh was gaining capital from Nagpur, as well. Pitambar Das, the party's president, lamented Congress' perverse fascination with Chinese planning, and skewered the "ever-changing land laws of Government [which] have created in the peasant's mind a feeling of insecurity in respect of his own rights, and he is not able to put in as much labour into his farm as he should."[97] In its electoral manifesto, the party vowed to "make the farmer master of his land," decrying cooperative farming as "detrimental to democracy and unsuited to the needs of increasing production per acre of land."[98] By contrast, opposition from the left accused the Congress of having retreated fully from the social aims of land reform. The Praja Socialist Party urged the Planning Commission – which "seems to have become lukewarm about land reforms" – to continue "to ensure the liquidation of capitalist farming and the provision of land to the tiller of the soil," urging a lowering of land ceilings and the restriction of ownership to cultivators alone.[99]

[95] *Report of the Study Team on the Working of the Cooperative Movement in Yugoslavia and Israel* (New Delhi: Ministry of Community Development and Cooperation, Government of India, 1960).
[96] *To Prosperity through Freedom.*
[97] Pitamber Das, *Presidential Address [to the] Eighth Annual Session, Raghuji Nagar, Nagpur, January 23, 24 and 25 1960* (New Delhi: Bharatiya Jana Sangh, 1960).
[98] Bharatiya Jana Sangh, *Election Manifesto 1962* (New Delhi: Bharatiya Jana Sangh, 1962).
[99] Mukut Behari Lal, *An Appraisal of the Third Five Year Plan* (New Delhi: Praja Socialist Party, 1961).

178   Hungry Nation

In campaign materials, Congress continued to trumpet its "many agrarian reforms which form the basis for rural progress," though made no mention of Nagpur and its aftermath. Voters' memories, however, were not so short: returning from canvassing in rural districts, Gulzarilal Nanda was "appalled to see that half my energy during the five weeks or so of the campaign had to be spent simply defending myself and the Congress on the question of cooperative farming. In that area, everybody was told the Congress wanted to take away the peasant's land."[100] These citizens had no doubt been inspired by the effective campaigning of the Jana Sangh and Swatantra, who made major gains in the elections. The Congress was still the overwhelming winner – but the Jana Sangh became the opposition party in Uttar Pradesh, and Swatantra in Bihar, Gujarat, Rajasthan, and Orissa, having capitalized upon a wellspring of support from ex-princes, former *zamindars*, and large landowners,

Nehru made one final push for land reform prior to his death. In 1961 India's Supreme Court issued a ruling in the case of *Karimbil Kunhikoman vs. State of Kerala*, declaring the Agrarian Relations Act whose passage P.P. Ananthanarayana Aiyar had so feared was unconstitutional in allowing seizures of certain "estates."[101] In effect, the ruling cast doubt on the constitutionality of the entire project of land reform. The Prime Minister responded by proposing a Seventeenth Amendment to the Constitution in 1963 which would protect a more capacious view of "estates" eligible for seizure and redistribution. Swatantra and the Jana Sangh were galvanized: the latter party declared that New Delhi was "seeking powers to seize land from the tiller of the soil under any kind of tenure for any purpose," and invoked fears of collectivization that had never truly died down among the peasantry.

The bill initially failed in the absence of a legislative quorum, and Nehru was dismayed that some Congress parliamentarians broke with the party to join the opposition to the bill. After a reintroduction in April 1964, the Seventeenth Amendment bill was passed into law. But legislative opposition had been fierce, and had continued to invoke the specter of Nagpur. A.P. Jain, the erstwhile Food and Agriculture Minister who had subsequently resigned from the Congress, campaigned with Swatantra against the bill, accusing his former party of threatening collectivization once more.[102] Those supporting the bill and other land reform measures, he wrote, "have never been near the land! They do not know what

[100] Frankel, *India's Political Economy*, 209.
[101] Graham, *Hindu Nationalism and Indian Politics*, 186.
[102] See Ajit Prasad Jain, *"Lawless Legislation": Why Swatantra Opposes the 17th Amendment* (New Delhi: Swatantra Party, 1963).

The Disabilities Which Peasant and Land Can Suffer   179

land is; they do not know what is grown on it; they do not know how it is grown."[103] Elsewhere, Swatantra campaigners warned that India's landlords were so repulsed by new ceiling legislation that they would withdraw their investments in agriculture in favor of more lucrative sectors.[104] And a young Jana Sangh parliamentarian, Atal Bihari Vajpayee, inveighed loudly in the Lok Sabha against the threat of cooperatives in the Parliament. "Whenever there is a food crisis," the parliamentarian declared, "we want to adopt techniques that neither fit a democratic structure nor pass the test of practicality. In respect of agriculture we look to communist countries and want to adopt communist methods, while the truth is that agriculture has not yet been properly organized in communist countries." He warned the Food Minister that "in case you entertain the hidden hope that one day you would rob the small landholders of their land, bring it together and do cooperative farming on that land, the people would never accept it."[105] Four decades later, after a new, muscular agrarian lobby had remade India's political landscape, Vajpayee would become India's tenth Prime Minister.

As the decade dawned, there were few sharper students of Asian land reform than Wolf Ladejinsky and Gunnar Myrdal. Ladejinsky, a Soviet refugee who had made his name in the United States' Department of Agriculture, had been a frequent consultant on land reform projects in Japan, China, Taiwan, and Vietnam.[106] Myrdal, the celebrated Swedish economist, had arrived in India in 1957, declaring himself obsessed with the "momentous human drama of the desperate strivings for national consolidation and economic development in the South Asian countries."[107] Over the next four years, Myrdal would haunt seminars across Delhi, and with help from a rotating cast of assistants, he would work to produce *Asian Drama: An Inquiry into the Poverty of Nations*, the most exhaustive account to date of India's economic potential.[108]

By the middle of the 1960s, both Ladejinsky and Myrdal were prepared to declare Indian land reform a washout. Even if land reform

[103] *17th Amendment vs. Farm, Family, Freedom* (Bombay: Swatantra Party, 1964).
[104] Sardar Bahadur Lal Singh, "Need for Re-Appraisal of Our Agrarian Policy," in *Swarajya Special Number 1962* (Madras: Barathan Publications, 1962), 193–195.
[105] Atal Bihari Vajpayee, "Ushering Economic Imperialism in the Name of Co-Operatives," in *Four Decades in Parliament*, ed. N.M. Ghatate, vol. 2: *State of the Economy* (New Delhi: Shipra Publications, 1996), 339–343.
[106] Wolf Ladejinsky, *Agrarian Reform as Unfinished Business: The Selected Papers of Wolf Ladejinsky*, ed. Louis Joseph Walinsky (New York: Oxford University Press, 1977).
[107] Yvonne Hirdman, *Alva Myrdal: The Passionate Mind* (Bloomington: Indiana University Press, 2008), 309.
[108] See William J. Barber, *Gunnar Myrdal: An Intellectual Biography* (Basingstoke: Palgrave Macmillan, 2008); and Benjamin Siegel, "On 'Asian Drama,'" *Humanity* 8, no. 1 (March 2017): 195–205.

180   Hungry Nation

had been more successful, Myrdal declared that it would have had little ameliorative effect upon India's food deficit. "A radical redistribution of land," he wrote, "might still reduce the volume of marketable foodstuffs. Once released from the obligation to part with a large share of their crop to landowners, former tenants might easily be tempted to augment their low levels of consumption. [T]he problem of feeding the non-agricultural population would continue and might very easily be aggravated by such a change."[109]

Ladejinsky offered an even dourer assessment. "All the disabilities which peasant and land can suffer," he wrote after a 1964 visit, "are to be found in many of the 600,000 villages of India." While there were pockets of agricultural dynamism, they contributed minimally to the nation's dire food situation. At independence, the Indian government had rightly sought "to ease the lot of the peasantry by a drastic overhaul of the land system, the complexity of which almost defies description."[110] There were abundant "handicaps" to land reform that Ladejinsky deemed unique to India: the nation's vast size, presumed overpopulation, and administrative decentralization, its fragmentation of land and a lack of good records, and scant opportunities in an anemic industrial sector. But none of these factors were sufficient to explain the colossal failure of land reform in India. "Most of the handicaps," Ladejinsky concluded, "are not always causes but in a large measure consequences of attitudes displayed by state politicians and legislatures. This anti-reform sentiment has proved to be a crucial element in thwarting India's expectations."[111]

There was a consensus view among foreign observers that land reform in India had reached its limits, and that further efforts offered little gain to the Indian granary. Large *zamindars* had seen their estates liquidated, and some had taken to rather unenthusiastic agricultural tinkering on their shrunken lands. An American observer noticed as much while touring the pruned estate of the Raja of Kasmanda, who showed off a new, ox-drawn disc harrow. "When I commented upon this newly found interest in agriculture," Thomas Metcalf wrote, "he replied, 'Ah well, it gets

---

[109] Myrdal, *Asian Drama*, 1373–1374. See also Daniel Thorner's rebuttal, "Predatory Capitalism in Indian Agriculture," *Economic and Political Weekly* 3, no. 43 (October 26, 1968): A3–A4.

[110] Wolf Ladejinsky, "Agrarian Reform in Asia," *Foreign Affairs* 42, no. 3 (April 1, 1964): 452–458.

[111] The political scientist Atul Kohli would come to a similar conclusion two decades later. Land reforms, Kohl wrote, "highlighted the incapacity of the Indian state to confront propertied interests ... As the consciousness of this political weakness took hold, the state altered its half-hearted confrontational attitude toward the landowner and, in the later 1960s, moved toward an explicit support for agrarian capitalism." Atul Kohli, *The State and Poverty in India* (Cambridge: Cambridge University Press, 1989), 67–72.

one out of doors into the air.' "[112] John P. Lewis, an influential American policy analyst, concluded that further land reform efforts were a dead end. "There are not enough large landholders left in India," he wrote, "for any politically feasible redistribution of land to narrow the range of holdings or broaden the ownership base very much, nor is there any convincing evidence that the larger cultivators cannot be effectively actuated by the same incentives that can appeal to the smaller ones." Effective cooperative or collaborative farming, even if politically feasible, relied so much on mechanization that its gains would "be largely irrelevant to India for a long time yet."[113]

Nehru had been among the last Congressmen to place his faith in the transformative power of land reform, and the Prime Minister's death in May 1964 was the end of the line. Food imports were up after an unwanted extension of the P.L. 480 agreement with the United States, and there was little political will to push for land ceilings or further redistribution. B.R. Ambedkar's Republican Party of India, upon Lal Bahadur Shastri's appointment as Prime Minister, sighed in a manifesto that "the Government of India appears to have completely ignored the interest of the landless laborers in India," leaving tillers "crushed in the villages under the dead weight of feudalism."[114] India's landless were still suffering; its godowns were still only half-full.

The failure of land reform marked the end of an era when political machination seemed to hold the answer to India's search for abundance. India could not transform the agricultural and social practices of its citizens, nor raise yields by sheer force of will. Its byzantine system of control and distribution in food could not magically eke grains from the ground. And while it was doubtful that collective or cooperative farms held the secret to plenty, an obdurate anti-reform sentiment and the influence of India's propertied classes made substantive land reform a political nonstarter. It was in this moment of diminished ardor for political reform that Indian planners grew more ready to embrace alternate models for growth – ones rooted in the promise of markets, the power of concentrated inputs, and new trust in technological advance.

In 1966, the Southern India Chamber of Commerce reflected upon India's food problem, which continued to defy planners' best intensions. "It is a sad commentary on India's economic progress," the author of

[112] Thomas R. Metcalf, "Landlords without Land: The U.P. Zamindars Today," *Pacific Affairs* 40, no. 1/2 (April 1, 1967): 5–18.
[113] John P. Lewis, *Quiet Crisis in India: Economic Development and American Policy* (Washington, DC: Brookings Institution, 1962), 147.
[114] *Charter of Demands Submitted to Shri Lal Bahadur Shastri* (New Delhi: Republican Party of India, 1964).

the Chamber's brochure wrote, "that even after nineteen years of political freedom and the execution of three Five Year Plans, 'Freedom from Hunger' continues to elude a satisfactory solution."[115] The Chamber made a predictable plea for freer markets and subsidies for irrigation, pesticides, and chemical fertilizers. But it also looked back at India's land reform efforts and lamented that two decades' efforts had yielded so little. "'Land to the tiller,'" the Chamber asserted, "is indeed a catchy and fashionable phrase but in the absence of vast tracts of uncharted lands, it becomes an inane slogan, which of course has its own political though not economic value. It has only succeeded in accentuating rural discontent and unrest and has acted as a damper on agricultural productivity."

A new generation of Indian politicians were increasingly in agreement with the Chamber of Commerce's analysis. An earlier drive for equity and socialistic policy had wilted, and Indian citizens, peasants, planners, and politicians were beginning to articulate the need for selective inputs, price incentives, and the advance of wealthier peasants over their subsistence counterparts. The disabilities of land and peasant would remain as a different set of transformations that remade the political, social, and economic frameworks of Indian agriculture.

[115] *The Food Situation: A Study* (Madras: Southern India Chamber of Commerce, 1966).

6 The Ideological Origins of the Green Revolution

Jawaharlal Nehru ran his fingers along an ear of corn, its kernels large and full. Glenn Peterson, the Illinois farmer from whose crop the ear had been selected, flanked the Prime Minister with his three sons, the family clad in matching plaid overshirts. They stood proudly next to Nehru as he admired the corn, ignoring the journalists' flashbulbs flaring behind them.[1]

The late October day in 1949 had been a long one: the Prime Minister's six-car motorcade had left Chicago's stately Drake Hotel early in the morning, cruising through the West Side's black and Mexican purlieus to Oswego Avenue, where Highway 34 bridges the city and its rural hinterlands.[2] Nehru sat in the back seat of a Cadillac Sixty Special next to Theodore Schultz, the University of Chicago economist who, three years earlier, had chaired the American Famine Mission to India. As the city receded from view, their motorcade arrived in the green fields of the Fox River Valley. A century earlier, the valley was the Potawatomi heartland, but by the early decades of the twentieth century, with its native peoples dispossessed, the valley had become one of the most fertile stretches of land in the United States, brimming with bumper crops of corn.

Professor Schultz had taken a break from his research on the transformation of agricultural economies to guide Nehru through three of the valley's farms. "The farms were chosen," Schultz wrote in his pre-tour notes, to show "the several major stages of the farm family as it ascends the 'agricultural ladder.'"[3] The visit would not only showcase new technologies, Schultz hoped, but it might also highlight "the spiritual aspects of these families, the religion which they hold, and the educational,

---

[1] *Prime Minister Nehru Examines Corn Grown on an Illinois Farm*, Photograph, October 1949, 72–608, Harry S. Truman Library and Museum.

[2] "Two Busy Days Face Nehru on Chicago Visit," *Chicago Tribune*, October 24, 1949.

[3] Theodore W. Schultz, "Three Illinois Farms and Their Families: Introducing Prime Minister Nehru and His Party to Middle Western Agriculture and Farm Living, October 27, 1949," National Agricultural Library, United States Department of Agriculture.

183

184   Hungry Nation

Figure 10 Prime Minister Jawaharlal Nehru examines corn grown on an Illinois farm, October 1949. (Credit: Department of State, Courtesy of Harry S. Truman Library)

social, and economic organization into which they fit as these four families strive to achieve certain material and economic goals within a larger framework of enterprise." India, Schultz contended, had much to learn from Illinois' daring farmers.

The first stop of the morning had been William Smith's jointly tended 210-acre farm, resplendent with green stalks. The Prime Minister and his entourage moved on to the Petersons' farm, and over that ear of corn, heard how new credit lines had allowed the Petersons to buy new harvesting equipment. Finally, the group stopped at Albert G. Mitchell's diversified farm, where the success of the corn business had allowed the Mitchells to move into livestock and dairy. Sustenance came in the form of an early "thresher's dinner" prepared by Albert's wife, and the Prime Minister joined a crowd tucking into full tables of meat and starch.[4]

[4] "Visit to Illinois Farms," *Times of India*, October 28, 1949.

The Ideological Origins of the Green Revolution 185

Cornbread at the Mitchell's farm was a stark contrast with the Prime Minister's Oval Office meeting with President Harry Truman two weeks earlier.[5] With Secretary of State Dean Acheson and G.S. Bajpai listening, Nehru had outlined India's need to increase agricultural productivity and build up a major stockpile of wheat; in turn, the Prime Minister had listened to the President explain how the number of Americans living by agriculture had drastically diminished, while still accumulating a major surplus. It was with these transformations in mind that Nehru had arrived in Chicago. The day before his farm outing, Nehru had taken a private tour of the International Harvester Tractor Works; riding back from the Fox River Valley to a reception at the University of Chicago's International House, the Prime Minister listened to Professor Schultz's analysis of how America had managed to produce more. Each farmer they had met, Schultz contended, had been the beneficiaries of credit, implements, seeds, and chemicals – a package which had allowed them to ascend the agricultural "ladder" towards productivity and prosperity.[6]

The Prime Minister returned to India intrigued but unconvinced that these investments were possible in the context of an insolvent state barely two years old. In the wake of his visit, he invited a small team of American experts to India to discuss collaborative research and extension projects that could be undertaken under the new Point Four Program, which had been announced earlier in the year.[7] Schultz, for his part, returned to his office at the University of Chicago to immerse himself in research. It would be fifteen years before the publication of *Transforming Traditional Agriculture*, a massively influential text contending that agriculturalists in developing countries were not inefficient, but rather were hampered by a lack of access to advanced agricultural research and material inputs.[8] Nehru and Schultz's meeting foreshadowed a transformation in India's own agriculture that would take at least another decade to materialize. But the short ride from Chicago to the Fox River Valley and back suggests that, long before the Green Revolution took root in Indian soil, the ideas and institutions undergirding it were already crackling to life.

---

[5] "Memorandum of Conversation with the President and Jawaharlal Nehru," October 13, 1949, Acheson Papers, Harry S. Truman Library and Museum.

[6] Schultz, "Three Illinois Farms," 13.

[7] Albert H. Moseman, Oral History Interview, June 14, 2004, Harry S. Truman Library and Museum.

[8] Theodore W. Schultz, *Transforming Traditional Agriculture* (New Haven: Yale University Press, 1964). Schultz's work drew extensively upon W. David Hopper, "The Economic Organization of a Village in North-Central India" (Ph.D. diss., Cornell University, 1951); and Sol Tax, *Penny Capitalism: A Guatemalan Indian Economy* (Washington, DC: United States Government Printing Office, 1953).

186   Hungry Nation

Accounts of the Green Revolution in India frame it as an epiphanic event. Over several years, these accounts hold, Indian agriculture was yoked out of stagnation through a coordinated transformation of practices and technologies.[9] Towards the middle of the 1960s, members of the Indian cabinet began pressing for a new emphasis on modern agricultural inputs and the establishment of price incentives, spurred on by the Ford and Rockefeller Foundations' efforts to import high-yielding varieties of seeds to India. By 1966, as the threat of a major famine loomed again, American officials pressured their Indian counterparts to adopt these new technologies and paradigms. The result was a "new strategy in agriculture" that soon became known as India's "Green Revolution."

The abundant critiques of the Green Revolution have focused on the ecological degradation and social inequity wrought of these new technologies and paradigms.[10] The most sophisticated analyses have called into question the scale of gains attributed to these transformations, drawing lines of continuity between pre- and post-revolution agricultural practices.[11] Yet these critical assessments have nonetheless elided

---

[9] Exemplary in this regard is John H. Perkins, "Wheat Breeding and the Consolidation of Indian Autonomy, 1940–1970," in *Geopolitics and the Green Revolution: Wheat, Genes, and the Cold War* (New York: Oxford University Press, 1997), 157–186. See also Chopra, *Evolution of Food Policy in India*; Nick Cullather, *The Hungry World: America's Cold War Battle against Poverty in Asia* (Cambridge, MA: Harvard University Press, 2010); and Jack Ralph Kloppenburg, *First the Seed: The Political Economy of Plant Biotechnology, 1492–2000* (Madison: University of Wisconsin Press, 2004). Accounts of the Green Revolution in Mexico have proven more thoroughly historicized than elsewhere; an early example is David A. Sonnenfeld, "Mexico's 'Green Revolution,' 1940–1980: Towards an Environmental History," *Environmental History Review* 16, no. 4 (1992): 29–52.

[10] Vandana Shiva's alarmist work is frequently cited in ecological critiques of the Green Revolution; Vandana Shiva, *The Violence of the Green Revolution: Third World Agriculture, Ecology, and Politics* (London: Zed Books, 1991). Yet nuanced assessments balancing quantitative growth against social and ecological distress have been part of Green Revolution accounts since its earliest days; see Clifton R. Wharton Jr., "The Green Revolution: Cornucopia or Pandora's Box," *Foreign Affairs* 47, no. 3 (April 1969); and Harry M. Cleaver, "The Contradictions of the Green Revolution," *The American Economic Review* 62, no. 1/2 (March 1, 1972): 177–186. Ecofeminist scholarship in the early 1990s dovetailed neatly and creatively with many Green Revolution critiques; see, for example, Carolyn E. Sachs, *Gendered Fields: Rural Women, Agriculture, and Environment* (Boulder: Westview Press, 1996). A proliferation of popular writing on food crises has tied the Green Revolution to larger critiques of global food systems and the specter of climate change; exemplary are Raj Patel, *Stuffed and Starved: The Hidden Battle for the World Food System* (Brooklyn: Melville House, 2008); David Rieff, *The Reproach of Hunger: Food, Justice, and Money in the Twenty-First Century* (New York: Simon and Schuster, 2016); and Paul Roberts, *The End of Food* (Boston: Houghton Mifflin Company, 2009).

[11] Christopher J. Baker, "Frogs and Farmers: The Green Revolution in India, and Its Murky Past," in *Understanding Green Revolutions: Agrarian Change and Development Planning in South Asia. Essays in Honour of B.H. Farmer*, ed. Tim Bayliss-Smith and Sudhir Wanmali (Cambridge: Cambridge University Press, 1984), 37–52.

The Ideological Origins of the Green Revolution 187

the ways in which Green Revolution transformations drew upon ideas and institutions which had lingered at the margins of political thought in the Nehruvian era. These ideas did not spring forth from international foundations' policy papers, nor were they foisted upon Indian planners by American diplomats and sympathetic insiders; rather, a focus on individual prosperity and concentrated inputs had been a constituent, if marginalized, part of Indian agricultural and political thought for decades.

Leftist politicians' commitment to democratic equity was an overriding priority in the years before the Green Revolution, and efforts to remold land use, markets, and citizenship itself were all conceived within this frame. Yet even before Nehru's encounter with American agriculture, there were schemes and institutions which hewed to the notion that targeted inputs and the selective privileging of certain farmers could actualize greater national productivity, even at the cost of social equity. If this vision was initially odious to the majority of Indian planners, it grew increasingly palatable over the first two decades of independence.

This chapter explores the ideological origins of the Green Revolution: moments where Indian individuals and institutions explored the notion that equity might be sacrificed for growth, and advanced the idea that the food problem might be solved in a way that did not presuppose the universal uplift of all producers. Surveying the landscape of international and Indian organizations working to advance agricultural development in the two decades prior to the Green Revolution, there appear moments when paradigms of inequitable growth moved closer to the center of mainstream political thought through a series of successful agricultural development programs – even as waves of discontent highlighted the perils of these approaches.

India's agricultural transformations in the twentieth century took place along institutional lines with roots in the late colonial world, subsequently remade by the ingresses of American and international developmental organizations. The independent nation had inherited an extensive network of institutions dedicated to improving crop yields, strains, and overall productivity, beginning with the early nineteenth-century founding of the Royal Agri-Horticultural Society in Calcutta.[12] Yet in spite of colonial investments in irrigation and canal schemes, particularly in Punjab and the Godavari, India lacked a national Department of Agriculture to coordinate improvement efforts until Lord Mayo's efforts to create the same in 1869.[13] India's Revenue and Agriculture Department was founded

[12] On colonial improvement, see David Arnold, "Agriculture and 'Improvement' in Early Colonial India: A Pre-History of Development," *Journal of Agrarian Change* 5, no. 4 (2005): 505–525.
[13] Ludden, *An Agrarian History of South Asia*, 11–12.

188   Hungry Nation

two years later, just prior to the "Great Famine" of 1876–1878, and did little to convince nationalists of the colonial government's interests in anything beyond agrarian extraction.

The pace of agricultural research and extension quickened with the publication of J.A. Voelcker's major report on Indian agriculture in 1893.[14] In the wake of another major famine in Bombay, India's new Viceroy, Lord Curzon, announced the formation of the Imperial Agricultural Research Institute in Pusa, Bihar, in 1905.[15] The IARI would become the institutional home for India's most dedicated agricultural researchers – most notably, Albert and Louise Howard, whose work on soil and compost would inspire the twentieth-century organic movement, and whose successful wheat strains were disseminated widely across India.[16] In 1926, a Royal Commission on Agriculture urged the formation of an Imperial Council of Agricultural Research, which was attached to the IARI before both shifted to Delhi in the wake of a massive earthquake. The ICAR sponsored India's first studies on malnutrition – studies on beriberi and prison diets in Bengal – before a more formal nutritional research program was founded in Coonoor in 1929, soon rechristened as the Nutrition Research Laboratories.[17] These research efforts yielded little in a quantitative sense: the best estimate of agricultural productivity in India in the half-century before independence was a rate of growth for all crops of no more than 0.01 percent per year. More alarmingly, foodgrain yield per acre declined by 0.18 percent annually in the same period; in the years between 1911 and 1947, foodgrain availability itself declined by a single percent each year.[18]

As independence neared, the nation's imperial institutions were slowly remade as Indian ones, albeit with a high degree of staff continuity. A network of research institutes blossomed under the aegis of the

[14] John Augustus Voelcker, *Report on the Improvement of Indian Agriculture* (London: Eyre and Spottiswoode, 1893).
[15] An account of the Institute's founding is given in Nitya Rao, "Agricultural Research and Extension in India: Changing Ideologies and Practice," *Economic and Political Weekly* 40, no. 13 (March 26, 2005): 1371–1375. A later review of the organization and its functions in postcolonial India is C. Thomas, *Indian Agricultural Research Institute: An Introduction* (New Delhi: Indian Agricultural Research Institute, 1983).
[16] See Albert Howard and Louise Howard, *The Development of Indian Agriculture* (London: Oxford University Press, 1927); Albert Howard, *An Agricultural Testament* (London: Oxford University Press, 1940); Albert Howard, *The Soil and Health: A Study of Organic Agriculture* (New York: Schocken Books, 1947); and Louise Howard, *Sir Albert Howard in India* (London: Faber and Faber, 1953).
[17] Arnold, *Science, Technology and Medicine in Colonial India*, 201–202.
[18] Blyn, *Agricultural Trends in India, 1891–1947*. Blyn's estimates remain the best available, but are hampered by poor statistical collection; see Tomlinson, *The Economy of Modern India, 1860–1970*, 31.

The Ideological Origins of the Green Revolution 189

ICAR, with institutions dedicated to the study of everything from food and cash crops to livestock and fishery management.[19] But with funds scarce, these institutions saw their work increasingly underwritten by the largesse of the United States Technical Cooperation Mission, alongside the Rockefeller and Ford Foundations.[20] The first two institutions would underwrite independent India's agricultural institutions and stoke the engine of fundamental research – but it was the latter group whose work would restructure the basic assumptions of India's planning for plenty.

"More than half the people of the world," President Truman had declared in his second inaugural address, ten months before his first meeting with Jawaharlal Nehru, "are living in conditions approaching misery. Their food is inadequate. They are victims of disease. Their economic life is primitive and stagnant. Their poverty is a handicap and a threat both to them and to more prosperous areas." For American planners, India's 400 million citizens represented a politically significant bloc of those impoverished humans, and the Point Four Program that Truman's address presaged held out much for them.[21]

It took three years before an agreement between Jawaharlal Nehru and American ambassador Chester Bowles led to the founding of the Indo-American Technical Cooperation Mission in January 1952, yet for the next decade and a half, the TCM would spearhead over 150 collaborative projects in India, sending around 400 agricultural experts to India to supervise development projects and welcoming an equal number to the United States for training. The TCM's work fell into three main areas. The most significant undertaking was the project of Community Development, which sought to weave Gandhian idioms of village life into the fabric of the state itself.[22] American workers charged with supervising

---

[19] M.S. Randhawa, *Agricultural Research in India: Institutes and Organisations* (New Delhi: Indian Council of Agricultural Research, 1958). A later history of the ICAR is M.S. Randhawa, *A History of the Indian Council of Agricultural Research, 1929–1979* (New Delhi: Indian Council of Agricultural Research, 1979). The ICAR regularly published and distributed pamphlets meant for farmers and consumers; see B. Choudhury, *Cultivation of Tomato and Brinjal*, Farm Bulletin (New Series) 31 (New Delhi: Indian Council of Agricultural Research, 1965); R.L. Kaura, *Gosadans in India* (New Delhi: Indian Council of Agricultural Research, 1964); and H.B. Singh, *Cultivation of Sweet Potato*, Farm Bulletin (New Series) 4 (New Delhi: Indian Council of Agricultural Research, 1964).

[20] On these foundations, see Inderjeet Parmar, *Foundations of the American Century: The Ford, Carnegie, and Rockefeller Foundations in the Rise of American Power* (New York: Columbia University Press, 2012). On their work in India, see Leonard A. Gordon, "Wealth Equals Wisdom? The Rockefeller and Ford Foundations in India," *Annals of the American Academy of Political and Social Science* 554 (November 1, 1997): 104–116.

[21] See Ekbladh, *The Great American Mission.*

[22] On Community Development, see Tridib Banerjee, "U.S. Planning Expeditions to Postcolonial India: From Ideology to Innovation in Technical Assistance," *Journal of*

190   Hungry Nation

ten to seventeen villages each sought to identify "natural leaders" who would guide projects on the ground, while providing any resources required beyond the seeds, livestock, or construction materials provided by the state. The TCM allocated its resources secondarily to large-scale modernization and industrialization schemes. And finally, TCM workers sought to advance the state of India's agricultural education and extension program, deriding India's research system as overly bookish and averse to the grit of experimentation and fieldwork.[23]

American experts deputed to India viewed extension as the missing link between research and "the man behind the plough." Spearheaded by Frank Parker, a USDA agricultural expert, the TCM's agricultural projects in India operated under the paradigm that there was no fundamental defect in Indian agriculture, merely an inability to transfer best practices to farmers toiling in fields. Parker lobbied for the creation of an extension wing in the Ministry of Agriculture and persuaded the Ford Foundation to underwrite it.[24] Yet far more significant was the import of hundreds of American agricultural experts tasked with teaching new practices to Indian farmers – a charge undertaken with missionary zeal and New Deal optimism.

American agricultural experts volunteered readily for service in India. The first to sign up was Malcolm Orchard, an agricultural information advisor from Tennessee who was attached to the ICAR, where he produced short films, festival plays, cartoons, posters, leaflets, and radio broadcasts on improved farming techniques.[25] A team of economists from Harvard

---

the *American Planning Association* 75, no. 2 (2009): 193–208; Frankel, *India's Political Economy*, 101–106 and passim; Walter C. Neale, "Indian Community Development, Local Government, Local Planning, and Rural Policy since 1950," *Economic Development and Cultural Change* 33, no. 4 (July 1, 1985): 677–698; and Benjamin Siegel, "The Village as Cold War Site"; and Benjamin Siegel, "Modernizing Peasants and 'Master Farmers': Progressive Agriculture in Early Independent India," *Comparative Studies of South Asia, Africa and the Middle East* 37, no. 1 (May 2017): 64–84. Daniel Immerwahr argues convincingly that the "small" scale of Community Development in India was not at odds with the conceits of "big" modernizers, but rather "part of a counter-tendency within Indian politics: a profound enchantment with the idea of the 'village community.'" Immerwahr, *Thinking Small*, 69–71.

[23] Uma Lele and Arthur A. Goldsmith, "The Development of National Agricultural Research Capacity: India's Experience with the Rockefeller Foundation and Its Significance for Africa," *Economic Development and Cultural Change* 37, no. 2 (January 1, 1989): 312.

[24] Frank W. Parker, "Proposed Extension Wing, Center Ministry of Agriculture and States," December 3, 1956, RG 469 / 600-A / Box 6 / India Projects 86-11-007, Agriculture and Home Science Training 1955, 56, 57, Correspondence, USNA; United States Technical Cooperation Mission, India, "Ministry of Food and Agriculture Establishes Extension Wing," April 8, 1958, RG 469 / 600-AA / Box 2 / 7.4 Economic Policy, USNA.

[25] "Point 4 in India: Special Edition," December 3, 1952, RG 469 / 600-AA / Box 2 / 7.4 Economic Policy, USNA.

The Ideological Origins of the Green Revolution   191

and the USDA worked to plan for better agricultural economics training.[26] A University of Illinois agronomist was deputed to the Allahabad Agricultural Institute to teach composting, manuring, weed control, and field education.[27] An Arkansas dairy expert was sent to Kerala to serve as that state's Extension and Development Advisor.[28] The outgoing head of the National Agricultural Library in Beltsville, Maryland, worked to plan a similar library system for India.[29] A Kansas State College poultry expert was named Poultry Husbandry Advisor to the Government of India, a dairy expert from the Minnesota Feed Service the Livestock and Animal Nutrition Advisor, and a US Operations Mission officer India's new Crop Production Advisor.[30] There was an egalitarian quality to this work: women from Ohio State, the University of Illinois, and the Tennessee Valley Authority were sent to work as home economics advisors, and as regional consultants to provincial governments.[31] Work was open to black Americans, as well, like John T. Bulls, an Alabama extension agent who was one of the first men to join the Indian mission.[32]

[26] John D. Black and Hugh L. Stewart, *Report on the Research, Teaching and Public Administration of the Economics of Agriculture for India* (New Delhi: Ministry of Food and Agriculture, Government of India, 1954), RG 469 / P 161 A / Box 7 / India Agriculture Reports, 1954–1956, USNA.

[27] Shuman, Frank H., "Extension for the People of India," *Extension* 3, no. 1 (January 1958): 5–22.

[28] Paul Carruth, *Two Year Terminal Report* (New Delhi: Division of Cooperation, Ministry of Agriculture, Government of India, 1957), RG 469 / P 161 A / Box 7 / India Agriculture Reports, Jun–Dec 1957, USNA. Other experts served similar roles in different states; see George R. Puckett, *Report on Second Two-Year Assignment with Madhya Pradesh State* (New Delhi: US Technical Cooperation Mission to India, August 1958), RG 469 / P 161 A / Box 7 / India Agriculture Reports, Jul–Dec 1958, USNA; and E.N. Sanders, "Report of Extension and Development Advisor, Himachal Pradesh," 1957, RG 469 / P 161 A / Box 7 / India Agriculture Reports, Jun–Dec 1957, USNA.

[29] Ralph R. Shaw and D.B. Krishna Rao, *Report on Library and Bibliographic Services for Agricultural Teaching and Research in India*, February 1957, RG 469 / P 161 A / Box 7 / India Agriculture Reports, Jun–Dec 1957, USNA.

[30] Loren L. Davis, *Indo-American Projects on Soils and Crop Production* (New Delhi: US Technical Cooperation Mission to India, October 1957), RG 469 / P 161 A / Box 7 / India Agriculture Reports, Jun–Dec 1957, USNA; Thor W. Gullickson, "Livestock Improvement in India and Feed, Fodder, and Forage Supply," 1958, RG 469 / P 161 A / Box 7 / India Agriculture Reports, Jul–Dec 1958, USNA; E.R. Halbrook and Tulsa Ram, *Poultry Development in India*, 1958.

[31] Dorothy Barbee, "Terminal Report of Two Year Assignment in India Western Region," October 1957, RG 469 / P 161 A / Box 7 / India Agriculture Reports, Jun–Dec 1957, USNA; Jeanette B. Dean, "Semi-Annual Report: University of Illinois – Allahabad Agricultural Institute," 1956, RG 286 / P446 / Box 9 / Reports – Quarterly Activity Reports 1959–1962, USNA; Ida L. Hildibrand, *Terminal Report of Regional Extension Home Economics Advisor in the Northern Region of India* (New Delhi: U.S. Technical Cooperation Mission to India, June 1958), RG 469 / P 161 A / Box 7 / India Agriculture Reports, Jan–Jun 1958, USNA.

[32] John T. Jr. Bulls, *Report on Second Two-Year as Extension Training Advisor in India* (New Delhi: Division of Cooperation, Ministry of Agriculture, Government of India, April

192   Hungry Nation

By the end of the decade, the TCM had spent $71 million on agricultural development schemes in India.[33] Over the course of the 1950s, as private foundation influence began to grow, the TCM began to consolidate its efforts on large-scale projects, most notably the establishment of modern agricultural universities.[34] In 1960, the first Indian "land grant" university was set up at Pantnagar, Uttar Pradesh; by 1966, American efforts had helped create eight such universities.[35] Yet the TCM never abandoned its focus on extension and outreach, continuing to sponsor mobile exhibitions, agricultural fairs, and pamphlets like *Pragati Mein Sazedar*, "Partners in Progress," which told the stories of the specialists who had arrived in India in what was the largest American development mission to date.[36] In 1959, farmers visiting the World Agriculture Fair in New Delhi could visit the American pavilion, where audiences were asked, rhetorically, "Can one farmer feed 23 people?" before being shown how, with borehole pumps, motorized tractors, and better wheat strains, such feats were indeed possible.[37] They might also have heard President Dwight D. Eisenhower extol the virtues of concentrated inputs at the Fair, or watched a short film on the Indian farmer "Ram Lal," who resisted new agricultural techniques until visiting the American exhibition.[38]

As short-sleeved Americans scraped dirt from their fingernails, trudged film projectors into villages, and fanned themselves in hot rooms in the Ministry of Agriculture, a cadre of private experts from New York was moving haltingly into India's agricultural morass. The Rockefeller Foundation had been involved in Indian developmental schemes for

1957), RG 469 / P 161 A / Box 7 / India Agriculture Reports, Jun–Dec 1957, USNA; wider context is given in Brenda Gayle Plummer, *Rising Wind: Black Americans and U.S. Foreign Affairs, 1935–1960* (Chapel Hill: University of North Carolina Press, 1996), 222.

[33] Agriculture Division, US Technical Cooperation Mission to India, "Summary of TCM Assistance to Indian Agriculture FY1951 – FY1961," February 10, 1960, RG 286 / P446 / Box 1 / Administration – Divisional Affairs – Agriculture 1960, USNA; a more general review is "The Indo-American Program: A Brief Resume (1952–1958)," 1959, RG 286 / P446 / Box 3 / Contracts – Indo-American Team 1955–1958, USNA.

[34] *Report of the Joint Indo-American Team on Agricultural Research and Education* (New Delhi: Indian Council of Agricultural Research, 1955); *Report of the Second Joint Indo-American Team on Agricultural Education, Research and Extension* (New Delhi: Indian Council of Agricultural Research, 1960).

[35] Arthur A Goldsmith, *Building Agricultural Institutions: Transferring the Land-Grant Model to India and Nigeria* (Boulder: Westview Press, 1990).

[36] *Pragati men Sazedar [Partners in Progress]* (Bombay: United States Information Service, 1957).

[37] "Handsome U.S. Hit in India," *Life*, January 25, 1960.

[38] Dwight D. Eisenhower, "Remarks at the Opening of the World Agriculture Fair" (New Delhi, December 11, 1959); *From This Land*, 16mm (United States Information Service, 1960).

The Ideological Origins of the Green Revolution 193

several decades before independence: the American missionary Sam Higginbottom had reached out to the Foundation for funding for the Allahabad Agricultural Institute in the 1910s, but the outbreak of war had stymied any substantive investment.[39] Nonetheless, by the 1920s, the Foundation had built up a network of institutions and investments in public health and tropical medicine in India, moving from a single chair at the School of Tropical Medicine in Calcutta to the establishment of the All India School of Hygiene and Public Health in 1932.[40]

Foundation officials were hesitant to deepen their investments in independent India, citing institutional and financial constraints as they turned down funding requests from P.C. Mahalanobis and others.[41] Hesitation stemmed partially from political logic: the Communist revolution had summarily ended Rockefeller projects in China, and officials feared a similar fate in India.[42] Yet Foundation trustees urged a continued, if cautious, involvement in India's development: Karl Taylor Compton, outgoing president of the Massachusetts Institute of Technology, urged the Foundation to continue supporting agricultural work, noting "the role which India seems destined to play in the international scene."[43]

In 1952, three high-ranking Rockefeller officials traveled to India to assess what projects the Foundation might realistically undertake in the country.[44] Their answer was clear. "The problem of food is so acute that practically all government officials are preoccupied with it," the team wrote in their report, adding that during their stay, "there was scarcely a day in which the newspapers did not have a front-page story on some aspect of the food problem." Rockefeller officials were damning in their assessment of existing agricultural ventures.[45] India's research organizations were "surprisingly good in plant and staff, but surprisingly unrealistic in the amount of articulation with the basic problems of India." Albert Mayer's Etawah project was laudable but "grandiose," and relied upon

---

[39] Gordon, "Wealth Equals Wisdom?," 107.

[40] John Farley, *To Cast out Disease: A History of the International Health Division of the Rockefeller Foundation (1913–1951)* (Oxford: Oxford University Press, 2004); Sunil S. Amrith, *Decolonizing International Health: India and Southeast Asia, 1930–65* (Basingstoke: Palgrave Macmillan, 2006).

[41] RBF, "Memorandum Regarding India and the Rockefeller Foundation's Program There," May 22, 1947, RG 1.2, series 460, box 1, folder 1, RAC.

[42] "Response to Warren Weaver's Memo Regarding Allahabad," January 30, 1951, RG 1.2, series 460, box 1, folder 1, RAC.

[43] Karl T. Compton, letter to Warren Weaver, November 3, 1949, RG 1.2, series 460, box 1, folder 1, RAC.

[44] Warren Weaver, J.G. Harrar, and Paul C. Mangelsdorf, "Notes on Indian Agriculture," April 11, 1952, RG 1.2, series 460, box 1, folder 4, RAC.

[45] "Notes on Discussion, India Conference (Including Pakistan and Ceylon)," March 26, 1952, RG 1.2, series 460, box 1, folder 4, RAC.

194   Hungry Nation

the fecundity of a single variety of wheat. American technical advisors in India were "sincere, devoted, confused and frustrated people." The team agreed to make a limited investment in agricultural education and hybrid breeding, but cautioned against undue optimism, since Indian scientists, "intelligent or even brilliant," still shunned direct field work.

The Foundation's cautious approach was expedited by a request from one particularly enterprising Indian official.[46] Vishnu Sahay, India's Secretary of Agriculture, approached Foundation officials in 1953 with a request for assistance in building a hybrid maize research program, having noted the success of the Foundation's efforts in Mexico under the direction of American agronomist Norman Borlaug. K.M. Munshi had approached American officials about a hybrid corn program in late 1950, but the American seed companies whom those officials approached in turn had been unenthused. Maize was barely consumed or cultivated in India at the time: at the beginning of the 1950s, only 3 percent of India's cultivated area was dedicated to the crop. Yet there was a certain political expediency to maize research: work on a relatively unpopular crop would not impinge upon the interests of Indian researchers protective of their own agendas, and the opportunity cost of failure would be proportionately lower than that of research on wheat or rice.[47] Foundation officials were skeptical of deputing experts to India in the absence of a preexisting research network, and the preliminary visits of two research scientists, veterans of Rockefeller programs in Mexico and Colombia, confirmed that there was reason for caution.[48] Yet when a more formal request came from India's Ministry of Agriculture in 1955, the Foundation agreed to the formation of a pilot Indian Agricultural Program.

The partnership was fraught from the start. Health Minister Rajkumari Amrit Kaur irritated Foundation President Dean Rusk with her demand that Rockefeller schemes be run under central government supervision.[49] "The situation since the British regime," she wrote, "has completely changed. We have now five year plans and everything has to be fitted into the picture." The Program's first director soon quit, handing over the reigns to a talented young agricultural scientist, Ralph W. Cummings. Cummings was a more resolute administrator, but by summer 1958 was already complaining that the meddling of India's new Finance Minister,

---

[46] F.D. Collins, "Hybrid Corn Program for India," November 30, 1950, RG 59 / 54D341 / Box 14 / Food, 1950, USNA; "Hybrid Corn Program for India," January 9, 1951, RG 59 / 54D341 / Box 14 / Food, General Correspondence, 1951, USNA.

[47] Lele and Goldsmith, "Development of National Agricultural Research Capacity," 314.

[48] *Rockefeller Foundation Annual Report* (New York: Rockefeller Foundation, 1954), 19–20.

[49] Rajkumari Amrit Kaur, letter to Dean Rusk, July 31, 1956, RG 1.2, series 460, box 1, folder 2, RAC.

The Ideological Origins of the Green Revolution 195

Morarji Desai, was making work impossible.[50] The future Prime Minister was also an anti-science provocateur who would later shock Barbara Walters, Dan Rather, and their American audiences with the proclamation that his morning glass of urine would stave off disease. In a September 1958 visit to the Foundation, he rattled Dean Rusk with his contention that while the Foundation's experts were sophisticated, "too much sophistication has done great harm in the world," and that India would be most readily assisted by funds which it could distribute autonomously, "giving extra help to those who need it most to keep up with the rest and restraining the others who might pull too far ahead."[51] His dismissal of the Foundation's authority came as an affront to its administrators, then pouring large sums of money into flagship institutions like the Indian Agricultural Research Institute, the All India Institute of Medical Science, the Virus Research Centre at Pune, and the International Cultural Centre, later renamed the India International Centre.[52]

Yet despite interpersonal conflicts and struggles over administrative control, the Foundation successfully undertook three early projects in India. The 1956 agreement paved the way for a sorghum and millet breeding program, and funds for the Indian Agricultural Research Institute's graduate school of agriculture. And as per Indian bureaucrats' initial requests, Rockefeller pilot plots helped develop four hybrid maize strains that would quadruple output by 1960.[53]

The gleaming curves of a Studebaker Champion bore little resemblance to the clunky Ferguson tractors that were the mainstay of India's most productive farms. Yet it was the man who had rescued that iconic American automobile company from insolvency who turned the Ford Foundation's attention to India. Paul Hoffman had left Studebaker in 1948 to join the United States' Economic Cooperation Administration; two years later, he was named president of the Ford Foundation. It was Hoffman who set India as an institutional priority, seeing the "staggering, appalling poverty" of India's "700,000 tiny villages" as kindling that could lead to communist revolution.[54]

Hoffman assembled a team of liberal New Dealers to oversee the Foundation's efforts in India, beginning with the recruitment of Douglas

[50] Ralph W. Cummings Jr., letter to Dean Rusk, July 25, 1958, RG 1.2, series 460, box 1, folder 2, RAC.
[51] "Interview with Morarji Desai," September 12, 1958, RG 1.2, series 460, box 1, folder 2, RAC.
[52] Dean Rusk, letter to C.D. Deshmukh, December 16, 1958, RG 1.2, series 460, box 1, folder 2, RAC.
[53] Lele and Goldsmith, "Development of National Agricultural Research Capacity," 314.
[54] Sackley, "Foundation in the Field," 237–238.

196   Hungry Nation

Ensminger, a well-respected agricultural sociologist from the USDA, as the Foundation's Field Representative. Ensminger had already been working in India with the Economic and Technical Evaluation Agency, but was frustrated with the United States' insistence on showboating instead of teaching self-reliance. It was a photo session with *Life* magazine that led Ensminger to agree to join Ford: Nehru had reportedly been outraged by the results of the shoot, which highlighted an American extension worker and placed his Indian colleagues in the background as observers.[55]

From its Delhi office, the Foundation worked to complement the work of the United States' Technical Cooperation Mission, allotting funds to projects that the Indian government could not persuade the TCM to fund, the vast majority of these projects in the realm of agricultural experimentation.[56] The Ford Foundation sponsored scores of instructional and experimental projects in Indian villages, teaching villagers crop rotation methods, fertilizer application, seed row planting, the use of bull-drawn ploughs in place of *desi* ones, and the establishment of extension wings at agricultural colleges.[57] The Foundation supported extension directors' study tours in Japan and the United States, and the publication of an agricultural monthly, *Dharti ke Lal* [Sons of the Soil], prepared at the ICAR and translated for farmers across the country. A Rockefeller trustee had marveled at the audacity of Ford's projects, exemplified by the large number of Texans it employed, "not a bit frightened by India or anything in India, including the languages. Only a Texan would be unafraid of India."[58] Dean Rusk referred to Ford as "the fat boy in the canoe" with a mix of admiration and jealousy.[59]

Yet even a cadre of steely Texans had a herculean task ahead of them if they intended to remake the paradigmatic foundations of independent India's agriculture. India's planners, by the middle of the 1950s, were steering the country towards a "socialistic pattern of society," a shift most evident in its approach to agricultural transformation. If Nehru had been impressed by the capitalist farmers of Illinois in 1949, he had been far more entranced by the statist models of the Soviet Union – or, in the middle of the 1950s, agrarian reform along Chinese lines. Yet Ford's experts were about to make a different case.

[55] Douglas Ensminger, interview by Harry S. Taylor, July 16, 1976, Harry S. Truman Library and Museum.
[56] *The Ford Foundation and Foundation Supported Activities in India* (New Delhi: Ford Foundation, January 1955).
[57] Goldsmith, *Building Agricultural Institutions*.
[58] "Notes on Discussion, India Conference."
[59] Gordon, "Wealth Equals Wisdom?," 111–112.

The Ideological Origins of the Green Revolution

Douglas Ensminger had become something of an informal consultant to India's Planning Commission, though in the summer of 1957, he was vacationing in the United States when a call came from India.[60] Agricultural production, he was told, had flatlined, and Ensminger made a beeline back to India to embark upon an ad hoc tour of the Indian countryside. After a promising meeting with Nehru, with whom he enjoyed an easy rapport, and V.T. Krishnamachari, then vice-president of the Commission, Ensminger approached the American ambassador to India and the head of USAID's New Delhi office to ask if the United States might consider launching an official agricultural mission. The Ford Foundation president was quickly rebuffed: any real effort to boost the agricultural output of one of the United States' major surplus importers would be met by loud resistance from the American farm lobby. But a private mission, they suggested, might raise fewer objections. Ensminger accepted these warnings, and recruited Sherman Johnson, Chief Economist of the USDA's research service, to lead a Ford Foundation mission.

Traversing India in early 1959, Johnson and his colleagues would have had little idea that their mission would remake the ideological underpinnings of Indian agriculture. The team comprised agricultural experts from Iowa State, the University of Arkansas, Kansas State, Cornell University, the University of Maryland, the US Department of Agriculture, and the Farm Credit Administration, as well as Indian officials from the Planning Commission, the Department of Agriculture, and the Soil Conservation Board. "Without food enough," the team concluded, "India's hopes for improving human welfare, achieving social justice, and securing democracy will become almost impossible of attainment."[61]

Drastic change, the team asserted, was necessary, and only possible through a set of ten interlinked points. India could offer new price incentives to farmers, and place a new priority on improved, hybrid strains of crops, intensified irrigation, chemical fertilizers, and credit. (India's fertilizer situation was particularly dire: two team experts concluded that India had 1 pound of fertilizer for every acre of crops grown, as compared with 40 pounds in the United States.[62]) And India, broadly, would

---

[60] George Rosen, *Western Economists and Eastern Societies: Agents of Change in South Asia, 1950–1970* (Baltimore: Johns Hopkins University Press, 1985), 74–75.

[61] Agricultural Production Team, Ford Foundation, *Report on India's Food Crisis and Steps to Meet It* (New Delhi: Ministry of Food and Agriculture and Ministry of Community Development and Cooperation, Government of India, 1959).

[62] Carl C. Malone and Sherman E. Johnson, "The Intensive Agricultural Development Program in India," *Agricultural Economics Research* 23, no. 2 (April 1971): 26.

198   Hungry Nation

need to stop starving agriculture in the name of industrialization: the
Nagpur resolution earlier that year had demonstrated that cooperative
agriculture was a non-starter in India, but the Ford Foundation's report
contended that it was bad agronomics, as well.[63]

The report provoked immediate controversy. The Indian members of
the team were barred by the government from signing the report, meaning that the *Report on India's Food Crisis and Steps to Meet It* was published
by the Ministries of Agriculture and Community Development and
Cooperation, but authored only by American experts. Nehru objected
to the term "crisis" outright, allowing it in the final document only after
Johnson presented a chart projecting a 20 million ton food shortage by
1970 that could not be made up for by imports. His criticism anticipated
that of longtime students of Indian agriculture like M.L. Dantwala,
V.K.R.V. Rao, Pitamber Pant, and Daniel and Alice Thorner. The latter pair argued, somewhat implausibly, that the Ford Foundation team
had exaggerated the severity of India's food crisis, perhaps as a means of
diverting increasing investment in industry back towards agriculture to
prevent competition with the United States.[64]

In spite of this skepticism, India's Planning Commission responded
to the report by increasing the outlay of resources to agriculture in the
Third Five-Year Plan from 16 percent to 23 percent.[65] But the greater
boon for advocates of major change came in the Government of India's
agreement, in early 1960, to a five-year trial project based on the report's
conclusions. Seven promising trial districts with a total population of
1.1 million farmers were selected: all seven were areas with good irrigation, predictable rainfall, and little chance of flooding. They enjoyed
good infrastructure for credit and marketing, reasonable road access,
secure land tenure, and a local leadership demonstratively receptive to
new ideas. Ford's contribution of $10.5 million represented a third of
the total monetary outlay.[66] The Intensive Agricultural District Program
was launched in Tanjore District on Pongal, the Tamil New Year, in early
April.[67]

The program's implementation was patchy from the start.[68] Indian
administrators had eschewed the Ford Foundation's recommendations
for price incentives, and farmers groused that fertilizers were scarce and

[63] John H. Perkins, *Geopolitics and the Green Revolution: Wheat, Genes, and the Cold War* (New York: Oxford University Press, 1997), 181–182.
[64] Rosen, *Western Economists and Eastern Societies*, 74–75.
[65] Frankel, *India's Political Economy*, 181.
[66] Malone and Johnson, "The Intensive Agricultural Development Program in India," 26.
[67] "New Urgency Given to Food Drive," *Times of India*, September 19, 1960.
[68] Rosen, *Western Economists and Eastern Societies*, 77.

The Ideological Origins of the Green Revolution 199

district officials patronizing. The Ministry of Food and Agriculture had also ignored the Ford Foundation's selection of districts, selecting several with poor irrigation facilities. And poor data collection stymied analysis until a major overhaul in the program's third year.[69] There were administrative problems, too: the senior official placed in charge of implementation was deputed to the Food and Agriculture Organization, and the Ministry of Food and Agriculture stalled in finding a replacement. In spite of these hurdles, the "package program" was scaled up in 1962, expanding into districts encompassing 2.6 million farms, 7.4 million laborers, and a total population of 23 million Indians.[70]

Assessed five years in, the success of the program was unclear. After much administrative wrangling, the Ford Foundation and the Government of India came to somewhat different conclusions.[71] An economist with Harvard's Development Advisory Service was brought in to provide clarity.[72] Package recipients' output, the economist concluded, was little better than that realized by India's most productive farmers who were not package recipients.[73] Optimistic voices, however, suggested that the problem with the program lay not in the plan, but in the execution.[74] Ford Foundation officials prepared to withdraw their support, until Douglas Ensminger personally escorted a trustee to an IADP district to make the case for a second five-year grant.[75]

Yet the package program would become far more transformative than these results suggested. In an era when modernization was a watchword, and "progressive farmers" were being extolled as key votaries of change, the program suggested to planners that Indian farmers would change their practices if given a robust enough set of resources. W. David Hopper, an agrarian economist who had been working in Uttar Pradesh

---

[69] *Package Programme Districts: Facts and Figures* (New Delhi: Farm Information Unit, Directorate of Extension, Ministry of Food and Agriculture, 1961).

[70] Malone and Johnson, "The Intensive Agricultural Development Program in India," 26.

[71] S.R. Sen, *Modernising Indian Agriculture: Report on the Intensive Agricultural District Programme, 1960–68* (New Delhi: Department of Agriculture, Government of India, 1969). Neil A. Patrick, *India's Package Program for Intensive Agricultural Development* (New Delhi: Ford Foundation, 1972); Howard Eugene Ray, *The First Decade of the Intensive Agricultural District Program* (New Delhi: Ford Foundation, 1974).

[72] Dorris D. Brown, *The Intensive Agricultural Districts Programme and Agricultural Development in Punjab, India* (Cambridge, MA: Development Advisory Service, Harvard University, 1967); Dorris D. Brown, *Agricultural Development in India's Districts* (Cambridge, MA: Harvard University Press, 1971).

[73] C.A. Robertson, G.R. Saini, and R.K. Sharma, "The Package Programme: An Appraisal (I)," *Economic and Political Weekly* 1, no. 2 (August 27, 1966): 79–85; C.A. Robertson, G.R. Saini, and R.K. Sharma, "The Package Programme: An Appraisal (II)," *Economic and Political Weekly* 1, no. 3 (September 3, 1966): 124–126.

[74] Malone and Johnson, "The Intensive Agricultural Development Program in India," 33.

[75] Rosen, *Western Economists and Eastern Societies*, 78–79.

200   Hungry Nation

since the 1950s, served as the IADP's official chronicler, and suggested in 1965 that the package had proven certain Indian farmers' readiness to adopt new inputs. Once he realizes, Hopper wrote, "that a particular innovation is both useful and within his means, he is as prompt as farmers in any other part of the world to accept it." Regardless of the quantitative results, planners were increasingly looking to the IADP as proof of this point. There was an essential innovation missing, however: the experimental seeds of Mexican stock sprouting in little patches across the country, waiting to find purchase on new fields.

In 1965, as the first iteration of the IADP came to a close, A.P. Jain found himself unimpressed with the state of Indian agriculture. The former Food Minister had grown increasingly estranged from the Congress Party in the wake of the 1959 push for collectivization. "There are far too many men," he wrote, "knowing and doing far too little at New Delhi and State headquarters, who day in and day out go on deciding the farmer's fate."[76] Jain recalled a trip to the United States years earlier, and the farmer who had attributed his bountiful corn harvest to lessons learned from University of Illinois extension workers – as well as the price policy which rewarded farmers appropriately for their good yields. "Money, water, fertilizers, tools, and technology are all necessary," Jain wrote, "but it is only the farmer possessing high human qualities and compelling urges who will utilize them fully and efficiently. It is our job to create that farmer."

Jain's take would have put him at odds with the late Jawaharlal Nehru, but his was a perspective consonant with the fashionable doctrines of modernization theory. Bureaucrats looked to the work of Walt Rostow with excitement, cheering his supposition that agricultural diffusion might be accelerated in the interests of industrial growth.[77] In 1964, fifteen years after escorting Nehru around Illinois farms, Theodore Schultz published his landmark *Transforming Traditional Agriculture*, which asserted that farmers in the developing world were every bit as rational and market-oriented as their counterparts in the developed world.[78] That they did not take readily to new innovations was a matter of policy, not innate conservatism: governments in developing countries set crop prices too low, taxed farmers too heavily, and did not provide the inputs or extension services needed to induce change. Work like Rostow's

[76] Ajit Prasad Jain, "A Wizard Who Made Two Count as Four," in *Rafi Ahmad Kidwai: A Memoir of His Life and Times* (New York: Asia Publishing House, 1965), 112–113.
[77] W.W. Rostow, *The Stages of Economic Growth* (Cambridge: Cambridge University Press, 1960).
[78] Schultz, *Transforming Traditional Agriculture*.

The Ideological Origins of the Green Revolution 201

and Schultz's suggested to planners that it would be possible to remake Indian agriculture along modern lines, provided that farmers received the right technical assistance and institutional support.

The technological transformations came first. In the early 1960s, the best varieties of wheat and rice in India – those used in the IADP and other trial programs – yielded an average of 20 percent to 30 percent more than their "unimproved" counterparts.[79] But grown long enough to yield these results, these crops would bend over and lodge, spoiling the harvest. One enterprising Indian scientist had noticed the problem of lodging long before the IADP. Since the early 1950s, the enterprising young biologist M.S. Swaminathan had headed a rice hybridization program at the Central Rice Research Institute at Cuttack, interbreeding strains of *indica* and *japonica* rice.[80] Yet he soon abandoned his work on rice for more promising research in wheat, importing a strain of dwarf seed from Washington State University in 1954, only to find it unsuited to Indian conditions.

It was a decade before Swaminathan found the right strains, tapping into collaborative research on maize and wheat undertaken by the Mexican Ministry of Agriculture and the Rockefeller Foundation led by Norman Borlaug. Swaminathan had met the American agronomist in Madison, Wisconsin, in 1953, but it was a decade before B.P. Pal, head of the Indian Agricultural Research Institute, agreed to the establishment of a dwarf wheat breeding program with Mexican materials. After a visit to India in March 1963, Borlaug arranged for shipments of seed stock to the IARI; before long, new Mexican-Indian hybrids like Kalyan Sona were being tested at field sites across the country. In 1965, the program was accelerated through the import of 250 tons of Mexican wheat; a year later, Indian scientists were dispatched to Mexico to collect 18,000 tons of Lerma Rojo 64 and Sonora 64 seed.

As Swaminathan collected wheat stock from the west, G.V. Chalam, head of the Seeds Corporation of India, was looking east for rice. In 1958, Taiwanese scientists had engineered a high-yielding strain of rice, Taichung Native One, which was soon cultivated on the experimental plots of the International Rice Research Institute in the Philippines. TN1 was soon joined by another promising strain, IR-8, which grew quickly and resisted both insects and lodging. In 1964, Chalam took note of TN1 during a visit to IRRI campus, importing 2 kilograms of seed to India in his own suitcase. Planting it successfully on his own grounds,

---

[79] On notions of "improved" seeds, see Lakshaman Yapa, "What Are Improved Seeds? An Epistemology of the Green Revolution," *Economic Geography* 69, no. 3 (1993): 254–273.
[80] Randhawa, *A History of Agriculture in India*, vol. 4: *1947–1981*: 366–371.

202   Hungry Nation

Chalam requested more stock: 5 tons arrived from the Philippines in October 1965, and 60 tons from Taiwan the year after.[81]

Administrative changes in New Delhi were hastening the pace of agricultural transformation. The new Prime Minister, Lal Bahadur Shastri, eager to reduce the Planning Commission's influence on policymaking, moved to fix members' terms and created a new Prime Minister's Secretariat to compete directly with the Commission. The reduction of the Planning Commission's influence led to new opportunities for the Minister of Agriculture, C. Subramaniam. Subramaniam's "new agricultural strategy" was a vast departure from the "institutional strategy" that vaunted equity over productive gains. It relied instead upon a combination of new technologies, bureaucratic reform, and price incentives. New technologies in the form of improved seeds were already available, and it was simple enough to force a bureaucratic transformation. In short order, Subramaniam replaced the political appointee then heading the ICAR with B.P. Pal; M.S. Swaminathan was then deputed to replace the talented Pal as head of the IARI. Subramaniam convened a committee of agronomists to appraise him on the workings of Indo-US trial programs, brought all Indian research organizations under the authority of the ICAR and established a research service to employ India's best agricultural scientists on a more permanent basis.[82]

Yet pressing the case for price incentives in the Cabinet was much harder. Subramaniam's arguments for guaranteed minimum food prices to farmers courted the vociferous objections of Finance Minister T.T. Krishnamachari, who suggested that the increased cost to urban consumers would be politically unpalatable.[83] The impasse was broken when L.K. Jha was asked to weigh in on the decision, and lent his support to the proposal. Meanwhile, Subramaniam organized a National Demonstration Program that facilitated the planting of new Mexican seed stock on a thousand experimental plots – a project underwritten by government-issued crop insurance and advised by capable extension officers.[84]

---

[81] Robert F. Chandler, *An Adventure in Applied Science: A History of the International Rice Research Institute* (Los Baños, Laguna, Philippines: International Rice Research Institute, 1982), 116; P.L. Jaiswal and M.L. Madan, eds., *Annual Report 1964–65* (New Delhi: Indian Council of Agricultural Research, 1965), 2.

[82] Govindan Parayil, "The Green Revolution in India: A Case Study of Technological Change," *Technology and Culture* 33, no. 4 (October 1, 1992): 750.

[83] "Prices and Production of Food Articles," 1964, Cabinet Secretariat – Executive Council Office – Progs., Nos. 37(7)-CF, 1964 (Vol. III), NAI.

[84] Varshney, *Democracy, Development, and the Countryside*, 64.

The Ideological Origins of the Green Revolution

Subramaniam's institutional gains were threatened by a renewed conflict with the Finance Minister. The Ministry of Food and Agriculture's August 1965 report on the new strategy cautioned against "betting on the strong," and warned of the 11.15 billion rupees – nearly $2.8 billion in foreign reserves – required to import fertilizers, pesticides, and seeds. T.T. Krishnamachari rallied members of the sidelined Planning Commission to support an alternate proposal: a return to Community Development schemes, Panchayat Raj institutions, and agricultural cooperatives. Yet as the debate grew heated, T.T. Krishnamachari found himself battling the mysterious resurfacing of the corruption charges which had forced his resignation in 1958. With Subramaniam's most powerful foe ousted, the "new agricultural strategy" could proceed as planned.

Even by the standards of the country's best astrologists, H.L. Pandya's track record was a remarkable one.[85] The astrologer from Dombivli, Maharashtra, had been right about Nehru's "controlling numbers" – 2, 7, and 5 – and the Prime Minister had indeed died on the twenty-seventh day of the fifth month of 1964. It was unfortunate, then, that so few men in power wanted to listen to him. In 1957, Pandya had been given an audience with the Chief Minister of Bombay State, where he had demonstrated that Bombay was not, in fact, short of foodgrains. But the Chief Minister had inexplicably rejected his invitation to sit for an hour daily for a single week to understand the error in his calculations. But now, Pandya was not even relying upon his powers of divination: his contention that *India Could and Can Export Food* was made from the facts and figures that the government itself had printed in its *Bulletin on Food Statistics*. And the numbers there were as clear as any found in the lunar mansions: if there were not already, there would soon be enough food in India for all its citizens, perhaps even enough to export abroad. Pandya was certain of this, even though his prediction flew in the face of the empty bowls and dry lands on the front page of every newspaper.

While Pandya consulted his *jyotisa* charts, a *New York Times* correspondent was reporting on a mounting crisis. In Kerala, in normal years, the rains brought forth "coconuts, tapioca, mangoes, bananas, pineapples, sweet potatoes, sugar cane, cashew nuts, peppers, tea, and coffee. The waters off its dazzling beaches teem with sardines, mackerel, shrimp and lobster."[86] But these foods, the correspondent wrote, were "mere side dishes for the only real food: rice." And as Indira Gandhi assumed the office of Prime Minister in the wake of Lal Bahadur Shastri's sudden

---

[85] H.L Pandya, *India Could and Can Export Food* (Bombay, 1966).
[86] J. Anthony Lukas, "Kerala Is Hungry, But Only for Rice," *New York Times*, February 7, 1966.

204   Hungry Nation

death, Kerala's rice was in gravely short supply. Usually, Kerala grew only enough rice to meet half its provincial demand, importing the rest from the surplus states of Madras and Andhra Pradesh. Yet this year's drought had reduced imports to a trickle, and even the declaration of emergency rule and the reduction of rice rations had not staunched the crisis.

The riots convulsing Kerala in the beginning of January 1966 were not the first in the state's history. In 1957, 200 demonstrators had accosted governor E.M.S. Namboodiripad as he left the Legislative Assembly, demanding lower rice prices.[87] Seven years later, students had raided shops and warehouses, angry over the delayed shipments of rice that Lal Bahadur Shastri had ordered from Andhra Pradesh.[88] But the 1966 riots were unprecedented in scale: in Trivandrum, students had thrown stones at policemen, burned government buildings, and tore up the train tracks that might otherwise have been used to ferry in rice. A.P. Jain, appointed emergency governor, decried the rioters as communist stooges, but could do nothing to stop livid demonstrations from crisscrossing the state's brackish canals.[89] Indira Gandhi had singled out Kerala in her inaugural address on All India Radio, vowing that "the first duty of Government" would be to "ensure food to our people in this year of scarcity."[90] Yet the Prime Minister was dissuaded by her advisors from traveling to Kerala to speak with rioters on grounds of safety.[91] As Communist leaders – including E.M.S. Namboodiripad – were jailed, Indira Gandhi harkened back to a familiar strategy. "I pledge," she told rioters, "to surrender my rice ration for the people of Kerala. I also pledge not to eat or serve rice until the food situation there is normal."[92]

Yet dire scenes were playing out in India's north and east in ways which would impel institution change in New Delhi. The November monsoon had failed in Maharashtra, Madhya Pradesh, and Rajasthan, but nowhere were matters worse than in Bihar: the state's poor harvest in 1965 had been compounded by a devastating drought and pockets of flooding the

[87] "Rice Prices Spark Riot in Red-Ruled India State," *New York Times*, July 14, 1957.

[88] "Indians Stage Food Riots in Kerala," *New York Times*, November 11, 1964. The riots, the *Economic Weekly* believed, were proof of the central government's inability to persuade surplus states to share their abundance with deficit ones.

[89] J. Anthony Lukas, "Kerala Students Join in Rice Protests: Violence Grows as Police Tear-Gas Demonstrators," *New York Times*, February 1, 1966; J. Anthony Lukas, "Food Protest in Kerala," *New York Times*, February 3, 1966.

[90] Indira Gandhi, "Inaugural Address to the Nation," All India Radio, New Delhi: January 26, 1966.

[91] "The Sounds of Hunger," *Time* 87, no. 5 (February 4, 1966): 39.

[92] "A Particular Hunger," *Time* 87, no. 6 (February 11, 1966): 44.

The Ideological Origins of the Green Revolution 205

year after.[93] Even before Indian officials were ready to acknowledge the existence of famine there, observers overseas were watching the horrific scenes on television sets.[94] From Washington, Lyndon Johnson had decried the "near famine conditions" that would necessitate an international response. Pope Paul VI pleaded for global assistance to India, where "people are literally dying of starvation," while the United Nations Secretary-General, U Thant, contended that shortages in India were already assuming famine proportions.[95]

Indian functionaries toed a careful line, hopeful for aid, but equally eager to project confidence and thus resist American demands for a rupee devaluation, decreased Indian cotton production, and relaxed controls upon the Indian private sector. Semantics grew ever-more important, with Indian officials quick to distance themselves from the term "famine" itself. "Today, when we talk of famine," Indira Gandhi declared on *Meet the Press*, "it is not in the sense in which we knew these words before independence. There is an acute shortage of food in our country in specific scarcity areas. There are no people dying of starvation." *Yojana*, the official publication of the Planning Commission, lamented that overseas, "the impression has been created that there is a widespread famine in India. Television programs have painted such a harrowing picture that little children in Europe have risen from the table and asked that the breakfast untouched by them be sent to India."[96] C. Subramaniam would only admit that the food situation in Bihar and elsewhere was "difficult." Yet the situation worsened throughout the winter, and the Congress government fell in early March 1967; the Bihar government declared famine in several districts a month later. By May, half the state's districts were designated "scarcity areas." All told, nearly 34 million people were affected by the crisis.[97]

The declaration of famine facilitated a massive expansion of aid, both public and private. The Bihar state government set up manual labor schemes with wages paid in food. New Delhi provided essentially unlimited cash to the state, but could only provide half of the 5 million tons of

[93] Paul R. Brass, "The Political Uses of Crisis: The Bihar Famine of 1966–1967," *The Journal of Asian Studies* 45, no. 2 (February 1, 1986): 246–247; Revenue Department, Government of Bihar, *Bihar Famine Report, 1966–67* (Patna: Secretariat Press, 1973).
[94] "Famine in Bihar," *ITN Reporting* (ITN News, April 12, 1967).
[95] Cullather, *The Hungry World*, 218–225.
[96] "Food, 1966," *Yojana* 10, no. 5 (March 20, 1966).
[97] Brass, "The Political Uses of Crisis," 246–247, 256; Alan Berg, "Famine Contained: Notes and Lessons from the Bihar Experience," in *Famine: A Symposium Dealing with Nutrition and Relief Operations in Times of Disaster*, ed. Gunnar Blix, Yngve Hofvander, and Bo Vahlquist, Symposia of the Swedish Nutrition Foundation 9 (Stockholm: Almqvist & Wiksell, 1971), 115.

206   Hungry Nation

grain the state had demanded, leaving the state's 20,000 new fair price shops perennially understocked.[98] Private aid made up the difference. Jayaprakash Narayan oversaw the activities of the Bihar Relief Committee and its 500 staffers as they set up camps, collected cash, food, *dhotis* and *saris*, installed pumping sets and boring rigs, and gave out vitamin tablets, drinking water, and cholera vaccines.[99] Occasionally accused of overselling the famine – and forced to recant a claim of starvation deaths in early 1967 – Narayan saw in shortage the failings of government and citizen alike, lamenting "that such a Nature-favored state should be reduced to its present plight in twenty years of *Swaraj*. This is the accumulated result of two decades of wrong policies and inept government."[100]

Meanwhile, foreign volunteers flocked to Bihar, galvanized by television reports and the machinations of international aid organizations. The Bihar crisis represented Oxfam's first on-the-ground relief program: it issued private ration cards, brought in Halco Tigers to irrigate dry districts, and facilitated the distribution of multipurpose food – a failed project undertaken by the Central Food Technological Research Institute fifteen years earlier – to famine zones.[101] Foreign volunteers from America, Britain, France, and Japan dotted the landscape.[102] In the small village of Daneri, famine victims made pilgrimages to a mud hut topped with palmyra leaves, named "Steve Bhavan" after the twenty-two-year-old Fulbright scholar conducting private relief operations from this modest dwelling. More famous Americans arrived in Bihar, as well: in early 1967, Marlon Brando, on a South and Southeast Asian tour, arrived in Bihar with a 16-millimeter camera to film a documentary on the famine.[103] Brando chaffed at his inability to persuade NBC to air his forty-five minute feature, but convinced the seventh-graders of Bangkok's International School to "adopt" Bihari children and pay for their food, water, and medicine.[104]

---

[98] Brass, "The Political Uses of Crisis," 259; Berg, "Famine Contained: Notes and Lessons from the Bihar Experience," 117.

[99] "Statement as President, Bihar Relief Committee," January 25, 1967, Jayaprakash Narayan papers (III) Speeches and Writings, folder 51, NMML.

[100] "Report of an Interview of J.P. about the Bihar Famine," 1967, Jayaprakash Narayan papers (III), Speeches and Writings, folder 72, NMML.

[101] Maggie Black, *A Cause for Our Times: Oxfam, the First 50 Years* (Oxford: Oxford University Press, 1992), 111–116.

[102] "Foreign Humanitarian Agencies Render Aid," *Times of India*, April 21, 1967. I am grateful to Steve Minkin of Brattleboro, Vermont, for his recollection of these relief efforts.

[103] Marlon Brando, *Brando: Songs My Mother Taught Me* (New York: Random House, 2011), 292–295.

[104] United Nations Children's Fund, "International School Students Follow Up Marlon Brando's Bihar Appeal," February 1967, CR/RAF/USAA/DB01/2003–04058, UNICEF Archives.

The Ideological Origins of the Green Revolution

Bihar represented the clear internationalization of an Indian crisis. But more significantly, planners saw in it the opportunity to pilot their own experimental schemes. For the first time, relief camps had largely eschewed observing caste restrictions in free kitchens.[105] American development workers used the crisis to promote its new infant food, Bal Ahar.[106] New Delhi's efforts to induce Indian citizens' use of long-term and permanent birth control methods received a fillip in the Bihar crisis. Towards its beginning, the Union government had standardized a payment of 11 rupees for an IUD insertion, 30 rupees for a vasectomy, and 40 rupees for a tubal ligation. Bihar had been the least compliant state prior to the crisis, with only 2,355 procedures undertaken in 1965; during the famine, those numbers spiked to 97,409 procedures in 1966 and 185,605 the year afterwards, frequently performed without so much as soap or sterile instruments.[107] Most fantastically, the American State Department secretly underwrote trials of a weather modification program, "Project GROMET," in Bihar and Uttar Pradesh throughout the early months of 1967.[108] Conducted with Indira Gandhi's knowledge under the guise of a meteorological survey, the project sought to seed clouds through aircraft-dispensed silver iodide in hopes of a better harvest, before the project was abandoned with the arrival of the summer rain.

Floods returned to Bihar in August, but the 1967 *kharif* crop was a normal one, and an end to the famine was declared in November. Decades removed from his own work in India, W.R. Aykroyd lauded Bihar famine relief as resoundingly successful. "In a book about the conquest of famine," he wrote, "the Bihar emergency of 1967 deserves a prominent and honorable place."[109] Yet Bihar's easy descent into famine conditions underscored the need for fundamental agricultural change. B.G. Verghese, press advisor to Indira Gandhi, noted that the children living on feeding center handouts seemed to be faring better than in non-famine years without state intervention.[110] One legislator lamented that

---

[105] R. Constantine, "Famine Effectively Tamed: Spot Report on Bihar," *Yojana* 11, no. 11 (June 11, 1967): 19–21.

[106] Bal Ahar files, RG 286 / P486 / Box 2 and Box 14, USNA.

[107] Connelly, "Population Control in India," 657–658.

[108] Kristine C. Harper and Ronald E. Doel, "Environmental Diplomacy in the Cold War: Weather Control, the United States, and India, 1966–1967," in *Environmental Histories of the Cold War*, ed. John Robert McNeill and Corinna R. Unger (Cambridge: Cambridge University Press, 2010), 115–137.

[109] The "famine contained" paradigm was advanced by a USAID administrator, Berg, "Famine Contained: Notes and Lessons from the Bihar Experience," 111; W.R. Aykroyd, *The Conquest of Famine* (New York: Reader's Digest Press, 1975), 142.

[110] B.G. Verghese, *Beyond the Famine: An Approach to Regional Planning for Bihar* (New Delhi: Bihar Relief Committee, 1967), 1–3.

208   Hungry Nation

"to some extent, [famine] is a normal condition. The landless and poor suffer like this normally."[111] Bihar, its dramatic crisis, and the recognition of its quotidian suffering suggested to planners the imperative for dramatic change. And in light of the structural machinations in Delhi, it was increasingly clear that the "new agricultural strategy" would be the primary institutional vehicle for this transformation.

Gobinda Lall Banerjee, former whip of the Bengal Congress Assembly Party, did not need to leave his Calcutta flat to know that there was a revolution underway.[112] He had heard the names whispered like mantras: Kalyan 227 and Sona 277, the two wheat varieties yielding up to 100 maunds per acre. Up in Srinagar, there were two quick-maturing rices speeding production there, as well. Even in Bihar, an experimental farmer was said to be growing six excellent crops in a single *bigha* of land. All these crops would soon be available across India, thanks to the new National Seeds Corporation – but they would yield little without Banerjee's plan.

Marx, Lenin, Gandhi, Aurobindo, M.N. Roy – these were the names of true revolutionaries, and Banerjee's name belonged among them. The politician had studied his history: first there had been a proletariat revolution, and then a bourgeois one. Now, it was time for a "Free-the-Food Revolution." The whole of government would have to be rearranged to ensure that the basic stuff of life was available to all. The men importing rice stock to India from the Philippines would be known, before long, as "pillars of this super revolution"; soon, the Prime Minister himself or herself would be asked to hold the portfolio of agriculture. All free government lands would be converted into farms, every village would be given a grain depot, and every citizen a card by which to claim her share of the nation's food. No matter if this reorganization of national priority raised the cost of living elsewhere. "If food is given free," Banerjee asserted, "it will not matter if a shirt or a trouser costs a little higher. These are matters for the economists to find the ways and means."

Banerjee's may have been the most optimistic of all predictions made in the wake of the new agricultural strategy's implementation. But as the Bihar famine reached its end, he was not alone in the belief that a new era had dawned. As C. Subramaniam pressed forth with his National Demonstration Program, members of the press were invited to see what new seeds, irrigation, and fertilizers could do in the hands of industrious farmers. A group of reporters was taken in mid 1966 to the village

---

[111] Brass, "The Political Uses of Crisis," 255.
[112] Gobinda Lall Banerjee, *Free the Food: A Super Revolution* (Calcutta: Frank K.L. Mukhopadhyay, 1967).

The Ideological Origins of the Green Revolution 209

of Jaunti, not far from Delhi.[113] Two years prior, the city's Cooperative Farming Society had returned from IARI with samples of Sonora 64 and Lerma Rojo wheat, planting them on Jawaharlal Nehru's birthday. Now, M. Swaminathan took journalists to the fields of Goburdhan Lal, Bhoop Singh, and Ishwar Singh to see single-hectare plots golden with wheat. The stalks "were dwarfish, sturdy and erect, each proudly holding aloft four or five heads packed with grain. Around that field were other plots where the local Indian variety of wheat stood tall and rather skeleton-like with heads scarce in grains." And while the wheat was said to taste as good as the local varieties, these steadfast farmers vowed to save the seeds to grow more the following year. (Journalists who did not wish to travel to Jaunti could instead dash over to C. Subramaniam's residence: the Food Minister had replaced the cricket pitch on his lawn with a plot of the same seeds.)

In late 1966, Daniel Thorner returned to the coastal districts of Andhra Pradesh, eager to see the results of the new strategy for himself. He had last visited the region in 1959, and had left India in 1962 after ten years in the country.[114] The region, he found, had been transformed: everywhere Thorner went, people enjoyed two or three meals a day, and in the earliest-adopting districts of East and West Godavari, even landless laborers were enjoying vegetables, chilies, dry fish, tea, coffee, and toddy with their large meals of rice. Peasants there had welcomed new seeds, bathing them in fertilizers and treatments before planting; some rich agriculturalists had become millionaires. In the biggest towns of the region, Thorner noted the mushrooming of shops advertising the repair of agricultural machines from Japan and the United States, and Sikh dealers touting fertilizers and tools.

Thorner did not have to search far for evangelizing farmers willing to speak to the efficacy of the new agricultural strategy. A wealthy Keralan industrialist, Erandath Puttanveedu Madhavan Nair, declared that he "did not know ABC of agriculture" when he had once left his 18 acres of paddy to the care of an elderly sharecropper.[115] But after procuring a handful of Tainan-3 seeds, Nair found himself reaping 3 or 4 tons of rice per acre each year, dreaming of even bigger yields to come. The reporter visiting his farm marveled at Nair's "cement-lined troughs, each spotting a variety of paddy, luscious and virile." In Thanjavur, one of the first

---

[113] Rosscote Krishna Pillai, "New Wheat in Old Farms," *Yojana* 10, no. 6 (April 3, 1966): 11–12.

[114] Daniel Thorner, "Coastal Andhra: Towards an Affluent Society," *Economic and Political Weekly* 2, no. 3/5 (February 1, 1967): 241–252.

[115] Bhabhani Sen Gupta, "Match-Maker Takes to Farming, Shows Unmatched Results," *Yojana* 11, no. 2 (February 5, 1967): 4–5.

210   Hungry Nation

IADP districts, farmers were reveling in the productivity of the ADT-27 hybrid, which allowed for double-cropping.[116] The district's farmers, worried that their overabundant crop would spoil, petitioned the Food Corporation of India to build thirty technical mechanical drying centers, and to dispatch a special forty-four-wagon train to the district to haul away the crop, with the word FOODGRAINS fastened proudly to the engine. In a village outside Madras, a wealthy farmer invited a group of farmers and journalists to his transformed estate, where they were hosted by his two sons, graduates in biochemistry and agriculture. The evening before the tour, the farmer asked his cook to prepare "IR-8 *idli*" for breakfast. His puzzled guests were informed that IR-8 rice had come to India from the Philippines, and the fluffy grains were as tasty as they were abundant. Over a breakfast of IR-8 *idli* and *dosa*, the guests were informed that these foods symbolized an end to India's food crisis.[117]

Beyond the manifold brochures produced by the Ministry of Information and Broadcasting, both informative and instructional, budding talent was recruited to help publicize the new agricultural strategy in India and abroad. Compared to the Indian blockbusters released that same year, *Paddy: High-Yielding Varieties* was a rather more modest production, shot over the summer with a shoestring budget and 540 meters of film. But while Vijay Bhatt's mountain-set thriller *Himalaya ki God Mein* took the 1966 Filmfare Award, *Paddy: High-Yielding Varieties* still managed the National Documentary Award.[118] *Paddy* showed life in a Thanjavur village completely transformed by the Taichung Native One hybrid seed. "The miracles brought by the high yielding varieties of paddy are the talk of our villages," the journalist Romesh Thapar declared, promising an income of 3000 rupees per hectare. Farmers needed only apply fertilizer at the right dose, irrigate well, and procure chemically treated stock from the National Seeds Corporation. "By following the package of improved agricultural practices," Thapar declared to swelling strings, farmers "will raise your yield per hectare and increase your income manifold, thus helping yourself and the country." For a film adapted in large measure from a Farm Information Unit instructional brochure, *Paddy* was a rather inspired production.[119] One diplomat wondered whether the film might be "suitable for developing countries of Asia

[116] "Thanjavur Never Had It So Good," *Yojana* 11, no. 21 (October 29, 1967).
[117] S.V. Raghavan, "I.R.-8 Iddlis," *Yojana* 12, no. 20 (October 13, 1968): 10.
[118] "Production of Films on Behalf of the Ministry of Food, Agriculture, CD&C – Paddy," January 1968, Information & Broadcasting – Film Censor – 15/3/66/FP, NAI.
[119] *How to Get High Yields with Taichung Native I Paddy* (New Delhi: Farm Information Unit, Directorate of Extension, Ministry of Food and Agriculture and Ministry of Community Development and Cooperation, 1966).

The Ideological Origins of the Green Revolution

Figure 11 A Rockefeller Foundation photographer captured this image (c. 1965–1966) of a farmer whose maize was now towering above him, thanks to the returns of the new agricultural strategy. (Credit: Rockefeller Archive Center)

212   Hungry Nation

and Africa" as they undertook their own schemes of agricultural development, and before long, the Ministry of Information and Broadcasting had dispatched copies of the film to Indian missions around the world.

Even if they took little notice of *Paddy*, foreign observers marveled at the changes taking place in India. Lyndon Johnson had encouraged India's transformation with a characteristic ham-fistedness, with a "short tether policy" designed to humiliate India into complicity.[120] Yet those less invested in bullying India into submission were equally impressed with India's mounting agricultural prowess. "As if overnight," one American journalist reported in 1968, "political and scientific leaders are witnessing dramatic changes in India's bleak agricultural picture, signs that the farmer is on the verge of emancipation from his fear of science and from his unproductive stewardship of the land."[121] A group of Soviet agricultural experts voiced their approval, as well, noting how well high-yielding wheat had worked in the USSR.[122] The *Economist* lauded the "cool-eyed scientists" who had made it conceivable that the "world's hungriest nation could feed itself and even export food within a few years."[123] Most memorable was the assessment of USAID administrator William Gaud at a meeting of the Society for International Development at the Washington, DC Sheraton.[124] India, he marveled, "hopes to achieve self-sufficiency in foodgrains in another three or four years. She has the capability to do so." The developments in India and elsewhere, he declared, "contain the makings of a new revolution. It is not a violet Red Revolution like that of the Soviets, nor is it a White Revolution like that of the Shah of Iran. I call it the Green Revolution." India's revolution was not of the sort which Gobinda Lall Banerjee had imagined – but now, at least, it had a name.[125]

The survivors in the Dalit ghetto on the outskirts of the village knew that Gopalakrishna Naidu was to blame for the slaughter.[126] It was Naidu

---

[120] Barry Riley, "LBJ, India, and the Short Tether," in *The Political History of American Food Aid: An Uneasy Benevolence* (Oxford: Oxford University Press, 2017), 256–305.

[121] Barbara J. Culliton, "Wheat and Revolution," *Science News* 94, no. 1 (1968): 19–20.

[122] "Soviet Experts Endorse Farm Strategy," *Times of India*, April 12, 1967.

[123] "India's Food: A Land of Plenty," *Economist*, May 13, 1967.

[124] William S. Gaud, "The Green Revolution: Accomplishments and Apprehensions" (presented at the Society for International Development, Washington, DC, March 8, 1968).

[125] The earliest use of the term in India seems to have been in 1969; see, for example, K.C. Naik, *Green Revolution*, Misc. Series 11 (Bangalore: University of Agricultural Science, 1969); and *Green Revolution: Delhi Villages Pulsating with New Life* (New Delhi: Directorate of Public Relations, Delhi Administration, 1971).

[126] This account is based upon "Gentlemen Killers of Kilvenmani," *Economic and Political Weekly* 8, no. 21 (May 26, 1973): 926–928; Thirumaavalavan, *Uproot Hindutva: The Fiery Voice of the Liberation Panthers* (Mumbai: Popular Prakashan, 2004), 10–11;

The Ideological Origins of the Green Revolution 213

who had led the mob to the *paracheri*, and who had cheered the men on as they reduced the hut to a pile of charred bodies and broken bangles. Eight women and children had managed to escape, but the slower ones had been cut apart with threshing sickles before being tossed back in the flames. As the bodies smoldered, Naidu had absconded in his automobile – the only private car in Thanjavur District.

The Communist Party of India (Marxist) had attracted so many Dalits in Thanjavur district that it was known locally as the *Paraiyan Katchi* – the Pariah's party. And as the district's low-caste laborers had seen the expensive wet paddy driers and special train cars which had arrived to process the glut of rice, they had risen up. Naidu, District Secretary of the Congress Party and the president of the local Paddy Producers' Association, had used tactics from a high-caste playbook long predating independence: a bout of whippings in the field, or a slurry of cow dung forced down the loudest agitators' throats. In time, most of the villages had replaced the hammer and sickle flags with the PPA's green and mustard standard, but Kizhavenmani's workers had proven harder to menace. Three leaders of Kizhavenmani's Agricultural Workers' Association had met particularly gruesome deaths before an ultimatum was delivered, alongside a savage beating, to the tea-stall owner turned organizer: join the PPA or face the consequences. The Dalits resisted: the body of an upper-caste scab was dragged back to the ghetto and hung from a spindly tree.

It was Christmas Day, and a conflagration was looming. As sun set over the paddy fields, the Dalit laborers locked up their women and children for protection. The thugs had shown up after midnight, on foot and in police cars commandeered for the occasion. With the streets to the ghetto blockaded, it did not take long for the swarm to find the hut. Long after midnight, the screams of dying women and children were punctuated only by gunshots – though local policemen would later swear that they had heard nothing.

Thirumaavalavan, *Talisman, Extreme Emotions of Dalit Liberation* (Mumbai: Popular Prakashan, 2003), 77; "11 Held: Arson and Clash in Thanjavur Village," *Times of India*, December 28, 1968; "Madras Is Reaping a Bitter Harvest of Rural Terrorism," *New York Times*, January 15, 1969; and Francine R. Frankel, *India's Green Revolution: Economic Gains and Political Costs* (Princeton: Princeton University Press, 1971), 112–118. The events of late 1968 in Thanjavur district were later fictionalized in a celebrated Tamil novel, Indira Parthasarathy, *Kuruthippunal [River of Blood]* (Madras: Tamil Puthakalayam, 1975); and more recently, in Meena Kandasamy, *The Gypsy Goddess* (London: Atlantic Books, 2014). The classic account of Thanjavur District is Kathleen Gough, *Rural Change in Southeast India, 1950s to 1980s* (New Delhi: Oxford University Press, 1989).

214   Hungry Nation

In the days that followed, there were arrests. C.N. Annadurai, Tamil Nadu's Chief Minister, wanted nothing more than the whole matter to disappear. These were optimistic days: the former Madras state had been given a proud Dravidian name, and its godowns were newly full with mountains of rice. But the state was electric with anger: Madras' Dalits had begun to fast under a statue of Ambedkar in protest, and across Thanjavur, laborers had occupied fields to demand the standardized, increased wages approved in the wake of the massacre.[127] An American reporter in Thanjavur wondered whether the crisis was "a sign that rural conflict may be an inescapable part of the so-called green revolution."[128]

It took three years for the case to snake its way through the judiciary, before the judge declared that an automobile owner could not possibly have orchestrated such horrors. Bodies aside, why were forty-two women and children in a space as small as that torched hut? To the rage of Kizhavenmani's survivors, Naidu was released alongside the other landlords. "My heart won't be at rest," one woman in the ghetto wailed, "until I skin him alive and make a roof for my hut with his skin." Her compatriots waited, watching Naidu strut across his fertile fields. One morning, the landlord did not wake up. "The people's forum," a Dalit Panther would later recall, "gave him the punishment of death penalty."

Even before the events in Kizhavenmani, it was dawning on planners that widening inequality and the specter of violence was baked into the Green Revolution package. Economist V.K.R.V. Rao had warned the year prior that its implementation would inevitably "increase inter-personal and regional inequalities among our farmers."[129] And as agrarian violence had erupted in villages from Tamil Nadu to West Bengal, officials in the Ministry of Home Affairs drew out its origins in the new agricultural strategy.[130] The Ministry's 1969 report on *The Causes and Nature of Current Agrarian Tensions* warned that the "widening gap between the relatively few affluent farmers and the large body of small landholders and landless agricultural laborers" would invariably "end in an explosion."[131] Her populist instinct alerted, Indira Gandhi sought to rally India's dispossessed with the cry of *garibi hatao* – "eradicate poverty." Yet beyond

---

[127] "Protest Fast against Caste Hindu Outrage," *Times of India*, January 14, 1969; "Paddy Harvested Forcibly in Thanjavur," *Times of India*, January 24, 1969.

[128] "Reaping a Bitter Harvest."

[129] Rajeshwar Dayal, *India's New Food Strategy* (New Delhi: Metropolitan Book Co., 1968), 85–90.

[130] Akshayakumar Ramanlal Desai, *Agrarian Struggles in India after Independence* (New Delhi: Oxford University Press, 1986).

[131] Research and Policy Division, Ministry of Home Affairs, *The Causes and Nature of Current Agrarian Tensions* (New Delhi: Ministry of Home Affairs, Government of India, 1969).

The Ideological Origins of the Green Revolution

sloganeering, agrarian violence unleashed prompted observers to ask whether a red revolution would be the natural consequence of the green one. A Ministry official had leaked copies of the report, and reviewing it, the *Financial Express* warned of the consequences of "big farmers in their village reaping the entire benefit of the green revolution." In a year of scarcity, "rural India will be in flames."[132]

As Indian bureaucrats wondered what unrest the new agricultural strategy had wrought, a cadre of foreign social scientists, economists, and journalists flocked to India to assess its true gains and costs. In 1969, a young political scientist, Francine Frankel, made a tour of Ludhiana, West Godavari, Thanjavur, Palghat, and Burdwan districts, speaking with rural development officers, irrigation and cooperation experts, project officers, and agricultural laborers. Convinced upon arrival that India's planners had abandoned "the social objective of reducing disparities in life," Frankel concluded that no scientific advance could actualize "the economic gains of modernization while avoiding the social costs of mass upheaval and disorder usually associated with rapid change."[133] Only in the historically fertile tracts of Punjab was there reason to posit a benefit to rural society as a whole.

Yet others disputed Punjab's exceptional quality. A team of economists camped out on a well-irrigated 10-acre farm in Punjab, watching as the Persian wheel, used for irrigation since Mughal times, was replaced with pump-sets, augmented in turn with wheat threshers, corn shellers, electric cane crushers, tractors, and wheat reapers.[134] Prior to the new agricultural strategy, they concluded, the average local labor demand for a farm like this was 51 man-days per season. With high-yielding seeds alone, that number swelled to 60 – but with increased mechanization, demand plummeted to 25. This was fantastic news for farmers who could afford new implements, and a poor omen for the laborers left with less and less paying work. The conclusion in Punjab echoed throughout India: the nation's leading agricultural economists met at Visakhapatnam to devise means to address the crisis of widening rural incomes. "Though the small farmer was not bypassed," the agricultural economists wrote with concern, "he was unable to keep pace with the big and middle farmers. As for the tenant and the laborer, they were left much behind even the small owner-cultivator."[135]

---

[132] "Year of Lost Opportunity," *Financial Express*, December 17, 1969.

[133] Frankel, *India's Green Revolution*, v.

[134] Martin H. Billings and Arjan Singh, "Labour and the Green Revolution: The Experience in Punjab," *Economic and Political Weekly* 4, no. 52 (December 27, 1969): A221–A224.

[135] C.H. Shah, "Fall-Out of Green Revolution," *Economic and Political Weekly* 5, no. 2 (January 10, 1970): 42–44.

216   Hungry Nation

Martin Abel was a Cornell-trained agricultural economist who had helped develop the food stamp program for the United States Department of Agriculture. In 1968, he had quit his post as Deputy Undersecretary for International Affairs at the USDA to work for the Ford Foundation in New Delhi, and from this vantage, he was one of the first to ask whether the Green Revolution was in fact revolutionary, "or merely a small 'palace revolt?'"[136] The enhanced production of grains, he contended, had done nothing to ameliorate an entirely deficient diet, and he worried whether "the social and political tensions that have been building up in the countryside for some time, and have been made more acute by the stark visibility of the uneven impact of the new seed-fertilizer technology, could play havoc with the whole development process." And B. Sen, whose breeding work at the IARI had been essential to the new agricultural strategy, sounded a similar note of dismay. Inequity, he contended, could be remedied through the commandeering of surplus capital into non-farm development – yet without the will to enact an agricultural tax worth the name, these schemes were mere pipe dreams.[137]

Two of the most sensitive foreign students of India's agricultural development, Daniel Thorner and Wolf Ladejinsky, undertook parallel tours of the nation to assess the prospects for equitable development, both zeroing in on changes in Punjab. With great prescience, Thorner contended that the revolution that Indian planners would need to contend with was neither red, nor green, but rather the "steel-gray" of industrial machination. It was the development of new industry in the Green Revolution that would soon be "responsible for the rise of a class of enterprising agriculturists" who would in short order remake India's political landscape.[138]

Ladejinsky, then at the World Bank, took note of the "sturdy, self-confident, innovation-minded small group of farmers who in a short span of years have succeeded in translating promise into reality."[139] Yet in a state where land values were skyrocketing, and the "occasionally, though rare sight of a camel pulling a traditional plough, or the more

---

[136] Martin E. Abel, "Agriculture in India in the 1970s," *Economic and Political Weekly* 5, no. 13 (March 28, 1970): A5–A14.

[137] B. Sen, "Opportunities in the Green Revolution," *Economic and Political Weekly* 5, no. 13 (March 28, 1970): A33–A40.

[138] Daniel Thorner, "Capitalist Farming in India," *Economic and Political Weekly* 4, no. 52 (December 27, 1969): A211–A212.

[139] Wolf Ladejinsky, "The Green Revolution in Punjab: A Field Trip," *Economic and Political Weekly* 4, no. 26 (June 28, 1969): A73–A82. Ladejinsky's account was one of the main sources for an influential, early critique of Green Revolution written by the Marxist economist Harry W. Cleaver, which appeared, somewhat unaccountably, in the *American Economic Review*; Cleaver, "The Contradictions of the Green Revolution."

The Ideological Origins of the Green Revolution   217

frequent sight of a Persian wheel doing its rounds appeals as an anachronism from a bygone age," there was reason to maintain a cynical air. Ladejinsky spoke with a retired doctor who had taken to farming. His career transformation, the doctor declared, had been undertaken "for the good of my country," though Ladejinsky noted wryly that "patriotism in his case did not exclude a good package of practice, two tube-wells, 55 maunds to the acre, and the search for still more improvements." As Ladejinsky watched the poorer peasantry seethe, he lamented the mothballing of an earlier paradigm that had set equity before growth. The technology powering the Green Revolution could perhaps reach all agriculturalists, but only if planners' "bias against institutional change gives way to recognition of the interdependence between technology and socio-economic reform." Yet there would be no backpedaling now: the rumblings of a discontented peasantry was no match for full godowns – nor, for that matter, for the maneuvering of wealthy farmers eager to consolidate their political and economic gains.

The mounting unease of agricultural economists and students of Indian politics did little to dim the luster of abundant grain; nor could the Arcadian fantasies of a nation awash in an ethos of equity bring that grain to the hungry in India's towns and villages. In 1970, Norman Borlaug was awarded the Nobel Peace Prize for his work on Green Revolution technologies; two years later, Wolf Ladejinsky could claim that "the green revolution in India is an often told story."[140]

Yet the familiarity of that story continues to elide a gloomy, counterrevolutionary landscape. As early as 1960, as new seeds began to arrive in India, even government statistics were beginning to show a widening gap in incomes and outputs in Indian agriculture; this cleave grew decidedly worse in the years after the new agricultural strategy.[141] Steeped in the doctrines of modernization theory, planners like C. Subramaniam had placed their faith in a "demonstration effect" of the sort that Nehru had been asked to observe on the Illinois farms ascending the "agricultural ladder." Yet lacking the credit needed to purchase implements, market conditions that would allow poorer farmers and tenants to compete with richer agriculturalists, and a renewed commitment to equitable growth from New Delhi, India's small farmers and its landless could only watch as the rich grew richer, and the hungry grew hungrier.

[140] Wolf Ladejinsky, "How Green Is the Indian Green Revolution?," *Economic and Political Weekly* 8, no. 52 (December 29, 1973): A133.

[141] Erich H. Jacoby, "Effects of the 'Green Revolution' in South and South-East Asia," *Modern Asian Studies* 6, no. 1 (January 1, 1972): 63–69.

218   Hungry Nation

A grim postscript to the violence in Kizhavenmani came in the form of a nutritional survey undertaken in the 1970s. In Thanjavur district, nearly half of all Dalits – and a quarter of all other castes – were living on less than half of United Nations subsistence levels.[142] Abundance alone had done nothing to lessen the burden of hunger nor to distribute food more equitably: the district was producing more than three times its requirements of rice, but was using it primarily for export and as feedstock. Further humiliation came in the fact that the export of rice was preventing the district's Dalits from a last-ditch source of protein: the rats which otherwise would have fed on grain stores in godowns.

The new agricultural strategy was indeed revolutionary in its effects on India's political landscape. In the years that followed, an empowered class of agrarian capitalists who had benefited from Green Revolution transformations would remake national politics and stymie further efforts at egalitarian reform. Yet this strategy represented the mere amplification of paradigms which had smoldered at an early moment characterized by a greater commitment to social equity. Two decades earlier, Jawaharlal Nehru had stood in an Illinois cornfield, intrigued by the innovations which had galvanized American postwar agriculture. Yet at the time, he had dismissed American methods as unsuited to Indian contexts, which required the vaunting of equity above all other values.

The lure of a different model, however, had lurked spectrally in many Indian schemes. Even India's earliest "Grow More Food" campaign had relied partially upon the selective application of inputs. For the first two decades of independence, agronomists, plant breeders, politicians, and powerful farmers themselves had frequently extolled productivism as an overriding principle, above concerns of equity. Yet it took the shifting of India's political dynamics, the death of a singular prime minister, and the rising lure of new technologies to render this embrace palatable. In 1969, Planning Commission member Pitamber Pant contended that the goal of increasing agricultural production had come to be seen by all involved as a more urgent goal than the aim of social equity.[143] This goal had not materialized ex nihilo, but had instead been enthusiastically reanimated at a moment of political transformation.

Twenty years before the new agricultural strategy boosted the output of India's most productive farmers, India's planners had already seen the possibilities of capitalist agriculture operating under the aegis of state support, initially rejecting this model out of the notion that even in a

---

[142] Kathleen Gough, "The 'Green Revolution' in South India and North Vietnam," *Social Scientist* 6, no. 1 (August 1, 1977): 54.
[143] Tomlinson, *The Economy of Modern India, 1860–1970*, 210.

The Ideological Origins of the Green Revolution 219

hungry nation, growth and equity had to come in tandem. In a changed climate, India's planners were far more willing to ignore the fundamental inequities of a new agricultural strategy privileging quantitative growth above all else, dismissing the looming ingress of corporate interests in agriculture, the concentration of land and output, and the increased economic marginalization of India's peasantry.[144] The consequences of this decision would become apparent in short order, as India contended with the rise of a new agrarian politics which has thus far done little to better the enduring specter of hunger and malnutrition, and to meet the hopes and aspirations of India's citizens.

---

[144] Akhil Gupta, *Postcolonial Developments: Agriculture in the Making of Modern India* (Durham: Duke University Press, 1998), 53–54.

Conclusion: Landscapes of Hunger in Contemporary India

Of every subject that Prithwis Chandra Ray discussed with friends in the drawing rooms of Calcutta, it was the problem of India's poverty that held his attention most grippingly at the turn of the last century. In the spirit of Dadabhai Naoroji and Romesh Chunder Dutt, the young economist had dedicated his first academic undertaking to the question, publishing the work in a well-received monograph.[1] But within several years, those spirited conversations and the famines in western India had led Ray to his real concern. Poverty was the problem, but Indians experienced that poverty chiefly as hunger, with evidence of misrule in empty bowls and skeletal frames. Ray put his thoughts together in a short text. "This pamphlet," he wrote, "is published on the opening day of the Twentieth Century. I hope that, before this century draws to its close, the miserable population of India will be better fortified against all freaks of climate and that famines will be less frequent in occurrence and less fatal in their results in this ancient and unhappy land in future."[2]

What would Ray, who died before Indian nationalists brought hunger to the forefront of their claim-making, make of the Republic of India in the opening decades of the twenty-first century? How might he account for a nation that holds in its godowns 70 million tons of grains – the world's largest store, which would fill sacks stretched to the moon and back – but which is home to a quarter of the world's starving population?[3] How would he, or any of the Indian economic thinkers wrestling with poverty at the turn of the last century, come to terms with a nuclear nation, beeping and chirping with smartphones, satellites, and supermarkets, but which lets 18 percent of its citizens go hungry?[4]

---

[1] Prithwis Chandra Ray, *The Poverty Problem in India; Being a Dissertation on the Causes and Remedies of Indian Poverty* (Calcutta: Thacker, Spink & Co., 1895).
[2] Ray, *Indian Famines.*
[3] Laul, "The Politics of Hunger."
[4] Virmani and Singh, "Malnutrition, Not Hunger, Ails India."

220

Conclusion

India's struggle for independence and its postcolonial accomplishments are both singular and spectacular – and its many success stories render the nation's nutritional failures even more jarring. Some seventy years ago, speaking at the inaugural session of the Food and Agriculture Organization, G.S. Bajpai struggled to quantify India's hunger at the cusp of independence. Before making a plea for technical assistance that would help India attain self-sufficiency, Bajpai cut through the morass of agricultural statistics, suggesting that about a third of the incipient nation's 400 million people were hungry, in spite of what he considered, "east of Suez, the best agricultural institute of research in the world."

Greater statistical clarity has allowed researchers to paint a sharper, if no less damning, portrait of India's contemporary landscape of hunger. A recent Global Hunger Index report offers a grim numerical assessment: in spite of a grain supply large enough to export in droves, 15 percent of India's citizens remain hungry.[5] India is the second worst-fed country in the region after Pakistan, and its index ranking of 28.5 puts it just ahead of clunkers like Zimbabwe and North Korea. India's levels of malnourishment remain far worse than sub-Saharan Africa's, in spite of far more robust economic growth. The report is not optimistic: by 2030, India is predicted to be scarcely better-off than today. Much has been made of Amartya Sen's contention that no famine has occurred in a true democracy.[6] Yet democratic India, Sen and his colleague Jean Drèze admit, has witnessed "alarming dips in food output and availability," and recurrent threats to "the entitlements of large parts of the population."[7]

These woes are starker when viewed along the axes of India's "unique cocktail of lethal divisions and disparities": those who looked eagerly at independence towards an egalitarian future would be crestfallen to see India's nutritional cleaves widen along lines of caste, religion, rurality, gender, and age.[8] Scheduled castes, scheduled tribes, and Muslims suffer far worse from hunger and malnutrition than their high-caste, Hindu counterparts.[9] And India's children, the worst fed in the world, suffer most of all. A 2012 survey of 73,000 Indian households found that nearly 42 percent of all children under age five suffer from malnutrition – a

---

[5] Klaus Bernstein von Grebmer et al., *2016 Global Hunger Index: Getting to Zero Hunger* (Washington, DC: International Food Policy Research Institute, 2016).

[6] Amartya Sen, *Development as Freedom* (New York: Knopf, 1999).

[7] Jean Drèze and Amartya Sen, *Hunger and Public Action* (New York: Oxford University Press, 1989), 211.

[8] Jean Drèze and Amartya Sen, *An Uncertain Glory: India and Its Contradictions* (New Delhi: Penguin, 2013), 213.

[9] Nidhi Sadana Sabharwal, "Caste, Religion and Malnutrition Linkages," *Economic and Political Weekly* 46, no. 50 (December 10, 2011): 16–18.

222   Conclusion

statistic which former Prime Minister Manmohan Singh decried as a "national shame."[10] In a comparative sense, India's children are far hungrier than their counterparts in sub-Saharan Africa, and the 43 percent who are underweight dwarf China's 4 percent.[11] Researchers are now documenting the ways in which early childhood hunger savagely stymies brain development.[12] A nation whose population has been ravaged both by developmental impairment and the health tolls of a growing obesity crisis – now estimated at 5 to 10 percent of the population – will have a hard time actualizing political elites' dreams of celebratory speeches at Davos.[13]

Yet at the same time, there is little political will to deal with questions of basic livelihood when poverty is increasingly cast as a choice made by the poor themselves. Glassy-eyed business school professors gush over India as a land of untapped entrepreneurship, while superstar Amitabh Bachchan, conscripted as India's "brand ambassador," declares that "there are two Indias," one "straining at the leash" to capitalize upon new market opportunities, while the other doubts, fears, and cowers.[14] It is difficult to innovate and disrupt, one presumes, when the government declares 32 rupees (USD $0.47) in villages and 48 rupees (USD $0.70) in cities to be a sufficient minimal daily income.[15]

The simple enunciation of a "right to food" is not sufficient to guarantee sustenance – though even enshrining that right as a starting point has proven a losing proposition, as legislators found in the Constituent Assembly debates seventy years ago.[16] In late 2013, half a year before being trounced at the polls, India's Congress government managed to push an ambitious National Food Security Act through Parliament.[17] Against protests of fiscal excess and electoral pandering, and the objections of the World Trade Organization, the Act's proponents extolled its provisions as the legislative safeguards and administrative reforms that would finally quash India's nutritional inequality.[18] Yoking together a

[10] Jim Yardley, "Malnutrition in India Is Widespread, Report Finds," *New York Times*, January 10, 2012.
[11] Drèze and Sen, *An Uncertain Glory*, 214–215.
[12] Rémi Radel and Corentin Clément-Guillotin, "Evidence of Motivational Influences in Early Visual Perception: Hunger Modulates Conscious Access," *Psychological Science* 23, no. 3 (2012): 232–234.
[13] "India Facing Obesity Epidemic: Experts," *The Hindu*, October 12, 2007; Praween Kumar Agrawal, "Emerging Obesity in Northern Indian States: A Serious Threat for Health," in *IUSSP Conference in Bangkok*, 2002.
[14] *India Poised* (Mumbai: Times of India, 2007).
[15] "New Poverty Line," *Times of India*, July 7, 2014.
[16] M. Ananthasayanam Ayyangar, November 9, 1948.
[17] *National Food Security Act (NFSA)*, 2013.
[18] Sudha Narayanan, "The National Food Security Act vis-à-vis the WTO Agreement on Agriculture," *Economic and Political Weekly* 49, no. 5 (January 23, 2014): 40–46.

Conclusion 223

coterie of schemes, the Act declared two-thirds of India's population as "priority households" eligible for 5 kilograms of heavily subsidized cereals a month. Rather than counting households as single units, the Act tied these guarantees to individual citizens. In certain poorer states, nearly 80 percent of citizens became eligible for these cheap grains – a victory for liberal economists and left-leaning politicians who had long agitated for universal or near-universal entitlements. Announcing its implementation, Congress President Sonia Gandhi ceremonially handed over packets of grain and new "smart" ID cards to poor Indians. "We made this scheme," she declared, "so that nobody remains hungry in the country and no one's child sleeps hungry."[19] At a speech in the Lok Sabha, Gandhi added that the bill's passage represented the fulfillment of Congress' long promise to "wipe out hunger and malnutrition."[20]

Yet by the time the Act's provisions were to have come into force, the new BJP-led government had assumed power in New Delhi. In states where the Act had been implemented quickly, like Chhattisgarh, Odisha, and Madhya Pradesh, the benefits were clear: coverage of beneficiaries increased, and the theft and waste that claimed nearly 90 percent of rations a decade earlier had been reduced to around 10 percent.[21] Yet other states took their cues from the new central government and stalled, eager to reduce spending on entitlements and subsidies; in February 2016, the Supreme Court reproached nine states and two union territories which had failed to implement the Act.[22] Perhaps unsurprisingly, activists and scholars studying those states surveyed a depressing status quo: missing ration cards and incomplete rosters, claims of inadequate supplies and overpricing, and grains unfit for human consumption. The new government, meanwhile, shows no terrible enthusiasm for the Act, preferring to focus on the showier, "value-added" sectors of food and agriculture like greenhouse and organic farming techniques, the construction of food processing units, and the opening-up of food marketing and retailing to foreign direct investment.

The ceding of responsibility for food security by the state has left the task to private initiative; unsurprisingly, the efforts of political parties and multinational corporations have yielded few substantive gains. The

---

[19] "Sonia Gandhi Launches Food Security Programme in Delhi," *The Hindu*, August 20, 2013.
[20] Vinay Kumar and Aarti Dhar, "Lok Sabha Passes Food Security Bill," *The Hindu*, August 27, 2013.
[21] Anumeha Yadav, "The Fruits of India's National Food Security Law Are Finally Showing on the Ground," *Scroll.in*, June 23, 2016.
[22] "Do You Want to Break Away from the Union, Court Asks Gujarat," *The Hindu*, February 1, 2016.

224   Conclusion

failure of ventures like Bharti-Walmart to rationalize food markets and lessen India's prodigious food wastage has done little to dissuade others from attempting to capitalize upon the nation's enduring nutritional woes.[23] Public health researchers worried about India's "dual burden" of cheek-by-jowl obesity and malnutrition were understandably cynical about KFC's recent pledge of a five-rupee donation to a private food bank for each bucket of deep-fried poultry sold in its popular outlets.[24] In Tamil Nadu, the state that pioneered the distribution of midday meals in the 1960s, "Amma Canteens" named after the late, mononymous Chief Minister Jayalalithaa, or "Amma," dole out subsidized fare to drum up support for the ruling AIADMK party. In 2017, the loudest agitation on matters of food is the ominously mounting assault on beef-eaters and alleged beef-eaters, with scant condemnation reserved for prosaic outrages of a secular nature.[25]

There are meaningful and effective roles for non-state actors to play in the amelioration of India's food crisis. Groups like the Abdul Latif Jameel Poverty Action Lab have brought the rigor of randomized controlled trials to issues like food security with compelling results.[26] Yet no entrepreneurial "disruption" has yet substituted for a scheme with the weight of a state behind it; no corporate social responsibility program has provided more than an incidental fillip to human welfare; and no party has sufficiently transcended politicking to reduce stark social disparities.

Anthropologist Akhil Gupta asks us to imagine a natural disaster claiming the lives and livelihoods of thousands of people. Those observing the disaster agree that it is impossible to aid all the victims, and that the best response is to focus on the improvement of the economy so that victims can find employment and better their own lots. "Would we not find such a state of affairs to be appalling," he asks, "and perhaps even outrageous?"[27] He asks us to consider the 140 million people who have died unnecessarily on account of hunger and preventable illness not as

---

[23] Nidhi Bagaria and Swarup Santra, *Foreign Direct Investment in Retail Market in India: Some Issues and Challenges*, SSRN Scholarly Paper (Rochester, NY: Social Science Research Network, January 31, 2014); Amy J. Cohen, "Supermarkets in India: Struggles over the Organization of Agricultural Markets and Food Supply Chains," *University of Miami Law Review* 68 (2013): 19–323.

[24] "KFC Launches Program 'Add HOPE™' to Fight Hunger," *Yum! Global Newsroom*, May 12, 2016.

[25] On cattle prohibition in modern India, see Rohit De, "Cows and Constitutionalism," *Modern Asian Studies* (forthcoming).

[26] See Abhijit V. Banerjee and Esther Duflo, *Poor Economics: A Radical Rethinking of the Way to Fight Global Poverty* (New York: PublicAffairs, 2011); and Sendhil Mullainathan and Eldar Shafir, *Scarcity: Why Having Too Little Means So Much* (New York: Times Books, 2013).

[27] Gupta, *Red Tape: Bureaucracy, Structural Violence, and Poverty in India*, 4–5.

Conclusion 225

tragic casualties of development, but as victims of murder. It is a proposition that Indian thinkers like Prithwis Chandra Ray might well have affirmed.

The imagery of the *kisan* – the peasant-farmer – is ubiquitous in Indian public life. So, too, do vestiges of India's struggle for self-sufficiency present themselves frequently beyond the daily headlines which chronicle India's nutritional woes. On the back of the five-rupee note, a robust peasant drives a tractor across rolling fields; until it was withdrawn from circulation in late 2016 in an effort to combat hidden and untaxed wealth, the thousand-rupee note set an oil rig, a CRT monitor, and a steel mill against a golden sheaf of wheat. The year I began this research, the dark farmer suicide comedy *Peepli Live* became a sleeper hit in cities, and the soaring price of onions threw India into an equally unexpected political crisis.[28]
Much of this book was researched in New Delhi; in the National Archives of India, I worked a few minutes away from Krishi Bhavan, the imposing office complex housing the Department of Food and Distribution. Not far off stood Yojana Bhavan, home of the Planning Commission, now defunct and replaced by NITI Aayog, a government-run "think tank" which has traded notions of social uplift for a laser-like focus on "entrepreneurship," "transformation," and ideas suited for the "global economy." On other days, I combed through the dusty library of the Indian Agricultural Research Institute, and looked out on fields where the first Green Revolution cultivars were tested in India. On mornings in the Nehru Memorial Museum and Library, I cut across a lawn where, sixty years prior, a young Indira Gandhi had tended to vegetables and tubers on her father's lawn in an act of showy civic pedagogy.
One day, not long after the end of a strike over foreign direct investment in India's food retail sector which had shut down shops and transportation, I found myself in conversation with an auto-rickshaw driver, a migrant from Bihar, who spoke with great intensity about the rising price of food. As I paid, we exchanged names: his was Jaikisan – "long live the farmer." Somewhere in his mid forties, Jaikisan would have been born when Prime Minister Lal Bahadur Shastri rallied the nation around the slogan of "*Jai jawan, jai kisan*"– long live the farmer, and long live the soldier, each responsible for the nation's well-being in times of emergency.
Yet while those who considered India's agrarian plight in the decades surrounding India's independence would recognize the rich symbology of the present, very few would readily comprehend contemporary India's

---

[28] On farmer suicides, see R.S. Deshpande and Saroj Arora, *Agrarian Crisis and Farmers' Suicide* (New Delhi: Sage Publications, 2010); and A.R. Vasavi, *Shadow Space: Suicides and the Predicament of Rural India* (Gurgaon: Three Essays Collective, 2012).

226   Conclusion

agricultural politics. The machinations of the 1950s and 1960s created the terrain for a new administrative order wherein agriculturalists have gained much political primacy. But the meaningful ends of agriculture – that is to say, food for a hungry populace – have lost out to the idioms of agrarian politics. This paradoxical configuration requires a brief recounting of the years between the Green Revolution and the present day.

The agricultural transformations of the mid 1960s, as the preceding chapter has demonstrated, did not solve the problem of want. And as the specter of violence in even the most productive districts underscored, the fundamental questions of welfare and citizenship which had animated an earlier moment of popular politics remained unresolved. The establishment of a state-run organization to compete on the market mean that the struggle for state control of India's food economy had been lost. The project of land reform remained similarly incomplete. And the terrain had been primed for a new political order in India.

This new order was beginning to take shape by the early 1970s. The establishment of the Food Corporation of India came alongside the creation of an Agricultural Prices Commission charged with recommending support and procurement prices, and determining the contributions that states would make to the pool of grains for fair price shops.[29] In effect, the Commission was given the politically charged task of deciding whether state policy would favor consumers seeking cheaper grains, or producers eager for inducements and incentives. As large farmers grew more politically powerful in the wake of the Green Revolution, they lobbied aggressively for seats on the committees, distrustful of urban technocrats.[30]

The result was a return to a chaotic status quo ante. "Farmers," Wolf Ladejinsky recounted, "sold or did not as suited them; wholesalers didn't sit idle; retailers indulged consumer-hoarders; and smugglers had a field day."[31] In 1973, galvanized by Indira Gandhi's slogan of "eradicating poverty," the Planning Ministry successfully pushed for the nationalization of the wheat industry. Private wholesale trade was eliminated, and the Food Corporation was designated as the sole purchasing agency for the state.[32] Yet the outbreak of food riots and the muscle of an emboldened agricultural class forced the state to beat a hasty retreat.

[29] D.S. Tyagi, *Managing India's Food Economy: Problems and Alternatives* (New Delhi: Sage Publications, 1990).
[30] Ashutosh Varshney, "Ideas, Interest and Institutions in Policy Change: Transformation of India's Agricultural Strategy in the Mid-1960s," *Policy Sciences* 22, no. 3/4 (January 1, 1989): 92.
[31] Ladejinsky, *Agrarian Reform as Unfinished Business*, 108.
[32] Lewis M. Simons, "Wheat Nationalization Tests India's Socialism," *Washington Post*, April 9, 1973.

Conclusion 227

These rumblings portended greater change to come. In 1977, Indira Gandhi's government was defeated by an unstable coalition under the banner of the Janata Party; the estimable peasant leader Charan Singh was made Home Minister.[33] Singh had long cast the goal of industrial development as inimical to India's agrarian character. He had built political capital as the steward of India's "middle peasantry," deepening this clout by lambasting Congress' ill-fated push for collectivization in 1959.[34] By the 1960s, Singh – now affectionately "Chaudhuri," the boss – had seen his political fortunes rise, bolstered by the ascent of India's new "bullock capitalists."[35]

The massive peasant rallies that Singh held in New Delhi as Home Minister were visible assertions of the farmer's political ascent. Singh called for "remunerative prices" to the farmer, and vastly increased government investment in agriculture. These populist cries antagonized the Congress faction of the Janata government, led by Morarji Desai, and led to Singh's ouster. Yet Desai's effort to defang agrarian politicking was a critical miscalculation. Singh promptly organized a massive rally in Delhi, bringing together somewhere between several hundred thousand to a million farmers. "The Government's policy," the septuagenarian Singh declared, "does not help the farmers. The farmers are forgotten by this Government. The things that farmers produce are selling cheap, and the things that they have to buy cost very much."[36] Singh rose back briefly to power on a platform of increased farmer representative on the Agricultural Prices Commission, parity prices in agriculture and industry, larger fertilizer subsidies, and the government promotion of agricultural exports.

The vision of India's "forgotten" farmers striking back to take their rightful share was not a new one. In 1958, an Uttar Pradesh agriculturalist named Ram Krishan Sharma published a fiery Hindi invective on India's food problem and its farmers. Its argument was scornful of government schemes, and consonant with Charan Singh's reading of the middle peasantry.[37] "Our Central and Provincial government," he wrote,

---

[33] On Charan Singh, see Brass, *An Indian Political Life*, 2011; Brass, *An Indian Political Life*, 2014; and Byres, "Charan Singh, 1902–1987: An Appreciation."

[34] Charan Singh, *Joint Farming X-Rayed: The Problem and Its Solution* (Bombay: Bharatiya Vidya Bhavan, 1959). See also Charan Singh, *Whither Co-Operative Farming?* (Allahabad: Superintendent, Printing and Stationery, Uttar Pradesh, India, 1956); and Charan Singh, *Agrarian Revolution in Uttar Pradesh* (Lucknow: Superintendent, Printing and Stationery, Uttar Pradesh, India, 1958).

[35] Rudolph and Rudolph, *In Pursuit of Lakshmi*, passim.

[36] "Farmers in India Rally to Support Rival of Premier," *New York Times*, December 24, 1978; "Peasant Leader Vying for Power in India: Chaudhury Charan Singh," *New York Times*, July 25, 1979.

[37] Ram Krishan Sharma, *Kheti aur Bhojan [Farming and Food]* (Allahabad: Lahar Prakashan, 1958), 6–13. See also *Dharti Dhan: Bhumi aur Krishi Sambandh 47 Utkrsht*

228 Conclusion

are trapped in their extensive plans, costing millions and trillions of rupees. They imagine that one day, rivers of milk, *ghee*, butter and honey will flow, and there will be verdant fields of fruits, flowers, and grains. Yet these well-intentioned people do not understand that it is more important to alleviate the sufferings of the present than dream of the future.

Those sufferings, he felt, were borne by farmers more than anyone else: the government celebrated its big dams, but neglected tools for farmers. It gave subsidies to products like refined sugar, and underwrote the production of vegetable *ghee*, which poisoned citizens and made virile men impotent.

"India today," Sharma wrote, "is independent but heading towards ruin." Its farmers, victims of a government drunk on notions of industrialization, were no better than slaves. "Will the screams of hunger be silenced by government proclamations? Absolutely not. No granaries will be filled in this hungry country by big speeches and big assurances, or laws passed in the Parliament." Only by empowering its farmers through correct politics could India's government escape the curse of "food produced by a rotten state, distributed only by ration card."

By the 1980s, thanks to the machinations of men like Charan Singh, the frustrations of farmers like Ram Krishan Sharma were bearing political fruit. Empowered by Singh's brief ascent – capped by a forgettable six-month stint as Prime Minister – India's agriculturalists converged throughout the decade into an alphabet soup of farmers' organizations, whose mass mobilizations became a staple of Indian public life.[38] Consistent in their demands for higher prices for agricultural produce, these groups blocked food transportation in massive *rasta roko* [road blockage] campaigns. They denied officials access to villages, withheld payment on outstanding tax, electricity bills, and bank loads, and kept crops from local markets to force up prices.[39] Two leaders, Maharashtra's Sharad Joshi and Uttar Pradesh's M.S. Tikait, emerged as national

---

Lekhon ka Sangrah [The Wealth of the Soil: A Collection of 47 Excellent Articles on Land and Agriculture] (Patna: Parijat Prakashan, 1959).

[38] On the "new farmers' movement," see Tom Brass, "Introduction: The New Farmers' Movements in India," in *New Farmers' Movements in India*, ed. Tom Brass (Ilford: Frank Cass, 1995), 3–4; Mangesh Venktesh Nadkarni, *Farmers' Movements in India* (Ahmedabad: Allied Publishers, 1987); and Utsa Patnaik, *Agrarian Relations and Accumulation: The "Mode of Production" Debate in India* (Bombay: Published for Sameeksha Trust by Oxford University Press, 1990).

[39] See Ian Duncan, "Agricultural Innovation and Political Change in North India: The Lok Dal in Uttar Pradesh," *Journal of Peasant Studies* 24, no. 4 (1997): 246–268; Sucha Singh Gill, "The Farmers' Movement and Agrarian Change in the Green Revolution Belt of Northwest India," *Journal of Peasant Studies* 21, no. 3–4 (1994): 195–211; and Partha Nath Mukherji, "The Farmers' Movement in Punjab: Politics of Pressure Groups and Pressure of Party Politics," *Economic and Political Weekly* 33, no. 18 (May 2, 1998): 1043–1048.

Conclusion

Figure 12 The "new farmers' movement" of the 1980s saw ascendant peasants assert their newfound political preeminence through massive demonstrations. Here, Uttar Pradesh's M.S. Tikait addresses one such rally.

figures, capable of mobilizing massive protests in the capital. In 1980, Joshi brought tens of thousands of farmers to Bombay to block the main railway line into the city; nine years later, Tikait did the same in Delhi.[40] In 1993, Joshi addressed a massive conference of farmers in Aurangabad, where he – knowingly or otherwise – borrowed language from C. Rajagopalachari's announcement of unilateral decontrol in Madras forty years prior. "You are free," he vowed,

from slavery to the state. Sell your crops wherever you want. Process your own products without waiting for licenses. Don't pour milk into the ground when there's too much to sell to the cities; make dairy products out of it. Make *gur* out of your sugarcane instead of giving it to the factories. Don't let the government confiscate your land. Don't pay extra taxes. And if officials or the police try to stop you, resist them![41]

---

[40] Cornelia Lenneberg, "Sharad Joshi and the Farmers: The Middle Peasant Lives!," *Pacific Affairs* 61, no. 3 (October 1, 1988): 446–449, 462.
[41] Gail Omvedt, "Farmers' Movement: Fighting for Liberalisation," *Economic and Political Weekly* 28, no. 50 (December 11, 1993): 2708–2710.

230   Conclusion

While marshalling human bodies, Joshi and Tikait were deploying a powerful alternate reading of modern Indian history itself: like Ram Krishan Sharma, Charan Singh, and others, they set an urban, industrial India at odds against a rural, agricultural *Bharat*. Declaring "India" to be the inheritor of the colonial state, Joshi growled that "'Indian' children take Ovaltine and toast for breakfast, don uniforms and go to costly schools for an 'Indian' education, whereas the children of Bharat munch a morsel of stale *bhakari*, kill their hunger with a mugful of water, pick up a stick and go out to tend animals." Joshi's powerful imagery did not reflect the rising purchasing power of his constituency, yet it gave new voice to an old resentment against the designs of the Nehruvian juggernaut – a resentment which, prior to the Green Revolution, had nucleated only in ephemeral institutions like the Swatantra party.

The "new farmers' movement" was never a fully coherent project, and its motley assemblage of caste and class alliances defied easy characterization. The earliest assessments of the movement focused on "bullock capitalists," suggesting that this was primary an undertaking of *kulaks*, or the middle-peasantry. "It is the rich farmer," an early analysis contended, "with his economic power enhanced by the so-called green revolution and commanding a strong social base and political clout who is going increasingly to dictate terms on the farm front."[42] Yet this assessment did not predict the wide range of lower castes who would give their political support to higher ones.[43] Subsistence farmers, too, have been swayed by the language of a rural India pitted against an urban counterpart, lending their support to larger farmers in ways that confound clear economic interests.[44]

Yet even as power and fertilizer subsidies flow to large agriculturalists, and subsistence farmers compete in the distorted market economy which ensues, a quantitative surplus of grain produced through industrial agriculture has been disconnected from the goals of nutritional equity.

[42] B.M., "Agricultural Policy Dictated by Rich Farmer," *Economic and Political Weekly* 23, no. 22 (May 28, 1988): 1107–1108.

[43] See Jim Bentall and Stuart Corbridge, "Urban-Rural Relations, Demand Politics and the 'New Agrarianism' in Northwest India: The Bharatiya Kisan Union," *Transactions of the Institute of British Geographers* 21, no. 1 (January 1, 1996): 27–48; Jaffrelot, "Rise of the Other Backward Classes"; Christophe Jaffrelot, *India's Silent Revolution: The Rise of the Lower Castes in North Indian Politics* (New York: Columbia University Press, 2002); and Craig Jeffrey, "'A Fist Is Stronger than Five Fingers': Caste and Dominance in Rural North India," *Transactions of the Institute of British Geographers* 26, no. 2, New Series (January 1, 2001): 217–236.

[44] Gail Omvedt, "'We Want the Return for Our Sweat': The New Peasant Movement in India and the Formation of a National Agricultural Policy," *Journal of Peasant Studies* 21, no. 3–4 (1994): 126–164. On rising *Hindutva* affinities among farmers, see Zoya Hasan, "Shifting Ground: Hindutva Politics and the Farmers' Movement in Uttar Pradesh," *Journal of Peasant Studies* 21, no. 3–4 (1994): 165–194.

Conclusion

231

Even by the mid 1970s, observers were noting that India had acquired a national granary large enough to feed all of its citizens, but that broad access to cereals was being hampered by distributional inadequacies.[45] A backlash ensued against the policy of "support prices," with a futile demand for a food subsidy to replace or accompany it.[46] Others contended that money spent on support prices be used to subsidize wider adoption of new agricultural technologies, instead.[47]

As India's agriculturalists and their allies were transforming the nation's politics, the rise of entitlement theory in economics, spurred on by the publication of Amartya Sen's *Poverty and Famines*, was suggesting to liberal planners the need for states to concentrate on distribution and access to food, as opposed to production alone.[48] The effort to secure these entitlements in India, however, proved underwhelming. India's much-maligned public distribution system was coming under new scrutiny for its alleged pro-rich and pro-urban bias, and two rounds of reform in the 1990s and early 2000s saw only limited success.[49] Liberalization saw massive shocks to India's agricultural economy: the nation's farmers' movements fractured over the question of whether or not to support economic reforms, and the public distribution system struggled to keep up with changes wrought by structural adjustment.[50]

All the while, the geography of India's hunger was shifting and worsening: an early post-liberalization survey suggested that malnutrition and hunger had become particularly dire in coastal states, and while rates

---

[45] James D. Gavan and John A. Dixon, "India: A Perspective on the Food Situation," *Science* 188, no. 4188, New Series (May 9, 1975): 541–549.

[46] Colin Clark, "Extent of Hunger in India," *Economic and Political Weekly* 7, no. 40 (September 30, 1972): 2019–2027; P.S. George, "Some Aspects of Public Distribution of Foodgrains in India," *Economic and Political Weekly* 19, no. 39 (September 29, 1984): A106–A110.

[47] Alain de Janvry and K. Subbarao, "Agricultural Price Policy and Income Distribution in India," *Economic and Political Weekly* 19, no. 51/52 (December 22, 1984): A166–A178.

[48] Sen, *Poverty and Famines*.

[49] On early efforts, see S. Mahendra Dev and M.H. Suryanarayana, "Is PDS Urban Biased and Pro-Rich?: An Evaluation," *Economic and Political Weekly* 26, no. 41 (October 12, 1991): 2357–2366; Stephen Howes and Shikha Jha, "Urban Bias in Indian Public Distribution System," *Economic and Political Weekly* 27, no. 19 (May 9, 1992): 1022–1030; and M.H. Suryanarayana, "Urban Bias in PDS," *Economic and Political Weekly* 29, no. 9 (February 26, 1994): 510–512. On the second round of reforms, see Madhura Swaminathan, "Revamped Public Distribution System: A Field Report from Maharashtra," *Economic and Political Weekly* 30, no. 36 (September 9, 1995): 2230; Jean Drèze, "The Task of Making the PDS Work," *The Hindu*, July 8, 2010.

[50] See Abhijit Sen, "Economic Liberalisation and Agriculture in India," *Social Scientist* 20, no. 11 (November 1, 1992): 4–19; Kirit Parikh, Shikha Jha, and P.V. Srinivasan, "Economic Reforms and Agricultural Policy," *Economic and Political Weekly* 28, no. 29/30 (July 17, 1993): 1497–1500; and Jos E. Mooij, "Public Distribution System as Safety Net: Who Is Saved?," *Economic and Political Weekly* 29, no. 3 (January 15, 1994): 119–126.

232   Conclusion

had declined in half of India's states, they had risen in the other half. Perhaps most troublingly, the most prosperous of India's states, and those with the greatest surplus quantities of food, appeared to be those with the highest rates of malnutrition and hunger.[51] One prescient analysis published in the immediate wake of economic reform assailed a new focus on export-oriented agribusiness, and "half-baked theories of the country having arrived at a point of saturation in regard to foodgrains production."[52]

The new farmers' movement and the reorientation of Indian politics towards agrarian interests would have pleased men like Ram Krishan Sharma. But even the most fervent advocates of India's farmers, as they decried the hubris and cluelessness of urban planners starry-eyed with dreams of steel and dams, would be confused to see an India where farmers and tech mavens vie for the future of state planning, and where even the empty rhetoric of equity and the promise of subsistence has been wholly abandoned.[53]

In April 1947, a Bombay resident lodged a complaint against the new Indian government taking shape in New Delhi. "Since the Popular Ministry came into power," Practical Homi wrote, true to his name,

there has been plenty of talk but nothing practical has been done to increase food-growing, which fact is amply proved by the shortage of essential cereals. A solemn promise was given to the people of this country by the Congress 'that their first duty towards this country would be to see that the people do not feel the pinch and want for ordinary bread.' Where is this bread or chapati?[54]

Yet even as this writer urged the nationalist government to give up tinkering with food canning and preservation in place of weightier projects like the wholesale takeover of lands for cereal production, others knew that growth alone was not the answer to India's woes. Just three years later, a young economist, writing in Hindi, asserted that the problem called for bigger interventions. "Our food crisis," Girraj Prasad Gupta

---

[51] Edison Dayal and Chandra Gulati, "Regional Changes in Food Poverty in India," *GeoJournal* 30, no. 2 (June 1, 1993): 167–177.

[52] "Too Much Food?," *Economic and Political Weekly* 30, no. 23 (June 10, 1995): 1339–1340.

[53] A dire assessment is Jayati Ghosh, "The Political Economy of Hunger in 21st Century India," *Economic and Political Weekly* 45, no. 44/45 (October 30, 2010): 33–38; a recent retrospective is M.S. Swaminathan, "From Bengal Famine to Right to Food," *The Hindu*, February 12, 2013. A recent collection of diverse essays and studies on India's food and nutrition predicament is Bill Pritchard et al., *To Feed India, to Feed the World: Livelihoods, Entitlements and Capabilities* (London: Routledge, 2013). For a representative collection of Hindi-language essays, see Mahasweta Devi, ed., *Khadya Sankata ki Cunauti [Challenge of the Food Crisis]* (New Delhi: Vani Prakasana, 2009).

[54] Homi, "Food Shortage."

Conclusion 233

wrote, "is not merely the problem of production, but of storage, and distribution as well."[55] He lambasted farmers who withheld their crops, the wastage of edible stores of food, and better statistics that would allow for smarter management of surplus where it arose. He called for fortitude to deal with the frustration of rationing until these projects could bear fruit. A well-managed economy would lead, in time, to the conditions facilitating a freer one.

Yet that Bombay letter-writer's question could well be posed today, and the young economist's plan reads like a quaint fantasy in light of the agrarian transformations which remade India's politics. This book has charted the ways in which the fantasies of the past have ceded to the disappointments of the present. It has shown how questions of food emerged as one of the most central sites of claim-making for Indian nationalists, animating the process of nation-building, and opening up a space for citizens to discuss and debate what welfare, citizenship, and markets might look like in an independent nation. It has also shown how these claims receded from political preeminence, as debates over land, markets, and technology elided dissent, technical solutions "resolved" matters once cast as political problems, and agricultural productivity allowed for surplus without addressing the fundamental questions of equity which had once animated civic life. India's food crisis endures because of this history, not in spite of it.

By recovering this history, we open certain possibilities for remaking it. We need not be romantic in this recovery – if perhaps more optimistic, the politics of early independence were neither more capable, nor somehow purer, than that afforded by India's present. Yet we can interrogate a moment wherein the question of state legitimacy grew sutured, for many citizens, to its ability to safeguard human welfare. Within this framework, spirited contestations buffeted state institutions and civic life, remaking them time and again. The purported resolution of these conflicts closed a space for political debate – with the eventual, ironic result of an exportable surplus, grains which rot in godowns, and human beings who remain among the world's most deprived. These deprivations remain as preventable, and as solvable, as they were when India's new citizens imagined an independent nation that would put human welfare at its core, looking to the future with dreams of plenty.

---

[55] Giriraj Prasad Gupta, *Hamari Aarthik Samasyayen [Our Economic Problems]* (Agra: Ramprasad and Sons Prakashan, 1952), 9.

Select Bibliography

MAJOR ARCHIVAL COLLECTIONS CONSULTED

India Office Records, British Library, London (IOR and MSS Eur)
National Archives of India, New Delhi (NAI)
National Archives of the United Kingdom, London
National Archives of the United States, College Park, Maryland (USNA)
Nehru Memorial Museum and Library, New Delhi (NMML)
P.C. Joshi Archives on Contemporary History, New Delhi
Rockefeller Archive Center, Tarrytown, New York (RAC)

NEWSPAPERS AND JOURNALS

Aaj [Varanasi]
Bombay Chronicle
Bombay Sentinel
Boston Globe
Chicago Tribune
Commerce [Bombay]
Eastern Economist [New Delhi]
Economic Times [Bombay]
Economic Weekly [Bombay]
The Economist [London]
Far Eastern Survey [New York]
Financial Express [Bombay]
Forward [Allahabad]
Free Press Journal [Bombay]
Harijan [Poona]
The Hindu [Chennai]
Hindustan Times [New Delhi]
Indian Express and Sunday Indian Express [Bombay]
Life [New York]
M.P. Chronicle [Bhopal]
New Age [New Delhi]
New Statesman [London]
New York Times
People's Age [Bombay]
Pravda [Moscow]
Roshni [Bombay]
Sansar [Bombay]

Select Bibliography 235

Shankar's Weekly [New Delhi]
Time [New York]
The Times of India [Bombay]
Vartman [Kanpur]
Washington Post
Yojana [New Delhi]

SOURCES IN INDIAN LANGUAGES

Abbas, Khwaja Ahmad. *Dharti ke Lal [Children of the Earth]*. Indian Progressive Theatre Association Pictures, 1946.

Bachchan, Harivansh Rai. *Bangal ka Kal [The Bengal Famine]*. Allahabad: Bharati-Bhandara, 1946.

Bandyopadhyay, Tarasankar. *Kalindi [Novel]*. Calcutta: Janvan Prakashan, 1951.

Devi, Mahasweta, ed., *Khadya Sankata ki Cunauti [Challenge of the Food Crisis]*. New Delhi: Vani Prakasana, 2009.

Dharti Dhan: Bhumi aur Krishi Sambandh 47 Utkrsht Lekhon ka Sangrah [The Wealth of the Soil: A Collection of 47 Excellent Articles on Land and Agriculture]. Patna: Parijat Prakashan, 1959.

Gupta, Giriraj Prasad. *Hamari Aarthik Samasyayen [Our Economic Problems]*. Agra: Ramprasad and Sons Prakashan, 1952.

Hindson ki Gavahi: Angrezi Raj mein Parja ke Dukh ki Kahani [India's Testimony: The Story of Sorrow Under British Rule]. San Francisco: Ghadar Press, 1915.

Hindustan ka Zar'ai Mas'alah [India's Agrarian Problems]. Bombay: Communist Party of India, 1950.

Jain, Jagdishchandra. *Hamari Roti ki Samasya [Our Food Problem]*. Bombay: National Information and Publications Limited, 1947.

Jalees, Ibrahim. *Bhooka Hai Bangal [Bengal Is Starving]*. Hyderabad: Nafees Academy, 1946.

Lalwani, Kasturba. *Bharat ki Arthik Samasyaye [India's Economic Problems]*. Ahmedabad: Navajivan Publishing House, 1950.

Malihabadi, Shad. *Sudharak Traikt [A Tract of Improvement]*. Lucknow: Rama Shankar, 1939.

Mugali, R.S. *Anna [Food]*. Dharwad: Manohar Grantha Mala, 1948.

Omkaranth. *Kisan Shreni Sajaga Ho! [For the Peasants' Class Consciousness]*. Allahabad: Harṣadeva, Bhāratī Bhavana, 1934.

Omprakash, Shri. *Hamari Khurak aur Aabadi ki Samasya [Our Food and Population Problem]*. New Delhi: Rajkamal Publications, 1947.

Paliwal, Krishna Dutt. *Kisan Raj [Peasants' Rule]*. Agra: Ramprasad and Sons Prakashan, 1945.

Pande, Mahendranatha. *Bhojana Hi Amrta Hai [Only Food Is Truth]*. Allahabad: Mahendra Rasayanasala, 1946.

Pant, Amba Datt. *Bharatiya Savidhan tatha Nagarikta [The Indian Constitution and Citizenship]*. Allahabad: Central Book Depot, 1959.

Parthasarathy, Indira. *Kuruthippunal [River of Blood]*. Madras: Tamil Puthakalayam, 1975.

236   Select Bibliography

Patil, A.K., ed., *Chini mein Krishi-Sahkari-Sansthayaen ke Aadhyayanarth Gaye Bharatiya Pratinidhi Mandal ka Report [Agricultural Cooperatives in China]*. New Delhi: Yojana Ayog, Bharat Sarkar, 1957.

Phabhat, Jhunnilal Prasad Kesari, and Gaurishankar Prasad Gupta. *Zamindar Kisan Natak [A Peasant–Landlord Drama]*. Varanasi: Bindeśvagī Prasāda Bukselara, 1950.

Pragati men Sazedar [Partners in Progress]. Bombay: United States Information Service, 1957.

Roy, Bimal Kumar. *Do Bigha Zameen [Two Bighas of Land]*. Bimal Roy Productions, 1953.

Saraswati, Sahajanand. *Kisan Sabha ke Samsara [The World of the Kisan Sabha]*. Allahabad: New Literature, 1947.

Sarvodaya Yojana [Planning Sarvodaya]. New Delhi: Sasta Sahitya Mandal, 1953.

Sharma, Ram Krishan. *Kheti aur Bhojan [Farming and Food]*. Allahabad: Lahar Prakashan, 1958.

Thakur, Jyotirmayi. *Aahar aur Aarogya [Diet and Health]*. Varanasi: Sahitya-Sevak Karyalay, 1948.

Varma, Devanarayan. *Bharat ki Lut [The Plunder of India]*. Calcutta: Deva-Citralaya, 1930.

SOURCES IN ENGLISH

17th Amendment vs. Farm, Family, Freedom. Bombay: Swatantra Party, 1964.

400 Millions to Be Fed. New Delhi: Bureau of Public Information, Government of India, 1945.

A Manual on the Organisation of Food Control and Rationing. Simla: Government of India Press, 1944.

A Short Memorandum on Food Control during the War in Bihar. Patna: Government of Bihar, 1944.

A Statement of Agriculture and Food Policy in India. New Delhi: Department of Agriculture and Department of Food, Government of India, 1945.

Abbas, Khwaja Ahmad. *I Am Not an Island: An Experiment in Autobiography*. New Delhi: Vikas Publishing House, 1977.

Abel, Martin E. "Agriculture in India in the 1970s." *Economic and Political Weekly* 5, no. 13 (March 28, 1970): A5–A14.

Abstracts of CFTRI Papers. Mysore: Central Food Technological Research Institute, 1966.

Adhikari, Gangadhar M. *Food in the Punjab*. Bombay: People's Publishing House, 1944.

Administration Report of the Civil Supplies Department for the Year 1961–62. Trivandrum: Civil Supplies Department, Government of Kerala, 1962.

Agrawal, Praween Kumar. "Emerging Obesity in Northern Indian States: A Serious Threat for Health." In *IUSSP Conference in Bangkok*, 2002.

Agrawal, Ram Gopal. *Price Controls in India since 1947*. New Delhi, 1956.

Agricultural Production Team, Ford Foundation. *Report on India's Food Crisis and Steps to Meet It*. New Delhi: Ministry of Food and Agriculture and Ministry of Community Development and Cooperation, Government of India, 1959.

Select Bibliography 237

Ahlberg, Kristin L. *Transplanting the Great Society: Lyndon Johnson and Food for Peace*. Columbia, MO: University of Missouri Press, 2008.

Ahluwalia, Sanjam. *Reproductive Restraints: Birth Control in India, 1877–1947*. Urbana: University of Illinois Press, 2008.

Ahuja, Ravi. "State Formation and 'Famine Policy' in Early Colonial South India." *Indian Economic Social History Review* 39, no. 4 (2002): 351–380.

Alamgir, Mohiuddin. *Famine in South Asia: Political Economy of Mass Starvation*. Cambridge: Oelgeschlager, Gunn & Hain, 1980.

Alexander, Horace. "Famine Returns to India." *Contemporary Review*, January 1944.

Ali, Muhammad Nasir. *Hindustan ke Ma'ashi Masa'il*. 2nd edn., Hyderabad: Idarah-yi Ma'ashiyat, 1945.

Ali Raza, Muhammad, Franziska Roy, and Benjamin Zachariah, eds., *The Internationalist Moment: South Asia, Worlds, and World Views, 1917–39*. New Delhi: Sage Publications, 2016.

All India Women's Conference, Cultural Section. *Education of Women in Modern India*. Anudh: Anudh Publishing Trust, 1946.

All India Women's Food Council. *Annapurna Recipes of Supplementary Foods*. 2 vols. New Delhi: All India Women's Food Council, 1951.

Allen, Keith. "Sharing Scarcity: Bread Rationing and the First World War in Berlin, 1914–1923." *Journal of Social History* 32, no. 2 (1998): 371–393.

Ambirajan, S. *Classical Political Economy and British Policy in India*. Cambridge: Cambridge University Press, 1978.

Amrith, Sunil S. *Decolonizing International Health: India and Southeast Asia, 1930–65*. Basingstoke: Palgrave Macmillan, 2006.

"Food and Welfare in India, c. 1900–1950." *Comparative Studies in Society and History* 50 (2008): 1010–1035.

Amrith, Sunil S., and Patricia Clavin. "Feeding the World: Connecting Europe and Asia, 1930–1945." *Past & Present* 218, no. suppl 8 (2013): 29–50.

Anderson, Robert S. *Nucleus and Nation: Scientists, International Networks, and Power in India*. Chicago: University of Chicago Press, 2010.

Anjaria, J.J. "A Review of Wartime Price Controls in India and the Consequences of Recent Decontrol," May 31, 1948. RD-634. International Monetary Fund.

Anjaria, Jonathan Shapiro. *The Slow Boil: Street Food, Rights and Public Space in Mumbai*. Palo Alto: Stanford University Press, 2016.

Ansari, M.S., R.P. Kataria, and S.K.A. Naqvi. *M.S. Ansari's Commentary on the Essential Commodities Act, 1955*. Jodhpur: Unique Law Publishers, 2011.

Ansari, Sarah. "Everyday Expectations of the State during Pakistan's Early Years: Letters to the Editor, Dawn (Karachi), 1950–1953." *Modern Asian Studies* 45, Special Issue 1 (2011): 159–178.

Appadorai, A. *Democracy in India*. Oxford Pamphlets on Indian Affairs 5. London: Oxford University Press, 1942.

Appadurai, Arjun. "Gastro-Politics in Hindu South Asia." *American Ethnologist* 8, no. 3 (August 1, 1981): 494–511.

"How Moral Is South Asia's Economy? A Review Article." *The Journal of Asian Studies* 43, no. 3 (May 1, 1984): 481–497.

238   Select Bibliography

"How to Make a National Cuisine: Cookbooks in Contemporary India." *Comparative Studies in Society and History* 30 (1988): 3–24.

Apte, Hari Narayan. *Ramji: A Tragedy of the Indian Famine*. London: T.F. Unwin, 1897.

Arnold, David. "Agriculture and 'Improvement' in Early Colonial India: A Pre-History of Development." *Journal of Agrarian Change* 5, no. 4 (2005): 505–525.

Colonizing the Body: State Medicine and Epidemic Disease in Nineteenth-Century India. Berkeley: University of California Press, 1993.

"Hunger in the Garden of Plenty." In *Dreadful Visitations: Confronting Natural Catastrophe in the Age of Enlightenment*, edited by Alessa Johns, 81–111. London: Routledge, 1999.

"Looting, Grain Riots and Government Policy in South India 1918." *Past & Present*, no. 84 (August 1, 1979): 111–145.

Science, Technology and Medicine in Colonial India. Cambridge: Cambridge University Press, 2000.

"Technology and Well-Being." In *Everyday Technology: Machines and the Making of India's Modernity*, 121–147. Chicago: University of Chicago Press, 2013.

Arondekar, Anjali R. *For the Record: On Sexuality and the Colonial Archive in India*. Durham: Duke University Press, 2010.

Austin, Granville. *The Indian Constitution: Cornerstone of a Nation*. New Delhi: Oxford University Press, 1999.

Aykroyd, W.R. *Notes on Food and Nutrition Policy in India*. New Delhi: Government of India Press, 1944.

The Conquest of Famine. New York: Reader's Digest Press, 1975.

Ayyar, S.V. "The Food Problem in India To-Day." In *The Indian National Congress, 64th Session, Nagpur, Souvenir*, B65–B68. Reception Committee, Indian National Congress, 1959.

Bagaria, Nidhi, and Swarup Santra. *Foreign Direct Investment in Retail Market in India: Some Issues and Challenges*. SSRN Scholarly Paper. Rochester, NY: Social Science Research Network, January 31, 2014.

Bagchi, Amiya Kumar. "Reflections on Patterns of Regional Growth in India During the Period of British Rule." *Bengal Past and Present* 95, no. 1 (1976): 247–289.

Baker, Christopher J. "Frogs and Farmers: The Green Revolution in India, and Its Murky Past." In *Understanding Green Revolutions: Agrarian Change and Development Planning in South Asia. Essays in Honour of B.H. Farmer*, edited by Tim Bayliss-Smith and Sudhir Wanmali, 37–52. Cambridge: Cambridge University Press, 1984.

Banerjee, Abhijit V., and Esther Duflo. *Poor Economics: A Radical Rethinking of the Way to Fight Global Poverty*. New York: PublicAffairs, 2011.

Banerjee, Gobinda Lall. *Free the Food: A Super Revolution*. Calcutta: Frank K.L. Mukhopadhyay, 1967.

Banerjee, Tridib. "U.S. Planning Expeditions to Postcolonial India: From Ideology to Innovation in Technical Assistance." *Journal of the American Planning Association* 75, no. 2 (2009): 193–208.

Select Bibliography 239

Bansil, P.C. *India's Food Resources and Population: A Historical and Analytical Study*. Bombay: Vora & Co., 1958.

Barber, William J. *Gunnar Myrdal: An Intellectual Biography*. Basingstoke: Palgrave Macmillan, 2008.

Bardhan, Gul. *Rhythm Incarnate: Tribute to Shanti Bardhan*. New Delhi: Abhinav Publications, 1992.

Bashford, Alison. *Global Population: History, Geopolitics, and Life on Earth*. New York: Columbia University Press, 2014.

"Nation, Empire, Globe: The Spaces of Population Debate in the Interwar Years." *Comparative Studies in Society and History* 49, no. 1 (January 1, 2007): 170–201.

Batabyal, Rakesh. *Communalism in Bengal: From Famine to Noakhali, 1943–47*. New Delhi: Sage Publications, 2005.

Baxi, Upendra. "The Justice of Human Rights in Indian Constitutionalism." In *Political Ideas in Modern India: Thematic Explorations*, edited by V.R. Mehta and Thomas Pantham, 263–284. New Delhi: Sage Publications, 2006.

Bayly, C.A. *Origins of Nationality in South Asia: Patriotism and Ethical Government in the Making of Modern India*. New Delhi: Oxford University Press, 1998.

Bengal Famine and Sind Merchants: Report of the Karachi Commercial Bodies' Famine Relief Committee for the Period Ending 31st December 1943. Karachi: Karachi Indian Merchants' Association, 1944.

Bentall, Jim, and Stuart Corbridge. "Urban-Rural Relations, Demand Politics and the 'New Agrarianism' in Northwest India: The Bharatiya Kisan Union." *Transactions of the Institute of British Geographers* 21, no. 1 (January 1, 1996): 27–48.

Bentley, Amy. *Eating for Victory: Food Rationing and the Politics of Domesticity*. Urbana: University of Illinois Press, 1998.

Berg, Alan. "Famine Contained: Notes and Lessons from the Bihar Experience." In *Famine: A Symposium Dealing with Nutrition and Relief Operations in Times of Disaster*, edited by Gunnar Blix, Yngve Hofvander, and Bo Vahlquist, 113–129. Symposia of the Swedish Nutrition Foundation 9. Stockholm: Almqvist & Wiksell, 1971.

Berger, Rachel. *Ayurveda Made Modern: Political Histories of Indigenous Medicine in North India, 1900–1955*. Basingstoke: Palgrave Macmillan, 2013.

"Between Digestion and Desire: Genealogies of Food in Nationalist North India." *Modern Asian Studies* 47, no. 5 (2013): 1622–1643.

Bharatiya Jana Sangh. *Election Manifesto 1957*. New Delhi: Bharatiya Jana Sangh, 1957.

Election Manifesto 1962. New Delhi: Bharatiya Jana Sangh, 1962.

Bhatia, B.M. *India's Food Problem and Policy since Independence*. Bombay: Somaiya Publications, 1970.

Bhattacharjee, Kalyani, ed., *Bengal Speaks!* Calcutta: Servants of Bengal Society, 1944.

Bhattacharjee, Kalyani, and Humayun Kabir. *War against the People: A Sharp Analysis of the Causes of Famine in Bengal*. Calcutta: People's Book Club, 1944.

Bhattacharya, Bhabani. *So Many Hungers!* London: V. Gollancz, 1947.

240   Select Bibliography

Bhattacharya, Sanjoy. *Propaganda and Information in Eastern India, 1939–45: A Necessary Weapon of War*. Surrey: Curzon, 2001.

Bhave, Acharya Vinoba. *From Bhoodan to Gramdan*. Tanjore: Sarvodaya Prachuralaya, 1957.

Billings, Martin H., and Arjan Singh. "Labour and the Green Revolution: The Experience in Punjab." *Economic and Political Weekly* 4, no. 52 (December 27, 1969): A221–A224.

Birla, Ritu. *Stages of Capital: Law, Culture, and Market Governance in Late Colonial India*. Durham: Duke University Press, 2009.

Black, Maggie. *A Cause for Our Times: Oxfam, the First 50 Years*. Oxford: Oxford University Press, 1992.

Blyn, George. *Agricultural Trends in India, 1891–1947: Output, Availability, and Productivity*. Philadelphia: University of Pennsylvania Press, 1966.

B.M. "Agricultural Policy Dictated by Rich Farmer." *Economic and Political Weekly* 23, no. 22 (May 28, 1988): 1107–1108.

Bose, Jyothi. *The Man-Made Famine*. Cambridge: Cambridge University Majlis, 1943.

Bose, Subhas Chandra. "Some Problems of Nation-Building." *Science and Culture* 1, no. 5 (October 1935): 258.

Bose, Sugata. *Agrarian Bengal: Economy, Social Structure, and Politics, 1919–1947*. Cambridge: Cambridge University Press, 1986.

His Majesty's Opponent: Subhas Chandra Bose and India's Struggle against Empire. Cambridge, MA: Belknap Press of Harvard University Press, 2011.

"Instruments and Idioms of Colonial and National Development." In *International Development and the Social Sciences*, edited by Frederick Cooper and Randall Packard, 45–63. Berkeley: University of California Press, 1997.

Peasant Labour and Colonial Capital: Rural Bengal since 1770. Cambridge: Cambridge University Press, 1993.

"Pondering Poverty, Fighting Famines: Towards a New History of Economic Ideas." In *Arguments for a Better World: Essays in Honor of Amartya Sen*, edited by Kaushik Basu and Ravi Kanbur, vol. 2: *Society, Institutions, and Development*: 425–435. Oxford: Oxford University Press, 2009.

"Post-Colonial Histories of South Asia: Some Reflections." *Journal of Contemporary History* 38, no. 1 (2003): 133–146.

"Starvation amidst Plenty: The Making of Famine in Bengal, Honan and Tonkin, 1942–45." *Modern Asian Studies* 24, no. 4 (October 1990): 699–727.

Bose, Sugata, and Kris Manjapra, eds., *Cosmopolitan Thought Zones: South Asia and the Global Circulation of Ideas*. Basingstoke: Palgrave Macmillan, 2010.

Bradlee, Ben. *India's Famine: The Facts*. London: The Communist Party, 1943.

Brass, Paul R. *An Indian Political Life: Charan Singh and Congress Politics, 1937 to 1961*. New Delhi: Sage Publications, 2011.

An Indian Political Life: Charan Singh and Congress Politics, 1967–1987. New Delhi: Sage Publications, 2014.

"The Political Uses of Crisis: The Bihar Famine of 1966–1967." *The Journal of Asian Studies* 45, no. 2 (February 1, 1986): 245–267.

Brass, Tom. "Introduction: The New Farmers' Movements in India." In *New Farmers' Movements in India*, edited by Tom Brass, 3–26. Ilford: Frank Cass, 1995.

Select Bibliography 241

ed., *New Farmers' Movements in India*. Ilford: Frank Cass, 1995.

Breckenridge, Carol Appadurai. "Food, Politics and Pilgrimage in South India, 1350–1650 A.D." In *Food, Society, and Culture: Aspects in South Asian Food Systems*, edited by R.S. Khare and M.S.A. Rao. Durham: Carolina Academic Press, 1986.

Breen, T.H. *The Marketplace of Revolution: How Consumer Politics Shaped American Independence*. Oxford: Oxford University Press, 2004.

Brennan, Lance. "Government Famine Relief in Bengal, 1943." *The Journal of Asian Studies* 47, no. 3 (August 1, 1988): 541–566.

Brown, Dorris D. *Agricultural Development in India's Districts*. Cambridge, MA: Harvard University Press, 1971.

The Intensive Agricultural Districts Programme and Agricultural Development in Punjab, India. Cambridge, MA: Development Advisory Service, Harvard University, 1967.

Brown, Judith M. *Nehru: A Political Life*. New Haven: Yale University Press, 2003.

Burma, D.P., and Maharani Chakravorty, eds., *History of Science, Philosophy, and Culture in Indian Civilization*, vol. 13, part 2: *From Physiology and Chemistry to Biochemistry*. New Delhi: Centre for Studies in Civilizations, 2010.

Butalia, Urvashi. *The Other Side of Silence: Voices from the Partition of India*. Durham: Duke University Press, 2000.

Byres, Terence. "Charan Singh, 1902–1987: An Appreciation." *Journal of Peasant Studies* 15, no. 2 (1988): 139–189.

Carpenter, Kenneth J. "The Work of Wallace Aykroyd: International Nutritionist and Author." *The Journal of Nutrition* 137, no. 4 (April 1, 2007): 873–878.

Chacko, George Kuttickal. *India: Toward an Understanding (A de Novo Inquiry into the Mind of India in Search of an Answer to the Question: "Will India Go Communist?")*. New York: Bookman Associates, 1959.

Chakrabarty, Dipesh. "'In the Name of Politics': Democracy and the Power of the Multitude in India." *Public Culture* 19, no. 1 (2007): 35–57.

Chakravorty, Sanjoy. *The Price of Land: Acquisition, Conflict, Consequence*. New Delhi: Oxford University Press, 2013.

Chand, Gyan. *India's Teeming Millions: A Contribution to the Study of the Indian Population Problem*. London: G. Allen & Unwin, 1939.

Chand, Shiv, and A.H. Kapoor. *Land and Agriculture of India: An Agronomic Study*. New Delhi: Metropolitan Book Co., 1959.

Chandler, Robert F. *An Adventure in Applied Science: A History of the International Rice Research Institute*. Los Baños, Laguna, Philippines: International Rice Research Institute, 1982.

Chandra, Bipin. *The Rise and Growth of Economic Nationalism in India*. New Delhi: People's Publishing House, 1996.

Chandra, Jag Parvesh. *Miss a Meal Movement: An Experiment in Voluntary Errors and National Co-Operation*. New Delhi: Constitution House, 1949.

Chandra, Romesh. *Who Starves Bengal To-Day Punjab To-Momorrow?: An Indictment of the Unionist Ministry*. Bombay: People's Publishing House, 1943.

Chandrasekhar, S. *Hungry People and Empty Lands: An Essay on Population Problems and International Tensions*. London: G. Allen & Unwin, 1954.

Charter of Demands Submitted to Shri Lal Bahadur Shastri. New Delhi: Republican Party of India, 1964.

242   Select Bibliography

Chatterjee, Dwarkanath. *Food and Nutrition in India*. Calcutta: D.N. Chatterjee, 1947.

Chatterjee, Partha. "Development Planning and the Indian State." In *The State, Development Planning and Liberalisation in India*, edited by T.J. Byres, 82–103. New Delhi: Oxford University Press, 1998.

Nationalist Thought and the Colonial World: A Derivative Discourse? London: Zed Books, 1986.

"The National State." In *The Nation and Its Fragments: Colonial and Postcolonial Histories*, 200–219. Princeton: Princeton University Press, 1993.

Chatterjee, Santosh Kumar. *The Starving Millions*. Calcutta: M.A. Ashoka Library, 1944.

Chatterji, Indubhusan. *Is Our Country Really in Deficit of Food?* Calcutta, 1951.

Chatterji, Joya. *Bengal Divided: Hindu Communalism and Partition, 1932–47*. Cambridge: Cambridge University Press, 1994.

"South Asian Histories of Citizenship, 1946–1970." *The Historical Journal* 55, no. 4 (2012): 1049–1071.

The Spoils of Partition: Bengal and India, 1947–1967. Cambridge: Cambridge University Press, 2007.

Chattopadhyay, Kamaladevi. "The Food Problem." *Modern Review*, November 1947, 357–360.

Chauhan, Devi Singh. "Task of Agrarian Reforms." In *Souvenir, 58th Plenary Session, A.I.C.C. 1953, Nanal Nagar*, 1953.

Chibber, Vivek. *Locked in Place: State-Building and Capitalist Industrialization in India, 1940–1970*. Princeton: Princeton University Press, 2003.

Chittaprosad. *Hungry Bengal: A Tour through Midnapur District, by Chittaprosad, in November, 1943*. Bombay: New Age Printing Press, 1943.

Chopra, R.N. *Evolution of Food Policy in India*. New Delhi: Macmillan, 1981.

Choudhary, Valmiki, ed. *Dr. Rajendra Prasad: Correspondence and Select Documents*. New Delhi: Allied Publishers, 1988.

Choudhury, B. *Cultivation of Tomato and Brinjal*. Farm Bulletin (New Series) 31. New Delhi: Indian Council of Agricultural Research, 1965.

Clark, Colin. "Extent of Hunger in India." *Economic and Political Weekly* 7, no. 40 (September 30, 1972): 2019–2027.

Cleaver, Harry M. "The Contradictions of the Green Revolution." *The American Economic Review* 62, no. 1/2 (March 1, 1972): 177–186.

Cohen, Amy J. "Supermarkets in India: Struggles over the Organization of Agricultural Markets and Food Supply Chains." *University of Miami Law Review* 68 (2013): 19–323.

Collingham, E.M. *Imperial Bodies: The Physical Experience of the Raj, c. 1800–1947*. Cambridge: Polity Press, 2001.

Collingham, Lizzie. *The Taste of War*. New York: Penguin, 2011.

Communist Party of India. *Draft Programme of the Communist Party of India*. Bombay: New Age Printing Press, 1951.

India's Food Crisis, Analysis and Solution: Memo of the Communist Party of India to the Government of the Indian Union. Bombay: People's Publishing House, 1947.

"Congress Food Policy." *Modern Review*, April 1946.

Select Bibliography   243

Connelly, Matthew. "Population Control in India: Prologue to the Emergency Period." *Population and Development Review* 32, no. 4 (December 1, 2006): 629–667.

Constituent Assembly Debates: Official Report. New Delhi: Lok Sabha Secretariat, 1967.

Cooper, Frederick. "Conflict and Connection: Rethinking Colonial African History." *The American Historical Review* 99, no. 5 (1994): 1516–1545.

Co-Operative Farming: The Great Debate between Jawaharlal Nehru, C. Rajagopalachari, Jayprakash Narayan, K.M. Munshi, M.R. Masani, N.G. Ranga, Shirman Narayan, Frank Moraes, and Others. Bombay: Democratic Research Service, 1959.

Corbridge, Stuart. *Seeing the State: Governance and Governmentality in India.* Cambridge: Cambridge University Press, 2005.

Cullather, Nick. "The Foreign Policy of the Calorie." *The American Historical Review* 112, no. 2 (April 1, 2007): 337–364.

The Hungry World: America's Cold War Battle against Poverty in Asia. Cambridge, MA: Harvard University Press, 2010.

Dang, Vimla. "Some Glorious Struggles of AISF." *New Age Weekly: Central Organ of the Communist Party of India* 52, no. 6 (February 8, 2004).

Darling, Malcolm. *Rusticus Loquitur; or: The Old Light and the New in the Punjab Village.* Oxford: Oxford University Press, 1930.

Das, Pitamber. *Presidential Address [to the] Eighth Annual Session, Raghuji Nagar, Nagpur, January 23, 24 and 25 1960.* New Delhi: Bharatiya Jana Sangh, 1960.

Das, Sisir Kumar. *History of Indian Literature, 1911–1956, Struggle for Freedom: Triumph and Tragedy.* New Delhi: Sahitya Akademi, 1991.

Dasgupta, Ajit K. *Gandhi's Economic Thought.* London: Routledge, 1996.

Dasgupta, Ajit Kumar. *A History of Indian Economic Thought.* London: Routledge, 1993.

Datta, Dvijadas. *Landlordism in India.* Taraporevala's Indian Economic Series. Bombay: Taraporevala, 1931.

Davis, Mike. *Late Victorian Holocausts: El Niño Famines and the Making of the Third World.* London: Verso, 2001.

Dayal, Rajeshwar. *India's New Food Strategy.* New Delhi: Metropolitan Book Co., 1968.

De, Rohit. "'Commodities Must Be Controlled': Economic Crimes and Market Discipline in India (1939–1955)." *International Journal of Law in Context* 10, no. 3 (September 2014): 277–294.

"Cows and Constitutionalism," *Modern Asian Studies* (forthcoming).

Litigious Citizens, Constitutional Law and Everyday Life in the Indian Republic, forthcoming.

Department of Agriculture, Government of India. *Proceedings of the All India Food Ministers' Conference Held in New Delhi on 9th and 10th August 1946.* Simla: Government of India Press, 1946.

Report of the Indian Delegation to the United Nations Conference on Food and Agriculture at Québec City. New Delhi: Government of India Press, 1946.

Desai, Akshayakumar Ramanlal. *Agrarian Struggles in India after Independence.* New Delhi: Oxford University Press, 1986.

Deshpande, R.S., and Saroj Arora. *Agrarian Crisis and Farmers' Suicide.* New Delhi: Sage Publications, 2010.

Select Bibliography

Dev, S. Mahendra, and M.H. Suryanarayana. "Is PDS Urban Biased and Pro-Rich?: An Evaluation." *Economic and Political Weekly* 26, no. 41 (October 12, 1991): 2357–2366.

Director of Public Information, Bengal Government. *Famine and the Government.* Alipore: Bengal Government Press, 1944.

Drèze, Jean, and Amartya Sen. *An Uncertain Glory: India and Its Contradictions.* New Delhi: Penguin, 2013.

Hunger and Public Action. New York: Oxford University Press, 1989.

Duncan, Ian. "Agricultural Innovation and Political Change in North India: The Lok Dal in Uttar Pradesh." *Journal of Peasant Studies* 24, no. 4 (1997): 246–268.

Dutt, Romesh Chandra. *Famines in India: Their Causes and Possible Prevention.* London: P.S. King & Son, 1876.

Open Letters to Lord Curzon on Famines and Land Assessments in India. London: Trübner, 1900.

The Economic History of India Under Early British Rule, vol. 1. London: Kegan Paul, Trench, Trübner, 1902.

Dutt, T.K. *Hungry Bengal.* Lahore: Indian Printing Works, 1944.

Ebb, Lawrence F. "Interstate Barriers in India and American Constitutional Experience." *Stanford Law Review* 11, no. 1 (1958): 37–93.

Ekbladh, David. *The Great American Mission: Modernization and the Construction of an American World Order.* Princeton: Princeton University Press, 2010.

Elenjimittam, Anthony. *Hindustan Hamara, Or, Our India.* Calcutta: Orient Book Co., 1949.

Engerman, David C. "Learning from the East: Soviet Experts and India in the Era of Competitive Coexistence." *Comparative Studies of South Asia, Africa and the Middle East* 33, no. 2 (2013): 227–238.

Planning for Plenty: The Economic Cold War in India. Cambridge, MA: Harvard University Press, forthcoming.

Ensminger, Douglas. Oral History Interview. Interview by Harry S. Taylor, July 16, 1976. Harry S. Truman Library and Museum.

Erdman, Howard L. *The Swatantra Party and Indian Conservatism.* Cambridge: Cambridge University Press, 1967.

Famine Enquiry Commission. *Report on Bengal.* New Delhi: Government of India Press, 1945.

Farley, John. *To Cast out Disease: A History of the International Health Division of the Rockefeller Foundation (1913–1951).* Oxford: Oxford University Press, 2004.

Ferguson, James. *The Anti-Politics Machine: "Development," Depoliticization, and Bureaucratic Power in Lesotho.* Minneapolis: University of Minnesota Press, 1994.

Five Years with the Grain Man: A Review (1965–1970). New Delhi: Food Corporation of India, 1971.

"Flag Hoisting Ceremony at the Indian Council of Agricultural Research." *Indian Farming* 8, no. 8 (August 1947): 380–381.

"Food." *Bulletin of Indian Women's Movement,* July 1946.

"Food." *Science and Culture* 13, no. 6 (December 1947): 211–213.

Food Corporation of India. *Review of Activities since Inception.* New Delhi: Food Corporation of India, 1967.

Forbes, Geraldine Hancock. *Women in Modern India.* New Cambridge History of India IV.2. Cambridge: Cambridge University Press, 1996.

Select Bibliography

Fourth All India Food Conference. New Delhi: Government of India Press, 1944.

Frankel, Francine R. *India's Green Revolution: Economic Gains and Political Costs.* Princeton: Princeton University Press, 1971.

India's Political Economy, 1947–2004: The Gradual Revolution. New Delhi: Oxford University Press, 2005.

Fraser, Bashabi. *Bengal Partition Stories: An Unclosed Chapter.* New York: Anthem Press, 2000.

From This Land. 16mm. United States Information Service, 1960.

Fuller, C.J., and Véronique Bénéï. *The Everyday State and Society in Modern India.* London: Hurst & Co., 2001.

Gandhi, Leela. *The Common Cause: Postcolonial Ethics and the Practice of Democracy, 1900–1955.* Chicago: University of Chicago Press, 2014.

Gandhi, Mohandas K. *Delhi Diary.* Ahmedabad: Navajivan Publishing House, 1948.

Food Shortage and Agriculture. Ahmedabad: Navajivan Publishing House, 1949.

Gangulee, Nagendranath. *Health and Nutrition in India.* London: Faber and Faber, 1939.

India's Destitute Millions Starving Today - Famine? London: Swaraj House, 1943.

Gaud, William S. "The Green Revolution: Accomplishments and Apprehensions." Presented at the Society for International Development, Washington, DC, March 8, 1968.

Gavan, James D., and John A. Dixon. "India: A Perspective on the Food Situation." *Science* 188, no. 4188. New Series (May 9, 1975): 541–549.

"Gentlemen Killers of Kilvenmani." *Economic and Political Weekly* 8, no. 21 (May 26, 1973): 926–928.

George, P.S. "Some Aspects of Public Distribution of Foodgrains in India." *Economic and Political Weekly* 19, no. 39 (September 29, 1984): A106–A110.

Ghosh, Durba. "Gender and Colonialism: Expansion or Marginalization?" *The Historical Journal* 47, no. 3 (September 1, 2004): 737–755.

Ghosh, Jayati. "The Political Economy of Hunger in 21st Century India." *Economic and Political Weekly* 45, no. 44/45 (October 30, 2010): 33–38.

Ghosh, Kali Charan. *Famines in Bengal: 1770–1943.* Calcutta: Indian Associated Publishing Co., 1944.

Gill, Sucha Singh. "The Farmers' Movement and Agrarian Change in the Green Revolution Belt of Northwest India." *Journal of Peasant Studies* 21, no. 3–4 (1994): 195–211.

Goel, Ram Sita. *China Is Red with Peasants' Blood.* Calcutta: Society for Defence of Freedom, 1953.

Goldsmith, Arthur A. *Building Agricultural Institutions: Transferring the Land-Grant Model to India and Nigeria.* Boulder: Westview Press, 1990.

Gordon, Leonard A. "Wealth Equals Wisdom? The Rockefeller and Ford Foundations in India." *Annals of the American Academy of Political and Social Science* 554 (November 1, 1997): 104–116.

Goswami, Manu. "From Swadeshi to Swaraj: Nation, Economy, Territory in Colonial South Asia, 1870 to 1907." *Comparative Studies in Society and History* 40, no. 4 (October 1, 1998): 609–636.

Producing India: From Colonial Economy to National Space. Chicago: University of Chicago Press, 2004.

246   Select Bibliography

Goswami, Omkar. "The Bengal Famine of 1943: Re-Examining the Data." *Indian Economic and Social History Review* 27, no. 4 (December 1, 1990): 445–463.

Gough, Kathleen. *Rural Change in Southeast India, 1950s to 1980s.* New Delhi: Oxford University Press, 1989.

"The 'Green Revolution' in South India and North Vietnam." *Social Scientist* 6, no. 1 (August 1, 1977): 48–64.

Gould, William. *Bureaucracy, Community, and Influence in India: Society and the State, 1930s–1960s.* London: Routledge, 2009.

"From Subjects to Citizens? Rationing, Refugees and the Publicity of Corruption over Independence in UP." *Modern Asian Studies* 45, Special Issue 1 (2011): 33–56.

Graham, Bruce Desmond. *Hindu Nationalism and Indian Politics: The Origins and Development of the Bharatiya Jana Sangh.* Cambridge: Cambridge University Press, 1990.

Grebmer, Klaus Bernstein von, Jennifer Thompson, Jill Bernstein, David Nabarro, Nilam Prasad, Fraser Patterson, Yisehac Yohannes, Shazia Amin, Andrea Sonntag, and Olive Towey. *2016 Global Hunger Index: Getting to Zero Hunger.* Washington, DC: International Food Policy Research Institute, 2016.

Green Revolution: Delhi Villages Pulsating with New Life. New Delhi: Directorate of Public Relations, Delhi Administration, 1971.

Greenough, Paul R. *Prosperity and Misery in Modern Bengal: The Famine of 1943–1944.* New York: Oxford University Press, 1982.

Gregory, Theodore. *India on the Eve of the Third Five-Year Plan.* Calcutta: Thacker Spink, 1961.

Report of the Foodgrains Policy Committee, 1943. New Delhi: Government of India Press, 1943.

Grover, Verinder. *Political Thinkers of Modern India, vol. 23: Dr. Rajendra Prasad.* New Delhi: Deep & Deep Publications, 1993.

Guha, Ramachandra. *India after Gandhi: The History of the World's Largest Democracy.* New York: Ecco, 2007.

"The LSE and India." *The Hindu.* November 19, 2003.

Guha, Ranajit. *A Rule of Property for Bengal: An Essay on the Idea of Permanent Settlement.* Paris: Mouton, 1963.

Guha, Sumit, ed., *Growth, Stagnation, or Decline? Agricultural Productivity in British India.* New Delhi: Oxford University Press, 1992.

Guha, Sunil. *India's Food Problem.* New Delhi: Indian National Congress, 1957.

Gupta, Akhil. "Agrarian Populism in the Development of a Modern Nation (India)." In *International Development and the Social Sciences,* edited by Frederick Cooper and Randall Packard, 320–344. Berkeley: University of California Press, 1997.

Postcolonial Developments: Agriculture in the Making of Modern India. Durham: Duke University Press, 1998.

Red Tape: Bureaucracy, Structural Violence, and Poverty in India. Durham: Duke University Press, 2012.

Gupta, Partha Sarathi, ed., *Towards Freedom: Documents on the Movement for Independence in India, 1943–1944, Part I.* New Delhi: Indian Council of Historical Research, 1997.

ed., *Towards Freedom: Documents on the Movement for Independence in India, 1943–1944, Part II.* New Delhi: Indian Council of Historical Research, 1997.

ed., *Towards Freedom: Documents on the Movement for Independence in India, 1943–1944, Part III.* New Delhi: Indian Council of Historical Research, 1997.

Gupta, S.C. *Freedom from Foreign Food: Pernicious Effects of PL480.* New Delhi: Blitz National Forum, 1965.

Halbrook, E.R., and Tulsa Ram. *Poultry Development in India,* 1958.

Hall-Matthews, David. "Colonial Ideologies of the Market and Famine Policy in Ahmednagar District, Bombay Presidency, c. 1870–1884." *Indian Economic and Social History Review* 36, no. 3 (1999): 303–333.

Hancock, Mary. "Gendering the Modern: Women and Home Science in British India." In *Gender, Sexuality and Colonial Modernities,* edited by Antoinette M. Burton, 148–160. London: Routledge, 1999.

"Home Science and the Nationalization of Domesticity in Colonial India." *Modern Asian Studies* 35, no. 4 (2001): 871–903.

Hardiman, David. *Feeding the Baniya: Peasants and Usurers in Western India.* New Delhi: Oxford University Press, 1996.

Harper, Kristine C., and Ronald E. Doel. "Environmental Diplomacy in the Cold War: Weather Control, the United States, and India, 1966–1967." In *Environmental Histories of the Cold War,* edited by John Robert McNeill and Corinna R. Unger, 115–137. Cambridge: Cambridge University Press, 2010.

Harper, T.N., and Sunil S. Amrith, eds., *Sites of Asian Interaction: Ideas, Networks and Mobility.* Cambridge: Cambridge University Press, 2014.

Harris, Marvin. "The Cultural Ecology of India's Sacred Cattle." *Current Anthropology* 33, no. 1 (February 1, 1992): 261–276.

Hasan, G. *The State of Rajasthan vs Nath Mal and Mitha Mal* (Supreme Court of India 1954).

Hasan, Zoya. "Shifting Ground: Hindutva Politics and the Farmers' Movement in Uttar Pradesh." *Journal of Peasant Studies* 21, no. 3–4 (1994): 165–194.

Hassan, Zoya. "Congress in Aligarh District, 1930–1946: Problems of Political Mobilization." In *Congress and Indian Nationalism: The Pre-Independence Phase,* edited by Richard Sisson and Stanley A. Wolpert, 330–351. Berkeley: University of California Press, 1988.

Haynes, Douglas E. *Small Town Capitalism in Western India: Artisans, Merchants and the Making of the Informal Economy, 1870–1960.* Cambridge: Cambridge University Press, 2012.

Herring, Ronald J. *Land to the Tiller: The Political Economy of Agrarian Reform in South Asia.* New Haven: Yale University Press, 1983.

Hill, A.V. *A Food Plan for India.* London: Royal Institute of International Affairs, 1945.

Hirdman, Yvonne. *Alva Myrdal: The Passionate Mind.* Bloomington: Indiana University Press, 2008.

Hodges, Sarah. *Contraception, Colonialism and Commerce: Birth Control in South India, 1920–1940.* Farnham: Ashgate Publishing, 2016.

Hofmeyr, Isabel, and Michelle Williams, eds., *South Africa and India: Shaping the Global South.* Johannesburg: Wits University Press, 2011.

248   Select Bibliography

Hopper, W. David. "The Economic Organization of a Village in North-Central India." Ph.D. diss., Cornell University, 1951.

How to Get High Yields with Taichung Native I Paddy. New Delhi: Farm Information Unit, Directorate of Extension, Ministry of Food and Agriculture and Ministry of Community Development and Cooperation, 1966.

Howard, Albert. *An Agricultural Testament*. London: Oxford University Press, 1940.

The Soil and Health: A Study of Organic Agriculture. New York: Schocken Books, 1947.

Howard, Albert, and Louise Howard. *The Development of Indian Agriculture*. London: Oxford University Press, 1927.

Howard, Louise. *Sir Albert Howard in India*. London: Faber and Faber, 1953.

Howes, Stephen, and Shikha Jha. "Urban Bias in Indian Public Distribution System." *Economic and Political Weekly* 27, no. 19 (May 9, 1992): 1022–1030.

Hundred and Thirty Six Years under Zamindaries: Being the Report of the A.P.C.C. Regarding the Conditions of Zamin Ryots with Concrete Proposals. Masulipatam: Andhra Provincial Congress Committee, 1938.

Husain, M. Afzal. "Food Problem of India (1946, Bangalore)." In *The Shaping of Indian Science: 1914–1947*, edited by K. Kasturirangan, 548–571. Hyderabad: Universities Press, 2003.

Immerwahr, Daniel. *Thinking Small: The United States and the Lure of Community Development*. Cambridge, MA: Harvard University Press, 2015.

Inauguration, January 14, 1965: The Food Corporation of India. Madras: Food Corporation of India, 1965.

India Food Situation 1943. London: His Majesty's Stationery Office, 1943.

Indian National Congress. *Resolutions [of the] Indian National Congress Sixtieth Session, Satyamurthinagar, Avadi, Madras, 21st to 23rd January 1955*. New Delhi: All India Congress Committee, 1955.

Islam, M. Mufakharul. "The Great Bengal Famine and the Question of FAD Yet Again." *Modern Asian Studies* 41, no. 2 (March 1, 2007): 421–440.

Israel, Milton. *Communications and Power: Propaganda and the Press in the Indian Nationalist Struggle, 1920–1947*. Cambridge: Cambridge University Press, 1994.

Jacoby, Erich H. "Effects of the 'Green Revolution' in South and South-East Asia." *Modern Asian Studies* 6, no. 1 (January 1, 1972): 63–69.

Jaffrelot, Christophe. *India's Silent Revolution: The Rise of the Lower Castes in North Indian Politics*. New York: Columbia University Press, 2002.

The Hindu Nationalist Movement and Indian Politics, 1925 to the 1990s: Strategies of Identity-Building, Implantation and Mobilisation (with Special Reference to Central India). London: Hurst & Co., 1996.

"The Rise of the Other Backward Classes in the Hindi Belt." *The Journal of Asian Studies* 59, no. 1 (February 1, 2000): 86–108.

Jain, Ajit Prasad. "A Wizard Who Made Two Count as Four." In *Rafi Ahmad Kidwai: A Memoir of His Life and Times*, 103–113. New York: Asia Publishing House, 1965.

"Lawless Legislation": Why Swatantra Opposes the 17th Amendment. New Delhi: Swatantra Party, 1963.

Select Bibliography

Jaiswal, P.L., and M.L. Madan, eds., *Annual Report 1964–65*. New Delhi: Indian Council of Agricultural Research, 1965.

Jalal, Ayesha. *Self and Sovereignty: Individual and Community in South Asian Islam since 1850*. London: Routledge, 2002.

Jalan, B.L. *Food Problem in India*, 1951.

Janvry, Alain de, and K. Subbarao. "Agricultural Price Policy and Income Distribution in India." *Economic and Political Weekly* 19, no. 51/52 (December 22, 1984): A166–A178.

Jayal, Niraja Gopal. *Citizenship and Its Discontents: An Indian History*. Cambridge, MA: Harvard University Press, 2013.

Jeffrey, Craig. "'A Fist Is Stronger than Five Fingers': Caste and Dominance in Rural North India." *Transactions of the Institute of British Geographers* 26, no. 2. New Series (January 1, 2001): 217–236.

Jha, L.K. *Report of the Jha Committee on Foodgrains Prices for 1964–65 Season*. New Delhi: Ministry of Food and Agriculture, Government of India, 1968.

Jinnah, Mohammad Ali. *Quaid-i-Azam Mohammad Ali Jinnah: Speeches, Indian Legislative Assembly, 1935–1947*. Karachi: Quaid-i-Azam Academy, 1991.

Joshi, P.C. *Who Lives If Bengal Dies?* Bombay: People's Publishing House, 1943.

Kabir, Humayun. *Bengal Famine*. Calcutta: Bengal Students' Federation, 1944.

Kalpagam, U. "Colonial Governmentality and the 'Economy.'" *Economy and Society* 29, no. 3 (January 2000): 418–438.

Kamaraj, K. *Presidential Address: Indian National Congress 69th Session, Durgapur, West Bengal, 9th January 1965*. New Delhi: All India Congress Committee, 1965.

Kandasamy, Meena. *The Gypsy Goddess*. London: Atlantic Books, 2014.

Kantor, Hayden S. "'A Dead Letter of the Statute Book': The Strange Bureaucratic Life of the Bihar Food Economy and Guest Control Order, 1950–1954." *South Asian History and Culture* 7, no. 3 (July 2, 2016): 239–257.

"'We Earn Less than We Eat': Food, Farming, and the Caring Family in Bihar, India." Ph.D. diss., Cornell University, 2016.

Karve, D.G. *Poverty and Population in India*. London: H. Milford, Oxford University Press, 1936.

Kaura, R.L. *Gosadans in India*. New Delhi: Indian Council of Agricultural Research, 1964.

Kelavkar, Shamrao Krishnarao. *Our Food Problem*. Kolhapur: Arya Bhanu Press, 1946.

Khan, Yasmin. *The Great Partition: The Making of India and Pakistan*. New Haven: Yale University Press, 2007.

Khare, R.S. *Culture and Reality: Essays on the Hindu System of Managing Foods*. Simla: Indian Institute of Advanced Study, 1976.

"Hospitality, Charity, and Rationing: Three Channels of Food Distribution in India." In *Food, Society, and Culture: Aspects in South Asian Food Systems*, edited by R.S. Khare and M.S.A. Rao, 277–296. Durham: Carolina Academic Press, 1986.

The Eternal Food: Gastronomic Ideas and Experiences of Hindus and Buddhists. Albany: SUNY Press, 1992.

250 Select Bibliography

The Hindu Hearth and Home: Culinary Systems Old and New in North India. Delhi: Vikas Publishing House, 1976.

Khare, R.S., and M.S.A. Rao. *Food, Society, and Culture: Aspects in South Asian Food Systems.* Durham: Carolina Academic Press, 1986.

Khilnani, Sunil. *The Idea of India.* New York: Farrar, Straus and Giroux, 1998.

Klingensmith, Daniel. *One Valley and a Thousand: Dams, Nationalism, and Development.* New Delhi: Oxford University Press, 2007.

Kloppenburg, Jack Ralph. *First the Seed: The Political Economy of Plant Biotechnology, 1492–2000.* Madison: University of Wisconsin Press, 2004.

Knight, Henry. *Food Administration in India, 1939–1947.* Palo Alto: Stanford University Press, 1954.

Kochanek, Stanley A. *The Congress Party of India: The Dynamics of a One-Party Democracy.* Princeton: Princeton University Press, 1968.

Kohli, Atul. *The State and Poverty in India.* Cambridge: Cambridge University Press, 1989.

Kolhatkar, Vasudeo Yeshwant. *Reconstruction of Indian Agriculture.* Bombay: Popular Book Depot, 1946.

Krishna Menon, V.K. *Unity with India against Fascism.* London: The India League, 1943.

Krishnamachari, V.T. *Report of the Grow More Food Enquiry Committee.* New Delhi: Ministry of Food and Agriculture, Government of India, 1952.

Kudaisya, Gyanesh, and Tan Tai Yong. *The Aftermath of Partition in South Asia.* London: Routledge, 2002.

Kudaisya, Medha. "'A Mighty Adventure': Institutionalising the Idea of Planning in Postcolonial India, 1947–60." *Modern Asian Studies* 43, no. 4 (October 2008): 939–978.

Kumar, Deepak. "Reconstructing India: Disunity in the Science and Technology for Development Discourse, 1900–1947." *Osiris* 15 (January 1, 2000): 241–257.

Kumarappa, Joseph Cornelius. *Our Food Problem.* Wardha: All India Village Industries Association, 1949.

Ladejinsky, Wolf. *Agrarian Reform as Unfinished Business: The Selected Papers of Wolf Ladejinsky.* Edited by Louis Joseph Walinsky. New York: Oxford University Press, 1977.

"Agrarian Reform in Asia." *Foreign Affairs* 42, no. 3 (April 1, 1964): 445–460.

"How Green Is the Indian Green Revolution?" *Economic and Political Weekly* 8, no. 52 (December 29, 1973): A133–A144.

"The Green Revolution in Punjab: A Field Trip." *Economic and Political Weekly* 4, no. 26 (June 28, 1969): A73–A82.

Lal, Bhawani, and Harbans Lal Mital. *The Law of Essential Supplies.* New Delhi: Federal Law Depot, 1951.

Lal, Mukut Behari. *An Appraisal of the Third Five Year Plan.* New Delhi: Praja Socialist Party, 1961.

Legg, Stephen. *Prostitution and the Ends of Empire: Scale, Governmentalities, and Interwar India.* Durham: Duke University Press, 2014.

Lele, Uma, and Arthur A. Goldsmith. "The Development of National Agricultural Research Capacity: India's Experience with the Rockefeller Foundation and

Select Bibliography

Its Significance for Africa." *Economic Development and Cultural Change* 37, no. 2 (January 1, 1989): 305–343.

Lewis, John P. *Quiet Crisis in India: Economic Development and American Policy.* Washington, DC: Brookings Institution, 1962.

Li, Tania Murray. "Beyond 'the State' and Failed Schemes." *American Anthropologist* 107, no. 3 (2005): 383–394.

Limaye, Madhu. *Food for All.* Bombay: Socialist Party, 1951.

Low, D.A. *The Egalitarian Moment: Asia and Africa, 1950–1980.* Cambridge: Cambridge University Press, 1996.

Ludden, David E., ed., *Agricultural Production and South Asian History.* New Delhi: Oxford University Press, 2005.

An Agrarian History of South Asia. The New Cambridge History of India 4. Cambridge: Cambridge University Press, 1999.

"The 'Discovery' of Malnutrition and Diet in Colonial India." *Indian Economic and Social History Review* 31, no. 1 (1994): 1–26.

Majumder, D. Dutta. "Subhas Chandra and National Planning." *Janata: A Journal of Democratic Socialism* 47, no. 2 (February 23, 1992): 11–17.

Malone, Carl C., and Sherman E. Johnson. "The Intensive Agricultural Development Program in India." *Agricultural Economics Research* 23, no. 2 (April 1971): 25–35.

Mankekar, D.R. *Lal Bahadur: A Political Biography.* Bombay: Popular Prakashan, 1965.

Markovits, Claude. *Indian Business and Nationalist Politics, 1931–1939: The Indigenous Capitalist Class and the Rise of the Congress Party.* Cambridge: Cambridge University Press, 1985.

Merchants, Traders, Entrepreneurs: Indian Business in the Colonial Era. Basingstoke: Palgrave Macmillan, 2008.

Marriott, McKim. "Caste Ranking and Food Transactions: A Matrix Analysis." In *Structure and Change in Indian Society,* edited by Milton B. Singer and Bernard S. Cohn, 133–172. New York: Wenner-Gren Foundation for Anthropological Research, 1968.

Masani, M.R. *Dangers of the Co-Operative Farming.* Nidubrolu: Peasant Protest Committee, 1959.

Why This Starvation?: Some Facts about Food. Bombay: New Book Company, 1943.

Your Food: A Study of the Problem of Food and Nutrition in India. Bombay: Padma Publications for Tata Sons, 1944.

Masani, Zareer. *Indian Tales of the Raj.* Berkeley: University of California Press, 1988.

Mathai, M.O. *My Days with Nehru.* New Delhi: Vikas Publishing House, 1979.

Mathur, Saloni. "History and Anthropology in South Asia: Rethinking the Archive." *Annual Review of Anthropology* 29 (2000): 89–106.

Mayer, P.B. "Inventing Village Tradition: The Late 19th Century Origins of the North Indian 'Jajmani System.'" *Modern Asian Studies* 27, no. 2 (May 1, 1993): 357–395.

McAlpin, Michelle Burge. *Subject to Famine: Food Crises and Economic Change in Western India, 1860–1920.* Princeton: Princeton University Press, 1983.

252   Select Bibliography

McCarrison, Robert. *Food: A Primer for Use in Schools, Colleges, Welfare Centres, Boy Scout and Girl Guide Organizations, Etc., in India.* Madras: Macmillan, 1928.

Megaw, John. *An Inquiry into Certain Public Health Aspects of Village Life in India.* New Delhi: Government of India Press, 1933.

Merillat, H.C.L. "Abstract of Law and Land Reform in India." *Law & Society Review* 3, no. 2/3 (November 1, 1968): 295–297.

Merrill, Dennis. *Bread and the Ballot: The United States and India's Economic Development, 1947–1963.* Chapel Hill: University of North Carolina Press, 1990.

Metcalf, Thomas R. "Landlords without Land: The U.P. Zamindars Today." *Pacific Affairs* 40, no. 1/2 (April 1, 1967): 5–18.

Millions on the Move: The Aftermath of Partition. New Delhi: Publications Division, Ministry of Information and Broadcasting, Government of India, 1949.

Ministry of Food and Agriculture, Government of India. *Report of the Foodgrains Enquiry Committee, November 1957.* New Delhi: Government of India Press, 1957.

Ministry of Food and Agriculture, Government of India, and Ministry of Information and Broadcasting, Government of India. *Towards Self-Sufficiency.* New Delhi: Publications Division, Ministry of Information and Broadcasting, Government of India, 1951.

Misra, Raghavendra Nath. *Bhoodan Movement in India: An Economic Assessment.* New Delhi: S. Chand & Co., 1972.

Mooij, Jos E. "Public Distribution System as Safety Net: Who Is Saved?" *Economic and Political Weekly* 29, no. 3 (January 15, 1994): 119–126.

Moore, Frank J. "Land Reform and Social Justice in India." *Far Eastern Survey* 24, no. 8 (August 1, 1955): 124–128.

More from Mother Earth. New Delhi: Publications Division, Ministry of Information and Broadcasting, Government of India, 1951.

Morris-Jones, W.H. "India's Political Idioms." In *Modern India: An Interpretive Anthology.* London: Macmillan, 1971.

"Shaping the Post-Imperial State: Nehru's Letters to Chief Ministers." In *Imperialism and the State in the Third World: Essays in Honour of Professor Kenneth Robinson,* edited by Michael Twaddle, 220–241. London: British Academic Press, 1992.

Moseman, Albert H. Oral History Interview. Interview by Raymond H. Geselbracht and Randy Sowell, June 14, 2004. Harry S. Truman Library and Museum.

Moskoff, William. *The Bread of Affliction: The Food Supply in the USSR during World War II.* Cambridge: Cambridge University Press, 1990.

Mudaliar, A.L. *Searchlight on Council Debates: Speeches of Sir A.L. Mudaliar in the Madras Legislative Council,* 167. Bombay: Orient Longmans, 1960.

Mukerjee, Madhusree. *Churchill's Secret War: The British Empire and the Ravaging of India during World War II.* New York: Basic Books, 2010.

Mukerjee, Radhakamal. *Food Planning for Four Hundred Millions.* London: Macmillan, 1938.

The Food Supply. Oxford Pamphlets on Indian Affairs 8. London: Oxford University Press, 1942.

Select Bibliography

Mukherjee, Janam. *Hungry Bengal: War, Famine and the End of Empire.* New York: Oxford University Press, 2015.

Mukherji, Partha Nath. "The Farmers' Movement in Punjab: Politics of Pressure Groups and Pressure of Party Politics." *Economic and Political Weekly* 33, no. 18 (May 2, 1998): 1043–1048.

Mullainathan, Sendhil, and Eldar Shafir. *Scarcity: Why Having Too Little Means So Much.* New York: Times Books, 2013.

Munshi, Kanaiyalal Maneklal. *The Ruin That Britain Wrought.* Bombay: Padma Publications for Bharatiya Vidya Bhavan, 1946.

Myrdal, Gunnar. *Asian Drama: An Inquiry into the Poverty of Nations.* New York: Twentieth Century Fund, 1968.

Nadkarni, Mangesh Venktesh. *Farmers' Movements in India.* Ahmedabad: Allied Publishers, 1987.

Nag, Sajal. "Bamboo, Rats and Famines: Famine Relief and Perceptions of British Paternalism in the Mizo Hills." In *India's Environmental History: Colonialism, Modernity, and the Nation,* edited by Mahesh Rangarajan and K. Sivaramakrishnan, vol. 2: 389–399. Ranikhet: Permanent Black, 2012.

Nagarjun. *Balacanama [Novel].* New Delhi: Vani Prakasana, 2009.

"Famine and After." *Indian Literature* 30, no. 3 (119) (May 1, 1987): 27.

Naidu, M. "The Bombay Plan." *Workers' International News* 5, no. 7 (December 1944): 1–4.

Naik, K.C. *Green Revolution.* Misc. Series 11. Bangalore: University of Agricultural Science, 1969.

Nair, K. Balakrishnan. "Mr. C. Subramaniam's Challenging Task: The Man the Smash 'The Graveyard of Reputations' Myth." *Food and Farming* 16, no. 6 (June 1964).

Nair, Kusum. *Blossoms in the Dust: The Human Element in Indian Development.* London: G. Duckworth, 1961.

Namboodiripad, E.M.S. *Agrarian Reforms: A Study of the Congress and Communist Approach.* New Delhi: People's Publishing House, 1956.

Food in Kerala. Bombay: People's Publishing House, 1944.

With the Ploughshare and the Sickle: Kisan Sabha in the Campaign for More Food. Bombay: Sharaf Athar Ali for the People's Publishing House, 1943.

Nanavati, Manilal B., and J.J. Anjaria. *The Indian Rural Problem.* Bombay: Indian Society of Agricultural Economics, 1944.

Nanda, Gulzar Lal. *Progress of Land Reforms in India.* New Delhi: All India Congress Committee, 1957.

Nandy, Srischandra. *Rationale of Food Crisis: A Plea for Rationing.* Calcutta: Cossimbazar House, 1943.

Naoroji, Dadabhai. *Poverty and Un-British Rule in India.* London: S. Sonnenschein, 1901.

Narayan, Jayaprakash. "Address at a Public Meeting Regarding Bhoodan Yagna, Secunderabad, 17 May 1953." In *Jayaprakash Narayan: Selected Works,* edited by Bimal Prasad, vol. 6: 338–340. New Delhi: Manohar Publishers and Distributors, 2006.

"Intervention in the Debate on General Secretary's Report, Betul, 16 June 1953." In *Jayaprakash Narayan: Selected Works,* edited by Bimal Prasad, vol. 6: 343–354. New Delhi: Manohar Publishers and Distributors, 2006.

254 Select Bibliography

"Letters to Freedom Fighters." In *Jayaprakash Narayan: Struggle with Values: A Centenary Tribute*, edited by Madhu Dandavate, 54–91. New Delhi: Allied Publishers, 2002.

Narayan, T.G. *Famine over Bengal*. Calcutta: Calcutta Book Company, 1944.

Narayanan, Sudha. "The National Food Security Act vis-à-vis the WTO Agreement on Agriculture." *Economic and Political Weekly* 49, no. 5 (January 23, 2014): 40–46.

Natarajan, Balasubrahmanya. *Food and Agriculture in Madras State*. Madras: Director of Information and Publicity, Government of Madras 1951.

Natesan, M.V. *A Scheme of Collective Effort to Promote the Health and Well-Being of the People of India through Proper and Sufficient Food*. Madurai: Sampath Press, 1944.

National Food Security Act (NFSA), 2013.

"Nation's Food Situation Described." *United States Foreign Broadcast Information Service Daily Reports*, April 11, 1956.

Neale, Walter C. *Economic Change in Rural India: Land Tenure and Reform in Uttar Pradesh, 1800–1955*. New Haven: Yale University Press, 1962.

"Indian Community Development, Local Government, Local Planning, and Rural Policy since 1950." *Economic Development and Cultural Change* 33, no. 4 (July 1, 1985): 677–698.

Needham, Mabel A. *Domestic Science for High Schools in India*. Bombay: Oxford University Press, 1929.

Nehru, Jawaharlal. *Independence and After: A Collection of Speeches*. New York: Day, 1950.

Jawaharlal Nehru on Science and Society: A Collection of His Writings and Speeches. Edited by Baldev Singh. New Delhi: Nehru Memorial Museum and Library, 1988.

Jawaharlal Nehru's Speeches, vol. 2. 3rd edn. New Delhi: Publications Division, Ministry of Information and Broadcasting, Government of India, 1963.

Letters to Chief Ministers, 1947–1964, vol. 1. New Delhi: Jawaharlal Nehru Memorial Fund; distributed by Oxford University Press, 1985.

Report of the National Planning Committee, 1938. New Delhi: Indian Institute of Applied Political Research, 1988.

Selected Works of Jawaharlal Nehru (Second Series). 70 vols. New Delhi: Jawaharlal Nehru Memorial Fund, 1984–2017.

The Discovery of India. New Delhi: Oxford University Press, 1989.

Nehru, Rameshwari. *Gandhi My Star: Speeches and Writings*. Patna: Pustakbhandar, 1950.

Newbigin, Eleanor. "Personal Law and Citizenship in India's Transition to Independence." *Modern Asian Studies* 45, Special Issue 1 (2011): 7–32.

The Hindu Family and the Emergence of Modern India Law, Citizenship and Community. Cambridge: Cambridge University Press, 2013.

Nichols, Beverley. *Verdict on India*. New York: Harcourt, Brace and Co., 1944.

Ó Gráda, Cormac. *"Sufficiency and Sufficiency and Sufficiency": Revisiting the Bengal Famine of 1943–44*. Dublin: UCD School of Economics, 2010.

Omvedt, Gail. "Farmers' Movement: Fighting for Liberalisation." *Economic and Political Weekly* 28, no. 50 (December 11, 1993): 2708–2710.

Select Bibliography 255

"'We Want the Return for Our Sweat': The New Peasant Movement in India and the Formation of a National Agricultural Policy." *Journal of Peasant Studies* 21, no. 3–4 (1994): 126–164.

Oommen, T.K. *Charisma, Stability, and Change: An Analysis of Bhoodan-Gramdan Movement in India*. New Delhi: Thompson Press, 1972.

Owen, Nicholas J. *The British Left and India: Metropolitan Anti-Imperialism, 1885–1947*. Oxford: Oxford University Press, 2007.

Paarlberg, Robert L. *Food Trade and Foreign Policy: India, the Soviet Union, and the United States*. Ithaca: Cornell University Press, 1985.

Package Programme Districts: Facts and Figures. New Delhi: Farm Information Unit, Directorate of Extension, Ministry of Food and Agriculture, 1961.

Palme Dutt, Rajani. *The Problem of India*. Toronto: Progress Books, 1943.

Pandian, Anand. "Devoted to Development: Moral Progress, Ethical Work, and Divine Favor in South India." *Anthropological Theory* 8, no. 2 (June 1, 2008): 159–179.

Pandya, H.L. *India Could and Can Export Food*. Bombay, 1966.

Parayil, Govindan. "The Green Revolution in India: A Case Study of Technological Change." *Technology and Culture* 33, no. 4 (October 1, 1992): 737–756.

Parekh, Bhikhu. "Nehru and the National Philosophy of India." *Economic and Political Weekly* 26, no. 1 (January 5, 1991): 35–39, 41, 43, 45–48.

Parikh, Kirit, Shikha Jha, and P.V. Srinivasan. "Economic Reforms and Agricultural Policy." *Economic and Political Weekly* 28, no. 29/30 (July 17, 1993): 1497–1500.

Parmar, Inderjeet. *Foundations of the American Century: The Ford, Carnegie, and Rockefeller Foundations in the Rise of American Power*. New York: Columbia University Press, 2012.

Parthasarathi, Prasannan. *The Transition to a Colonial Economy: Weavers, Merchants, and Kings in South India, 1720–1800*. Cambridge: Cambridge University Press, 2001.

Patel, Raj. *Stuffed and Starved: The Hidden Battle for the World Food System*. Brooklyn: Melville House, 2008.

Patil, P.C. *Food Problem in India in General and Kolhapur State in Particular*. Poona: V.H. Barve, 1948.

Patil, R.K. *Report of the Indian Delegation to China on Agrarian Cooperatives*. New Delhi: Planning Commission, Government of India, 1957.

Patnaik, Utsa. *Agrarian Relations and Accumulation: The "Mode of Production" Debate in India*. Bombay: Published for Sameeksha Trust by Oxford University Press, 1990.

Patrick, Neil A. *India's Package Program for Intensive Agricultural Development*. New Delhi: Ford Foundation, 1972.

Pattanayak, Gopal Chandra. *Planned Diet for India*. Allahabad: Kitabistan, 1946.

Patterson, Maureen L.P. "The South Asian P.L. 480 Library Program, 1962–1968." *The Journal of Asian Studies* 28, no. 4 (August 1, 1969): 743–754.

Patvardhan, V.S. *Food Control in Bombay Province, 1939–1949*. Poona: D.R. Gadgil, 1958.

Perkins, John H. *Geopolitics and the Green Revolution: Wheat, Genes, and the Cold War*. New York: Oxford University Press, 1997.

256   Select Bibliography

Phalkey, Jahnavi. *Atomic State: Big Science in Twentieth-Century India*. Ranikhet: Permanent Black, 2013.

Pinney, Christopher. *Photos of the Gods: The Printed Image and Political Struggle in India*. London: Reaktion, 2004.

Planning Commission, Government of India. *The First Five-Year Plan: A Draft Outline*. New Delhi: Government of India Press, 1951.

Plummer, Brenda Gayle. *Rising Wind: Black Americans and U.S. Foreign Affairs, 1935–1960*. Chapel Hill: University of North Carolina Press, 1996.

Prasad, Sarjoo, H.L. Capoor, D.D. Seth, and Jagdish Lal. *Sarjoo Prasad's Commentaries on Essential Commodities Act, 1955*. Allahabad: Law Publishers, 1980.

Premji, M.H. Hasham, and Bhani Ram Gupta. *India's Food Problem: Its Complex Nature*. New Delhi: Federation of All Indian Foodgrain Dealers' Associations, 1964.

Prime Minister Nehru Examines Corn Grown on an Illinois Farm. Photograph, October 1949. 72–608. Harry S. Truman Library and Museum.

Pritchard, Bill, Anu Rammohan, Madhushree Sekher, S. Parasuraman, and Chetan Choithani. *To Feed India, to Feed the World: Livelihoods, Entitlements and Capabilities*. London: Routledge, 2013.

Progress Evaluation Report about Cooperative Farming. New Delhi: Government of India, 1958.

Progress of Science. New Delhi: Publications Division, Ministry of Information and Broadcasting, Government of India, 1951.

Puri, Balraj. *Cooperative Farming: A Critique*. Calcutta: Institute of Political and Social Studies, 1959.

Puri, Ram Nath. *How to Conquer Poverty and Famine in India by American Methods*. Baroda: Padmaja Publications, 1947.

Radel, Rémi, and Corentin Clément-Guillotin. "Evidence of Motivational Influences in Early Visual Perception: Hunger Modulates Conscious Access." *Psychological Science* 23, no. 3 (2012): 232–234.

Rajagopalachari, C. "The Food Problem [All India Radio, July 6, 1949]." In *Speeches of C. Rajagopalachari, Governor-General of India. June 1948–January 1950*, 251. New Delhi: Superintendent, Governor-General's Press, 1950.

The Way Out, a Plea for Constructive Thought on the Present Political Situation in India. London: H. Milford, Oxford University Press, 1943.

Rajan, M.S. Nata. *Famine in Retrospect*. Bombay: Padma Publications, 1944.

Ramamurty, Sonti Venkata. *Looking across Fifty Years*. Bombay: Popular Prakashan, 1964.

Ramiah, V. *Independent India of Plenty: What Congress Government Ought to Do*. Madras: Andhra Publishing House, 1946.

Ramnath, Maia. *Haj to Utopia: How the Ghadar Movement Charted Global Radicalism and Attempted to Overthrow the British Empire*. Berkeley: University of California Press, 2011.

Ranadive, Bhalchandra Trimbak. *Food in Bombay Province*. Bombay: People's Publishing House, 1944.

Ranadive, Bhalchandra Trimbak, and C.N. Vakil. *Population Problem of India*. Studies in Indian Economics 4. Calcutta: Longmans, Green and Co., 1930.

Select Bibliography

Randhawa, M.S. *A History of Agriculture in India*, vol. 3: *1757–1947*. New Delhi: Indian Council of Agricultural Research, 1983.

A History of Agriculture in India, vol. 4: *1947–1981*. New Delhi: Indian Council of Agricultural Research, 1986.

A History of the Indian Council of Agricultural Research, 1929–1979. New Delhi: Indian Council of Agricultural Research, 1979.

Agricultural Research in India: Institutes and Organisations. New Delhi: Indian Council of Agricultural Research, 1958.

Out of the Ashes: An Account of the Rehabilitation of Refugees from West Pakistan in Rural Areas of East Punjab. Chandigarh: Public Relations Department, Punjab, 1954.

Randhawa, M.S., and U.N. Chatterjee. *Developing Village India: Studies in Village Problems*. Bombay: Orient Longman, 1951.

Ranga, N.G. *Revolutionary Peasants*. New Delhi: Amrit Book Co., 1949.

Rao, M. Thirumala. *Report of the Foodgrains Procurement Committee, 1950*. New Delhi: Government of India Press, 1950.

Rao, Nitya. "Agricultural Research and Extension in India: Changing Ideologies and Practice." *Economic and Political Weekly* 40, no. 13 (March 26, 2005): 1371–1375.

Rao, R.V. *Our Economic Problems*. Lahore: Lion Press, 1946.

Rasul, M. Abdullah. *A History of the All India Kisan Sabha*. Calcutta: National Book Agency, 1974.

Ray, Debidas. *Food Administration in East India: 1939–54*. Santiniketan: Agro-Economic Research Centre, Visva-Bharati, 1958.

Ray, Howard Eugene. *The First Decade of the Intensive Agricultural District Program*. New Delhi: Ford Foundation, 1974.

Ray, Krishnendu, and Tulasi Srinivas. *Curried Cultures: Globalization, Food, and South Asia*. Berkeley: University of California Press, 2012.

Ray, Prithwis Chandra. *Indian Famines: Their Causes and Remedies*. Calcutta: Cherry Press, 1901.

The Poverty Problem in India; Being a Dissertation on the Causes and Remedies of Indian Poverty. Calcutta: Thacker, Spink & Co., 1895.

Ray, Utsa. "Eating 'Modernity': Changing Dietary Practices in Colonial Bengal." *Modern Asian Studies* 46, no. 3 (2012): 703–729.

"The Body and Its Purity: Dietary Politics in Colonial Bengal." *Indian Economic and Social History Review* 50, no. 4 (October 1, 2013): 395–421.

Relief Organisations Fight Bengal Famine. Calcutta: Relief Co-ordination Committee, 1943.

Renu, Phanishwar Nath. *Tale of a Wasteland: An English Rendering of Parti Parikatha*. Translated by Madhusudan Thakur. New Delhi: Global Vision Press, 2012.

Report of the Congress Agrarian Reforms Committee. 2nd edn. New Delhi: All India Congress Committee, 1951.

Report of the Foodgrains Policy Committee, 1966. New Delhi: Ministry of Food and Agriculture and Ministry of Community Development and Cooperation, Government of India, 1966.

Report of the Indian Delegation to China on Agricultural Planning and Techniques. New Delhi: Ministry of Food and Agriculture, Government of India, 1956.

258 Select Bibliography

Report of the Joint Indo-American Team on Agricultural Research and Education. New Delhi: Indian Council of Agricultural Research, 1955.

Report of the Second Joint Indo-American Team on Agricultural Education, Research and Extension. New Delhi: Indian Council of Agricultural Research, 1960.

Report of the Special Meeting on Urgent Food Problem, Washington D.C., May 20–27, 1946. Washington, DC: Food and Agriculture Organization of the United Nations, 1946.

Report of the Study Team on the Working of the Cooperative Movement in Yugoslavia and Israel. New Delhi: Ministry of Community Development and Cooperation, Government of India, 1960.

Report Showing Action Taken by Central and Provincial Governments on the Recommendations Made by the Famine Inquiry Commission in Their Final Report. Calcutta: Government of India Press, 1948.

Research and Policy Division, Ministry of Home Affairs. *The Causes and Nature of Current Agrarian Tensions.* New Delhi: Ministry of Home Affairs, Government of India, 1969.

Revenue Department, Government of Bihar. *Bihar Famine Report, 1966–67.* Patna: Secretariat Press, 1973.

Rieff, David. *The Reproach of Hunger: Food, Justice, and Money in the Twenty-First Century.* New York: Simon and Schuster, 2016.

Riley, Barry. *The Political History of American Food Aid: An Uneasy Benevolence.* Oxford: Oxford University Press, 2017.

Robb, Peter, ed., *Meanings of Agriculture: Essays in South Asian History and Economics.* New Delhi: Oxford University Press, 1996.

Roberts, Paul. *The End of Food.* Boston: Houghton Mifflin Company, 2009.

Robertson, C.A., G.R. Saini, and R.K. Sharma. "The Package Programme: An Appraisal (I)." *Economic and Political Weekly* 1, no. 2 (August 27, 1966): 79–85. "The Package Programme: An Appraisal (II)." *Economic and Political Weekly* 1, no. 3 (September 3, 1966): 124–126.

Rockefeller Foundation Annual Report. New York: Rockefeller Foundation, 1954.

Rosen, George. *Western Economists and Eastern Societies: Agents of Change in South Asia, 1950–1970.* Baltimore: Johns Hopkins University Press, 1985.

Rostow, W.W. *The Stages of Economic Growth.* Cambridge: Cambridge University Press, 1960.

Roy, Krishna Benode. *Bengal Famine and Problems of Rehabilitation.* Calcutta: Bengal Provincial Kisan Sabha, 1945.

Roy, M.N. *National Government or People's Government?* Bombay: Renaissance Publishers, 1946.

Roy, P.N. Singh. *Food Policy in India.* Calcutta: British Indian Association, 1943.

Roy, Srirupa. *Beyond Belief: India and the Politics of Postcolonial Nationalism.* Durham: Duke University Press, 2007.

Rozin, Orit. "The Austerity Policy and the Rule of Law: Relations between Government and Public in Fledgling Israel." *Journal of Modern Jewish Studies* 4, no. 3 (2005): 273–290.

Rudolph, Lloyd I., and Susanne Hoeber Rudolph. *In Pursuit of Lakshmi: The Political Economy of the Indian State.* Chicago: University of Chicago Press, 1987.

Select Bibliography

Rudra, Sudhir Kumar. *Rationing of Foodgrains in the United Provinces during World War II*. Department of Economics and Statistics, U.P. Bulletin 4. Allahabad: United Provinces Department of Economics and Statistics, 1946.

Sabharwal, Nidhi Sadana. "Caste, Religion and Malnutrition Linkages." *Economic & Political Weekly* 46, no. 50 (December 10, 2011): 16–18.

Sachs, Carolyn E. *Gendered Fields: Rural Women, Agriculture, and Environment*. Boulder: Westview Press, 1996.

Sackley, Nicole. "Foundation in the Field: The Ford Foundation New Delhi Office and the Construction of Development Knowledge, 1951–1970." In *American Foundations and the Coproduction of World Order in the Twentieth Century*, edited by John Krige and Helke Rausch, 232–260. Göttingen: Vandenhoeck & Ruprecht, 2012.

"The Village as Cold War Site: Experts, Development, and the History of Rural Reconstruction." *Journal of Global History* 6, no. 3 (2011): 481–504.

"Village Models: Etawah, India, and the Making and Remaking of Development in the Early Cold War." *Diplomatic History* 37, no. 4 (2013): 749–778.

Saraswati, Sahajanand. *Sahajanand on Agricultural Labour and the Rural Poor: An Edited Translation of Khet Mazdoor*. Translated by Walter Hauser. New Delhi: Manohar Publishers and Distributors, 1994.

Sardesai, S.G. *Food in the United Provinces*. Bombay: People's Publishing House, 1944.

Sarkar, Sumit. "The Decline of the Subaltern in Subaltern Studies." In *Writing Social History*, 82–108. New Delhi: Oxford University Press, 1997.

The Swadeshi Movement in Bengal, 1903–1908. New Delhi: People's Publishing House, 1973.

ed., *Towards Freedom: Documents on the Movement for Independence in India, 1946*. New Delhi: Indian Council of Historical Research, 2007.

Sarkar, Tanika. *Hindu Wife, Hindu Nation: Community, Religion, and Cultural Nationalism*. Bloomington: Indiana University Press, 2001.

Sartori, Andrew. *Liberalism in Empire: An Alternative History*. Berkeley: University of California Press, 2014.

Schultz, Theodore W. *"Three Illinois Farms and Their Families: Introducing Prime Minister Nehru and His Party to Middle Western Agriculture and Farm Living, October 27, 1949,"* 1949. National Agricultural Library, United States Department of Agriculture.

Transforming Traditional Agriculture. New Haven: Yale University Press, 1964.

Scott, James C. *Seeing Like a State: How Certain Schemes to Improve the Human Condition Have Failed*. New Haven: Yale University Press, 1998.

The Moral Economy of the Peasant: Rebellion and Subsistence in Southeast Asia. New Haven: Yale University Press, 1976.

Sen, Abhijit. "Economic Liberalisation and Agriculture in India." *Social Scientist* 20, no. 11 (November 1, 1992): 4–19.

Sen, Amartya. *Development as Freedom*. New York: Knopf, 1999.

Poverty and Famines: An Essay on Entitlement and Deprivation. Oxford: Clarendon Press, 1981.

Sen, B. "Opportunities in the Green Revolution." *Economic and Political Weekly* 5, no. 13 (March 28, 1970): A33–A40.

Sen, B.R. *Towards a Newer World*. Dublin: Tycooly International Pub., 1982.

Select Bibliography

Sen, Ela. *Darkening Days: Being a Narrative of Famine-Stricken Bengal, with Drawings from Life by Zainul Abedin*. Calcutta: Susil Gupta, 1944.

Sen, S.R. *Modernising Indian Agriculture: Report on the Intensive Agricultural District Programme, 1960–68*. New Delhi: Department of Agriculture, Government of India, 1969.

Sengupta, Jayanta. "Nation on a Platter: The Culture and Politics of Food and Cuisine in Colonial Bengal." *Modern Asian Studies* 44, Special Issue 1 (2010): 81–98.

Shah, C.H. "Fall-Out of Green Revolution." *Economic and Political Weekly* 5, no. 2 (January 10, 1970): 42–44.

Shah, K.T. *National Planning Committee: Priorities in Planning (Food, Education, Housing)*. Bombay: Vora & Co., 1946.

Woman's Role in Planned Economy: Report of the Sub-Committee. National Planning Committee Series. Bombay: Vora & Co., 1947.

Shani, Ornit. "Gandhi, Citizenship and the Resilience of Indian Nationhood." *Citizenship Studies* 15, no. 6–7 (October 2011): 659–678.

Sharma, Sanjay. *Famine, Philanthropy, and the Colonial State: North India in the Early Nineteenth Century*. Oxford: Oxford University Press, 2001.

"The 1837–38 Famine in U.P.: Some Dimensions of Popular Action." *Indian Economic and Social History Review* 30, no. 3 (September 1, 1993): 337–372.

Shenoy, B.R. *P.L. 480 Aid and India's Food Problem*. New Delhi: Affiliated East-West Press, 1974.

Sherman, Taylor C. "From 'Grow More Food' to 'Miss a Meal': Hunger, Development and the Limits of Post-Colonial Nationalism in India, 1947–1957." *South Asia: Journal of South Asian Studies* 36, no. 4 (December 2013): 571–588.

Shiva, Vandana. *The Violence of the Green Revolution: Third World Agriculture, Ecology, and Politics*. London: Zed Books, 1991.

Shuman, Frank H. "Extension for the People of India." *Extension* 3, no. 1 (January 1958): 5–22.

Siegel, Benjamin. "Fantastic Quantities of Food Grains: Cold War Visions and Agrarian Fantasies in Independent India." In *Negotiating Independence: New Directions in the History of Decolonization and the Cold War*, edited by Elisabeth Mariko Leake and Leslie James, 21–42. London: Bloomsbury, 2014.

"Learning to Eat in a Capital City: Constructing Public Eating Culture in Delhi." *Food, Culture and Society: An International Journal of Multidisciplinary Research* 13, no. 1 (2010): 71–90.

"Modernizing Peasants and 'Master Farmers': Progressive Agriculture in Early Independent India." *Comparative Studies of South Asia, Africa and the Middle East* 37, no. 1 (May 2017): 64–84.

"On 'Asian Drama.'" *Humanity*, 8, no. 1 (March 2017): 195–205.

"'Self-Help Which Ennobles a Nation': Development, Citizenship, and the Obligations of Eating in India's Austerity Years." *Modern Asian Studies* 50, no. 3 (2015): 1–44.

Singh, Baljit. *Population and Food Planning in India*. Bombay: Hind Kitabs, 1947.

Whither Agriculture in India? A Study of the Re-Organisation of Agricultural Planning in India. Agra: N.R. Agrawal, 1945.

Select Bibliography

Singh, Charan. *Abolition of Zamindari, Two Alternatives*. Allahabad: Kitabistan, 1947.
— *Agrarian Revolution in Uttar Pradesh*. Lucknow: Superintendent, Printing and Stationery, Uttar Pradesh, India, 1958.
— *Joint Farming X-Rayed: The Problem and Its Solution*. Bombay: Bharatiya Vidya Bhavan, 1959.
— *Whither Co-Operative Farming?* Allahabad: Superintendent, Printing and Stationery, Uttar Pradesh, India, 1956.
Singh, H.B. *Cultivation of Sweet Potato*. Farm Bulletin (New Series) 4. New Delhi: Indian Council of Agricultural Research, 1964.
Singh, Sardar Bahadur Lal. "Need for Re-Appraisal of Our Agrarian Policy." In *Swarajya Special Number 1962*, 193–195. Madras: Barathan Publications, 1962.
Singh, Tarkeshwar Prasad. *Bhoodan and Gramdan in Orissa: A Social Scientist's Analysis (the First Inter-Disciplinary Study of India's Famous Land Gift Movement)*. Rajghat, Kashi [Varanasi]: Akhil Bharat Sarva Seva Sangh Prakashan, 1973.
Singh, Tarlok. *Poverty and Social Change: A Study in the Economic Reorganisation of Indian Rural Society*. London: Longmans, Green & Co., 1945.
Singh, T.N., ed., *Handbook for Congressmen*. New Delhi: All India Congress Committee, 1957.
Sinha, Bimal Chandra, and Haricharan Ghosh. *Food Problem in Bengal*. Calcutta: H.C. Ghosh, 1943.
Sinha, Lalan Prasad. *The Left-Wing in India, 1919–47*. Muzaffarpur: New Publishers, 1965.
Sinha, Subir. "Lineages of the Developmentalist State: Transnationality and Village India, 1900–1965." *Comparative Studies in Society and History* 50, no. 1 (2008): 57–90.
Sivaswamy, K.G. *The Exodus from Travancore to Malabar Jungles*. Coimbatore: Servindia Kerala Relief Centre, 1945.
Sivaswamy, K.G., J. Ananta Bhat, and Tadepally Shankara Shastry. *Famine, Rationing and Food Policy in Cochin*. Royapettah, Madras: Servindia Kerala Relief Centre, 1946.
Smith, Lilliam, Joseph Willen, Sidney Hertzberg, and Theodore W. Schultz. *India's Hunger: Report of the American Famine Mission to India*. New York: India Famine Emergency Committee, 1946.
Sokhey, S.S. "Planning for a New India: Food of the People." In *Report of the Sub-Committee on National Health*, edited by K.T. Shah, 135–139. National Planning Committee Series. Bombay: Vora & Co., 1948.
Solomon, Harris. *Metabolic Living: Food, Fat, and the Absorption of Illness in India*. Durham: Duke University Press, 2016.
Somani, G.N. *An Observation on the Food Production Drive of the Hon'ble Prime Minister Pandit Jawahar Lal Nehru*. Jaipur: The Manoranjan Press, 1949.
Sonnenfeld, David A. "Mexico's 'Green Revolution,' 1940–1980: Towards an Environmental History." *Environmental History Review* 16, no. 4 (1992): 29–52.
Sorensen, Reginald. *Famine, Politics – and Mr. Amery*. London: The India League, 1944.

262   Select Bibliography

Sovani, N.V. *Post War Inflation in India: A Survey.* Gokhale Institute Studies 21. Poona: Gokhale Institute of Politics and Economics, 1949.

Spivak, Gayatri Chakravorty. "Can the Subaltern Speak?" In *Marxism and the Interpretation of Culture,* edited by Cary Nelson and Lawrence Grossberg, 271–313. Urbana and Chicago: University of Illinois Press, 1988.

Sreenivas, Mytheli. *Wives, Widows, and Concubines: The Conjugal Family Ideal in Colonial India.* Bloomington: Indiana University Press, 2008.

Srimanjari. "War, Famine, and Popular Perceptions in Bengali Literature, 1939–1945." In *Issues in Modern Indian History: For Sumit Sarkar,* edited by Biswamoy Pati, 258–290. Mumbai: Popular Prakashan, 2000.

Sriraman, Tarangini. "Revisiting Welfare: Ration Card Narratives in India." *Economic and Political Weekly* 46, no. 38 (2011): 52–59.

Srivastava, Hari Shanker. *The History of Indian Famines and Development of Famine Policy, 1858–1918.* Agra: Sri Ram Mehra, 1968.

State Trading in Food. Calcutta: Employers' Association, 1955.

Stokes, Eric. "Dynamism and Enervation in North Indian Agriculture." In *The Peasant and the Raj: Studies in Agrarian Society and Peasant Rebellion in Colonial India,* 228–242. Cambridge: Cambridge University Press, 1978.

Stoler, Ann Laura. *Along the Archival Grain: Epistemic Anxieties and Colonial Common Sense.* Princeton: Princeton University Press, 2009.

Stolte, Carolien, and Harald Fischer-Tiné. "Imagining Asia in India: Nationalism and Internationalism (ca. 1905–1940)." *Comparative Studies in Society and History* 54, no. 1 (January 2012): 65–92.

Strahorn, Eric A. *An Environmental History of Postcolonial North India: The Himalayan Tarai in Uttar Pradesh and Uttaranchal.* New York: Peter Lang, 2009.

Subrahmanyan, V. "A Practical Approach to the Food Problem in India." *Science and Culture* 13, no. 6 (December 1947): 213–218.

Subramaniam, C. "Land and Food: Problems of Implementation of Congress Party Policy." In *Ooty Seminar: Papers Discussed,* 128–140. New Delhi: All India Congress Committee, 1959.

The New Strategy in Indian Agriculture: The First Decade and After. New Delhi: Vikas Publishing House, 1979.

Subramanyam, V. "Planning for Food Emergency." In *Food and Population and Development of Food Industries in India,* 131–134. Mysore: Central Food Technological Research Institute, 1952.

Subramanyam, V., D.S. Bhatia, M. Swaminathan, and G.S. Bains. "Rice Substitutes." *Nature* 174 (1954): 199–201.

Summary of Proceedings of the First Meeting of the Central Food Advisory Council Held at New Delhi on the 24th and 25th August 1942. New Delhi: Government of India Press, 1942.

Sur, Abha. "Scientism and Social Justice: Meghnad Saha's Critique of the State of Science in India." *Historical Studies in the Physical and Biological Sciences* 33, no. 1 (2002): 87–105.

Suryanarayana, M.H. "Urban Bias in PDS." *Economic and Political Weekly* 29, no. 9 (February 26, 1994): 510–512.

Svedberg, Peter. *Poverty and Undernutrition: Theory, Measurement, and Policy.* Oxford: Oxford University Press, 2000.

Select Bibliography 263

Swaminathan, Madhura. "Revamped Public Distribution System: A Field Report from Maharashtra." *Economic and Political Weekly* 30, no. 36 (September 9, 1995): 2230.

Swatantra Party. *Preparatory Convention, Bombay, August 1959.* Bombay: Popular Book Depot, 1959.

Talbot, Ian. "Punjabi Refugees' Rehabilitation and the Indian State: Discourses, Denials and Dissonances." *Modern Asian Studies* 45, Special Issue 1 (2011): 109–130.

Tambe, Ashwini. *Codes of Misconduct: Regulating Prostitution in Late Colonial Bombay.* Minneapolis: University of Minnesota Press, 2009.

Tauger, Mark B. "The Indian Famine Crises of World War II." *British Scholar* 1, no. 2 (2009): 166–196.

Tax, Sol. *Penny Capitalism: A Guatemalan Indian Economy.* Washington, DC: United States Government Printing Office, 1953.

Temple, R.C. "Agricultural Folk-Lore Notes." *The Folk-Lore Record* 5 (January 1, 1882): 33–49.

Tennyson, Hallam. *India's Walking Saint: The Story of Vinoba Bhave.* Garden City, NY: Doubleday, 1955.

Thakore, S.T. *Statement of Account up to 31-12-43 of Bengal Relief Fund.* Nairobi: Bengal Relief Fund, 1944.

Thakurdas, Purshottamdas. *Final Report, Foodgrains Policy Committee, 1947.* New Delhi: Government of India Press, 1948.

Thakurdas, Purshottamdas, J.R.D. Tata, G.D. Birla, Ardeshir Dalal, Shri Ram, Kasturbhai Lalbhai, A.D. Shroff, and John Mathai. *A Plan of Economic Development for India.* Bombay: The Commercial Printing Press, 1944.

The Flood of the Golden Grain. New Delhi: Food Corporation of India, 1972.

The Food Situation: A Study. Madras: Southern India Chamber of Commerce, 1966.

The Ford Foundation and Foundation Supported Activities in India. New Delhi: Ford Foundation, January 1955.

The Fourth Annual Meeting of the All India Women's Food Council, West Bengal Branch, 1954–55. Calcutta: All India Women's Food Council, 1955.

The Meaning of Self-Reliance. New Delhi: Publications Division, Ministry of Information and Broadcasting, Government of India, 1965.

The Servants of India Society Report for 1943–44. Poona: Servants of India Society, 1944.

The Servants of India Society Report for 1944–45. Poona: Servants of India Society, 1945.

Thirumaavalavan. *Talisman, Extreme Emotions of Dalit Liberation.* Mumbai: Popular Prakashan, 2003.

   Uproot Hindutva: The Fiery Voice of the Liberation Panthers. Mumbai: Popular Prakashan, 2004.

Thomas, C. *Indian Agricultural Research Institute: An Introduction.* New Delhi: Indian Agricultural Research Institute, 1983.

Thorner, Daniel. "Capitalist Farming in India." *Economic and Political Weekly* 4, no. 52 (December 27, 1969): A211–A212.

264 Select Bibliography

"Coastal Andhra: Towards an Affluent Society." *Economic and Political Weekly* 2, no. 3/5 (February 1, 1967): 241–252.

"Predatory Capitalism in Indian Agriculture." *Economic and Political Weekly* 3, no. 43 (October 26, 1968): A3–A4.

Prospects for Cooperation in Indian Agriculture. Paris: L'École des hautes études, 1960.

The Agrarian Prospect in India: Five Lectures on Land Reform Delivered in 1955 at the Delhi School of Economics. Columbia, MO: South Asia Books, 1976.

To Prosperity through Freedom: The Swatantra Party's Statement of Policy Adopted at the National Convention in Patna on March 19 and 20 1960. Swatantra Series no. 3. Bombay: Swatantra Party, 1960.

Tomlinson, B.R. *The Economy of Modern India, 1860–1970.* Cambridge: Cambridge University Press, 1993.

"Too Much Food?" *Economic and Political Weekly* 30, no. 23 (June 10, 1995): 1339–1340.

Tyagi, D.S. *Managing India's Food Economy: Problems and Alternatives.* New Delhi: Sage Publications, 1990.

United States House Committee on Agriculture, United States Congress. *Emergency Food for India. Hearing before the Committee on Agriculture, House of Representatives, Eighty-Ninth Congress, Second Session, on H. J. Res. 997. March 31, 1966.* Washington, DC: United States Government Printing Office, 1966.

Uppal, J.N. *Bengal Famine of 1943: A Man-Made Tragedy.* New Delhi: Atma Ram, 1984.

Vajpayee, Atal Bihari. "Ushering Economic Imperialism in the Name of Co-Operatives." In *Four Decades in Parliament,* edited by N.M. Ghatate, vol. 2: *State of the Economy:* 339–343. New Delhi: Shipra Publications, 1996.

Vakil, C.N. *Economic Consequences of Divided India.* Bombay: Vora & Co., 1950.

Varshney, Ashutosh. *Democracy, Development, and the Countryside: Urban-Rural Struggles in India.* Cambridge: Cambridge University Press, 1998.

"Ideas, Interest and Institutions in Policy Change: Transformation of India's Agricultural Strategy in the Mid-1960s." *Policy Sciences* 22, no. 3/4 (January 1, 1989): 289–323.

Vasavi, A.R. *Shadow Space: Suicides and the Predicament of Rural India.* Gurgaon: Three Essays Collective, 2012.

Vaswani, Khushiram Nebhraj. *Planning for a New India.* Lahore: Dewan's Publications, 1946.

Vegetable Growing in the Delhi Province. 2nd edn., ICAR Booklet 5. New Delhi: Imperial Council of Agricultural Research, 1946.

Verghese, B.G. *Beyond the Famine: An Approach to Regional Planning for Bihar.* New Delhi: Bihar Relief Committee, 1967.

Vinoba. *Democratic Values and the Practice of Citizenship: Selections from the Addresses of Vinoba Bhave, 1951–1960.* Rajghat, Kashi [Varanasi]: Akhil Bharat Sarva Seva Sangh Prakashan, 1962.

Virmani, Arvind, and Charan Singh. "Malnutrition, Not Hunger, Ails India." *Livemint,* September 22, 2013.

Visvesvaraya, Mokshagundam. *Planned Economy for India.* Bangalore: Bangalore Press, 1934.

Select Bibliography

Reconstructing India. London: P.S. King & Son, 1920.

Voelcker, John Augustus. *Report on the Improvement of Indian Agriculture*. London: Eyre and Spottiswoode, 1893.

Vyas, A.R. "Annapoorna: India's Democratic Restaurants." *March of India* 4, no. 2 (December 1951): 29–31.

Walsh, Judith E. *Domesticity in Colonial India: What Women Learned When Men Gave Them Advice*. Lanham, MD: Rowman & Littlefield Publishers, 2004.

Washbrook, David. "The Rhetoric of Democracy and Development in Late Colonial India." In *Nationalism, Democracy, and Development: State and Politics in India*, edited by Sugata Bose and Ayesha Jalal, 36–49. New Delhi: Oxford University Press, 1997.

Wattal, P.K. *Population Problem in India*. Bombay: Bennet Coleman, 1934.

Weigold, Auriol. "Famine Management: The Bengal Famine (1942–1944) Revisited." *South Asia: Journal of South Asian Studies* 22, no. 1 (1999): 63–77.

Weiner, Myron. *The Politics of Scarcity: Public Pressure and Political Response in India*. Chicago: University of Chicago Press, 1962.

Wharton, Clifton R., Jr. "The Green Revolution: Cornucopia or Pandora's Box." *Foreign Affairs* 47, no. 3 (April 1969).

Williams, Rebecca Jane. "Revisiting the Khanna Study: Population and Development in India, 1953–1960." Ph.D. diss., University of Warwick, 2013.

"Storming the Citadels of Poverty: Family Planning under the Emergency in India, 1975–1977." *The Journal of Asian Studies* 73, no. 2 (May 2014): 471–492.

Wiser, Charlotte Viall. *The Foods of a Hindu Village of North India*. 2nd edn. Bureau of Statistics and Economic Research, United Provinces. Allahabad: Superintendent, Printing and Stationery, United Provinces, 1937.

Wiser, William Henricks. *The Hindu Jajmani System*. Lucknow: Lucknow Publishing House, 1936.

Worboys, Michael. "The Discovery of Colonial Malnutrition between the Wars." In *Imperial Medicine and Indigenous Societies*, edited by David Arnold, 208–225. Manchester: Manchester University Press, 1998.

Wyatt, Andrew. "Building the Temples of Postmodern India: Economic Constructions of National Identity." *Contemporary South Asia* 14, no. 4 (December 2005): 465–480.

Yapa, Lakshaman. "What Are Improved Seeds? An Epistemology of the Green Revolution." *Economic Geography* 69, no. 3 (1993): 254–273.

Zachariah, Benjamin. *Developing India: An Intellectual and Social History, c. 1930–50*. New Delhi: Oxford University Press, 2005.

"Uses of Scientific Argument: The Case of 'Development' in India, c. 1930–1950." *Economic and Political Weekly* 36, no. 39 (2001): 3689–3702.

Zaidi, A.M., ed., *INC: The Glorious Tradition: Texts of the Resolutions Passed by the INC, the AICC and the CWC*. New Delhi: Indian Institute of Applied Political Research, 1989.

Zaidi, A.M., and S.G. Zaidi, eds., "Congress Working Committee, Bombay, March 12–15, 1946." In *The Encyclopaedia of Indian National Congress*, vol. 12: *A Fight to the Finish*: 495–496. New Delhi: S. Chand / Indian Institute of Applied Political Research, 1981.

Zamindar, Vazira Fazila-Yacoobali. *The Long Partition and the Making of Modern South Asia: Refugees, Boundaries, Histories.* New York: Columbia University Press, 2007.

Zimmermann, Francis. *The Jungle and the Aroma of Meats: An Ecological Theme in Hindu Medicine.* Berkeley: University of California Press, 1987.

Zook, Darren C. "Famine in the Landscape: Imagining Hunger in South Asian History, 1860–1990." In *India's Environmental History: Colonialism, Modernity, and the Nation,* edited by Mahesh Rangarajan and K. Sivaramakrishnan, vol. 2: 400–428. Ranikhet: Permanent Black, 2012.

Zutshi, C.N. *Starving India under the Ægis of Great Britain.* Muzaffarnagar, 1925.

Zweiniger-Bargielowska, Ina. *Austerity in Britain: Rationing, Controls, and Consumption, 1939–1955.* Oxford: Oxford University Press, 2000.

Index

Aadhar smart ID card scheme, 223
Abbas, K.A., 39–41
Abdul Latif Jameel Poverty Action
    Lab, 224
Abedin, Zainul, 37
Abel, Martin, 216
Abhyankar, N.G., 61
Acheson, Dean, 185
advertising, 71, 209
Agrarian Reforms Committee (1946), 158
agricultural credit, 176, 197
    from the *baniya* (creditor), 7
    impeded access to, 217
    in Kisan Sabha analysis, 155
    in the Bengal famine, 26
    in the United States, 184
    institutional support from the United
        States, 148, 169
    M.R. Masani's support for
        cooperative, 174
Agricultural Prices Commission, 226, 227
agriculture
    budget in First Five-Year Plan, 161
    ideologies of improvement, 185, 200
    imagery of, 225–226
    inputs, 154, 185, 200, 203
Ahmad, Ijaz, 59
Ahmad, Ziauddin, 56
Alexander, Horace, 41
All India Agricultural Federation, 175
All India Anna Dravida Munnetra
    Kazhagam (AIADMK), 224
All India Institute of Medical Science, 195
All India Radio
    C. Rajagopalachari's address on
        unilateral decontrol in Madras
        on, 133
    colonial officials' addresses on, 42, 58
    Herbert Hoover's address on, 58
    Indira Gandhi's address on, 204
    Jawaharlal Nehru's addresses on, 70,
        100, 104, 110

Lal Bahadur Shastri's address on, 149
    Rajendra Prasad's address on, 60
    rationing officials' addresses on,
        124, 130
All India Radio Jawaharlal Nehru's
    addresses on, 71, 76
All India School of Hygiene and Public
    Health, 193
All India Trade Union Congress, 123
Allahabad, 141
    protests and strikes in, 54
Allahabad Agricultural Institute, 191, 193
Ambedkar, B.R.
    and Dalit refugees, 65
    and Republican Party of India, 181
    Dalit fast in name of, 214
Amery, Lord Leo, 42
Amma Canteens, 224
Ananthasayanam, M., 78
Andhra Pradesh
    1951 elections in, 161
    new agricultural strategy in, 209
Annadurai, C.N., 214
Annapoorna (restaurant), 110
anthropology of food in South Asia,
    16–17, 91
Apte, Hari Narayan, 10
Argentina
    CPI criticism of wheat surplus in, 61
    foodgrain imports from, 74
    Indian mission to, 58
artificial rice, 88, 97, 106
    trials in Kerala, 106
astrology, 203
Aurangabad, 229
Australia, foodgrain imports from, 94, 139
Aykroyd, Wallace R.
    and dietary transformation, 95
    and the Bihar famine (1966), 207
    and the Woodhead Commission, 43
    and women, 108
Azad, Maulana, 44, 115

267

268 Index

Bachchan, Amitabh, 222
Bachchan, Harivansh Rai, 21, 49
Bajpai, G.S., 57, 185, 221
Bal Ahar (infant food), 207
Bandyopadhyay, Manik, 39
Bandyopadhyay, Tarasankar, 39, 160
baniya (creditor), 7
Baroda, strikes and protests in, 61
Basu, Jyoti, 22
below poverty line threshold, 222
Bengal famine (1943)
    American Famine Mission to India,
        58, 183
    and Axis propaganda, 34
    and drafting of postwar food plan, 44
    and theater, 40
    as demonstration of India's depleted
        health, 51
    as impetus for economic
        planning, 79, 83
    as impetus to move away from
        cereals, 93
    cyclone in Midnapore district, 27
    denial policy, 26
    historiography of, 24
    hunger marchers, 21
    in film and theater, 39–41
    in Kisan Sabha analysis, 155
    literature and poetry, 21, 34, 39, 47
    philanthropy, 27
    private relief efforts, 32, 33, 34, 36
    prostitution, 37
    Ram Nath Puri's account of the, 1
    reception in the United Kingdom, 41
Bengal Famine (1943)
    hunger marchers, 28
beriberi, 188
Bharat versus India, 230
Bharatiya Janata Party, 223
Bharatiya Vidya Bhavan, 86
Bhargava, Thakurdas, 77
Bharti-Walmart, 224
Bhattacharjee, Kalyani, 36
Bhattacharya, Bhabani, 47
Bhattacharya, Bijon, 40
Bhave, Vinoba. *See Bhoodan* movement
Bhoodan movement, 163–165
Bihar, 87
    protests and strikes in, 133
Bihar famine (1966), 204–208
    and family planning inducements,
        207
    short tether policy, 212
Biswas, C.C., 32
Biswas, Hemango, 39

Bombay, 53, 60
    All India Women's Council for
        Supplementary Foods work in, 110
    corruption among food officials in, 75
    exhibitions in, 110
    farmers' protests in, 229
    Food Advisory Committee, 139
    introduction of rationing in, 121
    protests and strikes in, 53, 121, 144
    rationing in, 124
    reintroduction of food control in, 130
    response to Bengal famine in, 30, 40
Bombay (State). *See* Maharashtra
Bombay Plan (1944), 46, 51, 52, 97
Borlaug, Norman, 201, 217
Bose, Subhas Chandra, 34, 92
Bourke, Richard (Lord Mayo), 187
Bowles, Chester, 144, 189
Boyd-Orr, Lord John, 70
Bradlee, Ben, 41
Brando, Marlon, 206
British Indian Association, 122
Buck, Pearl, 58
buffer stock, 88, 136–137, 142
bullock capitalists. *See* new farmers'
        movement
Burma, 26, 94

Cabinet Mission (1946), 40, 59
Calcutta, 29, 37, 65
    1946 recurrance of shortages, 54
    American troops in, 28
    Chinese community of, 33
    colonial excesses in, 25
    Direct Action Day, 59
    early rationing efforts in, 93
    hunger marchers in, 21
    private relief efforts in, 34
    protests and strikes in, 125, 144
    rationing in, 29
    School of Tropical Medicine, 193
    staging of Bengal famine theater in, 40
California Hindu Farmers' Association, 2
cartoons
    anti-colonial, 10, 28
    anti-Communist, 36
    of Jairamdas Daulatram, 71, 75
    of Jawaharlal Nehru, 173
    of K.M. Munshi, 87, 112
    on the Bengal famine, 37
Casey, Richard, 26, 42
caste
    and agricultural planning, 74, 83
    and feeding in refugee camps, 65
    and Green Revolution violence, 213

Index

and land reform, 160, 163
and nutritional outcomes, 218
and relief camps in the Bihar
famine, 207
correlation with malnutrition, 221
in the new farmers' movement, 230
censorship
of anti-colonial materials, 1
of anti-rationing sentiment, 122
of Bengal famine materials, 28,
30, 32, 33
Central Food Advisory Council, 27
Central Food Technological Research
Institute (CFTRI), 104, 106
Central Rice Research Institute,
Cuttack, 201
Chakravarty, Vasudha, 24, 36
Chalam, G.V., 201
Chandra, Jag Parvesh. *See* Miss a Meal
movement
Chattopadhyay, Kamaladevi, 46, 63
China, People's Republic of, 168
agricultural collectivization in, 164,
169, 171
agricultural economics in, 169
foodgrain imports from, 169
Indian delegations to, 138, 169, 170
influence on Indian agricultural
planning, 15, 154, 196
invasion of Tibet, 168, 176
nutritional comparison with
India, 222
Rockefeller Foundation projects
in, 193
Chittaprosad (Chittaprosad
Bhattacharya), 37
Circular-i-Azadi, 1
cloud seeding. *See* Project GROMET
Combined Food Board,
Washington DC, 54
Communist Party of India, 4, 25, 30
and criticism of P.L. 480, 136
and land reform, 140, 159
and rationing, 121, 132
and the *Bhoodan* movement, 164
criticism of Interim Government's food
administration, 61
criticism of substitute food drive, 112
founding of, 24
in Bengal, 30
in Kerala, 167, 204
joint protest with other parties, 54
protests and strikes, 144
relief efforts in Bengal, 34
student leaders in London, 22

Sunil Janah's photography for the, 37
wartime collaboration with the British,
22, 23, 36
Communist Party of India (Marxist), 213
Community Development, 177, 189,
198, 203
and the *Bhoodan* movement, 165
Compton, Karl Taylor, 193
Congress Working Committee, 92, 96
Constituent Assembly debates, 77–79, 222
cooperative agriculture, 162, 170, 174, 198
in Israel, 177
in Yugoslavia, 177
support of Jawaharlal Nehru, 158
versus collective agriculture, 178
corn (maize)
as substitute food, 97
in Illinois, 183, 200
in rations, 95, 96
Indian research on hybrid varieties of,
194, 195
planting by Jawaharlal Nehru, 101
Rockefeller Foundation research in
Mexico on hybrid varieties of, 201
Rockefeller Foundation's work on
Indian, 194
corruption, 36, 75, 126, 203
Council of Scientific and Industrial
Research, 99
crop lodging, 201
Cultural Workers' Committee for Fighting
Famine (Bombay), 53
Cummings, Ralph W., 194
Curzon, Lord George Nathaniel, 25, 188

Dalit Panthers, 214
Damodar Valley Project, 68
dams, 51, 80, 228
Dantwala, M.L., 158, 162, 198
Darling, Malcolm, 156
Das, Bhubanananda, 78
dates, imported from Iraq as substitute
food, 104
Daulatram, Jairamdas
and refugees, 65
Communist censure of, 112
correspondence with Jawaharlal
Nehru, 102
Jawaharlal Nehru's complaints about, 100
parliamentary censure, 68
satire of, 68, 75
Delhi
exhibitions in, 110
farmers' protests in, 229
flag raising in, 3

270   Index

Delhi (*cont.*)
  Food and Nutrition Exhibition in, 98
  opening of Annapoorna restaurant in, 110
  planting of food crops in, 100
  rationing in, 123
  refugees in, 18, 53, 65
  Vinoba Bhave's 1951 trip to, 164
Department of Food, 1943
    establishment of, 29
derivative discourse, Indian nationalism
    as a, 14
Desai, Morarji, 144, 195, 227
Development Advisory Office (Harvard
    University), 199
Dey, S.K., 166
Dharti ke Lal (1946 K.A. Abbas
    film), 39–41
dietary transformation, 51, 87, 88
  and women, 108–111
  putative impossibility of, 203
Dodd, Norris, 70
domestic science, 108
drain of wealth theory, 9
Drèze, Jean, 221
drought
  in Bihar, 204
  in Bombay and the Deccan, 53
  in Kerala, 204
dual burden (of obesity and malnutrition),
    6, 222, 224
Dufferin Enquiry (1888), 8
Dutt, Rajani Palme, 40, 41
Dutt, Romesh Chunder, 10, 220

economics and economists, 61, 67, 69, 79,
    80, 81, 92, 93, 96, 114, 122, 126,
    127, 130, 150, 159, 169, 171, 172,
    179, 183, 190, 199, 214, 215, 216,
    220, 221, 223
  and drafting of the Bombay Plan, 46
  and economic nationalism, 14
  assessment of Bengal famine, 25
  assessment of colonial malnutrition, 46
  British experts, 44
  late nineteenth-century, 9
Egypt, foodgrain imports from, 74
Eisenhower, Dwight D., 192
elections, 1951–1952, 161
elections, 1962, 177
Enlai, Zhou, 171
Ensminger, Douglas, 196, 197, 199
entitlement theory, 23, 231
equity, as guiding principle in Indian
    planning, 162, 187
Essential Commodities Act, 134–136, 146

Etawah, 193
Ethiopia, Indian efforts to secure aid
    from, 59
exhibitions on food and nutrition, 94,
    98, 110
expertise, 15

fair price shops, 139, 206, 226
Famine Inquiry Commission (1944), 25
famines (pre-1943), 5, 7, 9
  "Great Famine" of 1876–1878, 188
  in western India, 220
  Mughal relief efforts, 7
farmer suicides, 225
fertilizers, 79, 82, 210
  absence of funding for in Rajendra
    Prasad's first food plan, 61
  and the Planning Comission, 162
  as substitute for cow dung, 51
  in *Report on India's Food Crisis and Steps
    to Meet It* (1959), 197
film
  and substitute foods, 95
  and the new agricultural strategy, 210
  and the reversal of decontrol, 130
  at the 1959 World Agriculture Fair, 192
  contemporary, 225
  touring cinema vans, 71
Five-Year Plans
  First Five-Year Plan (1951–1956), 113,
    114, 117, 131
  First Five-Year Plan
    (1951–1956), 52, 77
  First Five-Year Plan (1951–1956), 161
  First Five-Year Plan (1951–1956), 162
  Second Five-Year Plan (1956-1961),
    138, 140
  Second Five-Year Plan
    (1956–1961), 166
  Second Five-Year Plan
    (1956–1961), 166
  Second Five-Year Plan
    (1956–1961), 170
  Second Five-Year Plan
    (1956–1961), 173
  Third Five-Year Plan (1961–1966), 198
Food and Agriculture Organization, 45,
    63, 199, 221
food control
  and restaurants, 139
  costs of, 131
  court cases concerning, 119–120
  decontrol experiment (1948), 127–130
  objections to, 120, 122, 139, 141, 143
  popular contempt for, 125, 132

Index

271

protests and strikes against, 124
regulation of foodgrains movement, 131, 139
religious petitions for exemptions from, 141
violations of, 119–120
Food Corporation of India, 115, 147–149, 226
food surplus, Indian, 6, 220, 231
foodgrain imports
  decision to end by 1951, 68–76
  from Argentina, 74
  from Australia, 94, 139
  from China, 169
  from Egypt, 74
  from Indonesia, 59
  from Iran, 59, 63, 74
  from Iraq, 63
  from Morocco, 74
  from Pakistan, 146
  from Southeast Asia, 139
  from the Soviet Union, 74
  from the United States, 60, 136–137
  from Turkey, 60
  from Yugoslavia, 74
  record amounts in 1949, 67
Foodgrains Enquiry Committee (1957), 114, 138
Foodgrains Policy Committee (1943), 44, 93, 97, 122
Foodgrains Policy Committee (1947)
  as antecedent to Subsidiary Food Production Committee, 105
  assessment of wartime Grow More Food campaign, 69
  call for removal of food controls, 67
  Communist criticism of, 112
  establishment of, 97
  Gandhi's support for, 127
Foodgrains Procurement Committee (1950), 75, 133
Foodgrains Stabilization Organization, 139
Ford Foundation, 189, 190, 195–200
foreign direct investment, 223, 225
foreign exchange, 3, 69, 80, 87, 139
Fox River Valley (Illinois), 183
Frankel, Francine, 215
French, Henry
  and B.R. Sen, 42
  and rationing, 41
  and the Bengal famine, 42

G.B. Pant University of Agriculture and Technology, 192
Gadgil, N.V., 134

Gandhi, Indira, 203
  1977 electoral defeat, 227
  and Bihar famine (1966), 205
  and famine in Kerala, 204
  and nationalization of the wheat trade, 226
  and populist campaigning, 214, 226
  and Project GROMET, 207
  and the founding of the Women's Food Committee, 110
  and tours of vegetable gardens, 101
Gandhi, Mohandas K.
  1915 tour of India, 36
  and development models, 5
  and refugees, 65
  and self-discipline, 103, 129
  and Vinoba Bhave, 163
  assassination of, 67, 129
  confluence with liberal thought, 120
  fast to protest partition, 63
  Gandhian economists, 79
  release from prison, 44
  suggestions for meeting the 1946 food crisis, 56
  support for decontrol, 67, 98, 127–128, 129
  village republic model, 79
Gandhi, Sonia, 223
Gandhian economics. *See* Kumarappa, J.C.
Gangulee, Nagendranath, 12, 41
garibi hatao, 214
Gaud, William, 212
Ghosh, Ajoy, 164
Ghosh, Kali Charan, 43
Global Hunger Index, 221
Godavari district
  1945 cyclone in, 53
  black marketeering in, 119
  colonial investments in agriculture in, 187
  new agricultural strategy in, 209
Goel, Sita Ram, 168
Gokhale, Gopal Krishna, 36
Gorwala, A.D., 56, 128
Great Bengal Famine (1770), 7
Great Depression, 11, 21, 155
Green Revolution
  access to technologies, 231
  and inequity, 214
  and William Gaud's naming, 212
  as alleged precursor to communism, 6
  Nobel Peace Prize (1970) to Norman Borlaug for work on, 217
  traditional accounts of, 186

272 Index

Gregory, Theodore, 93, 122
Grow More Food campaign (1942), 27, 52, 69
Grow More Food campaign (1949), 69–73, 100
growing of foodcrops in government buildings, 71
guest control orders, 101, 105, 112
Guha, Sunil, 171
Gupta, Akhil, 224

Haldar, Gopal, 39
Han-seng, Chen, 169
Henderson, Loy, 75
Herbert, John, 26
Higginbottom, Sam, 193
Hill, A.V., 44
Hindu Mahasabha, 30, 47, 102
  coalition with the Muslim League in Bengal, 26
  conflict with Muslim League and Communist Party in Bengal, 25
  joint protest with other parties, 54
hoarding, 32, 135
  and decontrol, 128
  and inflation, 76
  and the Essential Commodities Act, 136
  as alleged cause of Bengal famine, 29
  at independence, 4
  demand of death penalty for, 37
  in the wake of farmers' capture of the Agricultural Prices Commission, 226
  Lal Bahadur Shastri's efforts to combat, 146
Hoffman, Paul, 195
home economics, 94, 191
Hoover, Herbert, 58
Hopper, W. David, 199
Howard, Albert, 188
hunger in contemporary India, statistics, 220–222
Huq, Fazlul, 26, 27, 29
Husain, M. Afzal, 96
Hutchings, Robert, 54, 59

improved seeds, 197, 201
India International Centre, 195
India League, 41
Indian Agricultural Research Institute (IARI), 225
  basic research after independence, 68
  creation of graduate school of agriculture, 195
  establishment of dwarf wheat breeding program, 201

founding as Imperial Agricultural Research Institute, 11, 188
funding by the Rockefeller Foundation, 195
work of B. Sen at the, 216
Indian Air Force, 64
Indian Council of Agricultural Research, 3, 196, 202
  founding as Imperial Council of Agricultural Research, 188
Indian Council of Agricultural Research (ICAR), 68
Indian food missions, 4
Indian Institute of Sciences, 97
Indian Medical Service, 11, 91
Indian National Congress
  1950 power struggle within the, 162
  and development planning, 95
  and violence in Thanjavur (Tanjore) district, 213
  conflict with Muslim League and Hindu Mahasabha in Bengal, 25
  defeat in 2014 elections, 222
  expectations upon the, 12, 57
  fallout from Nagpur resolution, 178
  popular criticism of, 74, 83
  release of leadership, 44
  theater, 152
  underground units in the Bengal famine (1943), 28
  wartime detention, 27
Indian onion crisis (2010), 225
Indian People's Theater Association, 40
Indian Science Congress, 61, 96
Indonesia, foodgrain imports from, 59
industrialization, 216
  as inimical to India's agrarian character, 227
Institute of Political and Social Studies (Calcutta), 175
Intensive Agricultural District Program (IADP), 198–200
interim government, 59, 61
International Emergency Food Council, 60, 61, 126
International Monetary Fund, 130
International Rice Research Institute, 201
Iran, foodgrain imports from, 59, 63, 74
Iraq
  dates from, 104
  foodgrain imports from, 63
irrigation, 210
  colonial schemes in Punjab, 187
  demand for investment in, 61
  economists' support for improved, 81

Index

in *Report on India's Food Crisis and Steps to Meet It* (1959), 197
in the Grow More Food campaign (1942), 69
merchants' plans for better, 82
provisions for in the draft First Five-Year Plan, 162
Islam, Kazi Nazrul, 39
Ispahani, M.A.H., 29, 47
Israel
 cooperative agriculture in, 169, 175, 177
 Indian mission to, 177
Italy, hunger marchers in, 28

jai jawan, jai kisan [Long live the solider and the farmer!], 115, 225
Jain, A.P.
 and artificial rice, 107n. 116
 and China, 138
 and cooperative agriculture, 171
 and famine in Kerala, 204
 and Foodgrains Enquiry Committee (1957), 138
 and state trading in foodgrains, 140
 and Swatantra party, 178
 and the Indian farmer, 200
 appointment as Food Minister, 138
 criticism of C. Subramaniam, 145
 resignation of, 140, 176
 victory over C. Subramaniam, 176
jajmani system, 8
Jalees, Ibrahim, 39
Jana Sangh, 177, 178
 and state trading in foodgrains, 140
 efforts to abolish the Food Corporation of India, 148
Janah, Sunil, 37
Janata Party government (1977–1979), 227
Japan, new agricultural methods from, 18
Jayalalithaa, 224
Jha, L.K., 146, 202
Jinnah, Muhammad Ali, 31, 57, 59
Johnson, Lyndon, 205, 212
Johnson, Sherman, 197, 198
Joshi, P.C., 36, 37, 98, 140
Joshi, Sharad, 228
journalism, 33, 36

Kabir, Humayun, 22, 31
Kamaraj, K., 148
kans grass, 68
Karnal, 124
Kashmir, 136
Kaur, Rajkumari Amrit, 102, 194
Kenya and Tanganyika, Indians in, 35

Kerala
 1951 elections in, 161
 1966 rice shortage in, 204
 Agrarian Relations Act, 178
 anti-landlord sentiment, 167
 civic restaurants in, 94
 dock worker strike, 146
 Kerala Agrarian Relations Bill, 167
 new agricultural strategy in, 209
 rationing in, 124
 trials of artificial rice in, 106
 use of substitute foods in wartime, 106
 wartime shortages in, 28
Kesari (Marathi-language newspaper), 10
Keynes, John Maynard, 93
Khaitan, Debi Prasad, 93
Khandesh district, 73
Khanna, H.L., 63
Kirby, W.H., 93, 122, 123
kisan raj, 157
Kisan Sabha, 44, 155, 159
kitchen gardens, 109
Kizhavenmani. *See* Thanjavur (Tanjore) district, 1968 massacre in
Kolhapur, 50
Kripalani, J.B., 162
Krishak Praja Party, 26, 30
Krishnamachari, T.T., 140, 202
Krishnamachari, V.T., 197
Kumarappa, J.C., 80, 158, 164
Kumbh Mela, feeding of pilgrims at the, 141
Kunzru, H.N., 78

Ladejinsky, Wolf, 179, 216
Lady Irwin College, 94
Lahore, 1, 34
land ceilings, 160, 162, 168, 179, 181
land reform
 abolition of *zamindari*, 154, 156, 158, 160
 and Communist Party of India, 140
 failure of, 179
 ineffectiveness of, 160
 tension between growth and equity, 154
Lee-Warner, William, 89
liberalization, 231
 and impact on hunger, 223
literature and poetry
 and *kisan raj*, 156
 and the Bengal famine, 21, 34, 39
 and the Miss a Meal movement, 103n. 89
 medieval Jain, 7
 on the *baniya*, 7
 Telugu, 7
Lucknow, 124
 protests and strikes in, 54, 61

274 Index

Madras (Chennai), 3, 210
Mahajan, Mehar Chand, 135
Mahalanobis, P.C., 171
  and Bengal famine statistics, 36
  and Rockefeller Foundation, 193
  and Second Five-Year Plan
    (1956–1961), 138
  and Second Five-Year Plan
    (1956–1961), 166
  and Second Five-Year Plan
    (1956–1961), 171
Maharashtra, 53
  withholding of crops in, 132
Malabar. *See* Kerala
malnutrition, 51
  and liberalization, 231
  childhood, 221
  colonial surveys, 11, 91
  comparative indicators, 6
  in refugee camps, 66
  in Thanjavur (Tanjore) district, 218
Masani, M.R.
  address to Bombay's Commerce
    Graduates' Association, 143
  and the Bengal famine, 35
  assault on cooperative farming, 174
  condemnation of colonial
    government, 56
Mathai, John, 48, 127
Mathai, M.O., 112
Mayer, Albert, 193
Megaw, John, 11, 91
Mehta, Ashok. *See* Foodgrains Enquiry
    Committee (1957)
Mehta, G.L., 78
Menon, V.K. Krishna, 41, 63
merchants' groups
  All Indian Muslim Chamber of
    Commerce and Industry, 121
  Andhra Chamber of Commerce, 114, 132
  Andhra Pradesh Federation of
    Chambers of Commerce and
    Industry, 142
  Bombay Grain Dealers' Association, 121
  Federation of All India Foodgrain
    Dealers' Associations, 143, 148
  Federation of Indian Chambers of
    Commerce and Industry, 100, 115
  Gujarat Vepari Mahamandal, 148
  Indian Chamber of Commerce, 93
  Indian Grain Dealers' Federation, 141
  Indian Merchants' Chamber, 56, 61,
    127, 138, 143, 147
  Ismaili, 121
  Madurai-Ramnad Chamber of
    Commerce, 147, 148

Marwari Chamber of Commerce, 82
Muslim Grain Merchants'
    Association, 121
Southern India Chamber of
    Commerce, 181
Mexico
  Communist Party of, 24
  cooperative agriculture in, 175
  Indian seed mission to, 201
  Rockefeller Foundation hybrid maize
    program in, 194
midday meal scheme, 224
Midnapore district, 27
Military Evacuation Organization, 64
Ministries of Food and Agriculture
  and distribution of Iraqi dates, 104
  and food control, 67
  and food imports, 64, 74, 86
  and Grow More Food campaign
    (1949), 97
  and guest control orders, 101
  and planting of food crops in Delhi, 100
  and rationing, 131
  and restrictions on movement of
    food, 139
  and substitute foods, 97, 105, 110, 114
  and the Ford Foundation, 199
  and the Miss a Meal movement, 104
  and the *Report on India's Food Crisis and
    Steps to Meet It* (1959), 198
  as impossible government posting, 145
  assumption of control by Rajendra
    Prasad, 59
  confidential analysis by Food Ministry
    officials, 76
  corruption in the, 75
  creation of extension wing within, 190
  disagreement between wings over
    agricultural targets, 69, 100
  leadership vacuum under Jairamdas
    Daulatram, 68
  mission to Iraq and Iran, 63
  petitions to, 61, 140
  procurement efforts by, 139
  publicity efforts, 130, 161
  Rajendra Prasad's first address to the, 60
  request for Rockefeller Foundation
    assistance, 194
  victory of C. Subramaniam over Sanjiva
    Reddy, 144
Ministry of Finance, 194, 202
Ministry of Home Affairs, 32, 75
Ministry of Information and Broadcasting,
    98, 212
Miss a Meal movement, 102–104,
    112–113

Index

Miss a Meal movement, 115
modernization theory, 45, 200
monsoon, failure of the 1965, 204
Mookherjee, Shyama Prasad, 30
Moradabadi, Jigar, 39
moral economy, 8
Morocco, foodgrain imports from, 74
Mudaliar, A. Ramaswami, 56, 57
Mudaliar, A.L., 112
Mugali, R.S., 39
Mukerjee, Radhakamal, 12, 92
multipurpose food, 206
Munshi, K.M.
  adoption of religious idioms, 89
  and 1950–1951 shortages, 87
  and cooperative farming, 174
  and dietary transformation, 87
  and food control, 132
  and hybrid corn breeding, 194
  and women, 87
  appointment as Food Minister, 75
  critique of colonial rule, 44
  decision to end foodgrain imports by
    1951, 76
  early career, 86
  famine denial, 75
  popular contempt for, 87, 112
  Van Mahotsav (tree-planting
    campaign), 86
Munshi, Lilavati, 110
Muslim League
  1946 return to power, 47
  Bengal famine publicity efforts, 42
  Bengal famine relief, 22
  call for Direct Action Day, 59
  conflict with Hindu Mahasabha and
    Indian National Congress in
    Bengal, 25
  conflict with other parties, 30
  formation of new government in April
    1943, 29
  joint protest with other parties, 54
  meeting with American Famine Mission
    to India, 58
  Muhammad Ali Jinnah's
    defense of, 31
  perceived misadministration, 23
Myrdal, Gunnar, 179

Nagarjun, 39, 160
Nagpur resolution, 197
  and Jawaharlal Nehru's diminished
    authority, 141, 176
  as reaffirmation of existing Second
    Five-Year Plan commitments to
    cooperative joint farming, 173

Charan Singh's contempt for the,
  174, 227
impact on Congress planning, 176
Naidu, Gopalakrishna, 212
Nair, Kusum, 168, 172
Namboodiripad, E.M.S., 204
Nanavati, Manilal, 43, 46
Nanda, Gulzarilal, 171, 178
Naoroji, Dadabhai, 9, 220
Narayan, Jayaprakash
  and the Bengal famine, 31
  and the *Bhoodan* movement, 164, 165
  and the Bihar Relief Committee, 206
Narayan, Shriman, 165
Narayan, T.G., 37
National Development Council, 138, 140
National Food Security Act (2013),
  222–223
National Institute of Science, 92
National Institute of Virology, Pune, 195
National Planning Committee, 48, 96, 108
Nazimuddin, Khawaja, 29, 57
Nehru, Jawaharlal
  1949 trip to the United States, 73,
    183–185
  addresses on food, 61, 69, 70, 71, 76,
    100, 104, 110
  and All India Institute of Food
    Technology, 99
  and artificial foods, 99
  and China, 168
  and Congress Working Committee, 92
  and Constituent Assembly debates, 77
  and cooperative agriculture, 140,
    158, 167
  and decontrol, 134
  and Gandhian language, 99
  and Indian Science Congress, 61
  and National Development Council, 140
  and National Planning
    Committee, 48, 96
  and planting of food crops in Delhi, 100
  and sacrifice, 56, 102, 114, 117
  and substitute foods, 100, 101
  and the Bengal famine, 23, 48, 54
  and the Indian peasantry, 36
  and women, 109, 111
  appointment of Swaran Singh, 142
  campaign for self-sufficency by 1951, 74
  criticism of, 74, 75, 112
  death, 143
  development models, 79
  diminished authority in the wake of the
    Nagpur Resolution, 141
  discussions with Vinoba Bhave, 164
  goal of self-sufficiency by 1951, 106

276   Index

Nehru, Jawaharlal (*cont.*)
J.C. Kumarappa's criticism of, 80
letters to Chief Ministers, 88
Life magazine photo shoot, 196
planting food at Teen Murti Bhavan, 101
popular expectations of, 12
release from prison, 44
tryst with destiny speech, 3, 62
Nehru, Rameshwari, 108
new agricultural strategy, 117, 176, 186, 202, 203, 208–219
new farmers' movement, 228
Nichols, Beverly, 94
NITI Aayog, 225
Niyogi, Jnananjan, 43
Nutrition Research Laboratories, 11, 90, 95

obesity. *See* dual burden (of obesity and malnutrition)
oilseeds, export of, 51
Oxfam, 206

Pai, T.A., 115
Pakistan
1965 war with India, 114, 148
and Kashmir, 136
and productive land, 3, 62, 64
and the FAO, 59
foodgrain imports from, 146
Hindu Mahasabha linking of Bengal famine with demand for, 47
negotiations over wheat payment, 64
nutritional comparison with India, 221
refugees from, 65
Pal, B.P., 201, 202
Paliwal, K.D., 157
pamphlets, 51
anti-colonial Urdu language, 10
government-issued, 42, 95, 129, 161, 192
Hindi-language, 18, 48
on famines, 220
on nutrition, 67
on the Bengal famine, 31, 41
on the food problem, 50, 68, 73, 82, 83
Panchayat Raj, 173, 203
Pant, Pitamber, 198, 218
partition, 64, 81
Patel, Sardar Vallabhbhai, 44, 113, 161, 162
Patil, R.K.
and planting food at Teen Murti Bhavan, 101n. 76
appointment as Commissioner for Food Production, 70

Delegation to China on Agrarian Cooperatives, 170
publicity photographs of, 73
satire of, 75
Patil, S.K., 141
Peepli Live (2010 Anusha Rizvi film), 225
People's Age, 37, 61, 62, 112
Permanent Settlement (1792), 154
philanthropy, 48
and the Bengal famine, 27, 58
and the Bihar famine (1966), 206
Philippines, improved rice strains from the, 202
photography, 32
and government publicity of agricultural improvement efforts, 73, 196
and the Bengal famine, 33, 37, 48, 54
Pillai, K. Shankar. *See* Shankar's Weekly
Planning Commission, 174, 177, 197, 218
2014 abolition of, 225
and Chinese expertise, 169, 170
and cooperative agriculture, 140
and Daniel Thorner, 172
and Douglas Ensminger, 197
and land reform, 166
and P.L. 480, 142
and resources devoted to agriculture, 198
and support prices, 138
and T.T. Krishnamachari, 203
and the *Bhoodan* movement, 164
and the Bihar famine, 205
and the new agricultural stratregy, 145
and Vinoba Bhave, 163
establishment of the, 88, 160, 161
Lal Bahadur Shastri's efforts to diminish the influence of the, 202
Point Four Program, 185, 189
Pope Paul VI, 205
population, 11, 85, 89
Praja Socialist Party, 177
Prasad, Rajendra, 84, 133
addresses on food, 60, 128
and exhibitions on food and nutrition, 98, 110
and Miss a Meal Movement, 102
and substitute food, 106
and the Agrarian Reforms Committee, 158
and the Subsidiary Food Production Committee, 104
appointment of Foodgrains Policy Committee, 97
assumption of control of Food Ministry, 59
communication with V.K. Krishna Menon, 63

Index

critique of food imports, 59
petition to, 125
pledge to Vinoba Bhave, 164
speech at Indian Council of
Agricultural Research at
independence, 3, 62
Premji, M.H. Hasham, 143, 149
preventable deaths, estimates of, 224
prison diets, 188
procurement, 67, 74
protests and strikes
by the new farmers' movement, 228
colonial grain riots, 8
in Allahabad, 54
in Baroda, 61
in Bihar, 133
in Bombay, 53, 121, 128, 144
in Calcutta, 125, 144
in Kerala, 146
in Lucknow, 54, 61
in Punjab, 54, 124
in refugee camps, 65, 66
in Tamil Nadu, 53
over foreign direct investment, 225
Public Distribution System, 231
Public Law 480, 136–137, 138, 139, 141,
142, 181
publicity, government, 51, 94
of substitute foods, 95, 98, 107
of the Grow More Food campaign
(1949), 71
of the new agricultural strategy, 210
of the reversal of decontrol, 130
on the possibility of food riots, 3
Punjab, 1
colonial investments in agriculture
in, 187
new agricultural strategy in, 215
protests and strikes in, 54, 124
question of social disruption in, 215
Puri, Ram Nath, 1

Quetta, 122

Radhakrishnan, Sarvepalli, 144
railways, 32, 35, 53, 62, 83, 119, 121, 126,
148, 229
Rajagopalachari, C.
and Constituent Assembly Debates, 77
and food imports, 69
and founding of Swatantra Party, 175
and Grow More Food campaign, 100
and substitute foods, 100, 105
and transfer of power to popular
leaders, 31
correspondence with constituents, 174

influence on new farmers'
movement, 229
support for decontrol, 113, 133
Ramamurthy, Sonti, 56, 57, 58, 104, 106
Ranadive, B.T., 123
Ranga, N.G., 84, 175
and cooperative agriculture, 174
and *kisan raj*, 157
and the Agrarian Reforms Committee
(1946), 158, 159
and the Swatantra party, 175
leadership of the All India Kisan
Sabha, 155
Rao, V.K.R.V., 198, 214
rare earth minerals, 73
Rather, Dan, 195
rationing, 53
addresses on, 123
collapse of, 131, 132
estimates of extent of, 126
expansion of, 131
in Bombay, 124
in Calcutta, 29
in Kerala, 124
in Tamil Nadu, 124
Indira Gandhi and, 204
introduction in Bombay, 121
involuntary mixing of grains, 123
protests and strikes against, 124
ration cards, 19, 41, 83, 121, 124, 128,
206, 223, 228
Ray, Prithwis Chandra, 220
Reddy, Sanjiva, 144
refugees, 4, 18, 67
*Report on India's Food Crisis and Steps to
Meet It* (1959), 198
*Report on the Improvement of Indian
Agriculture* (1893), 11, 188
restaurants, and food control, 139
rice
improved varieties of, 201, 208,
209, 210
mill nationalization proposal, 143
milling of, 91
purported non-interchangability of, 95
Taichung Native One, 201
right to food legislation, 222
rights, 88, 103, 107
and the responsibilities of women, 109
and the responsibilities of women, 114
Rockefeller Foundation, 189, 192–195
Roosevelt, Franklin D., 36, 45
Rostow, Walt, 200
Roy, B.C., 102
Roy, Bidhan Chandra, 34
Roy, Bimal, 159

278 Index

Roy, M.N., 24, 31
Royal Agri-Horticultural Society, 187
Royal Commission on Agriculture
(1926), 188
Royal Commission on Indian Agriculture
(1928), 12, 41
Rusk, Dean, 194, 195, 196

sacrifice
government publicity to encourage,
96, 130
Jawaharlal Nehru's appeals for, 56,
102, 103
Maulana Azad's appeals for, 115
Mohandas Gandhi's appeals for, 98, 129
R.K. Patil's appeals for, 70
Rajendra Prasad's appeals for, 60, 126
Saha, Meghnad, 46, 92
Sahay, Vishnu, 64, 194
Sahney, B.L., 169
Saraswati, Swami Sahajanand, 157
Schultz, Theodore, 183, 200
Seeds Corporation of India, 201, 208, 210
Sen, Amartya, 23, 221
Sen, B., 216
Sen, B.R., 27, 42, 58
Sen, Ela, 37
Seventeenth Amendment, 178
Shah, K.T., 48
Shankar, Ravi, 40
Shankar's Weekly, 68, 71, 75, 87, 112
Shastri, Lal Bahadur, 143–147, 225
and Miss a Meal Movement, 115
and relationship with traders, 148
death, 203
protests in Kerala against, 204
reduction of Planning Commission's
influence, 202
Shastri, Srinivasa, 89
Shiva, Vandana, 186n. 10
Shivaji, 10
Shri Ram, Lala, 97, 104
Singh, Charan, 156, 160, 174
and the Janata Party government, 227
tenure as Prime Minister, 228
Singh, Manmohan, 222
Singh, Swaran, 142
Singh, Tarlok, 66, 158
Society for Defence of Freedom in Asia.
See Goel, Sita Ram
Sorensen, Reginald, 41
Southeast Asia, foodgrain imports
from, 139
Soviet Union
as developmental model, 79
collective agriculture in, 82, 84

collectivization in, 171
comparison of food control regime with
India, 126
development models, 15
foodgrain imports from, 58, 74
influence on Indian agricultural
planning, 154, 196
support for India's new agricultural
strategy, 212
Srivastava, J.P., 42, 44, 56
standard acre. *See* Singh, Tarlok
state trading in foodgrains, 137–140,
145, 176
C. Subramaniam's proposal for, 146
merchants' objections to, 147
nationalization of the wheat trade under
Indira Gandhi, 226
proposal for a Foodgrains Stabilization
Organization, 139
Stephens, Ian, 33
Subrahmanyan, V., 97, 99, 106
Subramaniam, C.
1957 plan for minimum support
prices, 138
and the Bihar famine, 205
and the National Demonstration
Program, 208
assessment of the Nagpur
resolution, 176
early views on state trading in
foodgrains, 145, 146
founding of the Food Corporation of
India, 147
meetings with merchants'
groups, 147
restructuring of Indian agricultural
research institutions, 202
rising influence in wake of Planning
Commission's diminished
influence, 202
sub-Saharan Africa, nutritional
comparison with India, 6, 222
Subsidiary Food Production Committee
(1949), 104, 106, 110, 113
substitute foods, 5, 56, 96, 98
in Kerala, 106
sugar, Indian efforts to trade for
foodgrains, 63
Suhrawardy, H.S., 29, 47
support prices
Agricultural Prices Commission's role in
determining, 226
C. Subramaniam's advocacy for
minimum, 202
Charan Singh's advocacy for
minimum, 227

Index

demand for concurrent food subsidy, 231

Food Ministers' eschewal of, 146

in developing countries, 200

J.C. Kumarappa's proposal for, 80

merchants' advocacy for, 82

new agricultural movement's demand for higher, 228

Swaminathan, M.S., 201, 209
and the Indian Agricultural Research Institute, 202

Swatantra party, 175, 177, 178, 230

Taiwan
improved rice strains from, 201

Tamil Nadu, 82
Intensive Agricultural District Program in, 198
midday meal scheme in, 224
new agricultural strategy in, 209
peasant intimidation in, 53
protests and strikes in, 9, 53
rationing in, 124
renaming of Madras state, 214
wheat propoganda officer in, 94

Tandon, Purshottamdas, 113, 162

Technical Cooperation Mission, Indo-American, 189–192, 196

Telangana, 163

Tennessee Valley Authority, 45, 81, 191

Terai region, 68

Texas, 196

Thakurdas, Purshottamdas, 52, 97, 127

Thanjavur (Tanjore) district, 198, 209, 210, 213, 214, 218
1968 massacre in, 212–214

Thant, U, 205

Thapar, Romesh, 210

The Causes and Nature of Current Agrarian Tensions (1969), 214

theater, 40, 152

Thorner, Alice, 198

Thorner, Daniel, 172, 198, 209, 216

Tikait, M.S., 228

Tilak, Bal Gangadhar, 10

tractors, 67, 71, 73, 166, 185, 192, 195, 215, 225

Travancore-Cochin. *See* Kerala

Trichur district, 168

Truman, Harry, 57, 185, 189

Turkey, foodgrain imports from, 60

United Kingdom
Bengal famine publicity, 41
industrial agriculture in the, 84
Ministry of Food, 41, 60, 62

United Nations, 57, 168, 205, 218

United States
assessment of First Five-Year Plan, 162
CPI criticism of wheat surplus in, 61
fear of communist revolution in India, 195
foodgrain imports from, 60, 73
influence on Indian agricultural development, 183–185, 200
universities, 190, 200, 201

United States Agency for International Development (USAID), 197, 212

United States Department of Agriculture (USDA), 190, 191, 196, 197, 216

Uttar Pradesh Consolidation of Holdings Act, 173

Vajpayee, Atal Bihari, 179

vanaspati (vegetable oil), 91

Varanasi (Benares), 144, 152

Vaswani, K.N., 79

Verghese, B.G., 207

violence, 144, 212–215, 225

Visakhapatnam, 119, 215

Voelcker, J.A. *See Report on the Improvement of Indian Agriculture (1893)*

Walters, Barbara, 195

Wardha, 163

wastelands, reclamation of, 68, 69, 81, 162

West Bengal, 22

wheat
imports from the United States. *See* Public Law 480
improved varieties of, 192, 201, 208, 209
nationalization of trade under Indira Gandhi, 226

Wipro, 143

Wisconsin, 201

Wiser, Charlotte Viall, 91

women
and development planning, 46
and dietary transformation, 88, 108–111
and food wastage, 127
and journalism, 36
and postwar food planning, 46
and promotion of public food distribution schemes, 58
and protests against decontrol, 128
Bengal famine relief efforts, 34, 36, 108
in social planning, 52
proposal for canteens staffed by, 95
protests and strikes by, 124, 144

280 Index

women's groups
All India Women's Committee, 58
All India Women's Conference, 46, 102, 109, 128
All India Women's Council for Supplementary Foods, 110
Mahila Atmaraksha Samiti, 108
Woodhead, John. *See* Famine Inquiry Commission (1944)
World Agriculture Fair (1959), 192
World Bank, 216
World Health Organization, 112

World Trade Organization, objections to National Food Security Act (2013), 222

Yojana (Planning Commission journal), 205
Yugoslavia
foodgrain imports from, 74
Indian mission to investigate cooperative agriculture in, 177

Zutshi, C.N., 12